Introducing Language Typology

Language typology identifies similarities and differences among languages of the world. This textbook provides an introduction to the subject which assumes minimal prior knowledge of linguistics. It offers the broadest coverage of any introductory book, including sections on historical change, language acquisition, and language processing. Students will become familiar with the subject by working through numerous examples of crosslinguistic generalizations and diversity in syntax, morphology, and phonology, as well as vocabulary, writing systems, and signed languages. Chapter outlines and summaries, key words, a glossary, and copious literature references help the reader understand and internalize what they have read, while activities at the end of each chapter reinforce key points.

EDITH A. MORAVCSIK is Professor Emerita in the Department of Linguistics at the University of Wisconsin-Milwaukee.

Cambridge Introductions to Language and Linguistics

This new textbook series provides students and their teachers with accessible introductions to the major subjects encountered within the study of language and linguistics. Assuming no prior knowledge of the subject, each book is written and designed for ease of use in the classroom or seminar, and is ideal for adoption on a modular course as the core recommended textbook. Each book offers the ideal introductory material for each subject, presenting students with an overview of the main topics encountered in their course, and features a glossary of useful terms, chapter previews and summaries, suggestions for further reading, and helpful exercises. Each book is accompanied by a supporting website.

Books published in the series
Introducing Phonology David Odden
Introducing Speech and Language Processing John Coleman
Introducing Phonetic Science Michael Ashby and John Maidment
Introducing Second Language Acquisition Muriel Saville-Troike
Introducing English Linguistics Charles F. Meyer
Introducing Morphology Rochelle Lieber
Introducing Semantics Nick Riemer
Introducing Language Typology Edith A. Moravcsik

Forthcoming:
Introducing Historical Linguistics Brian Joseph

Introducing Language Typology

EDITH A. MORAVCSIK

Professor Emerita of Linguistics
University of Wisconsin-Milwaukee

CAMBRIDGE
UNIVERSITY PRESS

CAMBRIDGE UNIVERSITY PRESS

Cambridge, New York, Melbourne, Madrid, Cape Town,
Singapore, São Paulo, Delhi, Mexico City

Cambridge University Press
The Edinburgh Building, Cambridge CB2 8RU, UK

Published in the United States of America by Cambridge University Press, New York

www.cambridge.org
Information on this title: www.cambridge.org/9780521152624

First published 2013

Printed and bound in the United Kingdom by the MPG Books Group

A catalog record for this publication is available from the British Library

Library of Congress Cataloging in Publication data

Moravcsik, Edith A.
    Introducing language typology / Edith A. Moravcsik, Professor Emerita of Linguistics,
University of Wisconsin-Milwaukee.
    pages   cm. – (Cambridge introductions to language and linguistics)
Includes bibliographical references and indexes.
ISBN 978-0-521-19340-5 (hardback) – ISBN 978-0-521-15262-4 (paperback)
1. Typology (Linguistics)   I. Title.
P204.M66   2013
415–dc23   2012028897

ISBN 978-0-521-19340-5 Hardback
ISBN 978-0-521-15262-4 Paperback

Additional resources for this publication at www.cambridge.org/moravcsik

Contents

Note: Every chapter begins with an outline and a list of key terms and ends with a summary, activities, and a list of further reading.

Figures

Preface

The goal of this book is to offer a few glimpses into the vast research area of linguistic typology – the study of the similarities and differences among languages that hold across genetic, areal, and cultural boundaries. It is meant for students and a general audience with some prior exposure to linguistics, such as an introductory course, but not necessarily anything more. No knowledge of foreign languages is presupposed. The glossary in the back of the book explains terms specific to language-typological research and provides references that define general grammatical terms.

Here are four features of the presentation. First, the survey of language-typological research is intended to be broad in topical coverage. Beyond the basic components of grammar – phonology, morphology, and syntax – it also offers a chapter on lexical semantics and brief sections on writing systems and sign languages. In addition to synchronic data, crosslinguistic generalizations about historical development, language acquisition, and language use are also discussed.

Second, the approach is broad in another way as well. Instead of adopting a particular descriptive framework, data are presented in a pretheoretical metalanguage that hugs the facts as much as possible. This feature should render the text relatively accessible to non-linguist readers.

Third, the pre-theoretical approach is also apparent in the selection of the crosslinguistic generalizations discussed. Hypotheses about language universals may be supported in three ways: by a set of crosslinguistic data, by a theory that predicts them, or by a combination of both. This book focuses on data-based, primarily inductive generalizations.

Fourth, a comprehensive survey of the literature on language typology is not attempted. The focus is mostly on analysis and documentation; the goal is to introduce the reader to the kind of argumentation used in crosslinguistic research and to show its close relationship to the modes of thinking employed in other sciences and in everyday life.

Here is a brief synopsis of the book.

Chapter 1 What is language typology illustrates differences and similarities among languages and presents the statement types that serve as tools to capture their similarities.

Chapter 2 The worlds of words is about similarities and differences in the meanings of words across languages, with a few comments on what this might mean for the way people actually see the world.

Chapter 3 Assembling words, Chapter 4 Dissembling words, and Chapter 5 The sounds of languages present crosslinguistic generalizations about syntax, morphology, and phonology, with a few remarks on writing systems and sign languages.

Chapter 6 Language in flux turns to the genesis of synchronic structure by presenting crosslinguistic generalizations about historical evolution, language acquisition, and language use.

Chapter 7 Explaining crosslinguistic preferences attempts historical, acquisitional, and usage-based explanations of synchronic crosslinguistic generalizations.

I am very grateful to my relatives, friends, and former students who have helped me with language data and comments. They are the following: Gustav Bayerle, Telle Bayerle, Yea-Fen Chen, Roberta Corrigan, Dina Crockett, Garry Davis, Fred Eckman, Nicholas Fleischer, Younghyon Heo, Gregory Iverson, John Kellogg, Ahrong Lee, Sooyeon Lee, Silvia Luraghi, Veronica Lundbäck, Julia Moravcsik, Corrine Occhino, Olesya Ostapenko, Hamid Ouali, Sueyon Seo, James Shey, Hyowon Song, Jae Jung Song, Jennifer Watson, Kathleen Wheatley, and Jessica Wirth.

My thanks go also to my linguist colleagues at the University of Budapest, the Linguistic Research Institute of the Hungarian Academy of Sciences, the University of Vienna, the University of Hawaii, the EUROTYP project, the WALS project, the Max Planck Institute for Evolutionary Anthropology, and the University of Wisconsin-Milwaukee, from whom I have learnt so much. I am also much indebted to Andrew Winnard of Cambridge University Press for his patience and encouragement, to Sarah Green, Ed Robinson, and Helena Dowson for their helpful guidance throughout the production process, to Jon Billam for his thorough copy-editing of the text and for many insightful suggestions, and to Sue Lightfoot for her careful work on the indexes.

I would not have been able to write this book without the guidance I was fortunate to receive in my early years as a linguist from Gerald A. Sanders, who was my professor at Indiana University, and from the late Joseph H. Greenberg, my project director at the Stanford Universals Project. I am profoundly grateful to both of them.

Copyright permissions

The following excerpts are reproduced by permission from the publishers.

Chapter 2, Section 2.4 (38): Oksapmin counting Nicholas Evans 2010. *Dying words. Endangered languages and what they have to tell us.* John Wiley and Sons, page 60.

Chapter 3, activity 5: Luiseño Ronald W. Langacker 1972. *Fundamentals of linguistic analysis.* New York: Harcourt Brace Jovanovich, page 69. By permission from Ronald W. Langacker.

Chapter 3, activity 4 Walmatjari, Chapter 4, activities 4 Agta, and 5 Cheyenne: Used by permission © **SIL**, William Merrifield *et al.* 1987. *Laboratory manual for morphology and syntax.* Summer Institute of Linguistics. Problems ##33, 94–95, 214.

Chapter 5, Section 5.5.2. (50b) ASL sign for 'father': Edward Klima and Ursula Bellugi 1979. *The signs of language.* Harvard University Press, page 134.

Chapter 5, Section 5.5.2 (51) ASL sign for paws: Ted Supalla 1986. The classifier system in American Sign Language. In Craig, Colette G. (ed.) 1986. *Noun classes and categorization.* Amsterdam/Philadelphia: Benjamins, page 209.

Chapter 5, activity 1: Mohawk Used by permission ©MIT, Morris Halle and G. N. Clements 1983. *Problem book in phonology. A workbook for introductory courses in linguistics and in modern phonology.* The MIT Press, page 59.

Chapter 5, activities 4 Akan and 5 Ulwa: Iggy Roca and Wyn Johnson 1999. *A workbook in phonology.* Oxford: Blackwell, pages 21, 124–125.

Chapter 6, Section 6.2.2 (21) Word order change: Murray Gell-Mann and Merritt Ruhlen 2011. The origin and evolution of word order. *Proceedings of the National Academy of Sciences* 108/42, page 17291.

Chapter 6, Section 6.3.1.2 (32) Spatial terms: Melissa Bowerman 1996. The origins of children's spatial semantic terms. John J. Gumperz and Stephen C. Levinson (ed.) *Rethinking linguistic relativity.* Cambridge University Press, figures 52A and 52B, pages 152–153.

Chapter 7, Section 7.4: Edith Moravcsik 2006. *An introduction to syntax.* New York: Continuum, pages 236–238. Revised version.

Chapter 7, Section 7.4: Mark Haddon 2001. *The curious incident of the dog in the night-time.* New York: Random House, page 143.

Abbreviations

Most of the abbreviations used here are taken from the Leipzig Glossing Rules (www.eva.mpg.de/lingua/files/morpheme.html).

A	the agent noun phrase of a two-argument verb
ABS	absolutive case
ACC	accusative case
ASP	aspect
CAUS	causative
CL	class
CLF	classifier
CMP	comparative
DAT	dative case
DC	declarative clause marker
ERG	ergative case
FEM	feminine
GEN	genitive case
GER	gerund
IMPF	imperfective
INDOBJ	indirect object
INF	infinitive
L1	first language (a language already acquired)
L2	target language (a language to be acquired)
MRK	marker
MSC	masculine gender
NEU	neuter gender
NMLZ	nominalizer
NOM	nominative case
OBJ	object
OM	object marker
ORD	ordinal
P	the patient noun phrase of a two-argument verb
PART	partitive case
PFV	perfective
PL	plural
POSS	possessive marker
PREF	prefix
PRF	perfect
PRIV	privative
PRT	particle

PST	past tense
S	the single noun phrase of a one-argument verb
SBJ	subject
SING	singular
SUP	superlative
1S	first person singular
2S	second person singular
3S	third person singular
1P	first person plural
2P	second person plural
3P	third person plural
A & B	A immediately precedes B
-	boundary between stem and affix
=	boundary between word and clitic
#	boundary between words
[...]	phonetic transcription
/.../	phonemic transcription
′	stress
' '	idiomatic translation
" "	literal translation

1 What is language typology?

CHAPTER OUTLINE

In this chapter, the goals of language-typological research will be defined as studying similarities and differences among languages that do not stem from shared genetic relationship, language contact, or shared environmental conditions. Some basic research tools will be introduced: language-typological generalizations of various kinds, ways of constructing language samples, and sources for obtaining language data.

1.1 Goals

You are riding in a crowded elevator; next to you stand two people conversing in a foreign language. You don't understand a word of what they are saying and couldn't even repeat any of it: their speech strikes you as just plain noise. Yet, the two people obviously communicate. One person says something whereupon the other breaks into a peal of laughter; he then responds and the first person comes back with another round of what sounds like complete gibberish. How can these odd noises make any sense to anybody?

What you have just experienced is a true fact: languages are different. The following examples further illustrate how different they can be. (2), (3), and (4) are Polish, Hungarian, and Turkish translations of the English sentence in (1).

(1) *Give us today our daily bread.*   English

(2) *Chleba   naszego   powszedniego   daj   nam   dzisiaj.*   Polish
     bread   our   daily   give   to.us   today

(3) *Mindennapi   kenyerünket   add   meg   nekünk   ma.*   Hungarian
     daily   our.bread   give   PREF   to.us   today

(4) *Gündelik   ekmeğimizi   bize   bogün   ver.*   Turkish
     daily   our.bread   to.us   today   give

While these examples and the "elevator-experience" suggest that languages are very different, languages also show surprising similarities. Look at the translations of sentence (1) in two additional languages.

(5) *Unser   tägliches   Brot   gib   uns   heute.*   German
     our   daily   bread   give   us   today

(6) *Vårt   dagliga   bröd   giv   oss   idag.*   Swedish
     our   daily   bread   give   us   today

Several of the words are similar in English, German, and Swedish:

(7) ENGLISH   GERMAN   SWEDISH
     our   *unser*   *vårt*
     bread   *Brot*   *bröd*
     give   *gib*   *giv*
     us   *uns*   *oss*

The fact that languages are both different and similar is a puzzle. Two questions arise:

(8) (a) How are languages different from each other and how are they similar?
     (b) What is the reason for their differences and for their similarities?

The first question addresses the **distribution** of structural properties among languages: what occurs and where? The second question in turn asks for an explanation of the distributional facts: why does a structural property occur where it does? There is hardly any issue more central to the science of linguistics than these two; and they are also the focus of this book.

The data cited in (1)–(7) have begun to answer the question in (8a) by showing crosslinguistic similarities and differences in vocabulary, word structure, and word order. Let us now turn to (8b), which asks for the reasons for crosslinguistic similarities. The vocabulary resemblances among English, German, and Swedish illustrated above have a straightforward explanation. About twenty-five-hundred years ago, these languages did not exist separately; instead, there was a single ancestral language – linguists call it Proto-Germanic – from which all three subsequently derived. The vocabulary similarities are due to inheritance: ancestral words have survived in the daughter languages albeit their forms have been somewhat altered over the centuries. The gradualness with which the three languages have changed away from each other is shown by the Old English version of the same sentence.

(9) | *urne* | *daghwamlican* | *hlaf* | *syle* | *us* | *to* | *dæg* | Old English |
     | our | daily | bread | give | us | to | day | |

The table in (10) shows that some of the Old English words are more similar to their German and Swedish equivalents than the Modern English ones because Old English, spoken about a thousand years ago, was closer in time to Proto-Germanic – their shared mother language.

(10) | GERMAN | SWEDISH | OLD ENGLISH | MODERN ENGLISH |
     | *unser* | *vårt* | *urne* | *our* |
     | *tägliches* | *dagliga* | *daghwamlican* | *daily* |

Polish, Hungarian, and Turkish (illustrated in (2), (3), and (4) above) are not Germanic languages; hence the differences.

The above materials point at one reason for similarities among languages: **shared historical origin**. However, languages may resemble each other even if they are not known to have evolved from the same ancestor. Take the word *sugar*. As we might expect, in Germanic languages (English, German, Swedish, Dutch, and others) it has roughly the same form.

(11) | ENGLISH | *sugar* |
     | GERMAN | *Zucker* |
     | SWEDISH | *socker* |
     | DUTCH | *suiker* |

But the word has similar forms even in languages outside the Germanic family.

(12) | SPANISH: | *azúcar* |
     | FRENCH: | *sucre* |
     | ITALIAN: | *zucchero* |
     | POLISH: | *cukier* |

A possible explanation may still be shared genetic origin: along with the Germanic family, the Romance languages (Spanish, French, and Italian) and Polish, a Slavic language, are all members of the larger group of Indo-European. Thus, the word for 'sugar' could be a legacy of Proto-Indo-European, their shared mother language (spoken about 5000–4000 BCE).

If this were the case, we would expect languages outside Indo-European to have completely different words for 'sugar.' However, this is not so.

(13)   HUNGARIAN: *cukor*
        TURKISH: *şeker*
        HEBREW: *sukkar*
        ARABIC: *soukar*
        JAPANESE: *satoo*
        SWAHILI: *sukari*
        INDONESIAN: *sakar*

These languages are not Indo-European: Hungarian is Finno-Ugric, Turkish belongs to the Turkic family, Hebrew and Arabic are Semitic, Japanese is an isolate, Swahili is Bantu, and Indonesian is Malayo-Polynesian. The extent to which some of these languages differ from English was illustrated in (3) on the example of Hungarian and in (4) for Turkish. Yet, the words for 'sugar' in these languages are still similar to the English word.

The explanation is again historical but of a different kind: not shared origin but **language contact**. The words for 'sugar' all come from Sanskrit *śarkarā*. Sugarcane was first cultivated in India, the home of Sanskrit. In the eighth century CE, Indian merchants began to export sugarcane; crusaders then brought it to Europe and traders spread it around the globe along with the word itself, with spelling and pronunciation somewhat modified according to the conventions of each language.

So far, we have seen two sources of similarities among languages: **shared historical origin** and **contact**. Might there be other reasons? In pondering this question, let us consider resemblances among things outside language. Take people. If you compare your friends, you will find that some are more like each other than others. In some cases, this may be due to the fact that they are related. If they are siblings, they may have inherited certain features – such as black hair or musical ability – from their parents or from their more remote ancestors. Thus, just as in the case of languages, genetic relatedness is a possible explanation for resemblances among people.

Now suppose you know two unrelated individuals who share an interest in butterflies. A different kind of explanation is needed here: they may have been long-time friends and one of them came to be interested in butterflies when prompted by the other. Contact and the attendant spread of characteristics from one individual to another can explain similarities among people as it does between languages shown on the example for the word for 'sugar.'

But let us consider a third scenario. Suppose you have two friends who are not related nor have they ever met; yet, they are both devoted to ice-fishing. Chances are that both came from parts of the world where there are severe winters that cover lakes and rivers with thick ice. Their shared interest is likely to be related to the environment that they both come from. Could the **same environment** – natural or cultural – result in similarities also among languages as it does among people?

Features of the natural setting of a speech community are often reflected in the vocabulary of the language. Nicholas Evans reports that in Kayardild (an Australian aboriginal language) there are five different verbs to describe hopping, one for each subtype of macropods – an animal species specific to Australia that includes kangaroos, wallaroos, and wallabies (1998: 164). Socio-cultural setting can also have an effect on language: if these conditions are similar, so may be some aspects of the languages. An example is word forms differentiated by degrees of respect. Two of the many languages that have a broad range of vocabulary items whose use is determined by social considerations are Guugu Yimidhirr, an Australian aboriginal language of Queensland, and Japanese. In Japanese, several kinship terms have alternative forms depending on whether you speak to members of your own family or to people outside it. For example, 'grandfather' is *ojiisan* when talking to family and *sofu* when talking to outsiders; 'father' is *otoosan* when talking to family but *chichi* when talking to outsiders (Inoue 1979: 282). In Guugu Yimidhirr, some words have special forms for talking to one's brother-in-law or father-in-law as opposed to talking to others. For example, the word for 'to go' is *balil* in the respectful brother-in-law style; the everyday form is *dhadaa* (Haviland 1979: 217–218). Note that Japanese and Guugu Yimidhirr are neither genetically related nor have they been in direct contact. Instead, their socially-conditioned vocabulary distinctions correlate with the stratified societies where these word distinctions developed.

These culturally conditioned vocabulary distinctions are somewhat comparable to the difference between the French second-person pronouns *tu* and *vous*, where the former is used to address a close family member or friend while the latter is reserved for formal relations. Similar distinctions hold in Spanish (*tu* and *usted*) and German (*du* and *Sie*). That such usages respond to societal conditions can be seen most clearly when social structure changes. In some European countries, such as Austria and Germany, where the second person pronoun of the language has an intimate and a polite form, the former is gaining over the polite version, very likely in response to societal leveling.

The three factors of **genetic relatedness**, **language contact**, and **shared cultural environment** go a long way addressing the question in (8b) about why languages are similar. However, they do not work in all cases: two additional reasons need to be invoked: **types** and **universals**.

Consider the following sentences from Hindi, Japanese, and Turkish, all translations of 'They bring water for the girl's mother.' Square brackets set off phrases.

(14) [Ve]   [larkiki   make   liye]   [pani]   [late   hai].   Hindi
      they   girl's   mother   for   water   bring   are

(15) [karera wa]   [ano   onnanoko   no   haha   ni]   [mizu   o]   [motte kuru]   Japanese
      they   SUBJ   the   girl   GEN   mother for   water   ACC   bring   give

(16)   [Kız   annesi   için]   [su]   [getiriler.]   Turkish
        girl   her.mother   for   water   they.bring

Although the words in these sentences are very different from each other, note that they are placed in the same order. All three are so-called "SOV languages," which means that first comes the subject of the sentence (if there is one; it is not present in the Turkish sentence), then the indirect and direct object, and then the verb.

In addition, the three languages share two other order patterns given in (17b) and (17c). (The symbol & indicates linear order.)

(17)   (a)   Subject & Object & Verb
            ("they water bring")
      (b)   Possessor & Possessum
            ("girl's mother")
      (c)   Noun Phrase & Adposition
            ("mother for")

The identical orderings of sentence constituents in these three languages is not due either to shared origin, or contact, or shared environment. These languages are not genetically related: Hindi is Indo-European and, as noted above, Turkish is Turkic and Japanese is an isolate. They have not been in close contact, nor are their natural and cultural conditions particularly similar.

Strikingly, these languages contrast with others that have near-mirror-image orders for all three sets of constituents, as in (18).

(18)   (a)   Verb & Subject & Object
            ("bring they water")
      (b)   Possessum & Possessor
            ("mother girl's")
      (c)   Adposition & Noun Phrase
            ("for mother")

Here are examples from Arabic and Rapa-Nui (the language of Easter Island; data from Chapin 1978). Arabic is Semitic, Rapa-Nui is Malayo-Polynesian; they are both genetically and geographically separate and share little by way of socio-cultural conditions.

(19)   (a)   Verb & Subject & Object   Arabic
            axaδa aşşinijjuna   almala
            took   the.Chinese   the.money
            'The Chinese took the money.'
      (b)   Possessum & Possessor
            bajtu arraʒuli
            house man.GEN
            'the house of the man'
      (c)   Adposition & Noun Phrase
            ila bosʈon
            to Boston
            'to Boston'

(20) (a) Verb & Subject & Object   Rapa Nui
         He   to'o   te   tenitō   i   te   moni.
         PAST take the Chinese ACC the money
         'The Chinese took the money.'
    (b) Possessum & Possessor
         te   hoi   o   te   tagata
         the horse GEN the man
         'the horse of the man'
    (c) Adposition & Noun Phrase
         ki Boston
         'to Boston'

Although the correlations between the alternative positions of the verb and the other two pairs of constituents are only a tendency across languages, most SOV languages do place the possessor before the possessum and use postpositions, and most verb-initial languages put the possessor after the possessum and have prepositions.

What might be the reason for genetically unrelated SOV languages in various parts of the world sharing these order patterns? And similarly, why do unrelated VSO languages scattered around the globe tend to have the opposite orders? An obvious idea is that the constituents whose ordering patterns form consistent clusters have something in common. If so, the otherwise puzzling clustering of THREE different orders would be reduced to just ONE pattern: the particular orders would fall out of a single regularity.

Several explanations along these lines have been proposed in the literature; they will be discussed in Chapter 7 (Section 7.3). One hypothesis is that the regularity has to do with the uniform ordering of heads and dependents (Vennemann 1973). What is meant by the "head" of a construction is the indispensable part and the one that determines the category of the entire construction. The "dependent" in turn is of a different category than the entire construction and it is often optional. The sorting of verbs, objects, possessums, possessors, adpositions, and noun phrase complements into the two categories of head and dependent is given in (21).

(21) HEAD   DEPENDENT
      Verb   Object
      Possessum   Possessor
      Adposition   Noun Phrase

In other words, the common denominator of verbs, possessums, and adpositions is that they are all heads, with object, possessor, and noun phrase complement being their respective dependents.

According to this theory, languages tend to adopt a single order rule for heads and dependents from which the ordering of verb and object, possessum and possessor, and adposition and noun phrase automatically follows. Languages thus belong to two different types: SOV languages (e.g. Hindi, Turkish, and Japanese), which adopt dependent & head order and therefore have "water bring," "John's book," and "Boston in"; and verb-initial languages (e.g. Arabic, Rapa-Nui), which opt for head & dependent order ("bring water," "book John's," "in Boston").

By way of a re-cap, the four types of explanations of crosslinguistic similarities discussed above are schematized in (22).

(22) Explaining crosslinguistic similarities...
      (a) ... by shared inheritance
           QUESTION: Why do English and German have similar words for 'bread'?
           ANSWER: Because both English and German are Germanic languages and they inherited this word from Proto-Germanic, their shared ancestral language.
      (b) ... by language contact
           QUESTION: Why do English and Swahili have similar words for 'sugar'?
           ANSWER: Because both languages adopted the Sanskrit word through contact.
      (c) ... by shared environmental conditions
           QUESTION: Why do Japanese and Guugu Yimidhirr have alternative words where the choice between them depends on the social relationship between speaker and addressee?
           ANSWER: Because in both languages, these distinctions evolved in response to the demands of stratified societies.
      (d) ... by reference to language types
           QUESTION: Why do both Hindi and Japanese place the possessor before the possessum?
           ANSWER: Because possessors are dependents and possessums are heads and both languages are of the dependent & head type.

These four types of explanations may be invoked in case we want to explain that **some** languages are similar to each other as opposed to others. But what about similarities that hold for **all languages**? As an example, consider the fact that all known languages have personal pronouns, such as *I*, *you*, and so forth. Let's try to apply the answer types discussed above to this fact.

(23) QUESTION: Why do all known languages have personal pronouns?
      ANSWER:
      (a) Because all languages are genetically related and the ancestral language from which they derived had personal pronouns.
      (b) Because all languages have been in direct or indirect contact with each other and the presence of personal pronouns has spread from one to the other.
      (c) Because all languages are spoken in the same cultural conditions that call for personal pronouns.
      (d) Because all languages belong to the same language type.

Let us evaluate these possible explanations. The first one posits a single source for all human languages: if this ancient language had personal pronouns, all of its daughter languages could have retained it. This is not an impossible hypothesis but it still leaves two questions open: why the source language had personal pronouns and why personal pronouns have consistently survived in the course of millennia when so many other structural properties have changed. The second hypothesis may also be correct: perhaps personal pronouns first evolved in one language and the idea then spread to all other languages; but the questions of ultimate origin and universal survival still remain open. The third hypothesis posits similar cultural conditions for all languages. In a sense, it is true that all languages share some of their environment: for example, they are all spoken in a human community. But why would this fact require personal pronouns?

The fourth explanation is correct by definition: to the extent that all languages have personal pronouns, we must say that they form a single type. But here we are not talking about a (sub)-type of languages but about all languages being a (sub)-type of communication systems. This yields a fifth kind of answer to why languages are similar.

(24)   QUESTION: Why do all known languages have personal pronouns?
       ANSWER: Because all languages belong to a type of communication
          systems where the presence of personal pronouns is required.

However, (24) simply states the fact rather than explaining it. The ultimate explanation must have to do with some or perhaps all of the three factors considered above: the origins of human languages, their contact with each other and their shared natural and social conditions, as well as with the universally manifested function of personal pronouns in thought and expression. The presence of personal pronouns in a language does not appear necessary: names or demonstrative pronouns (such as 'this' and 'that') could do just as well to identify 'me,' 'you,' and others. However, a name may be shared by several individuals and demonstratives like 'this' and 'that' also do not point at speaker and hearer as clearly as 'I' and 'you' do. Thus, preference for clarity in identifying speaker and hearer provides only a probabilistic explanation for the universal genesis and survival of personal pronouns across languages. More will be said about personal pronouns in Section 2.3.2. of Chapter 2.

Let us summarize the above discussion. First, two central questions of linguistics were raised: the crosslinguistic distribution of structural properties across languages and the reasons for their distribution. In contemplating possible reasons for similarities among languages, we explored five kinds of explanations: shared inheritance, contact, shared environment, language types, and language universals.

The field of linguistic research called language typology is the study of the latter two phenomena: typologically and universally shared features of languages. It focuses on the concept of a language type. The term "type" in everyday usage is synonymous with "kind": it refers to a subclass of a class of entities. In this broad sense, two languages belong to the same type if they have at least one characteristic in common regardless of whether this shared characteristic is due to shared inheritance or borrowing or similar environmental conditions. In actual linguistic usage, however, two languages are generally said to belong to the same type if their similarities hold across various genetic, areal, and cultural groups.

Before we begin to study language-typological implications and language universals in detail, we need to identify the conceptual tools needed for this study.

1.2 Tools

1.2.1 Statement types

In the previous section, we laid out the task of language typology: it is to find similarities among languages that are independent of genetic origin, areal influence, and shared environmental conditions. How do we capture the results of this investigation?

Let us begin by looking at the speech sound inventories of languages. We find the following:

(25) (a)   Some languages have oral stops (e.g. /t/).
      (b)   Some languages have alveolar nasals (/n/).

These statements simply declare the existence of languages that have such sounds. However, such existential statements do not provide us with distributional information: they do not tell us which languages have oral stops and which languages have /n/. They say that such sounds are possible in human languages since if at least one language has them, they must of course be possible. Thus, if we encounter a new language, what we know is that it may or may not have oral stops and alveolar nasals but we do not know if that particular language does or does not have them.

How could we turn these existential statements into distributional ones? Here is one attempt:

(26) (a)   All languages have oral stops.
      (b)   All languages have alveolar nasals.

These statements would be very useful: they define the set of human languages that have a particular property – namely, all languages. If we encounter a new language, these statements make predictions regarding its consonant inventory: that it will include oral stops and alveolar nasals.

But are these predictions true? As it turns out, (26a) is true: all languages known to us have oral stops. However, (26b) is untrue: indigenous languages spoken in the North-West area of the North-American continent – for example, Tlingit, a language of Alaska – have no alveolar nasals. Here is our problem: (25b), which states that some languages have alveolar nasals, is true but not predictive; (26b) is predictive but not true. Could we somehow combine the valuable universal scope of (26b) with the truth of (25b)?

The problem and its solution can be easily illustrated from everyday life. Suppose you are in a foreign city trying to learn the opening hours of food stores. Here is what you find:

(27)   Some food stores are open 7 days a week.

Well, but which are those stores? Your first guess may be this:

(28)   All food stores are open 7 days a week.

It then turns out that this is not so: some stores close on Sunday. In order to find out which are the seven-day stores, you will naturally look for a common characteristic of these businesses that distinguishes them from the others. Here is what you may discover:

(29)   All food stores **that carry fresh produce** are open 7 days a week.

By logical structure, (29) is like (28): it is a universal statement (since it includes the quantifier *all*) but it has an advantage over (28): it is correct. Both (28) and (29) are universal generalizations for sets of stores but they differ in how the sets are defined. (28) says something about the universe of all food stores in town; (29) says something about a sub-universe of the town's food stores: those that share the common denominator of carrying fresh produce. (28) is an unconditional, or unrestricted, universal; (29) is a conditional, or restricted, universal.

In this example, once the unrestricted universal (28) turned out to be incorrect for the entire domain of food stores, the solution was to find a characteristic that defined a subdomain of food stores for which the universal generalization held. Let us apply the same idea to solving the problem of the distribution of alveolar nasals. Given that we want to determine the universe of languages within which all languages have alveolar nasals but we know that this universe does not include all languages, we need to identify a characteristic that carves out the proper subdomain of languages within which the universal holds.

As it turns out, this characteristic is the presence of labial nasals. Thus, the following restricted universal holds true:

(30)   All languages **that have labial nasals** (/m/) also have alveolar nasals (/n/).

What the above examples show is that crosslinguistic generalizations may be existential or universal; and if they are universal, they may be unrestricted or restricted. Restricted universals are also called conditional or implicational; unrestricted ones are unconditional. These alternative terms will be used interchangeably throughout the book. Here are the schemata for these statement types:

(31)   (a)   Existential statements:
             Some languages have X.
       (b)   Universal statements:
             (aa)   unrestricted universals:
                    All languages have X.
             (bb)   implicational universals:
                    All languages that have Y also have X.

The typological clusters and universals mentioned in Section 1.1 can now be re-cast into these schemata.

(32) Unrestricted universal:
       All languages have personal pronouns.

(33) Implicational universals:
       (a) Most languages that have SOV order also have Possessor
            & Possessum and Noun Phrase & Adposition orders.
       (b) Most languages that have verb-initial order also have
            Possessum & Possessor and Adposition & Noun Phrase order.

(33a) and (33b) may be collapsed into the unrestricted universal in (34).

(34) Unrestricted universal:
       Most languages order heads and dependents uniformly.

What is the predictive force of these statement types? Unrestricted universals are about two logically possible languages types: languages that have X and those that do not have X; and the claim is that only one of the two exists. This is shown in (35). The star in front of a type means it is claimed not to occur; X is a structural feature; + and − stand for the presence and absence of a feature.

(35) Unrestricted universals

                    X
       Type I   +
      *Type II   −

Implicational universals in turn make a claim about four logically possible language types:

(36) Implicational universals

                   Y   X
       Type I   −   −
       Type II   +   +
       Type III   −   +
      *Type IV   +   −

Tables like (36) that compare the logically possible co-occurrence patterns of two properties with their actual occurrences are referred to in the literature as **tetrachoric tables** (from Greek *tettares* 'four').

That is, languages that have both characteristics (Type I) or that have neither (Type II) are both predicted to occur. However, of languages that have only one of the two features, only one type is said to occur (Type III); the other (Type IV) does not. In other words, the presence of Y is said to imply the presence of X: Y cannot occur without X.

Both restricted and unrestricted universals map out the logically possible distribution patterns of a structural characteristic: two for unrestricted universals − languages having the characteristic and those not having it − and four for implicational ones: languages having both characteristics, or neither, or one or the other. The actually observed patterns are then compared with the logical possibilities. As Frans Plank has remarked, "typology confronts possibility with reality" (Plank 1999: 285). If there is a gap − something that is logically possible does not actually occur − this is a highly valued finding because it calls for an explanation. If it seems something COULD occur, why does it NOT occur? More will be said about this at the end of the last chapter of this book.

What we have hit upon here is a powerful conceptual tool: distributional statements of a universal kind, either unrestricted or implicational. The applicability of such statements is not specific to studying the distribution of structural characteristics across languages: unrestricted and implicational universals can be usefully stated for any other domain of the world's phenomena as well. (28) and (29) showed how we use these tools in everyday life, such as in discovering opening hours of stores. These statement types are also basic staples in science. Here are some zoological universals.

(37) (a) An unrestricted universal
         All animals have reproductive systems.
     (b) An implicational universal
         All animals that have feathers are bipedal.

The respective charts are given in (38) and (39).

(38) All animals have reproductive systems.

	reproductive systems	EXAMPLES
Type I	+	all animals
*Type II	−	0

(39) All animals that have feathers are bipedal.

	having feathers	being bipedal	EXAMPLES
Type I	−	−	dogs
Type II	+	+	birds
Type III	−	+	humans
*Type IV	+	−	0

So far we have seen two basic divisions among crosslinguistic statements: whether they are **existential** or **universal**; and if the latter, whether they are **unrestricted** or **implicational**. There are three more variables that differentiate universal statements. One is their **modality**: whether they are absolute or statistical. Another has to do with the relationship between X and Y, called the implicans and the implicatum. And, thirdly, statements differ in whether X and Y are simple or complex. Let us look at examples.

An example of the varying **modality** of universals comes from the crosslinguistic distribution of nasal consonants as opposed to oral ones. Based on familiarity with English, German, Spanish, and so forth, we may state (40).

(40) Some languages have nasal consonants.

(40) is true; but it is not a universal statement and thus makes no firm prediction. Let's try an unrestricted universal.

(41) All languages have nasal consonants.

(41) makes a prediction but it is not true: languages in the NW areas of the North-American continent lack not only alveolar nasals (as discussed above) but they lack nasals in general. So let's try an implicational universal.

(42) All languages that have Y have nasal consonants.

Existential statements tell us about **possibilities**: the next language that you look at MAY or MAY NOT have a particular feature. Statistical statements are about **probabilities**: it is not only possible that the next language that you encounter has a particular feature – it is said to be PROBABLE. Absolute universals in turn are about **certainties**: they say that the next language you look at WILL have a particular feature.

This is a promising approach; but the problem is that no Y-feature has yet been found: that is, no property has been spotted that would differentiate languages with nasals and those without them. Do we therefore have to be content with the existential statement in (40)? No; there is a better option: we can state (43).

(43)   Most languages have nasal consonants.

By logical structure, (43) falls between an existential statement and a universal one: its scope does not include all languages but it says more than just the existential claim that some languages have them. It is a statistical statement. It does not make a sure-fire prediction about whether the next language that you look at does or does not have nasal consonants, but it makes it more likely that it will have them. The statements formulated about word order regularities in (33) and (34) are similarly of the statistical rather than absolute sort.

Next, let's turn to another factor by which crosslinguistic generalizations may differ: the relationship between implicans and implicatum of implicational statements. Here are three statements from outside language that differ in this respect.

(44)   (a)   All parts of the world that have bees also have flowering
                 plants.
         (b)   All animals that have feathers have two legs.
         (c)   All animal limbs that belong to primates are articulated.

(44a) relates two different objects – bees and flowering plants – that occur next to each other: the presence of one calls for the presence of the other. (44b) also relates two objects but they are parts of the same entity: an animal body. And (44c) relates two properties of the same animal body part: primate limbs are articulated. We will label the three types paradigmatic, syntagmatic, and reflexive universals (the last ones also called provisions).

Here are corresponding examples from language.

(45)   (a)   A paradigmatic universal
                 In all languages in which the inflected verb precedes the sub-
                 ject in yes/no-questions, it does so in *wh*-questions as well.
                 (Greenberg 1966a: #11a)
         (b)   A syntagmatic universal
                 In all languages in which the inflected verb precedes the
                 subject in wh-questions, the wh-word is normally initial.
                 (Greenberg 1966a: #11b)
         (c)   A reflexive universal
                 In all languages in which yes-no questions are differentiated
                 from declaratives by an intonation pattern, the position of this
                 pattern is reckoned from the end of the sentence rather than
                 from the beginning. (Greenberg 1966a: 110, #8)

These generalizations, just as those in (44), differ in how their implicans and implicatum are related to each other. In (45a), the claim is about the construction repertoire of languages: verb-before-subject order in yes/no-questions predicts the presence of the same pattern in another construction: wh-questions. Thus, implicans and implicatum are properties of different constructions: wh-questions and yes -no-questions. In (45b), this is not so: implicans and implicatum are both properties of a single construction: wh-questions. (45c) also applies within a sentence but implicans and implicatum are not distinct constituents of a construction; instead, they are properties of a single constituent. The statement refers to one feature of a constituent – an intonation pattern – and adds a detail about that feature: its position.

The diagrams in (46) show these three kinds of implicational universals. The rectangles are constructions of a language; Y and X are implicans and implicatum; arrows highlight the direction of prediction.

(46) (a) paradigmatic implication:

   If Y, then X (where Y and X are features of **different constructions of the same language**).

```
 _____       _____      _____
|   . . . Y . . .   |   |   . . . X . . .   |   |              |
|_____|   |_____|   |_____|
```

(b) syntagmatic implication:

   If Y, then X (where Y and X are features of **different constituents co-occurring in the same construction**).

```
 _____       _____      _____
| . . Y . . . X . . |   |              |   |              |
|_____|   |_____|   |_____|
```

(c) reflexive implication:

   If Y, then X (where Y and X are features of the **same constituent**).

```
 _____       _____      _____
|  . . . [ Y ] . . .  |   |              |   |              |
|      [ X ]      |   |_____|   |_____|
|_____|
```

We now turn to the last kind of division among implicational universals. Consider (47).

(47) In all languages that have prepositions and where the demonstrative follows the noun, the adjective also follows the noun. (Hawkins 1983: 71)

At first blush, the structure of this statement seems to deviate from a normal implication since it mentions not two but three structural characteristics: prepositions, noun-before-demonstrative order, and noun-before-adjective order. But notice that it still has the two basic terms: implicans and implicatum; it is just that the implicans consists of two conditions rather than one. (47) has a **complex** implicans: more than one condition needs to be met before a prediction results.

Similarly, implicata may also be complex, as in (48).

(48) In most languages where the adjective precedes the noun, both the
      demonstrative and the numeral also precede the noun. (Greenberg
      1966a: #18)

(48) is like a "two for the price of one" deal: from a single condition –
Adjective & Noun – two predictions fall out: Demonstrative & Noun and
Numeral & Noun. Needless to say, this pattern is preferable over (47),
which yields "one for the price of two." The statistical universals about
constituent order stated in (33) were also of the more useful kind: the position of the verb in the sentence predicts both the order of Possessor and
Possessum and the order of Adposition and Noun Phrase.
    Let us recapitulate the above survey of the typology of crosslinguistic
statements.

(49) (A) Crosslinguistic statements may be
             – existential statements:
                In some languages, there is X.
             – universal statements:
                In all languages, there is X.

      (B) Universal statements differ
           (a) in the universe they pertain to
                  – unrestricted universals:
                     In all languages, there is X.
                  – implicational universals:
                     In all languages where there is Y, there is also X.
           (b) in their modality
                  – absolute universals:
                     In all languages, there is X.
                  – statistical universals:
                     In most (or in 60% etc. of) languages, there is X.

      (C) Implicational universals differ
           (a) in the relationship between their terms
                  – paradigmatic implications:
                     In all languages, if there is Y, there is also X,
                     where Y and X are different constructions.
                  – syntagmatic implications:
                     In all languages, if there is Y, there is also X,
                     where Y and X are parts of the same construction.
                  – reflexive implications:
                     In all languages, if there is Y, there is also X,
                     where Y and X are features of the same constituent
                     within a construction.
           (b) in the complexity of their terms
                  – single implicans and/or implicatum:
                     In all languages where there is Y, there is also X.
                  – complex implicans and/or implicatum
                     In all languages where there is Y (and/or W), there is
                     also X (and/or Z).

There is one more task to attend to before we are ready to embark on the study of actual crosslinguistic generalizations that have been proposed in the literature: we should take a closer look at the terms mentioned in our statements. Consider the shared schema of unrestricted and implicational universals:

(50) In **all** (or most) languages (where there is **Y**), there is also **X**.

First, what exactly do we mean by "all languages"? And, second, how do we obtain information about the grammatical properties X and Y? The next two subsections will take up these questions in turn.

1.2.2 Language samples

In formulating language-universal statements, our goal is to find generalizations that hold for all human languages (or for most of them; or for (most of) a well-defined subset of them). Thus, our domain of inquiry includes not only languages that exist at the present but also those that existed in the past but have died out or changed into a different language, and even those that will evolve in the future. But clearly, we cannot possibly inspect all these languages. First and most obviously, we cannot know what future languages will be like. Second, we cannot know about all the languages that have ever existed in human history. By Daniel Nettle's estimate, human language first evolved at least 50,000 years ago and possibly before that. Since that time, about 233,000 languages have simply disappeared. Adding to this figure the 7,000 languages that are now in the world, the total number is about 240,000, of which today's languages form only about 3%.

So what about this 3%? Here is the third reason why we cannot inspect all languages: of the roughly 7,000 languages spoken today, we have descriptions for only about a third of them (Bakker 2011: 101–102). Large areas of Australia, South America, and other parts of the world are still *terra incognita* from a linguistic point of view. However, there are many doctoral dissertations and other monographs aiming at closing the gap between known and unknown. Three of the major institutions that produce new knowledge about hitherto unknown or insufficiently described languages are the Research Centre for Language Typology at La Trobe University in Melbourne, Australia, the Language and Culture Research Centre at the Cairns Institute of James Cook University also in Australia, and the Summer Institute of Linguistics International (SIL). At the two Australian institutions, descriptive work focuses on – but is by no means restricted to – the Aboriginal languages of Australia.

So far we have seen that claims about "all languages" cannot actually be assessed due to lack of information about future languages, about all past languages, and about all languages that exist today. This means that our largest available data base consists of some past languages and those present-day languages that have been described. In addition, there are also more practical considerations in the way of testing universal claims: even with today's extensive data bases, no linguist can consult all descriptions that are available. If we tried, we would have to deal with thousands of languages and the amount of time and effort involved would be enormous.

The first extant written documentation of a language is Sumerian tablets dating from around 3,000 BCE; we have no direct information about earlier languages. Nor do we have detailed information about some languages that were spoken in the more recent past, such as Etruscan (inscriptions dated from about 700 BCE).

SIL was founded in 1934. The goals of this faith-based but non-denominational organization include both language development in the speaker communities and linguistic research. Its workers – currently over 5,500 from about 60 countries – have produced linguistic accounts of 2,700 or more languages of the world.

To make the task more manageable, language typologists work with selected samples of languages. The question is: what languages should be chosen as part of a language sample?

The principles that guide sampling directly follow from the goals of language typology: we are interested in identifying similarities and differences among languages that are independent of genetic origin, language contact, and environment. Thus, a proper sample must be representative of all language families, all geographic areas, and all cultures.

A thoughtfully designed and widely influential sampling technique is one proposed by Matthew Dryer (1989). Dryer's focus is on establishing universal tendencies – that is, statistical universals – rather than absolute universals. His question is: under what conditions can the crosslinguistic distribution of a structural pattern be declared a universally valid tendency?

The first step is to insure genetic balance.

(a) GENETIC GROUPS
All languages are assigned to one of 322 groups called genera. Each genus contains related languages that can be traced back to an ancestor about 2,500 years ago. For example, Romance languages (Latin, Spanish, French, Italian, and others) form a genus and so do Germanic languages (English, German, Dutch, Swedish, and so forth).

The second step is to make sure the emerging sample is areally balanced.

(b) GEOGRAPHIC GROUPS
Each genus is assigned to one of five continent-size areas of the world: Africa, Eurasia, Australia & New Guinea, North America, and South America. For example, Romance and Germanic languages are part of the Eurasian area and so are some non-Indo-European genera such as Finno-Ugric (Finnish, Estonian, Hungarian, and so forth).

How is it then decided whether a particular structural feature's crosslinguistic distribution indicates a statistically significant tendency?

(c) MEASURE OF UNIVERSAL TENDENCIES
Given a particular structural feature – say front-rounded vowels, e.g. French /ü/ in *tu* 'you' – languages in the various genera are checked for the presence versus absence of this property. The pattern is said to represent a significant universal tendency if in all five geographic areas, the majority of the genera exhibit that feature.

If a genus has both languages that have that feature and languages that do not, the genus is divided into two sub-genera each counted separately as a genus.

Here is one of Dryer's examples. The question is whether SOV order (as in Turkish, Hindi, and so forth) is a crosslinguistically significant tendency over SVO order (as in English). The table in (51) presents his results (269–270). The five areas are listed on the top; the numbers are of the genera in each area that have SOV and SVO order. The boxes highlight the majority figures.

(51)

	Afr	Eura	Austr-NG	NorthAm	SouthAm	Total
SOV	22	26	19	26	18	111
SVO	21	19	6	6	5	57

Since SOV order is exhibited in more genera in every area than SVO order, SOV emerges as a significant crosslinguistic tendency.

This is in contrast with the distribution of SVO (English) and VSO (Rapa Nui, Arabic) orders. Here are the results (270–271).

(52)

	Afr	Eura	Austr-NG	NorthAm	SouthAm	Total
SVO	21	19	6	6	5	57
VSO	5	3	0	12	2	22

In this case, SVO may be viewed as a trend but, because in North America, VSO genera are more numerous than SVO genera, SVO fails to reach the level of a significant crosslinguistic tendency.

Given that our knowledge of the entire set of human languages, past, present, and future, is only partial and unavoidably so, our universal statements are mere hypotheses whose validity can never be proven. This holds regardless of whether the statement is absolute or statistical: the next language may be a counterexample to an absolute statement or may change the probabilities of a statistical one. They must be viewed as best-possible guesses. They involve extrapolations from what is KNOWN about SOME languages onto what ALL languages MIGHT be like.

1.2.3 Data sources

Here is again the general schema of language-typological statements:

(53) (repeated from (50))
    In **all** (or most) languages (where there is Y), there is also X.

In the preceding section, we probed into the meaning of the phrase "all (or most) languages." The other fundamental terms of this statement type are X and Y – the structural properties of languages whose distribution is at issue. The question is: given a language, what are sources of information for X and Y?

The primary data for general linguistic research come from oral language. Ideally, typological studies, too, should be based on live data gathered orally from speakers. In actuality, this is barely feasible given the extensive crosslinguistic samples that typological work requires. Another, more doable way of obtaining primary data is by relying on written information, such as questionnaires that request translations of relevant materials into various languages.

Most commonly, however, data for typological work are derived from secondary sources: published grammars, dictionaries, journal articles, and the like. In addition, information can also be obtained from the data bases available on the Internet. The website of the Association for Linguistic Typology (www.linguistic.typology.org) lists a number of relevant data bases. One of these is the World Atlas of Language Structures (www.wals.info), which provides articles and maps for the areal distribution of 142 grammatical features, such as relative clauses or consonant inventories. Another valuable source is the website of the Surrey Morphology Group (www.surrey.ac.uk), which offers crosslinguistic data and analyses on a number of morphosyntactic patterns, such as syncretism and agreement. The Typological Database System, whose home is the University of Amsterdam, is a collection of independently developed typological data bases (www.hum.uva.nl/TDS).

These sources are relevant for discovering new language-typological generalizations. Another endeavor crucial to the advancement of our knowledge about the distribution of grammatical properties is testing generalizations that have already been proposed in the literature. A prime source for such generalizations is The Universals Archive based in Konstanz, Germany (http://typo.uni-konstanz.de/archive). At the time of this writing (Summer 2012), it lists 2029 crosslinguistic generalizations gleaned from the typological literature. A separate branch of this website is an inventory of rare grammatical characteristics (to date, 147 are listed).

A printout of a crosslinguistic generalization in the Language Universals Archive is given in (54) (Figure 1.1). It has to do with the crosslinguistic distribution of certain body-part terms. The first line gives the serial number of the statement in the archive. Next comes the verbatim quote from the source followed by a restatement that makes the implicational structure explicit. The rest of the entries are self-explanatory; "achronic" means the generalization pertains to synchronic stages of present, past, and future languages. References are to the bibliographic list given on the website.

(54)		
	Number	1180 (used to be 1184 in the old version)
	Original	If in a given language there is a separate term for 'leg' (as opposed to 'foot') then there is also a term for 'arm' (as opposed to 'hand').
	Standardized	If there is a separate term for 'leg' (as opposed to 'foot'), THEN there is a term for 'arm' (as opposed to 'hand')
	Formula	'leg' ⇒ 'arm'
	Keywords	body parts
	Domain	Lexicon
	Type	Implication
	Status	Achronic
	Quality	Absolute
	Basis	41 languages in Brown 1976 (12 American Indian languages, 10 European, 5 sub-Saharan African, Mideastern and Western Asian, 5 Southeast Asian, 2 Chinese, 2 Micronesian)
	Source	Brown 1976, also mentioned in Anderson 1978: 352
	Counterexamples	—
	Comments	By Frans Plank 03.08.2006, 09:49 A term for 'leg' is present in most but not all language. According to Andersen's data, at least three languages, Hopi (Uto-Aztecan), Inupik (Eskimo-Aleut), and Tarascan (Chibchan), do not have 'leg' though they do have terms for subparts (e.g. 'thigh' ⇒ 'calf').

Figure 1.1
The distribution of terms for 'leg' and 'arm'.

Summary

This chapter presented the goals and tools of language typological research. The goals involve establishing the distribution of grammatical properties across genetically, areally, and culturally independent languages. The means whereby the results of this endeavor are captured are crosslinguistic statements of various kinds.

Existential statements tell us what can occur in languages; universals tell us what occurs under what conditions. Universals are unrestricted if they have all languages in their scope; they are implicational if they have a well-defined subset of languages in their scope. Implicational statements may vary in terms of the relationship between implicans and implicatum and in whether their terms are simple or complex. All of these statements may also differ in their modality: statistical statements hypothesize what is probable while absolute statements are hypotheses about what may be certain. For formulating crosslinguistic hypotheses, we work with genetically, areally and, as much as possible, culturally balanced language samples. Language data come mostly from published sources and from data bases.

In everyday discourse, we often think we know a lot of things – or at least we speak as if we think we do. When we stereotype people or institutions, we presume to know all from a few. We tend to think that we know the future based on past experience, that we know the causes of things including people's intentions behind their acts, and how things would have been if they had been different. In actuality, such inferences are mere possibilities or probabilities rather than certainties. In scientific discourse, researchers are more careful about distinguishing knowledge states: they form hypotheses rather than declare things as certain and, instead of sweeping generalizations, they describe what is possible (since it has occurred) and quantify probabilities as much as they can. These issues will be taken up again in the closing section of Chapter 7.

Activities

1. Look up the word for 'salt' in dictionaries of different languages. Are there any similarities? If so, what might be the reason?

2. Universals – both unrestricted and restricted – can also be stated for the distribution of structural characteristics within languages. An unrestricted universal for English words is that they all contain at least one vowel. But now consider the following: "All consonant-initial words of English start with /s/." This is clearly untrue: there are thousands of words like *table* or *paper* that do not start with /s/.
   Try to formulate a restricted universal of the following type: "All English words that have characteristic X start with /s/." For identifying X, consider words like *string*, *sprain*, *splint*, and others; also non-existing words like *ptring*, *tprain*, *kplint*, and others.

3. Consider the crosslinguistic generalizations in (a), (b), (c), and (d).
   A. Determine for each whether it is an unrestricted or an implicational universal and whether it is absolute or statistical.
   B. Determine each statement's predictive force for English by choosing one of the following answers:
      (i)   This statement makes a correct prediction about English.
      (ii) This statement makes an incorrect prediction about English.
      (iii) This statement makes no prediction about English.
   Here are the statements:
   (a) In most languages where the adjective precedes the noun, both the demonstrative and the numeral also precede the noun. (Greenberg 1966a, #18; cited above in (48))
   (b) In all languages in which the inflected verb precedes the subject in wh-questions, the wh-word is normally initial. (Greenberg 1966a: #11b; cited above in (45b))
   (c) Whenever the verb agrees with the subject or the object in gender, it also agrees in number. (Greenberg 1966a, #32)
   (d) In most languages, interdentals are fricatives.

4. In Section 1.1, it was noted that SOV and VSO languages tend to have mirror-image orders. Consider the order of Subject, Object, and Verb, Possessor and Possessum, and Noun Phrase and Adposition in English. Which of the two types does English belong to or stand closer to?

5. Here is a paradigmatic implicational universal (Greenberg 1966a: #24). If the relative clause precedes the noun either as the only construction or as an alternative construction, either the language is postpositional or the adjective precedes the noun or both.

What does this statement say about the language types "mimicked" by the following sentences? For each type, circle your answer. Relative clauses are bracketed; * indicates the structure is ungrammatical.

TYPE A: (a)   The [yesterday I bought] apples are sweet.
           (b)   sweet apples
           (c)   the store in
Answer: i.   predicts this type
           ii.   excludes this type
           iii. there is not enough data to decide
           iv.   does not say anything about this type

TYPE B: (a)   The [yesterday I bought] apples are sweet.
           (b)   apples sweet
           (c)   in the store
Answer: i.   predicts this type
           ii.   excludes this type
           iii. there is not enough data to decide
           iv.   does not say anything about this type

TYPE C: (a)   The apples [I bought yesterday] are sweet.
           (b)   *The [yesterday I bought] apples are sweet.
           (c)   sweet apples

Answer: i.   predicts this type
         ii.   excludes this type
         iii. there is not enough data to decide
         iv.   does not say anything about this type

TYPE D: (a)   The [yesterday I bought] apples are sweet.
         (b)   apples sweet
Answer: i.   predicts this type
         ii.   excludes this type
         iii. there is not enough data to decide
         iv.   does not say anything about this type

TYPE E: (a)   The apples [I bought yesterday] are sweet.
         (b)   The [yesterday I bought] apples are sweet.
         (c)   sweet apples
         (d)   in the store
Answer: i.   predicts this type
         ii.   excludes this type
         iii. there is not enough data to decide
         iv.   does not say anything about this type

··

Further reading

- Two comprehensive handbooks of language typology are Haspelmath *et al.* 2001 and Song 2011. See also issue 11/1, 2007, of the journal *Linguistic Typology* devoted in its entirety to what language typology is and how it relates to other endeavors within the science of linguistics. A careful assessment of the extent to which language universals exist at all is Evans and Levinson 2009 along with the detailed responses following the article.

- Textbooks on language typology include Ramat 1987, Comrie 1989, Whaley 1997, Song 2001, and Croft 2003.

- Nutshell grammars written in popular style are provided by Shopen (ed.) 1979a and 1979b. *The Atlas of Languages* (Comrie *et al.* 2003) surveys the languages of the world by continents; it is written in an easy style with lots of pictures. Comrie 1990 provides brief grammars of the world's major languages. *The Book of a Thousand Tongues* (Nida 1972) contains passages from the Bible in 1431 languages.

- The Internet addresses of the three institutions mentioned in the text are as follows:
  - Research Centre for Language Typology (La Trobe University): www.latrobe.edu.au/rclt
  - Language and Culture Research Centre (Cairns Institute, James Cook University): https://eresearch.jcu.edu.au/spaces/TLA
  - Summer Institute of Linguistics International: http://www.sil.org

- For detailed discussions of sampling issues including the optimal size of a sample, and of data sources, see Song 2001: 17–41, Croft 2003: 19–30, and Bakker 2011.

- For a comprehensive survey of linguistic diversity across genetic and areal groups, see Nichols 1992.

- For a survey of the languages of the world, see Pereltsvaig 2012.

2 The worlds of words

Lexical typology

CHAPTER OUTLINE

What do languages have words for? We will consider similarities and differences in vocabulary among languages in six semantic fields: body parts, kinship terms, personal pronouns, numerals, antonymic adjectives, and color words.

Summary generalizations will be presented about markedness relations and about the relationship between words and thoughts.

2.1 Introduction

Suppose you were to design a language that is easy to speak and understand. What would the words be like? Here are two features of what seems to be an ideal vocabulary.

(i)   There is a word for everything.
(ii)   From the way a word sounds, it is easy to tell what it means.

Let us see if these characteristics hold for English.

(A) WORDS FOR EVERYTHING?

Back in the 1980s, comedian and actor Rich Hall provided abundant evidence to show that English did not have words for everything. In his TV program and in his books (e.g. Hall 1984), he entertained his audience with "sniglets," which he defined as "any word that does not appear in the dictionary but should." Here are some of these tongue-in-cheek creations, proposed by either Hall himself and by other people who subsequently picked up on the idea.

(1)   (a) *downpause* n.
            The split-second interruption of rain as you drive your car
            under a bridge.
       (b) *lactomangulation* n.
            Manhandling the "open here" spout on a milk carton so badly
            that one has to resort to using the "illegal" side.
       (c) *cinemuck* n.
            The sticky substance on the floor of a movie theater.
       (d) *dasho* n.
            The area between a car's windshield and dashboard where
            coins, pencils etc. cannot be humanly retrieved.
       (e) *sashtuk* n.
            A belt lodged and hanging out of a closed automobile door.
       (f) *backspuddle* n.
            Dishwater that disappears down one drain of a double sink
            and comes up the other.
       (g) *blibula* n.
            The spot on a dog's stomach which, when rubbed, causes his
            legs to rotate widely.
       (h) *vegeludes* n.
            Individual peas or kernels of corn that you end up chasing all
            over the plate.

These "novelty items" show not only that our language does not have words for everything but also that it would be difficult to define what "everything" means. For an example, take the human hand. What would it be like to have a word for everything on it? Should the inside and outside of each of the ten fingers have distinct names? Should each knuckle

A couple of British sniglets:
(a) *happle* v.
To annoy people by finishing their sentences for them and then telling them what they really meant to say.
(b) *sketty* n.
Apparently self-propelled little dance a beer glass performs in its own puddle.
(c) *skibbereen* n.
The noise made by a sunburned thigh leaving a plastic chair.
(d) *duggleby* n.
The person in front of you in the supermarket queue who has just unloaded a bulging trolley onto the conveyor belt and is now in the process of trying to work out which pocket they left their cheque book in, and indeed in which pair of trousers.

be separately labeled? Should there be a separate word for each of the ten finger nails and for each white semicircle on each nail?

There are two organizing principles that underlie the English terms related to hand: segmentation and classification. Segmentation means dividing things into parts. The fact that we have a word *hand* distinct from *wrist* and *arm* reflects a **partonomic** decision: the hand is seen as something separate from the wrist and the arm, even though they are connected. Furthermore, within the hand we make a distinction between *palm* and *fingers*. There are of course clearly discernible joints between all these parts: one separates the hand from the arm and knuckles divide the fingers from the palm. Thus, segmentation does in part run along the lines present in reality. But there are also joints between the bones of each finger; yet, we do not have a word for each section. Thus, English vocabulary reflects the natural partonomy of the human hand to an extent but it does not follow it down to the last detail: not all parts are graced with a name.

In addition to delimiting relevant parts of things, the other tool involved in naming is defining **kinds**. Both the right hand and the left are called hands as if they were the same thing even though they are not exactly alike. Of the ten digits, each is distinguished from the other by a name – such as *pinky*, *thumb*, and so forth – but all of them can also be called *fingers*. The ten fingers resemble each other and this supports their shared labeling; but why are toes not included in the category? They, too, are similar to fingers in that they are all protrusions on limbs; yet, English does not call toes fingers. This shows that similarity is also a relative concept: we cannot just say that all things that are similar have the same name and those that are different do not. Type–subtype relations (**taxonomy**) are to a great extent in the eye of the beholder; and, as we saw above, the same holds for whole–part relations (**partonomy**).

If we now look beyond English and consider other languages, these two points jump out even more clearly: both partonomic and taxonomic divisions partially reflect what reality suggests but both concepts are negotiable. For example, in English, there are separate words for 'arm' and 'hand'; in Russian, the two may both be referred to as *ruka*. Thus, a partonomic split made in English is glossed over in Russian. Conceivable taxonomic splits may also be neglected in vocabulary: as mentioned above, in English, the difference between finger and toe is respected by there being different words for the two, while in Hungarian, it is their similarity that prevails: the same word *ujj* may be used to refer to either.

Reviewing the vocabularies of other languages, we find many other cases as well where partonomic or taxonomic distinctions are alternatively observed or disregarded. Distinctions not respected in English but honored in other languages include examples from German: it has two words for 'eat' depending on the eater: *essen* for humans and *fressen* for animals. German also has two words for 'student': *Schüler* in lower grades and *Student* for higher grades including university students. Likewise, Hungarian has distinct words for English *sister*: older sister is *nővér* and younger sister is *húg*. In other cases, it is English that makes a taxonomic cut where other languages do not: the difference between 'he' and 'she' is glossed over by Turkish, which uses the word *o* for both.

These observations suggest that if we wanted there to be a word for everything in a language, the very term "everything" would need to be defined by two decisions: how the world should be segmented into parts and how the parts should be categorized. Since there is virtually an infinite number of parts that the world could be segmented into and a similarly huge number of ways in which the parts may be categorized, there is no workable definition of the term "everything."

Aside from the differences between how vocabularies capture reality in various languages, we will see that there are also some crosslinguistic convergences as to what is named and how. Here is our first question.

(i)   What are crosslinguistic generalizations – absolute or statistical, unrestricted or implicational – about the **existence** of words for given meanings?

In an attempt to respond to this question, we will be looking for statements that conform to the following schemata (M, M-1, and M-2 stand for word meanings):

(a)   SCHEMA FOR UNRESTRICTED UNIVERSALS
        In all (or most) languages, there is a word for M.
(b)   SCHEMA FOR IMPLICATIONAL UNIVERSALS
        In all (or most) languages, if there is a word for M-2, there is also a word for M-1.

Before we begin our search, let us consider the second desirable characteristic of vocabularies as stated in (ii) at the beginning of this section: that the forms of words should suggest their meanings. Once again, we start with English: is this true in this language?

(B) DO THE SOUNDS OF WORDS REVEAL THEIR MEANINGS?

There are two ways in which this desideratum may be satisfied: onomatopoeia and compositional structure. **Onomatopoeia** refers to a pattern where the phonetic form of a word resembles its referent. Since phonetic form cannot possibly resemble shapes or colors, onomatopoeia can apply only to words that designate sounds. And, indeed, many sound words in English suggest their meaning by imitating that sound. Examples are *buzz*, *crash*, *boom*, and animal sounds such as *bow-wow*, *meow*, *bleat*, and *cock-a-doodle-doo*.

The other, more interesting way in which words can suggest their meanings applies to polymorphemic words. If the word consists of more than one morpheme each with its distinct meaning, the part-meanings taken together may or may not yield the total meaning. There are some cases where they do, such as in the list of compound words in (2). (These are all pronounced as single words even where spelling separates their components.)

(2) *bus ticket*
     apple seed
     paycheck
     dinnertime
     school day

In these words, the sum of the meanings of the parts at the very least approximates the meaning of the entire word; e.g. a *bus ticket* refers to a ticket for busses, and *dinnertime* refers to the time to have dinner. However, the match is not complete: a learner of English hearing *bus ticket* for the first time may think that it is a ticket that is sold on the bus as opposed to one sold at the bus station; and he may think *dinnertime* refers to the time it takes to have dinner. Thus, these words are compositional only to an extent. However, there are many other compound words in English that are even less compositional if at all.

(3) *airline*
     laughing gas
     ladybug
     lighthouse
     understand

If we tried to interpret these words compositionally, we would be likely to go astray: the components of the word *airline* suggest a line drawn in the air, *laughing gas* could be gas in a cartoon with a smiley-face; *ladybug* sounds like it refers to a female insect; and *lighthouse* may be any lit-up house. A learner of English first encountering these words is unlikely to zero in on the actual meanings. And when it comes to the word *understand*, all bets are off: the actual meaning has nothing to do with either *under* or *stand*.

How do other languages compare with English in how forms of words suggest their meanings? Onomatopoeia is common across languages; what is interesting, though, is that although the sound effects that the words are trying to imitate are presumably the same all over the world – roosters crow and balloons pop the same way in Louisiana, Lithuania, and Lebanon – it appears as if different languages "heard" the same noises somewhat differently. Here are two examples.

(4) rooster crowing:
     English: *cock-a-doodle-doo*
     Albanian: *kikeriki*
     Greek: *kikiriku*
     Hindi: *kukudukoo*

(5) balloon bursting:
     English: *pop*
     Arabic: *boof*
     German: *peng*
     Hungarian: *puff*

In the rest of this chapter, nothing further will be said about crosslinguistic onomatopoeia since the semantic domains we will discuss do not include sound. We will, however, see many instances of the other way in which words can suggest their meanings: by polymorphemic structure. Forming words by putting morphemes together is common across languages and, as in English, the resulting compounds may show varying degrees of compositionality. Here are some examples.

(6) (a) *petit   doigt*   'pinky'   French
            small   finger
      (b) *chemin de   fer*   'railroad'
            road   of   iron

(7) (a) *yào-diàn*   'drug store'   Mandarin
            drug-store
      (b) *huā-mù* 'vegetation'
            flower-tree

(8) (a) *daang-bakal*   'railroad tracks'   Tagalog
            road-iron
      (b) *hanap-buhay*   'livelihood'
            seeking-life

(9) (a) *wadu-bayiinda* 'tobacco'   Kayardild
            smoke-be.bitten   (Evans 1988: 166)
      (b) *dulja-winda* 'car'
            ground-runner

But even if a concept is expressed compositionally, there may be different ways of achieving this. Consider (10).

(10) (a) 80 in English: *eighty*
            80 in French: *quatre-vingt* "four twenty"
      (b) 19 in English: *nineteen*
            19 in Latin: *un-de-viginti* "one-out.of-twenty"

As shown in (10a), the English and French words for 80 are both compositional but in English, eight is multiplied by ten while in French, twenty is multiplied by four. And, as shown in (10b), the English word for 19 suggests the addition of nine and ten; Latin, however, uses subtraction: the three morphemes are *un* 'one,' *de* 'out of,' and *viginti* 'twenty.'

The examples above illustrate the various degrees and ways in which polymorphemic words may suggest their meanings. These observations give rise to a second question:

(ii) What are crosslinguistic generalizations – absolute or statistical, unrestricted or implicational – about the **morphological structure** of words for given meanings?

The schemata of the statements we will be looking for are given below. (M-1 and M-2 stand for word meanings; S-1, S-2 stand for various morphological structures, such as monomorphemicity, polymorphemicity, or a particular polymorphemic composition.)

(a) SCHEMA FOR UNRESTRICTED UNIVERSALS
     In all (or most) languages, the word for M-1 has morphological
     structure S-1.
(b) SCHEMA FOR IMPLICATIONAL UNIVERSALS
     In all (or most) languages, if the word for M-2 has morphological
     structure S-2, then the word for M-1 has the morphological
     structure S-1.

The two questions raised above – (i) and (ii) – provide an agenda for the rest
of this chapter. (i) probes into the crosslinguistic distribution of word meanings: whether there are unrestricted or implicational universals regarding
the existence of words for given meanings in languages. (ii) is about the
internal structure of words: whether there are unrestricted or implicational
universals regarding how words are constructed. Armed with this agenda,
we will now begin our crosslinguistic journey across the worlds of words.

2.2 Me. Words for body parts

There is no portion of the world more intimately connected to us than our
bodies. They form an inescapable ingredient of our personal reality: all of
our actions are inextricably connected with it. We are embodied crea-
tures: our self is centered on our body. The rest of the world only APPEARS
to us but the body is different: it IS us. Since our world is populated with
the bodies of other people as well, we know about the human body both
by experiencing our own bodies and by seeing, hearing, smelling, and
touching the bodies of others.

The human body is essentially the same all over the world and thus we
might expect that the words for its parts closely correspond to each other
across languages. Since, as we have already seen above, this is not entirely
so, studying body-part terminology will provide particularly striking
examples of how the SAME REALITY can be captured by alternative terminologies in different languages.

Let us recast the two general questions stated above for the particular
semantic domain of body parts.

(i)   What are crosslinguistic generalizations about the **existence** of
      body-part words?
(ii) What are crosslinguistic generalizations about the **morpholog-
      ical structure** of body-part terms?

We will consider these questions in turn.

(A) THE EXISTENCE OF BODY-PART TERMS

As mentioned in Section 2.1, when it comes to organizing the world
around us, the human mind operates on two fundamental principles:
delimiting parts of the world and assigning these parts to classes.

Segmentation (partonomy) and classification (taxonomy) are the two fundamental conceptual tools of naming. Accordingly, in trying to find crosslinguistic similarities in the existence of body-part terms, we should ask what parts of the body are singled out for naming in various languages and what the classes are that these parts of the body are assigned to in naming practices.

There is one unit that is unambiguously delimited by reality: the body itself. It is not permanently linked to other objects. Thus, one might expect that every language has a word for 'body.' And, indeed, several researchers have found this to hold true for extensive samples of languages (Brown 1976: 404, Andersen 1978: 352). Crosslinguistic generalizations below will be labeled as GEN(eralization) and sequentially numbered.

GEN-1: All languages have a word for 'body.'

There are also parts within the body that are fairly clearly delineated: they are linked to other parts but can be moved more or less independently. These are the head, the trunk, and the limbs; within the head, such units are the eyes, the ears, the nose, and the mouth; in the upper limbs, it is the hand, the wrist, the lower arm, the elbow, the upper arm, the armpit and the shoulder; and in the lower limbs, it is the foot, the ankle, the leg, the knee, and the thigh. But do all languages "see" these as separate units?

As noted earlier, in some cases, body-part terminology does follow the natural segmentation of the body: Elaine Andersen's classic article on the topic states that every language has words for 'head,' 'trunk,' 'arm' (possibly including 'hand'), 'eye,' 'nose,' 'mouth,' 'fingernail,' and 'toenail' (Andersen 1978: 352). There are nonetheless scattered examples of languages that lack some of these terms: there is no word for 'arm' in Lavukaleve (Terrill 2006) and there is no term for 'mouth' and 'face' in Jahai (Burenhult 2006). Similarly, a word for 'leg' (possibly including 'foot') occurs in most languages but, as noted in Section 1.2.3 (54), not in all (Andersen 1978: 352).

GEN-2: Most languages have separate words for 'head,' 'trunk,' 'arm' (possibly including 'hand'), 'eye,' 'nose,' and 'mouth'.

Although these major units are independently named in most languages, not all of the natural segments of the body are so labeled: some of the visible divisions between body parts may be glossed over so that the words span more than one natural segment. As mentioned in the introductory section, this is the case for the units of the fingers and toes that fall between the knuckles: languages don't have special words for each segment. More surprisingly, as noted above, hand and arm are not always separately named. Cecil Brown has found that while out of 617 languages, well over a half – 389 – differentiate them, 228 do not (Brown 2005a).

(11) Differentiation: Ngawun (Pama-Nyungan); also English:
     marl 'hand'
     palkal 'arm'
   No differentiation: Lonwolwol (Oceanic); also Russian:
     va: 'arm and hand'

A similar disregard for a joint between the terminal and pre-terminal sections of a limb holds for lower leg versus foot. In Hungarian, the same word *láb* may refer to the entire limb including leg and foot. 'Hand' and 'finger' may also be covered by the same word: Brown has found that out of 593 languages, the great majority (521) have different words for the two but 72 do not (Brown 2005b).

(12)   Differentiation: West-Central Oromo (Cushitic; Ethiopia, Kenya); also English:
        quba 'finger'
        harka 'hand'
    No differentiation: Warlpiri (Pama-Nyungan, Australia):
        rdaka 'hand and fingers'

Brown has found that the lack of distinction between words for hand and finger has cultural correlates: it occurs predominantly in hunter-gatherer societies.

While word meanings may extend over several contiguous segments of the body, a word's semantic scope may also include body parts that are not contiguous. In some languages, there is evidence that paired body parts are considered as a single entity. In Hungarian, the word *szem* 'eye' does have a plural: *szemek*, but the singular form *szem* may also refer to both eyes together. Thus, a person who has only one seeing eye may be said to be blind in half an eye: *fél-szemű* "half-eyed." Similarly, if somebody moves a crate with one arm, he can be said to have done it with half an arm: *fél-kéz-zel* "half-hand-with." The same holds for the words for other paired body parts such as 'ear,' 'arm,' 'knee,' 'leg,' 'kidney,' and even garments covering them such as 'sleeve,' 'glove,' 'shoe,' and 'sock'. If I have misplaced one of my socks, I can say I cannot find 'half of my sock' (*fél-zoknim*). In these cases, shared function and parallel position in the body prevail over discontinuity.

For some body-part words for whose existence no unrestricted universals can be stated, conditional generalizations do hold. That is to say, the naming of certain body parts may imply the naming of others.

GEN-3: If a language has words for individual toes, then it has
       words for individual fingers. (Andersen 1978: 352–353)
GEN-4: If a language has a word for foot, it also has a word for
       hand. (Andersen 1978: 352)

Having considered the **partonomic** cuts reflected in body-part terms, let us turn to **taxonomy**: what classes are body parts subsumed under? Generally, body parts that look alike form a single class, such as English fingers, toes, or limbs. Finger and toe are classed together in Rumanian and Spanish (Andersen 1978: 354); and several Mayan languages lump together head and knee by using the same word for both.

An overall pattern in body-part terminologies is that they are generally more detailed for the upper body and for the front. This preference is also evident in the morphological structure of body-part terms – the topic that we now turn to.

(B) THE MORPHOLOGICAL STRUCTURE OF BODY-PART TERMS

Some body parts are labeled with monomorphemic words in all languages investigated. These include 'leg,' 'hand,' and 'foot' – provided that a language has words for these parts (Brown 1976: 405). Andersen (1978: 353) adds 'head,' 'face,' 'eye,' 'mouth,' and 'ear' to this list. It is easy to see that monomorphemicity correlates here with the salience of the body parts referred to. But this is not always the case: strikingly, in Jahai, there are separate monomorphemic words also for as non-salient parts of the body as the upper lip and lower lip (Burenhult 2006).

As mentioned above, finger and toe may be different words (English, Finnish) or they may be the same (Hebrew, Spanish); but an additional pattern is also attested: one word may be derived from the other. In such cases, the base is always 'finger' rather than 'toe.' In other words, there are languages – such as Russian and Malay – where toes are named as the "fingers of the foot" but no languages where fingers are "toes of the hand". This again shows the primacy of the upper body over the lower one.

> GEN-5: The word for 'head' is monomorphemic in all languages.
> GEN-6: If words for a part of the upper body and a part of the lower
> are in a derivational relationship, the upper-body term is
> the base.

Other polymorphemic body-part words are for 'ankle,' which is "eye of foot" in Malay and "neck of leg" in Hausa; 'wrist' is "hand joint" in Lahu and 'foot' is "spoon of leg" in Hebrew (Andersen 1978: 355, 359). The composition of some polymorphemic body-part names recurs in languages: English's monomorphemic *nostril* is translated as "nose hole" not only in European languages such as German and Hungarian but also in Jahai (Burenhult 2006).

What are some general conclusions that emerge regarding our initial questions about the existence and morphological structure of body-part terms across languages? Regarding **existence**: as we saw above, there are unrestricted universals stating that some body parts are labeled by separate words universally – or at least in those languages that have been studied from this point of view. There are also implicational universals stating that the existence of some body-part words implies the existence of some others. For example, separate words for the different toes imply separate words for the different fingers (Andersen 1978: 352). Regarding **morphological composition**: there are body-part terms that are universally monomorphemic, e.g. head; and if an upper-body and a lower-body term are in a derivational relationship, the base is the upper-body term.

2.3 Me and others

2.3.1 Kinship terms

Body parts are permanent belongings: short of some drastic intervention, they stay with us for the rest of our lives. But there is also another set of permanent companions that we all have: relatives. Our relationships to them are defined once and for all: your sister remains your sister for life.

The permanent bondage with both body parts and relatives is reflected in many ways in language. For example, in Anindilyakwa (an Australian language spoken in the Northern Territory), family members may be referred to by touching various parts of the body: the nose refers to father, the breast signals mother, the leg calf stands for brother or sister (Leeding 1996: 232). While in this case, body parts symbolize relatives, the opposite metaphor also occurs and is in fact very common: relatives can provide names for body parts. In their survey of 118 languages, Cecil Brown and Stanley Witkowski (1981: 601–602) found 42 languages where digits of the hand or foot are named after relatives. For example, in Dakota, a Siouan language, the word for thumb is "mother of hand," in Quechua, an Andean-Equatorial language, it is "mother finger"; and in Maranao, a Northern Austronesian language, it is "father of hand." The striking similarity among these examples from genetically and areally unrelated languages indicates "shared cognitive processes underlying human behavior" – in particular, naming practices (Brown and Witkowski 1981: 597).

In addition to such metaphors, the likeness between body parts and kin is also apparent in grammar. In many languages, a person's relationships with his body parts and with his relatives are expressed in a unique way that is different from the expression of possessing other objects. (13) and (14) illustrate this from Tsimshian, an American Indian language of Northern British Columbia. "Alienable" possessions – such as house or stone – are marked with the prefix *ne-* and a possessive suffix; "inalienables," which include both body parts and kin terms, have the possessive suffix but no prefix. (Transcription is approximate.)

(13) alienable possession: Tsimshian
    (a) *walb* 'house'   **ne**-*walb*-**u** 'my house'
    (b) *lab* 'stone'   **ne**-*lab*-**u** 'my stone'

(14) inalienable possession:
    (a) *ban* 'belly'   *ban*-**u** 'my belly'
    (b) *negwad* 'father'   *negwad*-**u** 'my father'

In the brief crosslinguistic survey of kinship terms that follows, we will take up the two basic questions raised in Section 2.1, which, appropriately re-cast, guide vocabulary studies in all semantic fields:

(i)   What are crosslinguistic generalizations – absolute or statistical, unrestricted or implicational – about the **existence** of kinship terms?
(ii)   What are crosslinguistic generalizations – absolute or statistical, unrestricted or implicational – about the **morphological structure** of kinship terms?

(A) THE EXISTENCE OF KINSHIP TERMS

From the discussion of body parts in Section 2.2, some general conclusions may be derived. First, we saw that body-part terminology was founded on two organizational tools: establishing wholes and parts (partonomy) and classifying the resulting objects (taxonomy). Secondly, the crosslinguistic similarities and differences among body-part terms indicate that neither partonomic nor taxonomic cuts are faithful mirrors of external reality. Let us now see how these two general observations fare in the domain of kinship terminology.

Regarding segmentation: for body parts, the highest-level whole is a given: the human body itself, and it is the delimitation of the parts that is negotiable. In naming relatives, the opposite is true: the parts are given in that each relative is a separate person; what is negotiable is the wholes that the relatives belong to. In Western culture, the nuclear family counts as a whole; it is in turn a subpart of the extended family, which is part of the entire group of relatives. But in some other cultures, relatives are placed into other groups. In Guugu Yimidhirr, all relatives belong to one of two sets, called moieties. They are defined by unilateral descent. One moiety includes the speaker, his or her siblings, the father, and the father's siblings; the other contains the mother, her siblings, and the speaker's spouse (Haviland 1979: 213).

Let us turn to taxonomy. How are relatives classified? Consider first some kin terms of English.

(15) *father*   English
       mother
       grandfather
       grandmother
       brother
       sister
       sibling
       cousin
       son
       daughter
       mother-in-law
       brother-in-law

The classification of relatives reflected in this system is based in part on objective criteria. A real-life criterion is natural sex and it does indeed set apart some of the above terms, such as *father* and *mother*, *sister* and *brother*. But note that sex differentiation does not pervade the entire system: on the level of cousins, gender distinctions are not observed and the terms *parent*, *sibling*, and *in-laws* also rise above gender differences. The difference between *father* and *son* is **generational** – a second fact-based division. *Father* and *brother* in turn are distinguished by a third criterion, called **lineal** versus **collateral** relations. And, fourthly, the split between *father* and *father-in-law* is by blood relations versus relation by marriage (**consanguineal** versus **affinal** relations).

If we now begin to look at kinship terms in some other languages, we find two ways in which they differ from the English system. First, while the classificatory criteria that apply in English may be present in other languages as well, they may be used more or less extensively. For example, English *cousin* has no separate male and female forms but Spanish has *primo* for male cousin and *prima* for female cousin. Spanish thus makes a gender distinction where English does not. On the other hand, while sex distinguishes *grandson* and *granddaughter* in English, this feature is unexploited for grandchildren in Japanese: *mago* is grandchild and there are no separate words for male and female grandchildren.

A second way in which kin terms in other languages differ from those in English is by invoking additional distinguishing factors. Anthropologist Alfred Kroeber proposed a total of eight properties that underlie kinship term differentiations, with each present in at least one language of the world (cited in Greenberg 1966c: 87).

Four of Kroeber's dimensions are familiar from English as seen above and from other well-known languages. They are **sex** (e.g. *father* versus *mother*), **generation** (e.g. *father* versus *grandfather*), **lineal versus collateral relatives** (e.g. *father* versus *brother*), **consanguineal versus affinal relatives** (e.g. *father* versus *father-in-law*).

Sex-based splits may take additional forms in languages. In addition to the sex of the relative, the sex of the connective relative may also matter, as well as the sex of the speaker. The **sex of the connective relative** – a fifth criterion of Kroeber's – matters in languages where 'grandmother' is referred to by distinct words depending on whether she is father's mother or mother's mother. This is not entirely alien to English; while in English, the distinction is not honored by distinct words, it is paraphrasable as *paternal grandmother* and *maternal grandmother*.

If the **sex of the speaker** is relevant (a sixth factor), that means that, say, for '(someone's) child,' there are two words depending on whether the speaker is the father or the mother. Examples are in (16) (Haviland 1979: 214).

(16) *yumurr* 'child referred to by the father'   Guugu Yimidhirr
      dyuway 'son referred to by the mother'
      nguudhur 'daughter referred to by the mother'

In addition to the six properties mentioned so far, Kroeber offers two more: **relative age within generation** and **condition of life of the connective relative** (whether alive or dead). One example for the former was mentioned in Section 2.1: in Hungarian, there are separate words for older and younger sister, as well as for older and younger brother. Another example is Guugu Yimidhirr: *yaba* 'older brother,' *garga* 'younger brother'; *gaanhal* 'older sister,' *dyin-gurr* 'younger sister' (Haviland 1979: 214).

Since each of Kroeber's eight properties plays a role in differentiating kin terms in at least one language, each amounts to an existential generalization of the kind in (17).

(17) There are languages where kin terms are differentiated by X – where X is any one of Kroeber's eight properties discussed above.

Apart from **existential generalizations**, are there also **distributional statements** about kin terms across languages stating the conditions under which the different types occur? Greenberg proposes that of Kroeber's eight properties, three are universally present (Greenberg 1966c: 87).

GEN-7: Generational differences, the difference between consanguineal and affinal relatives, and sex differences of the
relatives are present in all languages.

Two further generalizations elaborate on sex distinctions.

GEN-8: In all languages, there are separate words for 'father' and
'mother' (although each word may also include other
relatives). (Greenberg 1966c: 74)

GEN-9: If sex is differentiated in the second descending generation,
it is also differentiated in the second ascending generations.
(Greenberg 1966c: 82).

GEN-8 is self-explanatory. GEN-9 means that if, for example, there are
separate words for 'grandson' and 'granddaughter,' there are also separate
words for 'grandfather' and 'grandmother.' In other words, of the four
logically possible types, only three exist.

	grandfather vs. grandmother	grandson vs. granddaughter	EXAMPLE LANGUAGE:
Type I	+	+	English
Type II	–	–	Lunda
Type III	+	–	Japanese
*Type IV	–	+	0

Let us now turn to the second question raised in the beginning of this
section: how are kinship terms internally structured?

(B) THE MORPHOLOGICAL STRUCTURE OF KINSHIP TERMS

In our discussion of body-part terms, we noted that some terms were
or tended to be monomorphemic across languages while others had a
complex structure. Furthermore, we saw that the distribution of
monomorphemicity and polymorphemicity among body-part terms
was not random: more prominent and presumably more frequently
used terms, such as those for head and arm, had simple structure
while less salient body parts, such as toes, tended to be complex. We
see a strikingly similar pattern in kinship terms. Compare the following English examples.

(18) (a) monomorphemic words: English
           father
           mother
           son
           daughter
      (b) polymorphemic words:
           grandfather
           grandmother
           grandson
           granddaughter

The difference between the simple and complex terms is generational distance from the speaker: those only one generation removed have simple names and those two (or more) generations removed have complex ones.

Apart from generational distance from the speaker, another criterion setting simple and complex terms apart is illustrated in (19).

(19) (a) monomorphemic terms: English
           father
           mother
           brother
           sister
      (b) polymorphemic terms:
           father-in-law
           mother-in-law
           brother-in-law
           sister-in-law

Here the division is between consanguineal and affinal relatives – another dimension of distance from the speaker.

As may be expected, an additional characteristic that correlates with simple (monomorphemic) versus complex (polymorphemic) structure is frequency. Text counts from English, Spanish, French, German, and Russian show that simple kin terms tend to be more frequent than complex ones (Greenberg 1966c: 81–82). This factor is not independent of the other two: terms that are close to the speaker by generational and blood relations are the ones that are also likely to be more frequent. If so, these correlations can be summarized in the following hypothesis:

> GEN-10: In all or most languages, kin terms that are frequent are semantically and morphologically simple; less frequent terms are semantically and morphologically complex.

The two-way correlation between frequency and structural simplicity (including simplicity in both meaning and form) holds for body-part terms as well: as noted above, simple terms such as *head* and *hand* are more frequent in texts than complex ones such as *toenail* and *earlobe*. In the following sections, we will see additional evidence for the pairing of frequency and structural simplicity.

In conclusion, we may note that kinship terminology largely follows factual, naturally given divisions. However, just as in the case of body-part terminology, not all possible natural divisions are picked up on by all languages, nor are the ones that do occur exploited to the same extent and in the same way.

2.3.2 Personal pronouns

Kinship terms serve to identify people differently from names like *Woody* and from descriptions such as *the furry animal in the corner*. This is because in addition to referring to persons, kin terms also specify the relationship between the self and another individual: *sister* is a particular person with a special relationship to me.

In addition to kin terms, there is also another set of words that both refer to a person and also describe the self's relationship to him: personal pronouns, such as *I*, *you*, and *he/she/it*. However, while our relationship with relatives is determined for life, the 'I-you-he' relationship varies with the speech situation. Change the speaker in a group and the assignment of 'I,' 'you,' and possibly 'he' will change as well.

Let us take a closer look at the meanings of personal pronouns. In order for an act of speech to happen, there have to be somebody who speaks and a person or persons addressed. Languages provide unique labels for them: a pronoun that refers to the speaker – such as English *I* – and a pronoun that refers to the hearer – such as *you*. In addition, there must be something or somebody to talk about. This may be 'me' or 'you'; but it may also be an entity other than the speaker and the hearer. Thus, most speech situations involve three protagonists: the speaker, the hearer, and whatever is the object of the verbal exchange, such as people or things in the world. We can therefore expect a minimal pronoun system to consist of the following:

(20) (a)   singular first person: 'I'
      (b)   singular second person: 'you'
      (c)   singular third person: 'the person or thing talked about'

This is almost as things really are. Based on an extensive language sample, Michael Cysouw (2003: 53–54) found only two exceptions to the generalization that, if a language has independent pronouns (i.e. pronoun words rather than affixes), there will be separate forms for all three persons. The list of 37 semantic units that proponents of the Natural Semantic Metalanguage framework hypothesize as having expressions in all languages also includes both 'I' and 'you' (cf. Goddard and Wierzbicka 1994: 37–38).

In each of the three person categories, there may be more than one individual involved. This is most obvious for the third person: we often speak about more than one person or thing, such as in *I would like to see* **them**. This calls for an additional pronoun.

(21) plural third person: 'more than one person or thing talked about'

Let us now see how plurality might apply to the first and second person.

(22) (a)   plural second person: more than one addressee
            E.g. *I want to praise* **you-all** *for your work*.
      (b)   plural first person: more than one speaker
            E.g. **We** *arrived in Milwaukee in 1976*.

The word *you-all* in (22a) is somewhat ambiguous. The group referred to by the third-person plural pronoun consists of a set of 'he'-s, 'she'-s, or 'it'-s: the word *they* refers to more than one third-person entity. If *you-all* expressed the same sense of plurality, it would have to refer to more than one addressee. This is indeed one of the interpretations of (22a): all of those receiving the praise may be present and listening. But the sentence may be spoken to a single addressee, in which case *you-all* refers to that person and others associated with him who are not present. In this case, the set of *you-all* is person-wise diverse: it consists of one 'you' and a set of third persons.

How about the plurality of the first person in (22b)? If the *we* in this sentence were a normal plural just as *they* is, it would have to refer to more than one speaker. And, indeed, the pronoun *we* may be used in this sense, such as when a crowd sings **We** *shall overcome*. But this use is rare; in most cases, *we* refers to a single speaker and some others, just as *you-all* may point at a person-wise heterogeneous set. In a normal nominal plural, such as *girls* or *tables*, and in the third person pronominal plural *they*, the set referred to is homogeneous: it contains more than one of the entity described by the noun. In the case of first- and second-person plurals, the set is mostly heterogeneous held together by cohesion rather than by similarity. It is for this reason that Cysouw (2003) re-labels the plurals of the first- and second-person pronouns as groups. In each case, there is a central person – 'I' for 'we' and 'you' for 'you-all' – and a set of others grouped around this focal individual.

For the second person plural *you-all*, the non-second-persons involved must all be third person. Which other persons can the first-person plural *we* refer to? Well, it depends. Consider the following sentences.

(23) (a) *Today* **we** *will discuss pronouns in Dutch.*
      (b) *My family moved to Chicago last year and* **we** *are very happy here.*

In (23a), announced by a teacher, the pronoun *we* includes the speaker, the listener(s) and possibly others who may not be present. In (23b), however, *we* does not include the listener: it includes only the speaker and the speaker's family or other associates.

English does not formally differentiate these two uses of *we*: the so-called inclusive use (where the addressee is included) and the exclusive use (where the addressee is not included), but there is reason to wish it did since the lack of two distinct words can lead to ambiguity. Notice the following dialogue:

(24) Wife entering the room with her daughter:
      Tonight **we** *are going out to see "Hunger games"!*
      Husband:
      (a) *Great; I have been wanting to see this movie.*
           OR
      (b) *Great; I will then watch TV while you are gone.*

The (a) response is based on the inclusive interpretation of *we*: the husband thinks he, too, is invited to go along. The (b) response in turn is based on the husband's assumption that the wife's *we* only includes herself and the daughter but not him.

In languages like Tok Pisin (an English-based Creole of Papua New Guinea), no such ambiguity would arise. If the woman wanted to include her husband in the pronoun, she would use *jumi*; if she wanted to exclude him, the pronoun would be *mifelo*. Similarly, Hawaiian would use *kakou* or *makou* to make the message clear. Here are the Tok Pisin and Hawaiian pronominal paradigms.

(25)   TOK PISIN   HAWAIIAN
    SING 1   *mi*   *owau*
    2   *yu*   *oe*
    3   *em*   *oia*
    PLU 1 inclusive   **jumi**   **kakou**
         exclusive   **mifelo**   **makou**
    2   *ju*   *oukou*
    3   *em*   *lakou*

In addition to the **person** and **number** distinctions discussed above, personal pronouns may also be differentiated for social factors: degrees and kinds of social relationship between the speaker and the other person. As was mentioned in Section 1.1 of Chapter 1, in several European languages, the second person has two forms depending on the relationship between the speaker and the addressee; Spanish *tu* and *usted* are an example. Also, in some languages, the inclusion of certain relatives in the reference of a plural pronoun calls for a special word. An example is the Mamu dialect of Dyirbal, an Australian language of North Queensland, where the first person pronoun has four forms (Dixon 1972: 50):

(26) 'I'   *ŋaḍa*   Dyirbal
      'I and one other person'   *ŋali*
      'I and more than one other person'   *ŋana*
      'I and spouse'   *ŋanaymba*

In some South Asian languages such as Vietnamese, kin terms themselves serve as second-person pronouns. For example, *anh* means 'elder brother,' 'cousin,' or 'husband' but it can also be used to address male equals (Cooke 1968: 127). Hungarian also uses 'uncle,' 'aunt,' and 'brother' for addressing unrelated older persons.

As we saw in the preceding section, in some languages, social relations play a role in differentiating kin terms although not as frequently as they do in pronouns. Another possible distinction that kin terms and pronouns have in common is **gender**. Note the following paradigms, where gender-differentiated pronouns are in bold. (M = masculine gender, F = feminine gender, N = neuter gender)

(27)		RUSSIAN	FRENCH	SYRIAN ARABIC	TURKISH
SING	1	*ja*	*je*	*ʔana*	*ben*
	2	*ty*	*tu*	**ʔənte** (M)	*sen*
				ʔənti (F)	
	3	**on** (M)	**il** (M)	**huwwe** (M)	*o*
		ona (F)	**elle** (F)	**hiyye** (F)	
		ono (N)			
PLU	1	*my*	*nous*	*nəḥna*	*biz*
	2	*ty*	*vous*	*ʔəntu*	*siz*
	3	*oni*	**ils** (M)	*hənne*	*onlar*
			elles (F)		

The four languages differ in whether they do or do not make gender distinctions in their pronouns and if they do, in which persons and in which numbers. First, here is an existential generalization: there are languages (such as Turkish) that make no gender distinction in any of their personal pronouns. Second, we can formulate two paradigmatic implications that hold for these data.

One is that if the second-person pronoun has a gender differentiation, so does the third-person pronoun. This is shown in Russian, French, and Syrian Arabic: Russian and French (just like English) have gender in the third person only, Syrian Arabic in both the second person and the third person. We have no example of a language with gendered second-person pronouns and ungendered third-person ones.

The other pattern is illustrated by Russian and French: if a plural pronoun has a gender differentiation, so does a singular pronoun. Russian (like English) has gender only in the singular, while French has it both in the singular and in the plural. There is no language in this sample with gender in the plural but not in the singular.

The two implications above express a preference for gender distinctions in the third person as opposed to the second, and in the singular as opposed to the plural. This makes sense. Since both speaker and addressee are aware of the addressee's gender but not necessarily of the person's talked about, it is understandable that marking gender in the third person should be preferred. And since a plural group may be mixed-gender, it is again understandable that gender distinctions should be preferentially made in the singular. Thus, it should come as no surprise that these implications hold for most, if not all, languages.

The two generalizations above have to do with the existence of pronouns and their subtypes in languages. But the data in (27) also invite two generalizations about the morphological structure of pronouns.

First, notice that if one of the two members in a pair of singular-plural pronouns is longer, it is the plural. This is true for French and Turkish. Second, notice that in Russian, French, and Turkish, the plural forms of the third-person pronouns are analyzable into the singular root and a suffix. Furthermore, as shown in (28), the suffix used to form the plural third-person pronoun is the same as what is used for noun plurals.

(28)

	Third-person pronoun		Noun	
	SING	PLU	SING	PLU
Russian:	*one/ona/ono*	*on-**i***	*kniga* 'book'	*knig-**i*** 'books'
French:	*il/elle*	*il-**s**/elle-**s***	*livre* 'book'	*livre-**s*** 'books'
Turkish:	*on*	*on-**lar***	*adam* 'man'	*adam-**lar*** 'men'

There are also languages, such as Mandarin Chinese, where not just the third person but all three persons form their plural with a nominal-plural affix.

(29) Pronouns   Noun   Mandarin

SING PLU   SING   PLU

1 *wǒ*   *wǒ-men*   *péngyǒu* 'friend'   *péngyǒu-men* 'friends'

2 *nǐ*   *nǐ-men*

3 *tā*   *tā-men*

However, no language has been reported in the typological literature where the first or second person pronoun would have a noun-like plural but not the third. This again makes sense in light of the special sense of plurality involved in first- and second-person pronouns as opposed to the third-person ones. As noted above, the third-person plural is person-wise homogeneous just like a noun plural is: 'they' is more than one third-person entity, just as 'friends' is more than one friend. But the first- and second-person plural pronouns are generally heterogeneous: they involve a mix of persons: 'we' = 1 + 2 + 3; 'you-all' = 2 + 3.

What conclusions can we derive about pronouns from the above discussion in response to the two basic questions regarding crosslinguistic similarities and differences in vocabulary: the existence of words and their morphological structure?

Here are some generalizations enriched by additional observations in the literature.

1.   Existence

GEN-11 Almost all languages that have independent pronouns have separate words for 'I,' 'you,' and 'other'. (cf. Greenberg 1966a: #42, Cysouw 2003: 53–54)

GEN-12 Most languages have some plural pronouns. (Greenberg 1966a: #42 proposes all languages do)

GEN-13 Some languages have the exclusive–inclusive distinction in first person.

GEN-14 For most languages, if they have gender distinctions in the first-person pronoun, they also have gender distinctions in the second- and/or third-person pronoun. (Greenberg 1966a, #44 says this for all languages; but see exceptions in Siewierska 2005a)

GEN-15 For most languages, if they have gender distinctions in plural pronouns, they also have gender distinctions in some singular pronouns. (Greenberg 1966a, #45 says this for all languages; but see numerous exceptions in Plank and Schellinger 1997: 93)

2.   Morphological structure

GEN-16 In all languages, if there is a derivational relationship between singular and plural pronouns, the plural is derived from the singular rather than vice versa.

GEN-17 In all languages, if the plural of first- or second-person pronouns is formed with a nominal plural affix, so is the plural of the third-person pronoun.

Several of these crosslinguistic generalizations are probabilistic rather than absolute. As Michael Cysouw wistfully remarks in conclusion to his extensive study of pronoun systems: "Nothing seems to be impossible, although certain structures are clearly less probable" (Cysouw 2003: 295).

2.4 How many? Words for numbers

Grammatical number distinctions – such as singular and plural, as in *porcupine* and *porcupines* – provide a bit of quantitative information about entities but not very much. A plural noun just says there is more than one thing referred to but does not specify how many. However, almost all languages have special words for more precise quantitative specification called numerals, such as *two*, *twenty-two*, and *five hundred*. We will now take a look at how these words resemble and differ from each other across languages.

Consider a set of English numerals.

(30) | *one* | *eleven* | *twenty-one* | English |
	---------	-------------	-------------------	---------
	two	*twelve*	*hundred-and-six*	
	three	*thirteen*		
	four	*fourteen*		
	five	*fifteen*		
	six	*sixteen*		
	seven	*seventeen*		
	eight	*eighteen*		
	nine	*nineteen*		
	ten	*twenty*		

This list suggests two ways in which number words may be constructed. First, a number can have an atomic, monomorphemic name, such as *one*, *two*, *three*, or *ten*. Second, numerals may be polymorphemic, composed of other numerals by some arithmetic operation. The words *thirteen, fourteen, nineteen* are not clearly separable into morphemes but they suggest components such as *three, four, nine*, and *ten* linked by the operation of addition. *Twenty* also reflects the faint images of two morphemes: *two* and *ten*. And numerals like *twenty-one* or *hundred-and-six* are clearly polymorphemic.

It is possible to imagine systems of numerals based on only one or the other of the two methods. A numeral sequence consisting solely of monomorphemic numeral words would have an unanalyzable word for every number. It would be like the English numerals 1–10 and then would continue with atomic labels like *crox* for 11, *poon* for 23, and so forth. A numeral system based exclusively on arithmetic operations would in turn have polymorphemic numerals only, as in (31).

(31) 1   "two-minus-one"
      2   "two-minus-one-plus-one"
      3   "two-minus-one-plus-two"
          and so forth

The former system, containing only single-morpheme words, would be very difficult to learn. If the number sequence were to go up into the millions and billions, a great many separate labels would need to be memorized. Each number word might be short and simple but the total amount of words would place a big burden on the language user. An exclusively polymorphemic number system would also be difficult to learn and to use. Although less memorization would be needed since one could compute each numeral from the others, each label would be long.

In light of these considerations, it is no wonder that almost no language follows just one of the two patterns; but at the same time, given the advantages of both methods, it is equally natural that languages should have developed both monomorphemic and polymorphemic number words. The ways numeral systems differ across languages are the varying balance of the two patterns – simplex and complex numerals – and the composition of the polymorphemic ones. We will consider these two issues in turn.

(A) MONOMORPHEMIC AND POLYMORPHEMIC NUMERALS

The English numeral sequence shows an increasing tendency upwards for complex structure. The numerals 1–12 are single-morpheme words; those between 13 through 20 are suggestive of complex structure although the component morphemes are barely recognizable. Beyond 20, however, the addenda are clearly separable: *twenty-one*, *eighty-six*, *one hundred and ten* and so forth.

The pattern of lower numbers being single-morpheme words and higher ones formed compositionally is crosslinguistically common. Here is a small sample from Swahili, a Bantu language of East Africa, where compositional structure already begins with 11.

(32) 1   *moja*   Swahili
      2   *mbili*
      10   *kumi*
      11   *kumi na moja*
      12   *kumi na mbili*

We will now consider the structure of polymorphemic numerals. Three questions arise: what are the components? what arithmetic operations are used to put the components together? and what is the linear order of the components?

(B-1) POLYMORPHEMIC NUMERALS: WHAT ARE THE COMPONENTS?

The English system involves 10 and its multiples as the base – that is, as the reference point for forming higher-number words. Although this seems entire natural to us speakers of English, there is a large number of

---

The difference between monomorphemic and polymorphemic number names is comparable to the difference between acronyms, such as *AIDS*, *ALS*, and *TB*, and their spelled-out versions: *acquired immune deficiency syndrome*, *amyotropic lateral sclerosis*, and *tuberculosis*. Acronyms are blissfully short but, like monomorphemic numerals, they need to be memorized individually. The full labels, just as polymorphemic numerals, "make sense" and thus they may be constructed "on the fly"; but due to their length, the tongue stumbles on them.

conceivable alternatives. Why not have a system based on, say, 4? It might look like this.

(33) 1 "one"
      2 "two"
      3 "three"
      4 "four"
      5 "four-plus-one"
      6 "four-plus-two"
      7 "four-plus-three"
      8 "two-times-four"
      9 "two-times-four-plus-one"
         and so forth

Languages show considerable variation in what bases they employ but only some are frequent, with 10 and 20 topping the list. A reason immediately leaps to the eye: these are the numbers of digits on the two hands and on the four limbs. The base of 20 shows up in French.

(34) 4   *quatre*   French
      10 *dix*
      20 *vingt*
      80 **quatre-vingt**
      90 **quatre-vingt-dix**

Meithei, a Tibeto-Burman language of India, also shows traces of the vigesimal (twenty-based) system. (*Kun* and *phú* are alternative forms for 'twenty.')

(35) 2   **əni**   Meithei
      3   **əhúm**
      20 kun
      40 **ni**-phú   "two-twenty"
      60 **húm**-phu   "three-twenty"

In addition to the fact that 10 and 20 are common bases in numeral systems, the bodily foundations of counting are also shown in other ways. In some languages, such as Oksapmin, a language of Papua New Guinea, numerals are named after 27 parts of the body.

(36) 1   *tipun* 'thumb'   Oksapmin
      12 *nat* 'ear'
      13 *kin* 'eye'
      15 *kin tən* 'other-side eye'
      16 *nat tən* 'other-side ear'
          and so forth

In counting, the Oksapmin speaker names the body part standing for a numeral and may also point at that part of the body. Thus, to say 'I have three children', you would say "I have middle-finger children" and 'I saw ten snakes' would be "I saw shoulder snakes" (Saxe 1981: 307; the image below [Figure 2.1] is reproduced from Evans 2010: 60–61). For a brief video

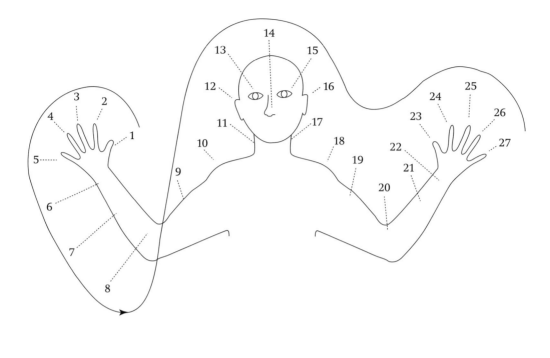

Figure 2.1
Counting in Oksapmin.

The figure shows a counting system using body parts:

14 *lum* "nose"

13	*kin* "eye"	*kin tən* "other-side eye"	15
12	*nat* "ear"	*nat tən* "other-side ear"	16
11	*gwel* "side of neck"	*gwel tən* "other-side side of neck"	17
10	*kat* "shoulder"	*kat tən* "other-side shoulder"	18
9	*tuwət* "upper arm"	*kat tuwət tən* "other-side upper arm"	19
8	*amun* "elbow"	*amun tən* "other-side elbow"	20
7	*bes* "forearm"	*bes tən* "other-side forearm"	21
6	*xadəp* "wrist"	*xadəp tən* "other-side wrist"	22
5	*xətxət* "little finger"	*xətxət tən* "other-side little finger"	23
4	*xətlip* "ring finger"	*xətlip tən* "other-side ring finger"	24
3	*bumlip* "middle finger"	*bumlip tən* "other-side middle finger"	25
2	*ləwatipun* "index finger"	*ləwatipun tən* "other-side index finger"	26
1	*tipun* "thumb"	*tipun tən* "other-side thumb"	27

clip showing an Oksapmin child displaying this counting system to his friends, go to www.culturecognition.com

A second question regarding the composition of complex numerals is the arithmetic operations that link the components.

(B-2) POLYMORPHEMIC NUMERALS: WHAT ARE THE OPERATIONS?

Consider the Latin data in (37).

(37)   1   *unus* (M), *una* (F), *unum* (N)   Latin

       2   *duo* (M, N), *duae* (F)

       7   *septem*

       8   *octo*

       9   *novem*

      10   *decem*

      11   *undecim*

      12   *duodecim*

      17   *semptendecim*

      18   ***duodeviginti***

      19   ***undeviginti***

      20   *viginti*

    100   *centum*

    200   *ducenti*

    300   *trecenti*

First of all, these data illustrate the two arithmetic operations for composing numeral words that are present in English and in the other examples above. The numerals 11 through 17 are formed by **addition** and 200 and 300 are formed by **multiplication**. But notice 18 and 19. If 18 and 19 were formed by addition like the rest of the teens, they would be *octo-decim* "eight-ten" and *novem-decim* "nine-ten." But these words do not exist; instead, there is *duo-de-viginti* "two-out.of-twenty" and "one-out.of-twenty." As noted in Chapter 1, these numerals are formed by **subtraction**. It is interesting that with the passing of centuries, this unusual formation has been eliminated in Latin's daughter languages in favor of addition; cf. Italian *diciotto* "ten-eight" for 18 and *diciannove* "ten-nine" for 19.

Subtraction involves reference to a higher numeral. A somewhat similar "forward-looking" system exists in Estonian. Note that *teist* is the irregularly-formed ordinal numeral for 'second.'

(38)   1   *üks*   Estonian

      2   *kaks*

    10   *kümme*

    11   ***üks teist kümmend*** "one of second ten"

    12   ***kaks teist kümmend*** "two of second ten"

    20   ***kaks kümmend*** "two ten"

    21   *kaks kümmend üks* "two ten one"

    22   *kaks kümmend kaks* "two ten two"

The numerals 21, 22 and so forth are formed by the common pattern of addition. But notice the teens: they are named with reference to the following 'ten' – that is, 'twenty' – rather than the 'ten' that comes before. The numeral 20 is 'two ten,' 11 is 'one of the second ten' and 12 is 'two of the second ten.'

The fourth basic arithmetic operation: division – also occurs although very rarely. In Meithei, the word for 50 is *yaŋkhɔy* "100-divide."

The third question about the structure of polymorphemic numerals is the order in which the component numerals are placed.

> The idea is similar to the way time is told in German: for example, 3:30 may be expressed not only by reference to the past hour (*drei dreissig* "three thirty") but also in reference to the hour to come: *halb vier* "half four". Dutch has the same pattern. French phrases like *dix heures moins vingt* "ten o'clock less twenty" for 9:40, or English *ten to five* for 4:50, are based on the same idea. In all these cases, a number is specified in view of a following value rather than a preceding one.

(B-3) POLYMORPHEMIC NUMERALS: ORDER OF COMPONENTS

Compare the order of morphemes in the following English, German, and Turkish numerals. (Elements of the higher place value capitalized.) In Turkish, *on* = 10, *yirmi* = 20, *otuz* = 30, *yüz* = 100, *bin* = 1,000.

(39)

	GERMAN	ENGLISH	TURKISH
14	vierZEHN	fourTEEN	ON dört
19	neunZEHN	nineTEEN	ON dokuz
21	ein-und-ZWANZIG	TWENTY-one	YIRMI bir
38	acht-und-DREISSIG	THIRTY-eight	OTUZ sekiz
121	HUNDERT-ein-und-zwanzig	HUNDRED-and-twenty-one	YÜZ yirmi bir
1100	TAUSEND-ein-hundert	ONE-THOUSAND-and one-hundred	BIN yüz

In German, the smaller element precedes the larger all the way up to 99; but beyond 100, 'hundred' comes first. English is like German up to 19 but it switches to larger-before-smaller already after 20. In Turkish, there is no switch: the larger number comes first throughout. These examples illustrate a crosslinguistic tendency: larger numerals favor the larger-before-smaller order of addenda. This does not seem unreasonable: if we assume that the most important piece of information should reach the addressee first, then it is useful for larger numbers to have the addendum with the higher place value to come first since it provides an approximate idea of the number involved, with detail left to the second component.

To sum up so far: we have seen that both single-morpheme and multi-morpheme numerals occur in languages and regarding the latter, we discussed the components (the base in particular), the arithmetic operations linking them, and the order of the components.

All of this had to do with the morphological composition of numerals. What about their existence? How many numerals do languages have? There are languages with very few numerals. Guana, an Arawakan language of South America, has only 1–5; and Pirahã (Brazil) is reported to have none.

The following statements summarize our discussion about numerals with some information added from the literature.

(A)   Existence of numerals
GEN-18 Most but not all languages can form an extensive set of numerals.

(B)   Structure of numerals
GEN-19 All languages have some monomorphemic numerals.
GEN-20 The two most common bases are 10 and 20.

GEN-21 Of the four fundamental operations – addition and its inverse: subtraction, and multiplication and its inverse: division – the existence of either inverse operation implies the existence of both direct operations; and the existence of multiplication implies the existence of addition. (Greenberg 1978a: 257–258)

GEN-22 In numerals formed by addition, there is a tendency for larger numbers to have the larger addend precede the smaller. (cf. Greenberg 1978a: 273)

2.5 What kind?

2.5.1 Antonymic adjectives

Switching from quantity to quality, in this section and the next one we will discuss adjectives that describe things. We will start with antonymic adjectives as those in (40).

(40) (a) *old – young*   English
     (b) *tall – short*
     (c) *large – small*
     (d) *deep – shallow*
     (e) *fast – slow*
     (f) *wide – narrow*
     (g) *thick – thin*
     (h) *much – little*
     (i) *far – close*

These adjectives have opposite meanings. As shown in (41), a person cannot be both old and young; a tree cannot be both tall and short; and a lake cannot be both deep and shallow.

(41) (a) *His mother is **not old**; she is young.*
     (b) *The gardener thought he had planted a **tall** tree but the tree grew up to be **short**.*
     (c) *The captain figured the lake would be **deep** but it turned out to be **shallow**.*

However, the examples in (42) seem to run counter to the concept of antonyms being contradictory.

(42) (a) *How **old** is this child?*
     (b) *How **tall** is Grumpy the Dwarf?*
     (c) *How **large** is a speck of dust?*
     (d) *How **deep** is this puddle?*
     (e) *How **fast** can a sloth climb?*
     (f) *How **wide** is a human hair?*
     (g) *How **thick** is this yarn?*

In (42), the interpretation of these adjectives is different from how they are generally used. In (42a), the adjective *old* is used in reference to a child that by its very nature cannot be old. In (42b), *tall* is used for Grumpy the

Dwarf even though dwarfs are not tall. Similarly in all the other examples of (42), an adjective is used for an object of which that property cannot be predicated: specks of dust are not large, puddles are not deep, sloths do not climb fast, a human hair is not wide, and a yarn is not thick.

Notice that this neutral interpretation is possible only for one member of each pair of adjectives – the one that designates 'larger extent' as opposed to the one referring to 'less extent.' The question *How long was the lecture?* expresses no expectation on the part of the speaker as to whether the lecture was long or short; but *How short was the lecture?* is a biased question showing that the speaker already knows that the lecture was short. The positive adjectives can be used in a question even if the speaker knows that the quality or quantity involved is on the negative side but the negative ones could not be used in this sense.

(43) (a) *I am told there is a gas station nearby. How **far** is it?*
 (b) *?I am told the gas station is far away. How **close** is it?*

What this shows is that one member in each antonymic adjective pair has two uses. On the one hand, it can designate one pole of an opposition, as in (41). On the other hand, it can be used in a neutral sense in reference to the entire dimension, as in (42) and (43). This is diagrammed in (44).

(44)

old	young
tall	short
large	small
deep	shallow
fast	slow
wide	narrow

how old?
how tall?
how large?
how deep?
how fast?
how wide?

The same neutral sense is apparent in the nominal forms of these adjectives: as shown in (45), *length*, *width*, and so forth refer to the entire dimension.

(45) *I am measuring the **length** of this mosquito.*
 *Note the tiny **width** of this hair.*
 *Psychologists research human **happiness**.*
 *Let's check the plums for **ripeness**.*

Our observations so far may be summarized as follows:

(46) In English, one member of each pair of antonymic adjectives may be used **both in a polar and in a neutral sense,** while the other member has only the polar interpretation.

There are two additional observations that underscore the asymmetry between members of antonymic adjective pairs. They have to do with form and frequency. First, note that in some cases, one of the two adjectives is morphologically derived from the other.

(47) *happy – unhappy*   (but not **unsad* for 'happy')   English
      ripe – unripe   (but not **ungreen* for 'ripe')
      wise – unwise   (but not **undumb* for 'wise')
      familiar – unfamiliar (but not **unstrange* for 'familiar')

In such cases, it is always the adjective with the neutral meaning that is the base of the derivation. We can therefore expand (46) as follows.

(48) In English, one member of each pair of antonymic adjectives may
      be used **both in a polar and in a neutral sense**, while the other
      member has only the polar interpretation; and if one of the two
      adjectives is derived from the other, **the one with the neutral
      sense is the derivational basis** for the other.

(48) says that one of two opposite adjectives has two properties that set it apart from its opposite: breadth of meaning and simplicity of form. An additional factor is frequency: it has been found that in English, adjectives like *good*, *many*, *long*, *wide*, and *deep* occur more commonly in text that their opposites (Greenberg 1966c: 53). This allows for a further expansion of (46).

(49) In English, in pairs of antonymic adjectives A-1 and A-2, if A-1 has
      both a polar and a neutral interpretation, then
      (a) if either of the two adjectives is derived from the other, **A-1 is
           the base of A-2**; and
      (b) if either of the two adjectives is more frequent than the other,
           A-1 is the more frequent one.

One wonders whether the clustering of these characteristics is specific to English or whether it is the same in other languages as well. Similar evidence has actually been found crosslinguistically. Joseph Greenberg, who first noted these correlations, cites Hausa as an example. In Hausa, 'wide' is expressed as "it is with width" and 'narrow' is "it is not with width"; similarly, 'shallow' has the form "lacking depth." In Spanish, 'deep' is *profundo*; 'shallow' is *poco profundo* ("a little deep"). This shows the same derivational relationship between antonymic adjectives as we see in English.

The correlation between neutral use and morphological simplicity was further tested for 29 languages by Jessica Wirth (1983). Here are some of her examples (p.c.).

(50) (a)   'abundant'   'scarce'
        Gêgbĕ   *sù nà gbɔ*   **mú** *sù nà gbɔ*
        Panare   *cure*   *cure* **ejque**
        Rapa Nui   *rahi*   *taʔe rahi*

(b)		'ripe'	'unripe'
	German	*reif*	**un**-*reif*
	Danish	*modne*	**u**-*modne*
	Gĕgbĕ	*sî*	*mú sìò*
	Yoruba	*pọn*	**ko** *pọn*
	Arabic	*mistiwiy*	**miš** *mistiwiy*

Tok Pisin, the English-based creole language of New Guinea, also provides an example: 'good' is *gut*; 'bad' is *nogut*.

However, evidence from antonymic adjectives for the clustering of neutral meaning, formal simplicity, and frequency as stated for English in (49) is not always complete. For Hausa, Gĕgbĕ, and the other languages mentioned in (50), we have morphological data but we don't know whether the adjectives that form the base for the derivations are used in a neutral sense and whether they are more frequent. We know that their English equivalents have neutral meanings and are more frequent; but this does not mean that the same holds in those languages. Also, the three-way correlation has not been tested for a larger language sample.

The clustering of broader meaning, simpler form, and more frequent occurrence is not unparalleled in other areas of vocabulary: the same has been noted in the preceding sections for body-part terms, kin terms, pronouns, and numerals. We saw that body parts that are frequently referred to tend to have short, monomorphemic forms; frequent kin terms are generally monomorphemic; singular and more frequent pronouns are generally shorter than plural ones; and lower numerals, presumably more frequent, also tend to be monomorphemic. Members of oppositions that have a simpler structure (simpler meaning and form) and are more frequent are labeled the unmarked members of an opposition, with the other member labeled marked.

In addition to the correlations between syntagmatic simplicity (simpler meaning and simpler form) and frequency, there is an additional property that frequently characterizes unmarked members of oppositions. Among body parts, those pertaining to the upper body are generally more differentiated than those of the lower body: as we saw above, English and other languages have a separate word for each finger but not for each toe. In the domain of kin terminology, close relatives are more likely to have sex-differentiated terms – e.g. *father* and *mother*, *sister* and *brother* – than more remote relatives such as *cousin*. For pronouns, we saw that gender differentiation was more common in the singular than in the plural. And for numerals, lower numerals, which have a greater text frequency, tend to have gender-differentiated forms more than higher ones. See, for example, the Latin numeral paradigm in (37) (Section 2.4): only *unus* 'one,' *duo* 'two' (and *tres* 'three') are differentiated for gender. This additional diagnostic of the unmarked may be called paradigmatic complexity, meaning that the unmarked member has more subtypes than the marked one.

If it is true that antonymic adjectives form unmarked–marked pairs, we would expect the unmarked adjective to show more paradigmatic complexity than the marked one. There is indeed some evidence for this: a semantic contrast is often articulated for the unmarked adjectives but glossed over for the marked. Consider English examples:

(51) (a) *tall – short*
 long – short
 (b) *hard – soft*
 loud – soft

In (51a), greater extension along the vertical and horizontal dimensions is expressed by separate words while the opposites are represented by a single word. In (51b), the tactile and auditory dimensions are kept apart for the more salient member of the pairs but are run together for their opposites.

While the pattern shown in (51) appears in other languages as well, there are also counterexamples. In English, the difference between *young* and *new* (animate and inanimate) is neutralized in *old*, which we know on independent grounds is the unmarked member of the opposition (because it has both a polar and a neutral sense), but kept at the other pole. Markedness would predict that the opposition is kept for *old* but eliminated for *young/new*. The same happens in German and Danish: a single polysemous word stands for 'old' both for animates and inanimates while the distinction is kept at the other end of the scale:

(52) 　　　　　'old'　'young/new'
　German:　*alt*　*jung*　　(people)
　　　　　　alt　*neu*　　(things)
　Danish:　*gammel*　*ung*　　(people)
　　　　　　gammel　*ny*　　(things)

In sum: there is a common clustering of properties for members of some antonymic pairs in some languages and the clusters follow the general pattern of markedness relations. However, the correlations of syntagmatic simplicity, paradigmatic complexity, and frequency in antonymic adjectives are yet to be tested for a large and representative sample of languages.

What answers can we derive from the above discussion of antonymic adjectives to the two questions that we have stated for crosslinguistic vocabulary studies in general: the existence of words of a given meaning and their morphological structure? No evidence is available about the existence of antonyms in languages; but regarding morphological structure, we can state GEN-23.

> GEN-23 In some languages, in pairs of antonymic adjectives A-1 and A-2, if A-1 has both a polar and a neutral interpretation, then
> (a) if either of the two adjectives is derived from the other, A-1 is the base of A-2;
> (b) if either of the two adjectives is more frequent than the other, A-1 is the more frequent one; and
> (c) if either of the two adjectival meanings has more subtypes by form, A-1 is the one with more subtypes.

GEN-23 conflates the following mutual implications for members of pairs of antonymic adjectives.

(53) (a) If greater frequency, then also neutral meaning, simpler form, and more subtypes.
  (b) If neutral meaning, then also simpler form, greater frequency, and more subtypes.
  (c) If simpler form, then also neutral meaning, greater frequency, and more subtypes.
  (d) If more subtypes, then also neutral meaning, simpler form, and greater frequency.

GEN-23 says that this pattern does occur in languages but it does not provide the distribution of the pattern: it leaves open the question of which are the languages where it does occur. It is therefore a conservative, existential statement. It is of the paradigmatic type rather than syntagmatic or reflexive (cf. Chapter 1, Section 1.2.1) because it is about the distribution of properties between two different structural entities of a language: two antonymic adjectives.

2.5.2 Words for colors

One of the most intriguing aspects of studying lexical typology is the relationship between words and the objects, qualities, and events that they describe. How do the categories reflected in vocabulary relate to the real boundaries among things in the world? To what extent do vocabularies cut the world along its natural joints?

For some areas of vocabulary discussed above, the real world does provide separable entities: people referred to by kin terms and by pronouns are distinct entities in the world. Body parts are less clearly delimited by reality: after all, they are all connected, and there are other domains that do not consist of segments at all: for dimensions of size, evaluative quality such as 'good' and 'bad,' temperature, sound, texture, taste, and smell, it is only language that provides the exact partitions.

One of these scalar dimensions is color. A rainbow shows some striping but the boundaries are fuzzy. Thus, one might expect that languages will label colors by dividing the color spectrum into arbitrary subfields. Due to lack of evidence to the contrary, this was indeed the view that anthropologists and linguists used to take. The first time that this position was confronted with empirical data on a large scale was in the late 1960s when two anthropologists at the University of California in Berkeley, Brent Berlin and Paul Kay, gathered information about color terms in 98 languages and presented their results in a ground-breaking study (1969 (1991)).

Berlin and Kay offered two major findings both indicating that color nomenclature did not vary arbitrarily across languages. First, they proposed that there was a finite pool of 11 colors from which languages picked their basic terms. Second, they found that while languages differed in how many of these colors they had words for, there was a universal hierarchy that determined the choice. GEN-24 presents the **restricted inventory** from which languages choose their basic color terms; GEN-25 in turn charts the **constraints on the choices from this set.** GEN-25 offers one unrestricted universal: that all languages have words for black and white. In addition, it represents a number of implicational universals: if a language has a term for any one of the colors, it also has terms for all the colors to the left.

> GEN-24 The inventory of basic color categories is as follows:
>   BLACK, WHITE, RED, YELLOW, GREEN, BLUE, BROWN, PINK,
>   PURPLE, ORANGE, GREY.
> GEN-25 The following implicational relations hold among the basic
>   color terms in languages (Berlin and Kay 1969: 5)

$$
\left.\begin{matrix} \text{BLACK} \\ \\ \text{WHITE} \end{matrix}\right\} < \text{RED} < \left\{\begin{matrix} \text{GREEN} < \text{YELLOW} \\ \\ \text{YELLOW} < \text{GREEN} \end{matrix}\right\} < \text{BLUE} < \text{BROWN} < \left\{\begin{matrix} \text{PINK} \\ \text{PURPLE} \\ \text{ORANGE} \\ \text{GREY} \end{matrix}\right.
$$

Here are examples of languages for some of the types.

(54) BLACK, WHITE: Jalé (Papua New Guinea)
     BLACK, WHITE, RED: Tiv (Nigeria)
     BLACK, WHITE, RED, YELLOW: Ibo (Nigeria)
     BLACK, WHITE, RED, GREEN: Ibibio (Nigeria)
     BLACK, WHITE, RED, YELLOW, GREEN: Tzeltal (Mexico)
     BLACK, WHITE, RED, YELLOW, GREEN, BLUE: Plains Tamil (India)
     BLACK, WHITE, RED, YELLOW, GREEN, BLUE, BROWN: Nez Perce
       (State of Washington)

The force of these claims in GEN-24 and GEN-25 is staggering. First, the pool of the 11 color terms is chosen from a literally infinite number of distinctions that could be made within the color spectrum. Second, the logically possible combinations of the 11 color terms amount to 2.048 types (such as "only brown," "only black and pink," "only red, blue and brown," and so forth). In contrast, the hierarchy allows for only a minute subset of the combinatory possibilities: 22 types. This situation represents a paradigm example of a scientific puzzle: the existence of a large gap between what is conceivable and what is actually found.

Since 1969, much more research has been carried out on color terminology and it has modified some of the original findings (see Hardin and Maffi 1997; Kay *et al.* 2009). This work has unearthed exceptions to the pool. For example, an additional basic color term – turquoise – has been found in at least one language, Tsakhur, a Nakh-Daghestanian language of the Caucasus. The hierarchy has also been modified somewhat: white and black cannot be said to be universal since some languages, such as Pirahã, have no color terms at all (Everett 2008: 119); and grey may have a higher position in the hierarchy.

More importantly, the very basis of the research has been questioned by some researchers (Lucy 1997; Wierzbicka 2008). The major point of criticism has to do with the nature of the data. Berlin and Kay presented speakers of languages with the color spectrum through the use of Munsell color chips and asked them to name the chips. The words provided by the consultants were then taken to be color terms in the respective languages. But how do we know that the words did not have some other more basic meaning, such as referring to some objects that happened to have that color? The words obtained from the different languages must have over-lapped in their referential range but before it could be established that they were color terms, we would need to probe into the typical uses of those words in each language. In fact, the very notion of color may not be a linguistic category in all languages; people may not be paying attention to color in all cultures. Wierzbicka makes this point in connection with the Australian language Warlpiri (2008: 420):

> The Warlpiri people do of course see what we call 'colours' and can be very sensitive to differences that we would think of as differences in colour. Judging by linguistic criteria, however, what we may see as a 'colour' (e.g. brown or purplish) they may see as 'something that looks like something else' (e.g. earth or smoke).

John Lucy (1997) provides an example of what he deems to be an analogous situation to Berlin and Kay's experiment. Imagine a chart depicting various kinds of luggage – the kind that is presented to some-body at an airport who has lost his bags so that airline personnel could identify the type of the errant luggage. Suppose you show this chart to speakers of different languages, point at the various pictures and ask them to name them. You cannot be sure that what you get is equivalents of the English terms *duffel bag*, *briefcase*, and so forth. Instead, consul-tants may come up with words that refer to objects that resemble those depicted, such as 'large object,' 'looks like a house,' etc. From such a test, one could not establish a set of "luggage universals" because the test would be fundamentally biased by the assumption that the notion of luggage and its various kinds are available in the various cultures. The same problem arises in connection with eliciting color terms by show-ing color chips.

Nonetheless, it seems uncontroversial that the inventory of universally available basic color terms is restricted and that there are some prefer-ences guiding the choice that languages make from among these terms. Given the very large number of logical possibilities noted above, the ques-tion arises how the enormous gap between possible and actual can be explained. Why is the pool restricted? Why are some colors preferentially chosen? And why does a particular language opt for one or the other from among the alternatives?

The explanation for the constraints on the pool and on the hierarchy must have to do both with the physics of color and with the way the human visual apparatus perceives colors. The answer to the third question – why a given language has one set of colors as opposed to another – may be social. Berlin and Kay noted a correlation between complexity of color terminology and cultural complexity: languages spoken in cultures with less developed technology – such as those of New Guinea – are the ones with simpler color terminology. It seems that people have a more differentiated view of color if they do not just see naturally occurring colors but they also create and manipulate them.

* * * *

In our vocabulary survey, it has become clear that the human perception of reality, rather than reality itself, is the basis of the meanings and structures of words. The vocabulary of a language is a depository of thoughts: of our perceptions and interpretations of the world. This much is non-controversial: thought creates words. But then a related question arises: is this a unidirectional causation? Or do words in turn affect thought? Is our perception of reality influenced by the way our language cuts up the world?

In our everyday life, we act as if we believe the answer is in the affirmative: if there are alternative ways of expressing the same meaning, we opt for one that steers thought in the right direction. Why do people prefer to use the phrase "if anything happens to me" rather than "if I die"? Why is the phrase "collateral damage" used in some military documents for civilian casualties? Why "visually handicapped" rather than "blind"? The use of these euphemistic expressions reveals our fear that the more direct words will channel thought in the wrong direction.

But what about cases where a language does not offer a choice of expressions? Pondering the great diversity of languages, the renowned Russian-American linguist Roman Jakobson said: "Languages differ essentially in what they must convey and not in what they may convey" (cited in Deutscher 2010: 151). Examples abound. In Turkish, it is quite possible to conduct a lengthy conversation about a person without his or her gender being revealed because, as we saw above, the third-person singular pronoun has a single gender-less form. In English, this would be near-impossible because the language forces us to choose between *he* and *she*. Does this mean that English speakers have a gendered view of the world while Turkish speakers have an ungendered perspective?

On one level, language clearly determines thought: for the purposes of speaking English, speakers have to keep gender in mind. As Dan Slobin has put it (2003: 158–161), "thinking for speaking" requires a specific thought pattern that is appropriate for the language. In other words, if we want to express something in a given language, the idea needs to be forced into the channels dictated by that language.

But does language influence thought also on a deeper, non-linguistic level? Do English speakers consider gender ONLY WHEN they want to use a third-person pronoun or does the gendered view pervade their entire perception of the world? According to Benjamin Whorf's and Edward Sapir's influential theory, the answer is yes: their view, known as the hypothesis of linguistic relativity, claims a strong effect on thought exerted by language. How can we test this claim? What would be decisive evidence to establish that language affects non-linguistic thought and behavior?

Chosen from among the large number of experiments that provide evidence for or against linguistic relativity, here follows a recent study about color differentiation. Psychologist Jonathan Winawer and his co-workers (2007) set up an experiment to test the ways in which English and Russian subjects differentiated shades of blue. The crucial point is that Russian has distinct basic terms for dark blue (*goluboj*) and light blue (*sinij*) while in English, the term *blue* covers both. Subjects were presented with sets of three color chips, one on the top and two at the bottom. The task was to determine which of the two chips at the bottom matched the one on the top. What the experimenters were interested in was reaction time: how easy was it for subjects to arrive at the right answer? Results showed that if the two bottom chips differed in that one shade belonged to *goluboj* and the other to *sinij*, the Russian subjects could decide in less time whether either of them was like the top chip than if the bottom chips were both shades of *goluboj* or *sinij*. For the English subjects, this did not make a difference. Thus, Russians perceived the colors as more different when they had separate terms for them. Winawer *et al.* arrived at the following conclusion: "(it) is not that English speakers cannot distinguish between light and dark blues but rather that Russian speakers cannot avoid distinguishing them" (7783).

Based on other relevant experiments, a similar opinion is articulated by Stanley Witkowski and Cecil Brown (1982: 411): "Our view is that lexical salience both mirrors and magnifies the inherent physical-perceptual salience of color referents and thus affects color behavior." Language does not determine the way people see the world but it frames reality for us by focusing attention on certain aspects of the world.

Probing into the vast differences among vocabularies of different languages is a broadening experience. If we only know one language, it seems that it is the only way for a language to be. Learning about other languages, we discover that just because something is familiar to us, it may not be the only option; there are diverse ways in which words can capture reality.

This is the same experience as learning about new cultures. We learn that one can consume calf's brain, dog meat, or buttered tea with relish; one can live without taking showers and even without bathrooms; and it is OK to bow rather than shake hands when meeting somebody. The experience is also comparable to how mankind's knowledge of astronomy has broadened over the centuries. Before Copernicus came around in the sixteenth century, people thought that the earth – their very own planet – was the center of the universe and that therefore it was something very special. Copernicus, however, demoted the earth from its sublime status when he proposed that it was the sun that was the center of the galaxy rather than the earth. Then, in the early twentieth century, astronomers came to realize that even our galaxy was not distinguished: it was one of countless billions of galaxies each containing billions of stars like our sun. We have thus gradually come to see our proper place in the 14-billion-years-old cosmos. In John Coleridge's words, mankind was getting "habituated to the vast."

In the course of their expanding knowledge, astronomers have learnt two things about the universe. One is its enormous expanse and the variability of its forms. The other is that there are general physical laws spanning the variation. The attempt to assess variation and to discover its limits is a common denominator uniting crosslinguistic studies, crosscultural studies, and the study of the universe. In the following chapter, we will continue to pursue this quest by viewing language structure beyond vocabulary.

Summary

In the introductory section of this chapter, two features of an ideal vocabulary were envisaged: (i) There is a word for everything. (ii) From the way a word sounds, it is easy to tell what it means.

Regarding (i): we saw that the concept of "everything" was blurry; but however it may be defined, it is not true that even a single language could comply with this requirement. Languages do have words for some things; but the very notion of a distinct "thing" is elusive: languages differ in how they segment and categorize the world. What is a name-worthy part and nameable kind in one language may not be that in another language.

Regarding (ii): we saw that languages make some use of compositionality: putting morphemes together so that the sum of the meanings of the morphemes at least approximates the meaning of a word; but they do so to varying extent and in varying ways.

With respect to the existence and the composition of words, we encountered both crosslinguistic variation and crosslinguistic invariance. A total of twenty-five crosslinguistic generalizations were presented (GEN-1–GEN-25). By way of a partial review, here are a few examples of our findings.

(A) THE EXISTENCE OF WORDS
   a. Variation
   There are languages that have separate words for toes and fingers and there are languages that do not have separate words for them.
   b. Invariance
   If a language has a word for 'purple,' it also has a word for 'red.'

(B) THE MORPHOLOGICAL STRUCTURE OF WORDS
   a. Variation
   Some languages use 'twenty' as a base in their numeral system; others do not.
   b. Invariance
   If a language forms the plural of the second-person pronoun with a nominal plural marker, it does the same for the plural of the third-person pronoun.

Furthermore, from the survey of the six semantic fields, a very general pattern emerged spanning both the existence of words and their morphological structure. This pattern is markedness. The picture is fragmented but its outlines are clear: there is a tendency for three basic characteristics of words to cluster: syntagmatic simplicity, paradigmatic complexity, and frequency. Examples include body-part terms for the upper body being simpler in structure, more variegated, and more frequent; consanguineal kin terms being more simple in structure, having more subdistinctions, and being more frequent; singular pronouns being monomorphemic, having gender-differentiated forms and being more frequent; lower numerals being monomorphemic, differentiated for gender, and more frequent; and adjectives of antonymic pairs referring to the salient pole of the dimension being morphologically simple, showing distinctions that are neutralized at the marked pole of the opposition, and being more frequent. Markedness patterns will continue to crop up in the following chapters on syntax, morphology, and phonology as well (Chapter 4, Section 4.2.2.2, Chapter 5, Section 5.3, and Chapter 7, Section 7.3).

Activities

1. Body part words are often polysemous: they are used in extended and figurative senses. Here are some examples for *finger*:
   (a) The **fingers** of this glove are too tight for me.
   (b) A long **finger** of the island reaches far into the sea.
   (c) The **fingering** of this violin piece is very complex.
   (d) Joe likes to have a **finger** in every pie.

   Similar extensions of meaning can also be found for the word *hand* as in *the hands of the clock*, or in *Give me a hand*. Find such extended or figurative uses for *head*, *face*, *shoulder*, *leg*, and *foot* and determine what are common properties of the various uses of any one of these words. Compare similar examples from other languages.

2. This exercise has to do with special uses of color words.
   (a) Color terms are at times used idiomatically to describe objects whose actual color does not match the meaning of the word. An example is *white wine*.
   (b) Some color words are specific to particular objects; such as *blond*, which is used only for hair and wood.
   (c) Color words may also be used metaphorically, such as *green with envy*.

   For each pattern, find additional examples in English and try to find reasons for the special uses. Collect examples from other languages as well and compare them with the English uses.

3. Words like 'minute,' 'hour,' 'day,' 'week,' 'month,' 'year,' 'decade,' and 'century' serve to segment the continuum of time. To what extent are they based on natural divisions?

4. In Section 2.3.2. on pronouns, four implicational universals were formulated (GEN-14, GEN-15, GEN-16, GEN-17). Work out the tetrachoric tables for each.

5. Here are the pronouns of Sierra Popoluca, a Mixe-Zoque language of Mexico. Which language mentioned in the text has the same type of pronoun system? (Simplified transcription.)

SNG	1	ʔʌč	PLU	1	ʔʌčiam
	2	mič		2	mičiam
	3	heʔ		3	heʔyah

Compare with čimpa 'dog'
             čimpayah 'dogs'

....

Further reading

- On body parts: see the entire issue of *Language Sciences* 2006: 28: 2–3, which provides relevant data from ten languages.

- On kinship terms: Jonsson 2001.

- On pronouns: see Bhat 2004, Siewierska 2004, Daniel 2005; also Völkel 2010, a fascinating book on Tongan culture showing how elaborate pronoun systems may be correlated with highly stratified societies. On the social bases of pronoun systems, see also Brown and Gilman 1960.

- On numerals: Hurford 1975, 1987; Wiese 2003; on oddities of numeral systems, see Hammarström 2010 and Hanke 2010. The website www.zompist.com/numbers.shtml provides lists of numerals 1–10 for over 5,000 languages.

- On color terms: see the data base www.icsi.berkeley.edu/wcs and the riveting and delightful account of the history and present status of research on color terms in Deutscher 2010.

- On vocabulary in other semantic domains, see Lehrer 1974 (on cooking terms); Newman 1998 (on terms of giving), 2002 (on words for sitting, standing, and lying), and 2009 (on words for eating and drinking); Talmy 2007 and Filipović 2007 (on verbs of motion); Deutscher 2010 (on space, gender, and color). For temperature words, see the materials of the workshop *Temperature in language and cognition* (http://ling-asv.ling.su.se/mediawiki/index.php/Main_Page). Koptjevskaja-Tamm 2008 and Evans 2011 provide thorough overviews of the field.

- On language and culture: Enfield 2002; Wierzbicka 1997; Boroditsky 2009; Niemeier & Dirven 2000; Gentner & Goldin-Meadow 2003; Evans 2010; Deutscher 2010.

- For a recent book on meanings and thoughts meant for the general public, see Jackendoff 2012.

- On a crosslinguistic study of sentential possession, see Stassen 2009.

3 Assembling words

Syntactic typology

CHAPTER OUTLINE

KEY TERMS

relative clause
resumptive
    pronoun
classifier
agreement
agreement
    controller
agreement target
agreement
    feature
Accessibility
    Hierarchy
Animacy
    Hierarchy
case
government
alignment
nominative
accusative
ergative
absolutive
subject

Some of the syntactic differences and similarities among languages will be surveyed and a sample of crosslinguistic generalizations will be documented. After a brief introduction, Section 3.2 illustrates crosslinguistic similarities and differences in the choice of words and word forms using the examples of resumptive pronouns as they occur in relative clauses, and of classifiers, agreement, and government. Section 3.3 illustrates frequencies of order patterns and statistical correlations between the orders of major sentence constituents, such as subject, object, and verb, and other phrases. On the example of the concept subject, Section 3.4 raises the issue of whether grammatical categories are crosslinguistically definable.

3.1 Introduction

Suppose you want to say something in a language unknown to you. You have a dictionary; but how do you put the words together into a sentence? A reasonable approach is to pick the words that jointly express the intended meaning and put them into some logical order, such as placing the more important words before the less important ones. This method might indeed work if the goal is just to convey the approximate meaning; but the resulting sentence is not likely to be a well-formed structure. This is for three reasons.

(a)   Languages differ in the choice of words that are used to express a given meaning.
(b)   Languages differ in the choice of word forms that are used to express a given meaning.
(c)   Languages differ in the order of words that are used to express a given meaning.

The choice and ordering of words and word forms is called syntax; crosslinguistic differences and similarities in syntactic structures is the topic of this chapter.

Here are examples to illustrate the three kinds of differences mentioned above.

(A) CROSSLINGUISTIC DIFFERENCES IN THE CHOICE OF WORDS

Consider the following English sentences and their translations in Serbo-Croatian, Russian, and Modern Standard Arabic. (The second-person form in the Arabic sentences is for masculine subjects. In the Serbo-Croatian examples, pitch is not marked.)

(1)

ENGLISH				SERBO-CROATIAN			RUSSIAN		ARABIC	
I	**am**	*a*	*student.*	*Ja*	**sam**	*student.*	*Ja*	*učenik.*	*ʔana*	*tˠaːlib*
You	**are**	*a*	*student.*	*Ti*	**si**	*student.*	*Ty*	*učenik.*	*ʔanta*	*tˠaːlib*
He	*is*	*a*	*student.*	*On*	**je**	*student.*	**On**	*učenik.*	*huwa*	*tˠaːlib*

The English sentences contain four words each, the Serbo-Croatian ones three, and the Russian and Arabic ones only two. What makes for these differences? Let us first focus on the bold-faced words in English and Serbo-Croatian. These are forms of the verb 'to be' (called the copula): while they are present in the English and Serbo-Croatian examples, they do not appear in the Russian and Arabic ones – even though, as a Slavic language, Russian is closely related to Serbo-Croatian. This is not because Russian and Arabic lack the verb 'to be': in the past-tense forms of these sentences, this verb appears: Russian *Ja* **byl** *učenik* and Arabic *ʔana* **kuntu** *tˠaːlib* "I was student." It is just that these languages – and many others – do not employ the copula in present-tense sentences of this kind.

In addition to tense, there are also other factors that may determine the presence versus absence of the copula in a sentence. In Hungarian, the copula is used if the subject is first or second person ('I am a student,' 'You are a student') but not if it is third person. In Cantonese Chinese, it is used if the predicate is a noun – e.g. 'I am a student' – but not if it is an adjective ('I am lazy').

Apart from the variable presence of the copula, there is also a second reason for the varying length of the sentences in (1): the presence versus absence of the indefinite article. In this respect, English is different from all three of the other languages: none of them have a word for *a(n)*.

The presence versus absence of the indefinite article exemplifies a type of crosslinguistic variation that is different from the case of the copula. As pointed out above, Russian and Arabic do have a copula verb but in present-tense equational sentences, this verb is not chosen. The indefinite article, however, does not exist at all in Russian, Serbo-Croatian, and Arabic: there is no corresponding word for *a(n)* in these languages. The case of the copula illustrates that languages can differ in the distribution of the available word categories across their sentence types. The case of the indefinite article in turn shows that languages can also differ in the very existence of word categories: they are variably distributed across languages.

> The same two patterns hold for cultural objects outside language. Butter is like the copula: it is used both in American and Tibetan cuisine but in different ways: in Tibet, butter is used to flavor tea while in American cooking it does not serve this purpose. Soy sauce in turn is like the indefinite article: it is a staple in Chinese cooking but it is not at all available in traditional American cuisine.

(B) CROSSLINGUISTIC DIFFERENCES IN THE CHOICE OF WORD FORMS

Once a word has been chosen to be part of a sentence, its form may still vary depending on the language. Here is our first set of examples. The Japanese, Spanish, and Swahili phrases are translations of the English ones.

(2)

ENGLISH		JAPANESE		SPANISH		SWAHILI	
small	*spoon*	*tiisai*	*saji*	*cuchar-a*	*pequeñ-a*	**ki**-*jiko*	**ki**-*dogo*
small	*spoon-s*	*tiisai*	*saji*	*cuchar-a-s*	*pequeñ-a-s*	**vi**-*jiko*	**vi**-*dogo*
small	*child*	*tiisai*	*kodomo*	*niñ-o*	*pequeñ-o*	**m**-*toto*	**m**-*dogo*
small	*childr-en*	*tiisai*	*kodomo-tati*	*niñ-o-s*	*pequeñ-o-s*	**wa**-*toto*	**wa**-*dogo*

In English and Japanese – two unrelated languages – the adjective is indifferent to the singular versus plural form of the noun. In Japanese, in fact, only 'child' has a plural, 'spoon' does not; but regardless, the adjective remains invariant whether the noun is interpreted as plural or singular. The other two equally unrelated languages are different from English and Japanese but similar to each other. In Spanish, nouns (the first words in the examples) have gender markers (-*o* for masculine and -*a* for feminine) as well as a suffix for the plural (-*s*), and the adjective faithfully mirrors nominal inflection: its endings also change with gender and number. In Swahili, too, nouns (again the first words of the examples) have different inflections for gender and number although the two are blended into single morphemes (Class 1 and 7 indicate gender classes):

(3) *ki-*   'singular, Class 7'   Swahili

     vi-   'plural, Class 7'

     m-   'singular, Class 1'

     wa-   'plural, Class 1'

Both the Spanish and the Swahili adjectives exemplify what is called **grammatical agreement**: the adjective agrees in gender and number with the noun.

Grammatical agreement is a pattern where a word in the sentence varies its inflection depending on the choice of another word. There is also another grammatical pattern where one word dictates the form of another. (4) provides examples.

(4)

(a)   ENGLISH: GERMAN:

      I follow **him**.   *Ich   folge*   **ihm**.

                                             I   follow   he.**DAT**

(b)   ENGLISH: FRENCH:

      dissatisfied **with** *something*   *mécontent*   **de**   *quelque   chose*

                                             dissatisfied **GEN** some   thing

(c)   ENGLISH: RUSSIAN:

      three **boys**   *tri   mal'chik-a*

                                             three   boy-**SING.GEN**

These examples show crosslinguistic differences in the choice of grammatical case even though the words that dictate distinct case forms have the same meaning. In English, the verb *to follow* takes the direct-object case, called accusative, of its complement while in German, the complement has to be in the indirect-object case called dative. In English, the adjective 'dissatisfied' requires the instrumental preposition *with* while in French, it takes the genitive preposition *de*. And in English, the numeral 'three' is followed by the subject form of a noun while in Russian, the noun following 'three' has to be in the genitive case.

While in both (2) and (4), one word determines the form of another word, there is a difference between the two. In (2), it is the same characteristics that show up on the noun and the adjective: gender and number. In (4), this is not so: there is nothing direct-object-like or indirect-object-like in the English and German verbs for 'follow,' nor is genitivity a property of the Russian numeral for 'three.' In other words, in (4), the case forms dictated by the other words do not reflect the forms of the governing words. As noted above, the pattern exemplified in (2) is called agreement, (4) in turn provides instances of government. As shown by the

English and French examples, required case forms may not be affixal: they may be adpositional.

All in all, the examples in (2) and (4) show that languages differ in whether there is or isn't agreement between adjective and noun and also in the case requirements that words impose on other words by government.

Having seen examples of how languages resemble and differ in the choice of words and word forms, let us turn to the third syntactic parameter of variation: the order of words.

The difference between the two patterns is comparable to a school principal that requires the teachers to wear the same attire as he does, as opposed to one that prescribes a particular uniform that is not like what he wears.

(C) CROSSLINGUISTIC DIFFERENCES IN WORD ORDER

Consider the examples in (2) again. In addition to adjective–noun agreement, they also show that languages differ in how adjective and noun are ordered. In English and Japanese, the adjective precedes the noun; in Spanish and Swahili, it follows.

In Section 1.1 of Chapter 1, we saw other examples of how word order varies across languages. Sentences from Hindi, Japanese, and Turkish were shown to have dominant SOV order (Subject & Object & Verb) as opposed to Arabic and Rapa Nui, which are VSO languages. Here are two other languages of the SOV and VSO types.

(5) (a) Subject & Object & **Verb**   Ainu

   Totto   *amam esose.*   'The mother borrowed rice.'

   mother rice **borrowed**

   (b) **Verb** & Subject & Object   Samoan

   Sa sogi *e   Ioane le   ufi.*   'John cut the yam.'

   PST cut SBJ John the yam

So far in this section, we have seen both similarities and differences in the syntactic patterns of languages involving the choice of words and word forms and the order of words. As a result, we can formulate **existential statements**, such as "Some languages have noun-adjective agreement and others don't" and "Some languages put the verb at the end of the sentence and others at the beginning."

But what is the **distribution** of these patterns across languages? In particular, how **frequent** are they and what are the **conditions** under which one or the other occurs? The main thrust of this chapter is to address these questions.

3.2 The choice of words and word forms

3.2.1 Which words?

We have already seen some evidence that languages differ in the choice of words to express a given meaning in a sentence (cf. (1)). First, there was the copula: while all four languages we considered do have a verb meaning 'to be,' English and Serbo-Croatian employ it in present-tense equational sentences while Russian and Arabic do not. This example showed that languages could differ in the distribution of the words that they have available. Second, there was the indefinite article: it occurs in the English sentences but not in those of the other three languages: the indefinite article is simply not available in Serbo-Croatian, Russian, and Arabic. These two cases show that there are differences both in the language-internal distribution of words and also in the crosslinguistic distribution of word categories. In what follows, we will see additional examples of both.

3.2.1.1 Resumptive pronouns

As noted at the beginning of this chapter, when we construct a sentence, most of the words are chosen because of their meaning: each contributes a part of what we want to say. If I want to say that this apple is sweet, I will have to pick the words for 'apple' and 'sweet.' But not all the words that need to appear in a sentence are semantically motivated. The copula verb is semantically empty: as we saw above, a meaning like 'I am a student' is expressed in English and Japanese with the copula present but in Serbo-Croatian and Arabic, without it; yet the same meaning comes through either way. To be sure, the verb 'to be' may be used meaningfully, as in the sentence *I am*, where it expresses existence; but in copulative sentences, the existential meaning fades out.

We will now consider two other examples of semantically idle uses of words that nonetheless need to be parts of sentences: a kind of pronoun and a kind of noun. This section takes up pronouns.

Consider the following sentences.

(6)   (a)   *The man was my uncle; I gave milk to **him**.*   English

      (b)   *? The man that I gave milk to **him** was my uncle.*

The occurrences of the word *him* in the two sentences differ in function. In (6a), it refers back to *the man*. In (6b), it does not have an identifying function: the word *that* seems to refer back to *the man* all by itself with *him* being redundant.

The sentence in (6b) is highly colloquial; in even moderately formal English style, *him* would not appear: *The man that I gave milk to ___ was my uncle*. Given that it does not contribute to the meaning of the sentence, its absence seems sensible. However, in some languages this pronoun is required. Consider the following Persian relative-clause construction.

(7)   *mardi*   *ke*   *man*   *shir-râ*   **be**   **u**   *dadâm*   Persian

    man   that   I   milk-ACC   to   him   gave:1S

    'the man that I gave milk to'

The phrase without *u* 'him' would be ungrammatical.

There are also several other languages that require so-called resumptive pronouns in some of their relative clauses. In a classic study of relative clause constructions, Keenan and Comrie reported 26 such languages (1977: 93). They found that the distribution of these pronouns across the various kinds of relative clauses in a language showed a clear pattern. For an initial illustration, consider an expanded set of data from Persian.

(8) (a) subject relativized; no pronoun   Persian

      mardi   *ke*   *az*   *Irân*   *amâd*

      man   that from Iran   came:3S

      'the man that came from Iran'

   (b) direct object relativized; pronoun optional

      mardi   *ke*   *man*   (**u**-*ra*)   *zadam*

      man   that I   (**him**-ACC) hit:1S

      'the man that I hit'

   (c) indirect object relativized; pronoun required (repeated from (7))

      mardi   *ke*   *man* *shir-râ*   **be u**   *dadâm*

      man   that I   milk-ACC **to him** gave:1S

      'the man that I gave milk to'

In (8a), there is no resumptive pronoun; in (8b) there is an optional one; and in (8c), the resumptive pronoun is obligatory. What differentiates the three constructions? In (8a), the head noun 'the man' is referred to as the subject in the relative clause ('the man came from Iran'); in (8b), it is referred to as the direct object of the clause ('I hit the man'); and in (8c), it is the indirect object ('I gave milk to the man'). Using standard terminology, we say that in (8a), it is the subject that is relativized, in (8b), the direct object is relativized, and in (8c), the indirect object is.

A similar pattern is manifested in all 26 languages cited by Keenan and Comrie that use resumptive pronouns in relative clauses: the distribution of these pronouns follows the scale called the Accessibility Hierarchy (Keenan and Comrie 1977: 66):

(9) Accessibility Hierarchy
    SU > DO > IO > OBL > GEN > OCOMP

Each category on the scale stands for a relativized constituent. SU stands for Subject (e.g. *the man* **who** *arrived*), DO stands for Direct Object (e.g. *the man* **whom** *I hit*), IO stands for Indirect Object (e.g. *the man* **to whom** *I gave a book*), OBL stands for Oblique Object (e.g. *the table* **on which** *I placed the book*), GEN stands for Genitive (possessor phrase) (e.g. *the man* **whose** *son is a student*), and OCOMP stands for Object of Comparison (e.g. ?*the man* **who** *my brother is taller* **than**).

Here is the crosslinguistic regularity: as we proceed to the right on the scale, there is an increasing tendency for resumptive pronouns to occur.

GEN-1 (a) If in a language, a resumptive pronoun is obligatory at any one point on the Accessibility Hierarchy, it is obligatory at all points to the right as well.

(b) If in a language, a resumptive pronoun is optional at any one point on the AH, it will not be obligatory to the left.

The sparse use of resumptive pronouns for relativized subjects ("the man that he arrived") is documented by Comrie and Kuteva's study (2005: 495–496): out of 166 languages, they found only 5 that have this pattern – that is, about 3%. For relativized oblique objects, ("the man that we talked about him"), which are toward the lower end of scale, however, the percentage is much higher: out of a sample of 112 languages, about 18% (20 languages) were found to use resumptive pronouns for oblique objects.

The generalization stated in GEN-1 amounts to five chained paradigmatic implications: the use of resumptive pronouns for relativized subjects (SU) implies their use for relativized DO; resumptive pronouns for relativized direct objects (DO) in turn imply their use for relativized indirect objects (IO); and so forth. Here are language types that are predicted and some that are ruled out. + stands for the obligatory or optional presence of the pronouns, – stands for their absence. Note that, as stated in GEN-1 (b), obligatoriness can increase only to the right.

(10) (a) Predicted types

	SU	DO	IO	OBL	GEN	OCOMP
TYPE I:	−	−	−	−	−	−
TYPE II:	+	+	+	+	+	+
TYPE III:	−	+	+	+	+	+
TYPE IV:	−	−	+	+	+	+
TYPE V:	−	−	−	+	+	+
TYPE VI:	−	−	−	−	+	+
TYPE VII:	−	−	−	−	−	+

(b) Types ruled out

	SU	DO	IO	OBL	GEN
*TYPE i:	+	−	+	+	+
*TYPE ii:	−	+	−	−	−

and so forth

Persian is a Type III language: as shown in (8), no resumptive pronoun is used for relativized subjects. Pronoun use in Persian begins with relativized direct objects, where the pronoun is optional, and it is obligatory for relativized indirect objects as well as for the other types to the right.

Hebrew is another language of Type III. Here are examples for all six types of relative clauses (Dina Crockett, personal communication).

(11) (a) subject relativized; no pronoun   Hebrew

      ha-ish   *she-ba*   *me-iran*

      the-man   that-came   from-Iran

      'the man who came from Iran'

   (b) direct object relativized; pronoun optional

      ha-ish   *she(-**oōōto**)*   *hiketi*

      the-man   that(-**him**)   I:hit

      'the man that I hit'

   (c) indirect object relativized; pronoun required

      ha-ish   *she-natati*   ***lo***   *chalav*

      the-man   that-I:gave   **to:him**   milk

      'the man that I gave milk to'

   (d) oblique object relativized; pronoun required

      ha-ish   *she-naasati*   *ito*

      the-man   that-I:traveled   **with:him**

      'the man that I traveled with'

   (e) genitive relativized; pronoun required

      ha-ish   *she-ha-ben*   ***shelo***   *hu*   *student*

      the-man   that-the-son   **his**   is   student

      'the man whose son is a student'

   (f) object of comparison relativized; pronoun required

      ha-ish   *she-yochanan*   *joter*   *garo-ha*   ***mimenu***

      the-man   that-John   more   tall   **from.him**

      'the man that John is taller than'

A Type IV language is Hausa: resumptive pronouns are not used if the relativized constituent is subject or direct object, they are optional for relativized indirect object, and obligatory to all structures to the right on the scale, such as for relativized genitives (Newman 2000: 537–538).

(12) (a) subject relativized; no pronoun   Hausa

      mùtumìn   *dà*   *bâ*   *shi*   *dà*   *kuδī*

      the.man   that   not   he   with   money

      'the man that has no money'

   (b) direct object relativized; no pronoun

      zōbèn   *dà*   *ya*   *ɓōyè̀*

      the   ring   that   he   hid

      'the ring that he hid'

(c)   indirect object relativized; pronoun optional

likitàn	*dà*	*na*	*gayà*	*wà*
the.doctor	that	I	tell	to

OR

likitàn	*dà*	*na*	*gayà*	*masà*
the.doctor	that	I	tell	to:him

'the doctor I told it to'

(d)   genitive relativized; pronoun obligatory

mùtùmin	*dà*	*ruwā*	*ya*	*rūshè*	*gidan*-**sà**
the:man	that	rain	it	destroyed	house-**his**

'the man whose house the rain destroyed'

Note that in (12a), there is a subject pronoun *shi* but it is not a resumptive pronoun: it is there in the corresponding main clause as well, as in (13):

(13)
mùtumìn	*bâ*	*shi*	*dà*	*kuδī*
the.man	not	**he**	with	money

'The man has no money.'

Why should the distribution of resumptive pronouns in relative clauses follow the Accessibility Hierarchy? Notice that a relative clause with a resumptive pronoun is more explicit about the intended meaning. A structure such as *the man that I hit **him*** includes a main clause that can be understood by itself: *I hit him*, while the structure *the man that I hit* has a truncated clause in it: *I hit*. In other words, the presence of the pronoun renders the clause compositional.

Now, if relative clauses with resumptive pronouns are easier to interpret, such added clarity may be expected in contexts that are difficult to comprehend on other grounds. There is some indication that relativization down the Accessibility Hierarchy gets more difficult: in many languages, relativization is simply not possible at all points on the scale and when this is the case, it is always the lower structures that are missing. In English, we can relativize down to the Genitive – *the man whose sister arrived* – but relativizing Object of Comparison – as in *the man that John is taller than* – is awkward. In Basque, only the top three constituents – Subject, Direct Object, and Indirect Object – can be relativized: the language has no structural equivalents of *the man that I talked to*, *the man whose book I am reading*, and *the man that John is taller than*.

If the crosslinguistic sparsity of relativization down the hierarchy can be taken to mean that these structures are more difficult, this explains the distribution of resumptive pronouns: they step in to aid the interpretation of more complex relative clause structures. But are relative clause structures down the hierarchy really more difficult? This hypothesis is based only on the diminishing presence of these structures across languages. Additional evidence coming from sentence processing will be adduced in Chapter 6 (Section 6.4.1).

The present section is about the different uses of words: how instances of the same word type available in a language can be differently distributed over the structures of a single language and of different languages. Resumptive pronouns provided our first example: third-person pronouns exist in almost all languages and while they are generally used meaningfully, in some languages they are also used redundantly in certain relative-clause constructions. Our second example shows a similar phenomenon for nouns.

3.2.1.2 Classifiers

What does it take to make an English noun plural? In most cases, all we need is the plural morpheme -*s* (or its allomorphs, such as -*z*, -*əz*) suffixed to the noun.

(14) (a) *Jack has delivered the tulip-**s**.*   English

    (b) *Two nail-**s** will be enough.*

    (c) *The ox-**en** returned from the meadow.*

But this simple process does not always work. Suppose you want to pluralize nouns like *coffee* or *wine*. The problem is that there is simply no entity that could be pluralized. Pluralization presupposes distinct units of which there can be one or many, but the nouns *coffee* and *wine* do not designate such units: they refer to unbounded masses. It is only units of coffee and units of wine that can be pluralized, such as *two cups of coffee, a pot of coffee, two glasses of wine,* or *ten carafes of wine*.

The necessary unitization of mass nouns for pluralization is recognized across languages. Here are some examples.

(15)

ENGLISH	RUSSIAN			KOREAN			JAPANESE		
three	*tri*	*čaški*	*čaja*	*cha*	*se*	**jan**	*kotsya*	*san*	**hai**
cups of tea	three	**cup**	tea	tea	three	**cup**	tea	three	**cup**
three **sheets**	*tri*	**lista**	*bumagi*	*jongi*	*se*	**jang**	*kami*	*san*	**mai**
of paper		three	**sheet**	paper	paper	three	**sheet**	paper	three	**sheet**

These examples show a shared pattern in the pluralization of mass nouns in four languages. But here is an interesting difference among them. When it comes to pluralizing nouns that refer to naturally delimited units such as 'chair' or 'child,' the languages part ways: as shown in (16), English and Russian directly pluralize such count nouns while Korean and Japanese use the same construction as what they use for mass nouns.

(16)

ENGLISH	RUSSIAN		KOREAN			JAPANESE		
three chairs	*tri*	*stula*	*euija*	*se*	***gae***	*isu*	*san*	***kyaku***
	three	chairs	chair	three	CLF	chair	three	CLF
three children	*tri*	*rebjonka*	*ai*	*se*	***myeong***	*kodomo*	*san*	***nin***
	three	children	child	three	CLF	child	three	CLF

Notice that the extra word in the Korean and Japanese examples, glossed as CLF, is different for 'chair' and 'child': it varies with the choice of the noun. Chairs, as well as tables, fruits, etc. belong to the class that requires *gae* in Korean; tables and other legged furniture take *kyaku* in Japanese; children as well as women, persons, etc. take *myeong* in Korean and *nin* in Japanese. Since these elements reflect a classification of nouns, they are called **sortal (or numeral) classifiers**. In Japanese and Korean grammatical terminology, numeral classifiers are referred to as counters.

Languages differ greatly in the kinds of constructions where numeral classifiers are used, in the noun classes defined by them, and, as we saw above, whether they do or do not have such classifiers at all. The number of classifiers will range from 1 (in Cebuano) all the way to 200 or more (in Vietnamese and Burmese) (Rijkhoff 2002: 77). They may be obligatory or optional and may accompany nouns not only when they occur with numerals but also if they occur with other nominal satellites such as demonstratives, and even if the nouns occur by themselves. Nonetheless, there are some crosslinguistic generalizations that apply to their use and their occurrence across languages. We will discuss three such generalizations, two about the crosslinguistic distribution of classifiers and one about their semantics.

(A) WHICH LANGUAGES HAVE NUMERAL CLASSIFIERS?

Numeral classifiers are not overwhelmingly frequent across languages. In a sample of 400 languages, David Gil has found that somewhat more than half – 260 – lack this category (Gil 2005: 226). While Gil notes that their geographic distribution is strikingly broad around the world, the main concentration is in East and South-East Asia (for more on the areal distribution of classifiers, see Aikhenvald 2000: 121–124). Beyond this geographic skewing, which suggests the influence of language contact, the question is whether the presence of numeral classifiers correlates with other grammatical properties of the languages that have them. Several such correlates have been proposed in the literature (for a sample of them, search for "classifier" in the Konstanz Universals Archive). We will consider two such hypotheses.

> GEN-2 All languages that have sortal (numeral) classifiers also have
> mensural classifiers. (Greenberg 1977: 285)
> GEN-3 Most languages that have sortal classifiers have optional or
> no plural marking on nouns. (Greenberg 1977: 286 (citing
> Mary Sanches))

GEN-2 makes reference to mensural classifiers: these are classifiers used to measure amounts of mass nouns rather than classifying countable nouns. The generalization sounds strange: don't all languages have mensural classifiers such as *cup* in *a **cup** of coffee*? If they did, the implication would be vacuous since it would state a condition for the occurrence of a pattern that is unconditionally present in all languages. However, Greenberg notes (1977: 185) that several American Indian languages and some languages of New Guinea have no mensural classifiers. Thus, the proposed generalization does have empirical significance by carving out a subset of human languages where mensural classifiers occur. The much greater frequency of mensural classifiers over sortal (numeral) ones suggests that sortal classifiers are historically secondary: they must have been an extension of mensural classifiers from mass nouns to count nouns.

The force of GEN-3, according to which languages with sortal classifiers tend not to have obligatory noun plural, can be illustrated with Korean.

(17) (a) *i*   *euija*   'this chair'   Korean
         this   chair

    (b) *i*   *euija(-deul)*   'these chairs'
         this   chair(-PLU)

The plural marker *deul* is optional: a noun phrase can be interpreted as plural even without it. While this implication holds for many languages, there do exist languages that have both classifiers and obligatory plural markings on nouns; for these, see the Konstanz Universals Archive under "classifier."

(B) THE SEMANTICS OF NUMERAL CLASSIFIERS

Consider the kinds of nouns that occur with the Japanese classifier *hon* (Lakoff 1986: 25–30)

(18) (a) sticks, candles, trees, dead snakes
    (b) hits in baseball
    (c) shots in basketball
    (d) Judo matches
    (e) verbal contests between a Zen master and his disciple
    (f) rolls of tape
    (g) telephone calls
    (h) letters
    (i) movies
    (j) medical injections

At first glance, the class seems fairly arbitrary: what do its members have to do with each other? Nonetheless, it does make same sense. One underlying principle is **similarity**: there are certain properties that some of the various objects share. Sticks, candles, trees, and dead snakes are similar in that they are all long, thin, rigid objects. Also, Judo matches and verbal contests are similar in that they involve a competitive interaction between people.

Classifications based on taxonomic and partonomy are also observable in everyday life. Suppose you are in a grocery store looking for raisins. You may find them on the shelf alongside dried apricots, nuts, and almonds. The rationale is similarity: they are all readily edible natural products that come in small bits. Alternatively, you may find raisins next to baking mixes and frostings. These items are not similar but they are likely to be used together: if you bake a cake, you may need raisins. Or if you go to a hardware store looking for a hammer, where do you find one? Hammers may be where other tools are – such as rakes and shovels – or they may be next to nails. The first arrangement is based on similarity, the second, on partonomy: hammers and nails are parts of a single act by their users. The two

But similarity does not hold for all of these objects. For example, a roll of tape is not a long thin rigid object: only part of it – the tape – is long and thin once it has been pried off the roll. Nevertheless, the entire roll is classified with *hon*: the whole object is placed in a class that, by mere similarity, only a part of that object would be sorted into. Or take baseball shots: they are not long, thin, and rigid objects themselves, either, but they are associated with baseball bats which do have these properties. In such instances, what ties the items together is metonymy: properties of a part are attributed to the whole. The idea is based on part–whole relations: partonomy. Things that occur in what Lakoff calls the same experiential domain – i.e., that are part of the same instance of human experience – are classified together.

The role of similarity and part–whole relations seen above in Japanese recurs across languages in how classifiers categorize nouns. Here is a crosslinguistic generalization to capture this fact.

> GEN-4 In many languages, noun classes are defined either by taxonomic or by partonomic relations among the referents.

The two classificatory criteria – taxonomy and partonomy – were also evident in our survey of body-part terms (Chapter 2, Section 2.2). Due to their similar shapes, fingers and toes are referred to by the same word in some languages. But when the word for 'leg' also includes 'thigh' and 'foot,' this is due to their being parts of the same whole rather than to their similarity.

As a rule, classifiers are redundant: they spell out an obvious category that a noun belongs to (as in "**child** three **human**," etc.). In other cases, however, they are used to add meaning. Nouns that occur with classifiers may not have a unique classification of their own; instead, it is the classifiers that assign the nouns to one or other class. Rather than simply re-iterating the genus of the noun, the classifier supplies the genus. This is shown in the following data from Thai.

(19)	(a)	klûay	sìi	**bay**	'four bananas'	Thai
		banana	four	**CL(round thing)**		
	(b)	klûay	sìi	**wîi**	'four bunches of bananas'	
		banana	four	**CL(bunch)**		
	(c)	klûay	sìi	**tôn**	'four banana trees'	
		banana	four	**CL(long vertical thing)**		

The Thai word for 'banana' all by itself does not refer either to a single banana or to a bunch of bananas or to a banana tree: it is the classifier that specifies the meaning.

Given that in classifier languages, the constructions for 'two cups of tea' and 'two tables' are alike in that both include a classifier, the question naturally arises whether in these languages, 'table,' 'chair,' and 'child' are actually viewed by speakers as shapeless things on a par with 'tea' or 'wine.' There is evidence, however, that this is not the case. If the referents of the Korean and Japanese words for 'apple' were construed as amorphous masses, expressions such as 'round apple' would not be possible: the presumed shapeless image of 'apple' would conflict with the adjective 'round.' However, as shown in (20), such expressions are possible: one can say 'round apple' in Korean or Japanese (but not 'round water,' etc.).

> relations of taxonomy and partonomy are fundamental tools of human conceptualization and thus no wonder they also underlie classifier assignment.

(20) (a) *dongeuran* *sagwa* 'round apple'   Korean
            round   apple

      (b) *marui*   *ringo* 'round apple'   Japanese
            round   apple

Perhaps nouns like 'apple' are alternatively conceptualized in these languages as mass nouns when they are numerated by means of classifiers, and as count nouns when they occur with adjectives expressing shape or size. That the referent of a noun can be construed sometimes as mass and other times as count can be illustrated from English. (21) shows the count and mass uses of *egg*, (22) shows the double use of *house*.

(21) (a) *Jim bought two **eggs**.*   English

      (b) *Jim had **egg** on his chin.*

(22) (a) *For two-million dollars, you get a lot more **houses** in this neighborhood than in the suburbs.*

      (b) *For two-million dollars, you get a lot more **house** in this neighborhood than in the suburbs.*

Or consider the English words *suggestion* and *advice*. They have roughly the same meaning, yet, *advice* is a mass noun requiring a mensural classifier in the plural while *suggestion* is a count noun.

(23) (a) *The principal offered **suggestions** to the teachers.*   English
          The principal offered **bits of suggestion to the teachers.*

      (b) **The principal offered **advices** to the teachers.*
          *The principal offered **bits of advice** to the teachers.*

The occasional blurriness of the distinction between what is a count noun and what is a mass noun is also shown by how some nouns of the same meaning are variably pluralizable in different languages. The English word *information* is not pluralizable: instead of **informations*, the plural requires a mensural classifier: *bits of information*. In German, however, the word has a regular plural: *Information-en*. Similarly, the German word for 'advice' – *Rat* – has a regular plural: *Räte*, while in English it does not.

All of these examples show that countability is negotiable: to an extent, it is in the eye of the beholder. While the real nature of things may have a role in drawing the linguistic distinction between masses and countable entities, there is much that is left to interpretation.

The topic of this section has been how words may be used differently in different languages. In addition to pronouns, classifiers also provide an example of such varying uses of words because classifiers are in many cases independent nouns themselves. This is not only true for mensural classifiers, such as English *cup*, but also for sortal classifiers. In (24a), Korean *saram* is a noun meaning 'person.' In (24b), it is a classifier for persons, such as workers; and, strikingly, in (24c), it is its own classifier.

(24) (a) **saram**   *se*   *myeong*   'three persons'   Korean

           person three   CLF

      (b) ilkkun   *se*   **saram** 'three workers'

           worker   three   **CLF**

      (c) **saram**   *se*   **saram** 'three persons'

           person three   **CLF**

However, not all classifiers have independent nominal use: for example, *myeong* – the classifier in (24a) – cannot be used as a noun in Korean. Thus, for some classifiers in some languages, a separate word class needs to be posited distinct from nouns. In this case, what is involved is not the cross-linguistically variant distribution of nouns over different contexts – a situation comparable to the copula seen above – but the crosslinguistically variant existence of word classes over different languages as in the case of articles.

3.2.2 Which word forms?

As we have just seen, for formulating a sentence it is not enough to choose the words that are necessary to convey the intended meaning: languages may require additional words – such as resumptive pronouns or classifiers – even though they make no semantic contribution.

However, as we saw in Section 3.1, even if the choice of words is in compliance with the grammar of the language, a sentence may still not be grammatical: over and above being present, words have to have the right forms as required by the context. Just as the choice of the words differs across languages, what is the right form for a word is also cross-linguistically variable. This is shown by the examples in (25). Does the verb 'met' have the same or different form in the (i) and (ii) sentences? And do the noun phrases 'I' and 'the tall teacher' have the same or different forms?

(25) (a) (i)   *I* MET *the tall teacher*.   English

      (ii) *The tall teacher* MET **me**.

  (b) (i)   **Saja**   *MENTEMUI*   *guru*   *tinggi*   *itu*. Indonesian
          I   met   teacher   tall   the
          'I met the tall teacher.'

      (ii) *Guru*   *tinggi*   *itu*   *MENTEMUI*   **saja**.
          teacher   tall   the   met   me
          'The tall teacher met me.'

  (c) (i)   **Ego**   *magistrum*   *magnum*   *CONVENI*.   Latin
          I   teacher   tall   met
          'I met the tall teacher.'

      (ii) *Magister*   *magnus*   **me**   *CONVENIT*.
          teacher   tall   me   met
          'The tall teacher met me.'

Regarding the verb forms: in English and Indonesian, there is no difference in the (i) and (ii) sentences. In Latin, however, there are two different
forms: *conveni* and *convenit*. This is because the subject in (i) is the first-
person 'I' while in (ii), it is third person: 'the tall teacher.' The switching
around of the two verb forms would result in ungrammatical sentences,
such as *Ego magistrum magnum convenit*. As noted in Section 3.2, this grammatical pattern is called **agreement**: the Latin verb agrees with the subject in person (also in number, but this is not shown by the examples).

Regarding the noun phrases: in the (i) sentences, 'I' is the subject and
'the tall teacher' is the object; in the (ii) sentences, the reverse is the case.
In Indonesian, this makes no difference: both 'I' and 'the tall teacher' have
the same form whether subject or object. In English, 'the tall teacher' does
not change but the pronoun does: *I* for subject and *me* for object. In Latin,
both the pronoun and the full noun phrase take on different forms: *ego*
versus *me* for the pronoun and *magister magnus* vs. *magistrum magnum* for
the full noun phrase. (*Ego magister magnus conveni* and other combinations
are ungrammatical.) As also noted in Section 3.1, the choice of case forms
depending on the verb or some other sentence part is called **government**.
In Indonesian, the verb does not govern different cases for subject and
object; similarly, in English it does not for nominal subjects and objects
but it does for pronouns (e.g. *I* vs. *me*)'; and in Latin, the case of both pronouns and full noun phrases is governed by the verb.

In the examples of agreement given in (2), we saw that in Spanish and
Swahili, the adjective agrees with the noun in gender and number; but
there is no such agreement in English and Japanese. In (25c) above, the
Latin verb agrees with the subject in person and number but it does not
agree in Indonesian or in the past tense in English. This shows that the
exact patterns of agreement vary across languages. The same is true for

government. In the Latin examples in (25c), it is the verb that governs the case of its subject and object. The English, German, French, and Russian examples in (4) showed that not only verbs but also adjectives and numerals can govern cases. All in all, even our small sample of examples illustrates that not only their occurrence but also the details of agreement and government vary across languages. Our task is to see if there are properties of the two patterns that are nonetheless invariant across languages.

3.2.2.1 Agreement

There is a wide variety of agreement patterns in terms of what can be an agreement target (the constituent that agrees, such as the verb or the adjective), the agreement controller (the constituent that the target agrees with, such as the subject of the verb or the noun that the adjective goes with), and the agreement features (the properties that the target copies from the controller, such as person, number, and gender). Nonetheless, there are crosslinguistically valid constraints on this variation. This section will offer a small glimpse into both the crosslinguistic variation of agreement and the constraints that limit it. First, we will look at possible controllers of verb agreement; second, we will consider how different targets exhibit different agreement features.

While, as we saw above, past-tense verbs in English do not agree with any of their arguments, there is verb agreement in the present tense, shown most extensively by the verb *to be*. This verb agrees with the subject in number and, in the singular, also in person.

(26)   *I am*   English

     you are

     he is

     we are

     you are

     they are

Beyond agreement with the subject, verbs can also agree with other arguments in languages. The data in (27) show Swahili verb agreement both with the subject in person and number and with the direct object in gender (cited in Lehmann 1982: 212).

(27)   **Ni-li-mw-**ona   **m**-toto.   Swahili

     SBJ.1S-PST-**OBJ.CL.1**-see   CL.1-child

     'I saw the child.'

Lebanese Arabic offers an even broader range of arguments controlling verb agreement. (28) illustrates gender agreement of the verb with subject and direct object (the agreement marker for masculine subject is zero, indicated by 0).

(28) (a) *huwwe* *šaaf-**0-u***   *la*   *l*   *walid*   Lebanese

      he   saw-**MSC.SBJ-**   Arabic

            MSC.OBJ   OBJ.MRK   the   boy

      'He saw the boy.'

(b) *hiyye* *šaaf-**it-u***   *la*   *l*   *walid*

      she   saw-**FEM.SBJ-MSC.OBJ**   OBJ.MRK   the   boy

      'She saw the boy.'

(c) *huwwe* *šaaf-**0-ha***   *la*   *l*   *bint*

      he   saw-**MSC.SBJ-FEM.OBJ**   OBJ.MRK   the   girl

      'He saw the girl.'

(d) *hiyye* *šaaf-**it-ha***   *la*   *l*   *bint*

      she   saw-**FEM.SBJ-FEM.OBJ**   OBJ.MRK   **the**   **girl**

      'She saw the girl.'

(29) in turn illustrates verb agreement with subject and indirect object in gender (*Samir* is a man's name, *Salma* is a female.)

(29) (a) *la*   *Samiir huwwe baảt-**0-lu***   *l*   *walad*   Lebanese

      to   Samir he   sent-**MSC.SBJ-**   Arabic

            MSC.INDOBJ   the   boy

      'He sent the boy to Samir.'

(b) *huwwe* *baảt-**0-la***   *l*   *walad*   *la*   *Salma*

      he   sent-**MSC.SBJ-**   the   boy   to   Salma

      FEM.INDOBJ

      'He sent the boy to Salma.'

The above examples of English, Swahili, and Lebanese Arabic suggest the following implications:

    GEN-5 Controller Hierarchy

  In most languages,
(a)   if the verb agrees with the indirect object, it also agrees with the direct object; and
(b)   if the verb agrees with the direct object, it also agrees with the subject.

GEN-5 states two patterns that are prevalent but not universal because there are languages where the verb agrees with indirect objects but never with direct objects and others where there is direct-object agreement but no subject agreement (for discussion and examples, see Siewierska and Bakker 1996, esp. 122–123).

Regarding (a): while most languages that have indirect-object–verb agreement do indeed also have direct-object–verb agreement, this is to be interpreted as a paradigmatic generalization, not a syntagmatic one. That is to say, in ditransitive sentences (i.e. those with both direct and indirect object), verb agreement with the indirect object may take precedence over the direct object. This is true for Lebanese Arabic as shown in (29): while in this language, there is both direct-object and indirect-object agreement, there are ditransitive sentences where the verb agrees with the indirect object but not with the direct one.

What might be the explanation for the prevalence of subject agreement over direct-object and indirect-object agreement?

The historical origins of verb agreement shed light on this issue. Verb-agreement markers evolve from personal pronouns that refer to topicalized noun phrases. An example of this construction is English *John, **he** is a friend of mine*. In some languages (e.g. Arabic or Swahili), agreement markers still carry their anaphoric pronominal function: the noun phrases they refer to are optional. This anaphoric function may get lost over time: agreement markers come to redundantly re-iterate some characteristics of a noun phrase that is also present in the sentence.

If the origin of verb agreement markers is tied to topicalization, we can expect verb agreement to occur primarily with noun phrases that are most likely to be topicalized. Foremost of these are subjects: topicalization favors noun phrases that are definite and subjects of transitive sentences generally are. This suggests that verbs should most commonly agree with subjects – a true fact. Direct objects are not generally definite but there is a telling pattern: if in a language the verb agrees with indefinite objects, it also agrees with definite ones. This is so in Lebanese Arabic: the examples in (28) show verb agreement with definite direct objects ('the boy,' 'to the girl') but if the object is indefinite, there is no verb agreement with it. The fact that in a given sentence, verb agreement with indirect objects takes precedence over agreement with direct objects (as in (29) above) may have to do with indirect objects being animate while direct objects mostly are not. Animate noun phrases are often more topical than inanimate ones.

To summarize so far: crosslinguistically preferred **verb-agreement controllers** line up along the Controller Hierarchy given in GEN-5 (which, as you may have noticed, is a subpart of the **Accessibility Hierarchy** seen in Section 3.2.1.1). Furthermore, there is also a second crosslinguistically valid ranking of agreement patterns which constrains not agreement controllers but the **agreement features** that various **agreement targets** exhibit. Formulated by Greville Corbett (2006: 206–237; 2011: 190–196), the Agreement Hierarchy can be illustrated as follows.

In American English, the noun *committee* takes singular verb agreement; however, as Corbett points out, in British English it normally takes plural verbs.

(30) (a) *The committee **has** met.*   American English

     (b) *The committee **have** met.*   British English

In other words, in American English, what is mirrored by verb agreement is the singular form of the subject noun, while in the British variety, the plural meaning of the noun prevails in determining agreement: committees consist of more than one individual. Semantic agreement may also apply to the relative pronoun and the anaphoric pronoun:

(31) (a) *the committee **who** have met*

      (b) *The committee have met. **They** have come to a decision.*

However, the possibility of semantic agreement does not hold for all targets: the demonstrative must conform to the singular form: *this committee*, and not **these committee*.

Another example to show how targets can differ in whether they take formal or semantic agreement is the German word *Mädchen* 'the girl.' This noun ends in the diminutive suffix -*chen* and as all other such nouns in German, it is formally neuter. The definite and indefinite article, the demonstrative pronoun, and the adjective faithfully reflect the neuter form of the noun and so does the relative pronoun.

(32) (a) *das*   *Mädchen*   'the girl'   German

           the.NEU   girl

      (b) *ein*   *schönes*   *Mädchen*   'a pretty girl'

           a.NEU   **pretty.NEU** girl

      (c) *dieses*   *Mädchen*   'this girl'

           this.NEU   girl

      (d) *das*   *Mädchen,*   ***das***   *angekommen*   *ist*

           the.NEUT   girl   **that.NEU**   arrived   is

           'the girl that arrives'

However, in colloquial style, the feminine form *sie* of the anaphoric pronoun is favored over the neuter *es*.

(32) (e) Das   Mädchen ist angekommen. **Sie/es**   ist   von   Berlin.

           the.NEU girl   is   arrived   **she/it** is   from   Berlin

           'The girl has arrived.   She is from Berlin.'

Based on such examples from languages from various parts of the world, Corbett suggests the following crosslinguistic generalization (2006: 207; 2011: 191).

GEN-6 The Agreement Hierarchy

attributive > predicate > relative   > personal

                             pronoun   pronoun

For any controller that permits alternative agreements, as we move rightwards along the Agreement Hierarchy, the likelihood of

agreement with greater semantic justification will increase monot-
onically (that is, with no intervening decrease).

The increasing tendency to use semantic agreement with constituent
types to the right, and especially with anaphoric pronouns, suggests that,
with increasing syntactic distance from the controller, form fades in the
memory of the speaker with meaning trumping it. Thus, in the case of
German *das Mädchen*, the neuter form of the noun calls for neuter agreement on articles, demonstratives, adjectives, and relative pronouns that
are placed close to the controller noun but the anaphoric pronoun, which
is at some distance from it, picks up on the natural feminine gender of the
referent.

3.2.2.2 Government

Given a transitive sentence – that is, a sentence with two noun phrase arguments such as *Jill hit Joe* – how does the listener know who performs the act
described? Is it Jill who hit Joe or did Joe hit Jill? In English, word order is
the most obvious signal: in general, the subject comes before the object.

There are, however, English sentences where word order is actually
redundant: as illustrated above in (25a), there are additional formal markers differentiating subject from object. This is also shown in (33).

(33) (a)   *I **am** hiring Joe.*   English

      (b) *Joe **is** hiring **me**.*

In addition to word order, there is verb agreement: *am* for a first-person
singular subject and *is* for third person. But beyond that, there is the difference between *I* and *me*. Most English personal pronouns have different
subject and object forms: for first-person singular subject, the form is *I*;
for object, the form is *me*. Different forms of noun phrases (in this case,
pronouns) dictated by the verb of the sentence are called case forms. The
case of the subject is termed nominative; the case of the direct object is
labeled accusative. Transitive verbs like *hit* and *hire* are said to govern the
nominative case for subjects and the accusative case for direct objects. As
was shown in (4), not only verbs but also adjectives and numerals can
serve as governors.

Case has an important role if it keeps subject and direct object apart
and thus helps the listener interpret the sentence. Notice, however, that
English pronouns have special case forms not only in transitive sentences,
where they have a differentiating function, but also in intransitive sentences, which only have a single noun phrase:

(34) (a)   *I   resigned.* (***Me** *resigned*.)   English

      (b) ***He** resigned.* (***Him** *resigned*.)

As (34) shows, the subject of intransitive sentences is in the nominative
case. But logically speaking, there is no reason why this should be the
case: why not the accusative, as in (35)?

(35) (a) **Me**   resigned.

    (b) **Him**   resigned.

One could argue that the choice has to do with semantics: both the subject of a transitive verb and the subject of an intransitive verb are initiators, or agents, of the act performed: they act intentionally. This is indeed the case for the subjects of transitive verbs such as *hit*, and *hire* and for some intransitive verbs like *resign* and *leave*. But, as (36) shows, not all intransitive verbs have volitional subjects.

(36) (a) *She* **fell**   *over.*   English

    (b) *He* **burst into laughter.**

In these sentences, the referents of the subjects undergo an action rather than initiating it. Semantically, they are patient-like and thus more similar to the direct object of a transitive sentence than to its subject.

Since some intransitive verbs have agent-like subjects and others have patient-like ones, we might expect agentive subjects in intransitive sentences to be in the nominative and non-agentive ones in the accusative, as in (37):

(37) (a) Transitive sentences: Pseudo-English

        He hit **her.**

    (b) Intransitive sentences:

        – Subject is Agent: **He** *resigned.*

        – Subject is Patient: **Her** *fell over.*

This is not so in English. However, if we take a look at the case-marking of subjects and objects in other languages, what we find is that, in addition to the English pattern, the other two plausible scenarios exemplified do occur; namely, that all intransitive subjects are case-marked as objects as in (35), or that some intransitive subjects are case-marked as transitive subjects and others as objects as in (37). The diagrams below show these two options in (38b) and (38c) along with the actual English pattern in (38a). These are the abbreviations used:

A (Agent) = transitive subject
P (Patient) = direct object
S = the single noun-phrase argument of an intransitive sentence
S_A = agentive S
S_P = patient-like S.

(38) (a) Accusative alignment:

                               A and S in the nominative case

                               P in the accusative case

(b) Ergative alignment:

A in the ergative case

P and S in the absolutive case

(c) Active alignment:

A and S_A in the agentive case

P and S_P in the patientive case

Regarding the labels accusative alignment and ergative alignment, note that each is named after the case that is unlike the other two in the system.

Here are real-language examples for (b) and (c). (0 stands for zero case marking.)

(39) Ergative alignment in Samoan (Langacker 1972: 174)

    (a) E   sogi   **e**   le   tama   **0**   le   ufi.

         PRS   cut   **ERG** the   boy   **ABS** the   yam

         'The boy cuts the yam.'

    (b) E   pa'ū   **0**   le   ufi.

         PRES   fall   **ABS** the   yam

         'The yam fell.'

(40) Active alignment in Georgian (Comrie 2005a: 399; glosses are simplified)

    (a) nino-**m**   ačvena   surat-eb-**i**   gia-s

         Nino-**AGT**   showed   picture-PL-**PAT** Gia-DAT

         'Nino showed pictures to Gia.'

    (b) nino-**m**   daamtknara

         Nino-**AGT**   yawned

         'Nino yawned.'

    (c) vaxt'ang-**i**   ekim-i   igo

         Vakhtang-**PAT** doctor-**PAT** was

         'Vakhtang was a doctor.'

Many languages have a mixture of the three types; suprisingly, English itself is an example.

(41) (a) Intransitive sentence: *She_S is running.*   English

                                    He_S is running.

      (b) Active sentence: *She_A followed **him_P**.*

      (c) Passive sentence: *He_P was followed by her_A.*

If we compare (41a) with (41b), the pattern is accusative-style: S and A are both in the nominative with P in the accusative. But when (41a) is compared with (41c), alignment is ergative-style: it is S and P that are in the nominative. It is only due to the greater text frequency of active sentences over passive ones and the fact that the passive has the more complex structure of the two that English is labeled an accusative language and not an ergative one.

There are also other parts of English grammar where the ergative pattern crops up. The basic idea behind ergativity is that S and P behave alike as opposed to A. This similar behavior of S and P does not have to be case marking: it can also be other aspects of grammatical behavior. Consider the following examples of English word formation.

(42) (a) nouns derived from intransitive verbs with -*er*:   English

    runner, sleeper, speaker, etc.

 (b) nouns derived from transitive verbs with -*er*:

    employer, reader, reporter, etc.

(43) (a) nouns derived from intransitive verbs with -*ee*:

    attendee, retiree, etc.

 (b) nouns derived from transitive verbs with -*ee*:

    employee, nominee, parolee, etc.

The suffix -*er* derives nouns that refer to the agent of an intransitive verb and, similarly, to the agent of a transitive verb. In contrast, the suffix -*ee* derives nouns that refer to the agent of intransitive verbs but when added to transitive verbs, the derived noun refers to the patient, rather than the agent. For example, a reader is one who reads but an employee is not one who employs; rather, he is one who is employed. Thus, noun derivation with -*er* complies with the accusative pattern; noun derivation with -*ee* in turn follows the ergative alignment.

The three case-marking alignment systems considered above – accusative, ergative, and active – do not exhaust all logical possibilities. Even if we disregard patterns where, as in the active system, an argument type is split into two subtypes, there are three additional options. (44) diagrams all five patterns with un-split arguments. Identically-case-marked arguments are in bold and large font.

(44)
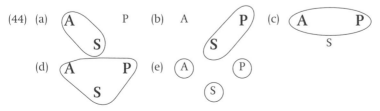

They are illustrated with real and imaginary English examples in (45).

(45) (a) **He** hit him. (b) He hit **him**. (c) **He** hit **he**.

        He ran.   **Him** ran.   Hoo ran.

    (d) **He** hit **he**. (e) He hit him.

        He ran.   Hoo ran.

(44a), exemplified in (45a), shows accusative alignment, (44b), exemplified in (45b), shows ergative alignment. In both, two of the three noun phrases are classed together. This is so also in (44c–45c) but here transitive subject and object have the same case, with intransitive subject being different. In (44d–45d), all three noun phrases are in the same case; in (44e–45e), all three are different.

The crosslinguistic frequency of these five alignment systems is heavily skewed. The accusative system is more numerous than the ergative system and the active system is very rare (Comrie 2005a: 399). The following statistical generalization may thus be stated:

> GEN-7 In most languages, case marking follows either the accusative or the ergative alignment, with accusative alignment being more frequent.

The uneven distribution of these five logically possible systems makes some sense. If the primary role of case marking is to differentiate subjects and objects of transitive sentences, the accusative and the ergative systems ((44a) and (44b)) are equally useful: they fulfill this task. But when subject and object are marked the same way (as in (44c) and (44d)), case marking fails to do the job. Finally, (44e) does differentiate subject and object but it goes overboard in that it also differentiates these noun phrases from the intransitive subject even though they do not occur in the same sentence and thus do not call for different markings.

Why accusative alignment should be more numerous than ergative alignment is an open question. Similarly, it is somewhat surprising that active alignment is so infrequent given that, from a semantic point of view, it is the most telling one since it differently marks agentive and non-agentive intransitive subjects while both the accusative and the ergative alignment systems obliterate this division. The accusative system extends the semantically expected marking of agentive intransitive subjects to the non-agentive ones. The ergative system does the opposite: it generalizes the marking of non-agentive intransitive subjects to agentive ones.

This section has been about the choice of words and word forms for making sentences. Once appropriate words and word forms have been chosen, the next question concerns the order in which they are placed. This is the topic of the next section.

3.3 The order of words

How COULD words be sequenced? There are many conceivable possibilities but only some occur with any frequency across languages. First, we will consider some of the logical options and state their distribution in terms of crosslinguistic frequency. This survey will yield statements like "Order pattern X is (in)frequent across languages." Second, we will consider a set of implicational universals showing that the distribution of the various order clusters relative to each other is not random: certain correlations occur more often. This investigation will yield statements such as "In all (or most) languages, if there is order pattern Y, there is also order pattern X." Since the term "order" is somewhat ambiguous, the terms "linear order," "linear pattern" or "linearization" will be used instead.

(A) FREQUENCIES OF LINEAR ORDER PATTERNS

The logical possibilities of the linear ordering of words can be assessed by considering the terms of ordering patterns and considering the ordering relations among the terms. Here is the list of logical possibilities:

THE TERMS OF LINEAR ORDER PATTERNS

1. Classes of words (e.g. "nouns")
2. Classes of phrases and clauses (e.g. "noun phrases")
3. Individual lexemes (e.g. "boy")
4. Numerical position (e.g. "after any first word in the sentence")

THE RELATIONS OF LINEAR ORDER PATTERNS

5. Precedence regardless of adjacency ("place A before B regardless of distance")
6. Adjacency regardless of precedence ("place A next to B regardless of whether before or after")
7. Both precedence and adjacency (=immediate precedence) (e.g. "place A immediately before B")
8. Neither adjacency nor precedence ("free order") ("place A anywhere")
9. Interlocking order (e.g. "place A between parts of B")

Let us look at some examples.

1. Linearization by word class

Examples of word-class-based ordering are ubiquitous. For instance, English grammar does not need to list all the adpositions – *in, one, over, below*, etc. – that are preposed to the noun phrase; it is sufficient to state a general rule: adpositions are preposed. Similarly, a general word-class-based rule stating that demonstratives precede nouns takes care, in a single stroke, of the pre-nominal order of the words *this, these, that*, and *those*.

2. Linearization by phrase and clause class

Consider the bold-faced parts of the following sentences.

(46) (a)   *Jack picked* **three juicy plums** *off the tree.*   English

   (b)   **Three juicy plums** *were picked off the tree by Jack.*

The order of the three words *three*, *juicy*, and *plums* is prescribed by a word-class-based rule that says numerals precede adjectives and adjectives in turn precede nouns. But now consider the order of this entire three-word sequence relative to the other parts of the sentences. What accounts for the post-verbal position of these words in (46a) and their pre-verbal position in (46b)? The reason is that they are parts of a larger whole: a noun phrase, which is the object of (46a) and the subject of (46b); and that English has a rule which says objects follow the verb and subjects precede it. Thus, the three words are ordered relative to the rest of the sentence as parts of a phrase: they get a free ride from the "vehicle" that they sit in.

Beyond phrases, there are also larger units that linearization rules may apply to. Just as the phrase-based rules, clause-based rules seize the words that occur within a clause and put them all in a particular position. It is like when all the furniture of a home is placed on a pallet and moved into a new place in one single move rather than each piece moved separately. Acting on the Whole amounts to acting on the Parts as well.

Here are examples of clausal order.

(47) (a) *Jack climbed the plum tree* **that was closest to the garage**.

  (b) *Jack promised to send me his latest book* **but he has not done so**.

Why do the boldfaced words stand where they do? Their order does not follow from the class membership of any of the individual words. Instead, it results from the fact that they jointly form clauses that have a particular position: English relative clauses follow the noun that they modify and *but* clauses follow the main clause of the sentence.

3.   Linearization by individual lexemes

Words are normally sequenced by rules that refer to the taxonomic or partonomic entities that the words belong to – that is, to word classes and to classes of larger units such as phrases and clauses. Nevertheless, there are sporadic instances where linearization rules apply to individual words. One example is the English adposition *ago*. As noted above, adpositions in English are preposed, such as in **before** *last year*. However, *ago* is a postposition: *a year* **ago**. English grammar must state *ago*'s exceptional position by specific mention of this lexical item.

A more complex example comes from Tagalog. Consider the following sentence (Schachter and Otanes 1972: 414).

(48) *Nagtatrabaho*   **nga**   **rin**   *daw*   *kayo*   *roon*.   Tagalog
     work   **indeed**   **too**   **they (say)** you   there

     'They say it is true that you are working there too.'

The order of some of these words follows general categorial patterns. Tagalog is a verb-first language, so *nagtatrabaho* 'work' starts the sentence;

the order of *kayo* and *roon*, 'you' before 'there' also obeys a general rule: the subject precedes the adverb. But the order of the three bold-faced words is idiosyncratic: there is no generalization that it would follow from. The rule must make mention to these particular words: *nga* must precede *rin*, which must precede *daw*. There are no other words in Tagalog that would alternate with these words in these positions and thus there are no classes for these words to be subsumed under.

4.   Linearization by numerical position

Consider another set of sentences from Tagalog (Schachter and Otanes 1972: 183–193). What is the rule that places *siya* 'he' into the slot where it occurs?

(49) (a) *Masaya*   **siya** *ngayon.*   'He is happy today.'   Tagalog

          happy   **he**   today

      (b) *Hindi*   **siya** *masaya*   *ngayon.*   'He is not happy today.'

          not   **he**   happy   today

      (c) *Bakit*   **siya** *hindi*   *masaya*   *ngayon?*

          why   he   not   happy   today

          'Why is he not happy today?'

From (49a), it would seem that *siya* must follow the predicate *masaya* 'happy'. However, this cannot be right since in (49b), *siya* follows *hindi* 'not' with the predicate 'happy' following *hindi*. But *siya* doesn't always follow either the predicate or the negator: in (49c), it follows *bakit* 'why' with both negator and predicate coming after. The pattern that emerges is that *siya* follows whatever word begins the sentence: it takes second position in the sentence.

There is no reason why numerically defined positions – second in the sentence, third in the sentence, etc. – would not be common across languages but in fact they are not. First, last, and second positions are the only ones that occur. Tagalog illustrates second-position order; another example is German. Here are three versions of 'Julia saw a dog in the garden.'

(50) (a) *Julia*   **sah**   *einen*   *Hund*   *im*   *Garten.*   German

          Julia   **saw**   a   dog   in.the   garden

      (b) *Einen*   *Hund*   **sah**   *Julia*   *im*   *Garten.*

          a   dog   **saw**   Julia   in.the   garden

      (c) *Im*   *Garten* **sah**   *Julia*   *einen*   *Hund.*

          in.the   garden   **saw**   Julia   a   dog

The verb follows different phrase types: the subject in (50a), the object in (50b), and an adverbial phrase in (50c). Thus, its position cannot be defined with respect to any one class of constituents; instead, it has to follow the first phrase whatever it is regardless of whether that phrase consists of a single word or more than one. Alternative orders with two phrases before the verb or with the verb sentence-initial are ungrammatical:

(51) (a) *Julia   einen   Hund   **sah**   im   Garten.   German

           Julia   a   dog   **saw**   in.the   garden

      (b) ***Sah**   Julia   einen   Hund   im   Garten.

           saw   Julia   a   dog   in.the   garden

The order pattern requiring second position for a constituent is labeled Wackernagel's Law named after the Swiss philologist Jacob Wackernagel (1853–1938), who first identified it. In numerical order patterns of this kind, a specified constituent – the subject pronoun in Tagalog and the verb in German – is ordered relative to an unspecified one, i.e., the first constituent of the sentence whatever it may be.

To summarize so far: words are generally ordered by reference to the superordinate taxonomic or partonomic units (classes of words and of phrases or clauses) that they belong to. Linearization of individual words and the ordering of words into numerically defined positions are rare. We will next turn to the kinds of linear relations that words are placed into.

5.   Precedence without adjacency

What are logically possible temporal relations between words? Here is a common linearization statement:

(52) The Adjective immediately precedes the Noun.

This statement includes two constraints: the Adjective comes before the Noun and it stands directly next to it. But the two relations of temporal precedence and adjacency are separable: given two entities, one may hold without the other.

For illustration, let us take a non-linguistic example. If you read the morning newspaper and you watch the TV news immediately after or some time later, the two activities are in a linear precedence relation: one comes after the other but not necessarily in an immediate sequence. If on some days you read the paper first and other days you watch the news first but you never take time to have breakfast between the two, the two activities are always adjacent, with precedence variable.

Immediate precedence – the combination of precedence and adjacency – figures in the word order patterns of individual languages; but crosslinguistically common orderings tend to involve either precedence or adjacency but not both. For an example of a crosslinguistic precedence pattern, let us take the three basic sentence constituents: Subject, Object, and Verb. They may occur in six logically possible orders: SOV, SVO, VSO, VOS, OVS, and OSV. All six orders occur as basic patterns in the simple declarative sentences of languages but not with equal frequency. In an extensive sample consisting of 1228 languages, Dryer has found the following distribution (2005a: 330):

S & O & V: 497 languages
S & V & O: 435 languages

V & S & O: 85 languages
V & O & S: 26 languages
O & V & S; 9 languages
O & S & V: 4 languages
Lacking a dominant order: 172 languages

These figures show two things. First, SOV and SVO are by far the most common patterns. What is unique to these two types is that the subject precedes both the object and the verb. Second, the next most frequent pattern – VSO – also has something in common with SOV and SVO: the subject still precedes the object, although not the verb.

Thus, in characterizing the two most common types and the three most common ones, we need to mention the relation of linear precedence ("A comes before B") without regard to adjacency ("A stands next to B").

S & O & V: 497 languages ⎫   S before both O and V
S & V & O: 435 languages ⎭
                                              ⎫ S before O
V & S & O: 85 languages   ⎭

V & O & S: 26 languages

O & V & S: 9 languages

O & S & V: 4 languages

6.   Adjacency without precedence

The two most frequent types – SOV and SVO – have a further feature in common: while the linear precedence relation between verb and object is not the same, the two constituents are next to each other (this also holds for the fourth and fifth most frequent types: VOS and OVS).

S & O & V: 497 languages ⎫
S & V & O: 435 languages ⎭   O and V are adjacent
V & S & O: 85 languages

V & O & S: 26 languages

O & V & S: 9 languages

O & S & V: 4 languages

This additional shared feature of SOV and SVO languages is an adjacency relation regardless of precedence: V and O are next to each other regardless of which comes first.

The fact that in the overwhelming majority of languages of Dryer's sample, the verb and the object occur next to each other reflects a very general principle of word order famously proclaimed by Otto Behaghel, a German linguist of the first half of the twentieth century: "The foremost law is this: whatever semantically belongs close together is also placed close together" ("Das oberste Gesetz ist dieses, dass das geistig eng Zusammengehörige auch eng zusammengestellt wird" Behaghel 1932: 4).

In other words, constituents that have a close semantic relationship are placed next to each other.

That objects do indeed have a closer semantic relationship to verbs than subjects is shown by many facts. Transitive verbs are often different depending on the choice of their object while subjects generally do not influence the choice. For example, depending on whether it is solid food or liquid food that is consumed, English – and many other languages – have two verbs *eat* and *drink* regardless of who does the action; and whether somebody *kills* or *assassinates* somebody depends on the social status of the person that the object refers to but not on who does the killing.

In addition to object and verb, two other constituents that are generally ordered next to each other are adjective and noun. Languages differ in the precedence relation between them; as we saw in (2), in English and Japanese, the adjective precedes the noun but in Spanish and Swahili, it follows it. But under most circumstances, the two are adjacent.

7. Both precedence and adjacency and
8. neither adjacency nor precedence ("free order")

No universal patterns have been reported in the literature that involve immediate precedence – that is, where two words or other sentence constituents must be both next to each other and in a strict sequence. Let us therefore go on to the last pattern: free order.

As just seen in Dryer's table above, out of 1228 languages, there are 172 which do not have a preferred order pattern for subject, object, and verb. In such "free-order" languages, these three constituents can occur in any of the six logically possible orders without any one being the most frequent. For example, English – a strictly SVO language today – allowed for all six of the logically possible orderings of subject, object, and verb in the Old-English period about thirteen hundred years ago. The following six sentences all mean 'The man slew the king.'

(53) (a)   SVO: *Se man sloh thone kyning.*   Old English

    (b)   SOV: *Se man thone kyning sloh.*

    (c)   VSO: *Sloh se man thone kyning.*

    (d)   VOS: *Sloh thone kyning se man.*

    (e)   OSV: *Thone kyning se man sloh.*

    (f)   OVS: *Thone kyning sloh se man.*

"Free-order" languages may nonetheless have constraints on the linear order of phrases but these constraints are not definable in terms of the categories subject, object, and verb. Such languages march to the beat of a different drummer. In Hungarian, for example, subject and object can occur in any of the six possible orders but there is a strict immediate precedence constraint: the constituent that is focused (that is, emphasized over other parts of the sentence) must directly precede the verb regardless of whether it is subject, object, or anything else. Thus, in this language the classes of noun phrases relevant for linearization are not subject and object but focal and non-focal. These classes cross-cut those of subject and object. Complete freedom of word order is very rare across languages if it exists at all.

9.   Interlocking order

A few paragraphs ago, the example of reading the morning paper and watching TV news was cited to illustrate two distinct temporal relations that may hold between things in the world: precedence and adjacency. But there is also a third relevant pattern. Suppose you read part of the paper, then watch a bit of the TV news, then return to the paper before watching the end of the news. In this case, the two activities are split into interlocking parts: parts of one surround a part or parts of the other.

This linearization pattern also occurs in languages although not commonly. Words are not known to be interlocked with other words but phrases may be, although rarely and usually involving only the simplest case of one phrase dissembled into two parts and surrounding another one. An example is French negative expressions, such as *Je **ne** sais **pas***. 'I don't know.' Here the negative marker has two parts: *ne* and *pas*, with the verb positioned between the two. Perhaps due to the complexity of this pattern, it has been simplified in today's colloquial French with only the second part kept: *Je sais **pas***. Instead of interlocking, the new rule involves immediate precedence: the negative element directly follows the verb.

Another example of interlocking order is inpositions – that is, adpositions that are placed inside a phrase. Dryer cites a Tümpisha Shoshone example (Dryer 2005b: 346): in the sentence 'He died from a mean cold,' the phrase 'from a mean cold' is expressed as "cold.OBJ **from** mean.OBJ." The adposition 'from' is placed inside the noun phrase 'mean cold' and it governs the case of both the noun preceding it and the adjective following it.

To summarize so far: we have seen that some linearization patterns are common in languages while others are rare or non-existent. This defines merely **quantitative** distributions for these patterns. Let us now turn to **conditions** that favor one word order pattern over another. In other words, we are looking for typological implications.

(B) CLUSTERS OF LINEAR ORDER PATTERNS: CORRELATION PAIRS

In Section 1.1 of Chapter 1, examples were given of two linearizations of subject, object, and verb: we saw that in Hindi, Japanese, and Turkish, the order is SOV, in Arabic and Rapa Nui, it is VSO. In addition, we noted that these languages also differed in two other word order patterns: in the ordering of possessor and possessum and of adposition and noun phrase. Here are the two types:

(54) Hindi, Japanese, Turkish: Arabic, Rapa Nui:

S & O & V   V & S & O

Possessor & Possessum   Possessum & Possessor

NounPhrase & Adposition   Adposition & NounPhrase

There is also another pair of constituents that shows a fairly consistent difference in linearization in the two language types: the relative clause generally precedes the noun in SOV languages and follows it in VSO languages. Here are examples from Turkish and Rapa Nui, with the relative clause between brackets:

(55) (a) **RelCl** & Noun (Underhill 1976: 276)   Turkish

            [*yemeğe*   *gelen*]   *adam*   'the man who came to dinner'

            [to.dinner   coming]   man

    (b) Noun & **RelCl** (Chapin 1978: 149)   Rapa Nui

            te   *tani*   *rapanui*   [*noho oruga*   *o*   *te*   *miro*]

            the   other   Rapa.Nui.people   [stay upon   GEN the boat]

            'the   other   Rapa Nui people   who stay(ed) on   the boat'

(56) offers examples from Ainu, an SOV language, and Fijian, a VSO language, showing the consistent ordering of all four pairs of constituents. The Fijian data are from the Boumaa dialect (Dixon 1988: 300, 120, 152, 43).

(56) (a) Subject & Object & **Verb**   Ainu

            Totto   *amam*   **esose.**   'The mother borrowed rice.'

            mother   rice   **borrowed**

    (b) Possessor & **Possessum**

            sapo   **ninkarihi**   'sister's earrings'

            sister   **earrings**

    (c) Noun & **Adposition**

            pis   **ta**   'at the shore'

            shore   **at**

    (d) Relative Clause & **Noun**

            Tokaci   *wa*   *ek*   **perekur**

            Tokachi from come **young.person**

            'the young man who came from Tokachi'

(57) (a) **Verb** & Subject & Object   Fijian

            e   *aa*   **raici** *Mere* *o*   *Jone*   'John saw Mary.'

            3SG PST see   Mary the John

    (b) **Possessum** & Possessor

            a   **ligai** *Jone*   'John's hand'

            the hand John

    (c) **Adposition** & Noun

            i-na   *oro*   'to the village'

            to-the village

(d)   **Noun** & Relative Clause

    u   **pua'a** *'eirau*   *'auta*

    the pig   1DU.EXCL   brought

    'the pig which we two brought'

(58) provides a table with all four correlations:

(58) Hindi, Japanese, Turkish, Ainu: Arabic, Rapa Nui, Fijian:

      S & O & **V**   **V** & S & O

      Possessor & **Possessum**   **Possessum** & Possessor

      NounPhrase & **Adposition**   **Adposition** & NounPhrase

      Relative Clause & **Noun**   **Noun** & Relative Clause

These clusterings are widespread in languages. For his extensive sample of several hundreds of languages, Matthew Dryer has found the following implicational generalizations to hold:

<u>S, V, O and possessive constructions</u> (Dryer 2005c: 350)

(a)   If a language has OV order, it usually has the possessor before the possessum.

(b)   If a language has VO order (other than SVO), it usually has the possessor after the possessum.

<u>S, V, O and adpositional phrases</u> (Dryer 2005d: 387)

(a)   If a language has OV order, then it usually has postpositions; and if a language has postpositions, then it usually has OV order.

(b)   If a language has VO order, then it usually has prepositions; and if a language has prepositions, then it usually has VO order.

<u>S, V, O and relative clause constructions</u> (Dryer 2005e: 391)

(a)   If a language has VO order, then it usually has the relative clause after the noun.

(b)   If a language has the relative clause before the noun, then it usually has OV order.

As noted in Section 1.1 of Chapter 1, the widely recurrent correlations among the orderings of these pairs of constituents – O and V, possessor and possessum, adposition and noun phrase, and relative clause and noun head – is puzzling. If these constituents are as distinct as their class labels show them to be, why should they be ordered alike? The answer must be that in spite of their differences, they are also alike in some way. The challenge is therefore to find the crucial property that places object, possessor, noun phrase complement of adpositions, and relative clause into one class, and verb, possessum, adposition, and noun head of a relative clause into another class.

As also mentioned in Chapter 1, among the various alternative theories that have been put forth in the literature, one proposal is to divide syntactic constituents into two classes: heads and dependents. Heads are the indispensable parts of a phrase; dependents are optional.

(59) HEADS: DEPENDENTS:
      Verb   Object
      Adposition   Noun Phrase
      Possessum   Possessor
      Noun   Relative Clause

According to this theory, it is head-hood versus dependent-hood that provides the common denominator for these otherwise different constituents and that explains their similar linear behavior (cf. Vennemann 1973). The four distinct pairs of constituents are ordered by a single stroke either as dependent before head (in OV languages) or as head before dependent in (VO languages). This proposal has nonetheless proven to be controversial. What is the problem with it? And what are alternative explanations? We will take up these questions in Chapter 7 (Section 7.3).

Let us sum up our discussion of word order. As stated in the introduction of this chapter, we have been looking for two kinds of generalizations: frequencies of individual word order patterns and distributional generalizations concerning the occurrence of various word orders. We have identified a set of generalizations about more frequent and less common linearization patterns and also some statistically valid implicational relations among order patterns.

GEN-8 TERMS
  (a) Frequent:
       • the ordering of words by word classes
       • the ordering of words by phrases and clauses

  (b) Rare:
       • the ordering of individual words
       • the ordering of words into numerically defined positions

GEN-9 RELATIONS
  (a) Frequent:
       – precedence patterns
       – adjacency patterns

  (b) Rare:
       – immediate precedence patterns
       – interlocking order

GEN-10 THE DISTRIBUTION OF LINEARIZATION PATTERNS

(a) In most OV languages, the noun phrase precedes the adposition, the possessor precedes the possessum, and the relative clause precedes the noun.

(b) In most VO languages, the adposition precedes the noun phrase, the possessum precedes the possessor, and the noun head precedes the relative clause.

3.4 Syntactic categories

As we saw earlier, languages differ not only in the distribution of their word categories across their constructions but more basically, in what categories of words and phrases they have to begin with. Some languages have articles, others do not; some languages have sortal classifiers, others do not. But what about the most basic categories, such as subject and object, noun, verb, and adjective? Are they present in all languages or only in some?

From the enormous wealth of data invoked in the literature to come to grips with these questions and the widely different interpretations of these data, we will take up only one category: subject. There are references at the end of the chapter concerning discussions on the crosslinguistic validity of other syntactic categories.

The term "subject" has been used throughout this chapter. Both the Accessibility Hierarchy of relativizability (Section 3.2.1.1) and the ranking of the Controller Hierarchy (GEN-5 in Section 3.2.2.1) assign prime status to subjects. Similarly, some word order regularities make crucial mention of subjects. This suggests that subjects form a crosslinguistically valid, universal category. In actuality, this is not the case: in the literature, cross-linguistic references to subject are generally based on semantics: the noun phrase referring to the more active participant of an action is designated as the subject. But this semantic definition does not always square with morphosyntactic properties. For example, in passive sentences of English, the more active participant is expressed with a *by*-phrase, which bears none of the formal properties of subjects of active sentences: it is not pre-verbal nor does it control verb agreement.

What we are dealing with here is a very general, fundamental issue in language typology and indeed in grammatical description in general. How are classificatory labels assigned to various structural units such as morphemes, words, phrases, and clauses? As is the case in any categorization, items are lumped together into a class when they have certain properties in common. However, while shared characteristics form a necessary condition for membership in a given category, they are not sufficient. Take, for example, English words that start with *s* and end in *l*, such as *skill, seal, seagull*, etc. Even though they have these two characteristics in common, they do not form a category of English grammar because there is nothing further to say about them. The real purpose of placing things into category is to facilitate the statement of generalizations. As Frans Plank put it: "Grammatical categories are justified if grammatical rules … make reference to them; or rather, if such rules can be best stated by reference to them" (Plank 1984: 491; my translation – EAM). In other words, setting up categories is not the ultimate goal. The goal is to state generalizations and categories are created as tools in the service of this goal. The usefulness of a category depends on the number of properties its members share. If the category is instrumental in stating a single generalization, this already justifies its existence; but the more patterns the category figures in, the more useful and thus better justified it is.

In English, the category "subject" is maximally useful because the term unites noun phrases that have a number of properties in common so that from the presence of one property the presence of another follows. First of all, the same noun phrases that, in their pronominal variety, occur in the nominative case (*I, he, she, we, they*) are the ones that the present-tense verb agrees with and that, in most sentences, stand before the verb. Second, in addition to these characteristics that can be observed at a glance – case, agreement, and word order, called coding properties – the noun phrases referred to as subjects also behave alike in other respects. For example, in a pair of coordinated clauses, the noun phrase suppressed in the second clause must be the subject: *Sue helped Jill do her homework and then left the house* is understood as Sue being the one who left the house, not Jill. Also, subjects control reflexivization: they themselves cannot be reflexivized (e.g. *Peter shaved himself*, **Himself shaved Peter*). Thus, rules of nominative case marking, verb agreement, word order, ellipsis in coordinate structures, and reflexivization all make crucial reference to subjects and this amply justifies positing this category for English (for a more detailed analysis showing instances of mismatch among subject properties even within English, see Newmeyer 2003).

But is the concept of subject a useful tool for stating crosslinguistic generalizations? For example, in accusatively aligned case-marking systems such as English, the term is used for the agent of transitive sentences and the single noun phrase of an intransitive verb. But what is the subject in an ergative language? Is it the ergatively marked A of transitive sentences? Or is it the absolutively marked P and S?

If we found that in all human languages, the five subject properties mentioned above clustered together as they tend to do in English, subject would be a universal category. However, there are two reasons why this is not so. First, some of these properties are simply not applicable to some languages. In a language like Vietnamese, which does not case-mark arguments nor has verb agreement, the concept "subject" cannot be justified by reference to case marking or verb agreement.

Second, even if all property types that justify "subject" in English are present in a language, they may not cluster exactly as they do in English: each may carve out a different set of noun phrases. In some languages, case marking and control of verb agreement involve the same class of noun phrases but word order does not. German and Russian are examples: nominative case-marking and control of verb agreement apply roughly to the same set of noun phrases but word order is more variable than in English and thus it does not provide a criterion for defining subject.

In other languages, even case marking and verb agreement part ways. Consider Nepali (Bickel 2011: 400 (Bickel's "NOM" is changed here to "ABS")):

(60) (a) *ma   ga-ẽ*   Nepali

       I.ABS go-1SG.PAST

       'I went.'

    (b) *mai-le   timro ghar   dekh-ẽ*

       1SG-ERG   your house.ABS   see-1SG.PAST

       'I saw your house.'

Case marking shows ergative alignment, with the absolutive case of S and P zero-marked and A having the ergative suffix *-le*. Verb agreement, however, is accusative-style: the verb agrees with 'I' in both sentences even though 'I' is in the absolutive case in (60a) and is marked ergative in (60b). This is a fairly typical example: accusative-style verb agreement is common in ergatively case-marked languages (Siewierska 2005b: 406).

Such lack of homogeneity among constituents that form a single class in English is more the rule than the exception across languages. In a classic paper, Paul Schachter (1976) showed how in transitive sentences of Tagalog, certain features of English subjects appear on the semantic Actor (the term used in Tagalog grammar for the more active participant) while others appear on the Topic (a noun phrase whose referent is known to both speaker and hearer). For example, reflexivization is controlled by Actors rather than Topics; but only Topics of the relative clause can be relativized regardless of whether they are Actors or not. This is shown in (61) and (62).

In (61), TM stands for Topic Marker: the preposition *ang* (Schachter and Otanes 1972: 138).

(61) *Sinaktan   ko   ang   aking   sarili.*   Tagalog

    hurt   I   TM   my   self

    'I hurt myself.'

In (61), the Actor of the sentence – the pronoun *ko* – controls reflexivization; the Topic is reflexivized. To this extent, the Tagalog Actor behaves like the transitive subject in English.

But this conclusion is scuttled if we consider relativization, as in (62). As was seen in Section 3.2.1.1 where the Accessibility Hierarchy was discussed, subjects are the most commonly relativized noun phrase constituents. Based on evidence from reflexivization, which showed the Actor to be subject-like, we might expect the Actor of the relative clause to be relativizable. However, in Tagalog, it is not the

Actor but the Topic that is relativized; Actors can be relativized only if they also happen to be Topics. In both (62a) and (62b), 'the newspaper' is relativized. (62a) is grammatical because 'newspaper' is the Topic of the relative clause as signaled by the verbal prefix *bi-*. (62b) in turn is ungrammatical because here 'the man' is the Topic of the relative clause rather than 'the newspaper' as shown by the verbal prefix *bu-* (Schachter 1976: 500).

The following abbreviations are used: TM = Topic marker; AM = Actor marker; GT = the marker on the verb signaling that the topic is the Goal argument (i.e., the Patient); AT = the marker on the verb signaling that the topic is the Actor argument. (In both (62a) and (62b), the head noun 'newspaper' is preceded by the topic marker *ang* but this is irrelevant since it has to do with it being the topic of the main sentence.)

(62) (a) *Interesante   ang diyaryong   [bi-nasa   ng   lalaki]*   Tagalog

          interesting   TM   newspaper   **GT**-read   AM   man

          'The newspaper that the man is reading is interesting.'

    (b) **Interesante   ang diyaryong   [bu-masa ang lalaki]*

          interesting   TM   newspaper   **AT**-read   TM   man

          'The newspaper that the man is reading is interesting.'

Thus, in Tagalog, two properties of English subjects: control of reflexivization and relativizability, are split between two noun phrase types – Actor and Topic – rather than applying to the same constituent as they do in English.

So what can we conclude about the universality of the category of subjects? There appear to be no single property and no set of properties that would define subjects for all languages. The subject functions of one language clustering on a single noun phrase may be delegated to various subclasses of noun phrases in other languages and some of the properties may not be present at all. If we start out with the properties of English subjects, we find that in some other languages, we have to posit multiple subjects each for a given purpose: one for formulating a rule about case marking, another one for verb agreement, a third one for reflexivization, and so forth. As Balthasar Bickel suggests (2011: 401), grammatical relations – such as subject, but also direct object, and indirect object – are best regarded as specific to different rules and how these relations cluster varies across languages. Other linguists in turn have altogether called into question the viability of crosslinguistic categories at least in the traditional sense (cf. Croft 2001, Haspelmath 2010).

These conclusions highlight the crucial significance of definitions: rather than taking the crosslinguistic validity of traditional category labels such as subject for granted, typologists must make explicit the criteria that they employ for defining the terms whose crosslinguistic distribution they are attempting to study. More will be said about this issue in the corresponding sections on categories in Chapters 4 and 5.

Summary

In this chapter, 10 (sets of) crosslinguistic generalizations have been discussed; some are frequency statements, others implications. Relativizability and the distribution of resumptive pronouns follow the Accessibility Hierarchy (3.2.1.1). Sortal classifiers occur in languages that also have mensural classifiers and that generally have no obligatory plural marking on nouns, and the noun classes that they carve out are predominantly defined by taxonomic and partonomic relations (3.2.1.2). Controllers of verb agreement show implicational relationships and whether agreement is form-based or meaning-based is determined by the Agreement Hierarchy (3.2.2.1). From among the various alignment patterns, accusative alignment is the most frequent, followed by the ergative system (2.2.2). Of the various linearization patterns, some are more frequent than others and there is a strong statistical tendency for the clustering of the order of certain syntactic constituents (3.3). The category "subject" was found not to be crosslinguistically definable by morphosyntactic properties (3.4).

Activities

1. Nouns like *wine* and *coffee* are mass nouns and thus generally require mensural classifiers in the plural. Yet, the waiter in a restaurant having received orders from the customers, may pass them on to the kitchen as "Two wines and three coffees, please!" How can you explain this?

2. In Section 3.2.2.2, the English derivational affixes *–er* and *–ee* were analyzed from the point of view of whether they follow accusative or ergative alignment. What about the affix *–able* (as in *readable, tolerable, perishable,* etc.)?

3. In the text it was stated that in English, word order, case marking, and control of verb agreement jointly characterize subjects. Is this true in *there*-sentences, such as *There is a lion on the loose*?

4. Here is a set of data from Walmatjari (Merrifield *et al.* 1987: #214).
   A. What kind of alignment determines case marking?
   B. Translate the following:
       (a) The dog trod on the man with his foot.
       (b) The goanna saw the man.
       (c) The dog bit the man on his foot.
       (d) The man saw the goanna.

   (1) *kunyarr*   *pa*   *laparni*

        dog   it   ran

        'The dog ran.'

(2)   *kunyarr   pa   laparni   manajarti*
      dog   it   ran   stick
      'The dog ran with a stick.'

(3)   *kunyarr   pa   pinya   nganpayirlu   kurraparlu*
      dog   he   hit   man   hand
      'The man hit the dog with his hand.'

(4)   *kakaji   pa   laparni*
      goanna   it   ran
      'The goanna ran.'

(5)   *nganpayi   pa   kurrapa   pajani   kakajirlu*
      man   it   hand   bit   goanna
      'The goanna bit the man on the hand.'

(6)   *kunyarr   pa   pinya   nganpayirlu   manajartirlu*
      dog   he   hit   man   stick
      'The man hit the dog with a stick.'

(7)   *mana   pa   nyanya   nganpayirlu*
      stick he   saw   man
      'The man saw the stick.'

(8)   *jirnal   pa   kanyjirni   nganpayirlu   jinarlu*
      spear   he   trod   man   foot
      'The man trod on the spear with his foot.'

(9)   *jirnal   pa   kanyjirni   nganpayirlu   puutjartirlu*
      spear   he   trod   man   boot
      'The man trod on the spear with his boot.'

5. In addition to case marking and verb-agreement, the following data from Luiseño (Langacker 1972: 69) also show an interesting pattern in the choice of verbs. Work out the rules for case marking, verb agreement, and verb choice. What are the alignment patterns involved?

(1)   *nóo kwótaq*   'I am getting up.'

(2)   *húnwutum ʔehéŋmayumi*   'The bears are killing the
      qeʔéewun   birds.'

(3)	*čáam tóowwun ʔehéŋmayi*	'We see the bird.'
(4)	*húnwutum ŋóoraan*	'The bears are running.'
(5)	*čáam wuváʔnawum ʔehéŋmayumi*	'We are hitting the birds.'
(6)	*nóo pókwaq*	'I am running.'
(7)	*ʔehéŋmay wíilaq*	'The bird is flying.'
(8)	*čáam móqnawun húnwuti*	'We are killing the bear.'
(9)	*húnwut wuváʔnaq čáami*	'The bear is hitting us.'
(10)	*čáam waráavaan*	'We are getting up.'
(11)	*nóo húnwuti móqnaq*	'I am killing the bear.'
(12)	*húnwut néy tóowq*	'The bear sees me.'
(13)	*čáam wótiwun húnwuti*	'We are hitting the bear.'
(14)	*nóo qeʔéeq húnwutumi*	'I am killing the bears.'
(15)	*ʔehéŋmayum wáapaan*	'The birds are flying.'
(16)	*nóo hunwúti wótiq*	'I am hitting the bear.'
(17)	*húnwutum čáami tóowwun*	'The bears see us.'
(18)	*nóo húnwuti tóowq*	'I see the bear.'
(19)	*čáam ŋóoraan*	'We are running.'
(20)	*húnwut pókwaq*	'The bear is running.'

....

Further reading

- On classifiers in Japanese, see Downing 1996.

- For a theoretical crosslinguistic investigation of copular sentences within the framework of Noam Chomsky's Minimalist program, see Dalmi 2010.

- On agreement, a classic paper is Lehmann 1982. On the historical evolution of agreement markers analyzed in the Minimalist framework, see Gelderen 2011.

- On case, see the comprehensive handbook edited by Malchukov and Spencer (2009).

- On parts of speech, such as noun and verb, see Hengeveld 1992; Vogel and Comrie 2000; Evans 2000; Evans and Osada 2005 and discussion in the same issue of *Linguistic Typology*; Langacker 2008: 93–127; Dixon 2010: 37–114; and Bisang 2011.

- For a comprehensive and clear account of constituent order correlations, see Dryer 2007. A recent survey of word order research is provided in Song 2012.

4 Dissembling words

Morphological typology

CHAPTER OUTLINE

The chapter discusses morphological patterns that are either very rare or very frequent across languages. Crosslinguistic generalizations regarding the forms, meanings, co-occurrence patterns, and orderings of morphemes will be presented, followed by a discussion of the crosslinguistic validity of some of the key terms of morphological typology.

KEY TERMS

word
morpheme
allomorph
analytic structures
synthetic structures
agglutination
fusion
prefix
suffix
infix
introfix
synonymy
polysemy
zero allomorph
zero morpheme
reduplication
the Relevance
    Principle
derivation
inflection
clitic
syncretism
monosemous
    morphemes
polysemous
    morphemesy
cumulative patterns
separatist patterns

4.1 Introduction

In Chapter 3, we discussed how words come together to form sentences. In the present chapter, we will take the reverse view: how morphemes are joined to form words. Examples of words composed of smaller meaningful units were already given in Chapter 2, but in what follows, we will take a more systematic view of morphological composition. The basic question is: what combinations of morphemes make well-formed words in various languages?

The best way to begin to answer this question is by considering ill-formed words and identifying the sources of their failures. In (1), examples of English words that miss the mark are given with the correct forms on the right.

> The same three kinds of requirements hold for the well-formedness of any complex object inside and outside language. For example, in order for a food recipe to turn out well, you have to use the right ingredients; the ingredients have to take the right form (e.g. sticks of butter may have to be melted and tomatoes may have to be chopped); and they have to be mixed together in the right order. Or if you want to build a piece of furniture, you need the right pieces of wood; they have to be sized and shaped correctly; and they have to be put together in a given order.

(1) (a) *bright-ing   bright-en-ing   English
          *bak-ed-ing   bak-ing
          *fast-ly   fast
     (b) *ox-es   ox-en
          */lɔv-t/   /lɔv-d/ (=loved)
          *im-tolerable   in-tolerable
     (c) *ed-cook   cook-ed
          *cook-ed-un   un-cook-ed
          *ing-play   play-ing

The three sets of examples illustrate three kinds of pitfalls in word construction. In (1a), a morpheme is missing (*bright-ing) or a morpheme is present even though it does not belong there (*bak-ed-ing, *fast-ly). This shows that one of the requirements of correct word structure is the right choice of morphemes.

(1b) reveals that it is not sufficient to select the right morphemes: it is equally important to have the right forms of the chosen morphemes. The plural morpheme, the negative prefix, and the past suffix have alternative shapes and, depending on the environment, one or the other has to be chosen. The noun *ox* makes its plural with *-en*, rather than *-(e)s*. The past-tense morpheme must be /d/ rather than /t/ following a voiced sound, as in *loved*. And the negative form of the adjective *tolerable* takes *in-* rather than *im-*.

Thirdly, the examples in (1c) illustrate that having the right morphemes in their correct forms still does not ensure the well-formedness of a word: the morphemes have to be placed in the required order. Thus, the affixes *-ed* and *-ing* must be suffixed while *un-* is a prefix.

In sum, in order for a word to be well-formed, it has to contain the right morphemes in their right form in the right order. This basic principle is the same for syntax: as seen in Chapter 3, the well-formedness of sentences depends on the right choice of words, the right choice of their forms (as required by rules of agreement and government), and their correct order.

These considerations provide us with three general dimensions along which the morphology of languages may differ: the choice of morphemes, the choice of morpheme forms, and the order of morphemes. And, indeed, languages do differ in all three ways. Let us look at some examples.

(A) CROSSLINGUISTIC DIFFERENCES IN THE CHOICE OF MORPHEMES

Here are two sentences from Thai and Turkish.

(2)   (a)   *Khāw nâŋ loŋ.*   Thai
          he   sit   down
          'He sat down.'
          (Comrie 1990: 773; punctuation added)

      (b)   *Gít-me-di-m.*   Turkish
          go-not-PST-1S
          'I didn't go.'

The Thai sentence consists of three words, each monomorphemic; the Turkish sentence is a single word made up of four morphemes. The Thai-like parsimony of morphological structure, called **analytic**, and the complex word structure seen in Turkish, labeled **synthetic**, may be further illustrated by examples from Mandarin, Hmong, Chukchi and Hungarian.

(3)   Analytic structures

      (a)   *Nèi chǎng yǔ   xià   de   hěn dà.*   Mandarin
          that CLF   rain descend EXTENT very big
          'That rain came down hard.'
          (Li and Thompson 1981: 92; glossing simplified,
          punctuation added)

      (b)   *Daim ntawv ko   yog kuv txiav hov.*   Hmong
          CLF   paper there is I   cut   really
          'I cut that piece of paper.'

(4)   Synthetic structures

      (a)   *Tə-meyə-levtə-pəɣt-ərkən.*   Chuckchi
          1S-big-head-ache-IMPF
          'I have big headaches.'
          (Iturrioz Leza 2001: 716; punctuation added)

      (b)   *leg-meg-veszteget-het-etlen-ebb-ek-nek*   Hungarian
          SUP-PRF-bribe-POSS-PRIV-CMP-PL-DAT
          'to those who are least bribable'

Analytic and synthetic structures – those that show a one-to-one relation-ship between morpheme and word and those where the relationship is many-to-one – do not strictly divide languages into two types: the two kinds may coexist within a single language. While English tends to be analytic (e.g. *We love spring*), it also has polymorphemic words such as the infamous *anti-dis-establish-ment-arian-ism* sporting six morphemes. Similarly, Mandarin, which is generally analytic, has polymorphemic compounds, such as *kāi-guān* "open-close" 'switch.' Languages are labeled as analytic or synthetic not because they have exclusively one or the other word structure but because one or the other is predominant.

Provided a language allows for multiple morphemes to form a word, the question is what kinds of morphemes can co-occur in words? There are two basic classes of morphemes: **stems** and **affixes**. Stems carry the brunt of the word's meanings, while affixes add grammatically relevant information, such as whether the word is a noun or a verb or whether the word is singular or plural. In the word *impossible*, the stem is *possible*; *im-* is an affix. In the word *childlessness, child* is the stem for the affix *-less* and *childless* is in turn the stem for *-ness*. There is a special term for monomorphemic stems, such as *possible* and *child* above: they are called roots.

> This is similar to the convention of labeling languages as SVO or as having accusative-style alignment: SVO languages may have other word orders and accusative languages may have ergative structures as well: they are classified by their majority patterns.

Given stems and affixes, three logically possible word structures emerge:

(a)   Stem combined with Stem
(b)   Stem combined with Affix
(c)   Affix combined with Affix

Here are examples of each:

(5)   Stem combined with Stem (called **compound**)

(a)	*black-board*		English
	high-school		
(b)	*ma'ta-hari*	'sun'	Malay
	eye-day		
	o'rang-oe'tan	'ape'	
	man-forest		

(6)   Stem combined with Affix:

(a)	*ten-**th***		English
	*un-grate-**ful***		
(b)	*jang-sapoe'loe*	'tenth'	Malay
	ORD-ten		
	*dja'lan-**in***	'make somebody walk'	
	walk-**CAUS**		

(7)   Affix combined with Affix

(a)	***től-em*** 'from me'		Hungarian
	from-my		
	(compare with *kert-**től***	'from garden'	
	garden-**from**		
	*kert-**em***	'my garden'	
	garden-**my**)		

(b)　***nek-ed***　'to you'
　　　to-your
　　　(compare with *Billy-**nek*** 'to Billy'
　　　　　　　　　　Billy-***to***
　　　　　　　　　　*kert-**ed*** 'your garden'
　　　　　　　　　　garden-***your***)

Here is therefore our first parameter of possible crosslinguistic variation in morphology regarding the choice of morphemes in a word:

(a)　STEMS AND AFFIXES
　　　What combinations of stems and affixes are possible
　　　in a language?

As we saw above ((2) through (4)), languages differ in how hospitable their word structure is to morphemes; they may or may not accommodate more than one morpheme per word. However, for polymorphemic words, languages do not set numerical limits on the number of morphemes tolerated in a word: instead, the number of affixes occurring in a word is related to the amounts of meanings conveyed by them. Provided that a language has affixing at all, it can be reasonably expected that if affixes have simple meanings, more of them will be needed to convey the entire word-meaning than if a single affix conveys more than one meaning element at the same time. This is illustrated in (8).

(8)　(a)　***ev-ler-i***　　　　　'the houses (ACC)'　　　　　Turkish
　　　　　house-PL-ACC
　　　(b)　***dom-os***　　　　　'(the) houses'　　　　　　　Latin
　　　　　house-PL-ACC

In Turkish, number and case are expressed by separate affixes and thus both are needed for the expression of the two meanings. In the Latin example, a single affix suffices since it carries both number and case. The Turkish affix pattern is termed **separatist**; the Latin is **cumulative**.

Thus, one factor that influences the choice of affixes in a word is how much meaning each affix has. But there is also another meaning-related property of affixes that influences the choice. While the Latin example in (8b) showed that a single affix could contain more than one meaning element **at the same time**, affixes may also have **alternative** meanings. This is shown by the plural case paradigm of the Latin word *uxor* 'wife' in (9).

(9)　Nominative:　*uxor-**es***　　　　'wives (NOM)'　　　　Latin
　　　Accusative:　　*uxor-**es***　　　　'wives (ACC)'
　　　Genitive:　　　*uxor-**um***　　　　'of wives'
　　　Dative:　　　　*uxor-**ibus***　　　'to wives'
　　　Ablative:　　　*uxor-**ibus***　　　'from wives'

The suffix *-es* has two alternative meanings: nominative and accusative. Similarly, *-ibus* can mean either dative or ablative. In other words, the suffixes *-es* and *-ibus* are **polysemous**, in contrast with the suffix *-um*, which is monosemous (at least in this paradigm): it signals the genitive only. When it comes to the choice of affixes, those with alternative meanings will necessarily occur in a larger number of contexts than those that only have one meaning.

In sum: in addition to (a) – the possible combinations of stems and affixes in a word – we have delimited two additional parameters along which languages – or more precisely, individual constructions – can differ. Both have to do with the meanings of affixes which of course influence the choice of affixes for the expression of particular meanings.

> (b) SEPARATIST VS. CUMULATIVE AFFIXES
>   Does an affix have only one meaning or more than
>   one meaning at the same time?
> (c) MONOSEMOUS VS. POLYSEMOUS AFFIXES
>   Does an affix have only one meaning or more than one
>   alternative meaning?

Having seen examples of how languages can vary in the choice of morphemes that make up words, let us now turn to the choice of the specific forms of these morphemes.

(B) CROSSLINGUISTIC DIFFERENCES IN THE CHOICE OF MORPHEME FORMS

As we saw above in connection with the English examples in (1b), in addition to the semantics of morphemes, the choice of morphemes for constructing words also depends on their forms. Affixes are very prone to having variant forms each suited to a particular environment. Allomorphic differences depending on the phonological environment are illustrated by English and Turkish examples in (10).

(10)	(a)	*cat-s*	/kæt-s/	English
		dog-s	/dɔg-z/	
		kiss-es	/kɪs-əz/	
	(b)	*adam-lar*	'men'	Turkish
		man-PL		
		ev-ler	'houses'	
		house-PL		

In English, the three principal allomorphs of the plural are conditioned by the last sound of the stem. In Turkish, the plural suffix also has variant forms: Turkish being a vowel-harmony language, the vowel of the suffix is front or back mirroring the stem vowel's frontness or backness.

Apart from such phonologically conditioned variants, a morpheme may take different forms depending on the lexical environment – i.e., what stem it is added to regardless of the phonological composition of the stem. The Serbo-Croatian singular case paradigms in (11) illustrate this. 0 stands for a zero-morpheme: the lack of overt expression of a meaning.

(11)

		'woman'	'student'	'money'	Serbo-Croatian
NOMINATIVE:		žèn-**a**	student-**0**	nòvac-**0**	
ACCUSATIVE:		žèn-**u**	student-**a**	nòvac-**0**	
GENITIVE:		žèn-**e**	student-**a**	nòvc-**a**	
DATIVE:		žèn-**i**	student-**u**	nòvc-**u**	
INSTRUMENTAL:		žèn-**om**	student-**om**	nòvc-**em**	

Each of the three nouns is case-marked somewhat differently. There is only one suffix that is the same for the three nouns: apart from a probably phonologically conditioned variant in *nòvc-em*, the instrumental case marker is uniformly *-om*. At the other end, the accusative has the most variants: *-u*, *-a*, and zero. The nominative, genitive, and dative each have two variants with 'student' and 'money' having one suffix and 'woman,' a different one. There are no phonological conditions involved here. Case paradigms like in (11) are called **declensions**; nouns that are assigned case endings are said to be **declined**.

The point of the Serbo-Croatian examples is that, apart from the instrumental, there is no single affix that would have the same form in all three declensions. Instead, there are synonymous variants: sets of distinct forms that all express the same meaning of accusativity, dativity, etc. Other combinations of stem and affix, such as **student-i* for the dative of *student* formed with the dative affix of *žena*, are ungrammatical.

While Serbo-Croatian has variant forms of case affixes, other languages do not. In Finnish – apart from some phonologically conditioned allomorphs (not shown below) – each case affix has a single invariant form regardless of the noun it is added to.

(12)

	'cupboard'	'Matti'	'school'	Finnish
NOMINATIVE:	kaappi-**0**	Matti-**0**	koulu-**0**	
GENITIVE: ('of')	kaapi-**n**	Mati-**n**	koulu-**n**	
ELATIVE: ('from')	kaapi-**sta**	Mati-**sta**	koulu-**sta**	
ADESSIVE: ('at')	kaapi-**lla**	Mati-**lla**	koulu-**lla**	
INESSIVE: ('in')	kaapi-**ssa**	Mati-**ssa**	koulu-**ssa**	

Morphemes with and without variant forms can occur in a single language as well. In English, the past morpheme has both phonologically and lexically conditioned allomorphs (as in *bake-d* versus *came*) but also invariant morphemes such as *-ing*.

We can now formulate the next crosslinguistic parameter to be added to the three listed above ((a), (b), and (c)).

(d) INVARIANCE VERSUS VARIANCE OF AFFIX FORMS
Do affixes have single forms or do they have variants?

This parameter is closely related to (b) and (c) above in that all three pertain to an issue that is fundamental for the study of any semiotic system: the numerical correspondence between forms and meanings (one-to-one, one-to-many, etc.). By asking whether an affix conveys a single meaning element or more than one at the same time, parameter (b) probes into the syntagmatic form–meaning relationship in affixes. This is shown in (13).

(13) Separatist vs. cumulative affixes
    (a) Separatist: Form-1 – Meaning-1
    (b) Cumulative: Form-1 – Meaning-1 **AND** Meaning-2…

Parameters (c) and (d) in turn pertain to **paradigmatic** form–meaning relations by exploring possible many-to-one relationships between affix forms and affix meanings. (c) has to do with the **polysemy** of affixes: single affix forms having alternative meanings; (d) has to do with the **synonymy** of affixes: the same affix meanings having alternative expressions. The respective diagrams are shown in (14) and (15).

(14) Monosemous vs. polysemous affixes
    (a) Monosemy: Form-1 – Meaning-1
    (b) Polysemy: Form-1 – Meaning-1 **OR** Meaning-2 …

(15) Single-form vs. synonymous affixes
    (a) Single form: Form-1 – Meaning-1
    (b) Synonymy: Form-1 OR Form-2 – Meaning-1

A further, somewhat unexpected issue in choosing the correct morpheme form is whether, given an affixal meaning to convey, there IS a form available at all to carry that meaning. To see the problem, consider the singular case paradigm of Latin *uxor* 'wife.'

(16) Nominative: *uxor*   'wife (NOM)'   Latin
       Accusative: *uxor-**em*** 'wife (ACC)'
       Genitive: *uxor-**is***   'of wife'
       Dative: *uxor-**i***   'to wife'
       Ablative: *uxor-**e***   'from wife'

The inventory of affixes appears to be incomplete: there is no affix to express the nominative case. Or, putting it differently, the nominative affix is zero: the very absence of any affixal material: *uxor-0*. For other examples of zero affixes, see (11) and (12). This gives rise to the next parameter of affix choice.

    (e) OVERT VERSUS ZERO AFFIXES
          What kinds of affixes have overt forms and what kinds are zero?

There is some cross-constructional and crosslinguistic variation in this regard as well. Note the marking of singular and plural in the following examples:

(17)

	SINGULAR	PLURAL
LATIN:	*uxor* 'wife'	*uxor-es* 'wives'
SOUTHERN BARASANO:	*kahe-a* 'eye'	kahe 'eyes'
SWAHILI:	*ki-su* 'knife'	*vi-su* 'knives'
MANDARIN:	*ren* 'man'	*ren* 'men'

In Latin, it is the plural that has an affix with the singular missing one; Southern Barasano does it in reverse (at least in this example); Swahili has affixes for both singular and plural; and Mandarin has one for neither.

Here is a diagrammatic representation of the relevant alternatives:

(18) <u>Overt or zero affixes</u>
    (a) Overt affix: Form-1 – Meaning-1
    (b) Zero affix: 0 – Meaning-1

One might naturally wonder whether the opposite lopsided relation may also occur: affixes without meanings. Although morphemes, including affixes, are defined as carrying meaning, there is sometimes phonological material in a word that makes no semantic contribution. An example is the *s* in the middle of some German compounds, such as *handlung-s-fähig* "action-s-capable" 'capable to act' or *arbeit-s-los* "work-s-less" 'unemployed.' These elements, albeit meaningless, are sometimes admitted into the category of morphemes.

Having seen examples of variation in the composition of words from stems and affixes and in whether affix forms vary or not, we will turn to the third dimension of morphological variation noted in the beginning of this section: the order of morphemes.

(C) CROSSLINGUISTIC DIFFERENCES IN THE ORDER OF MORPHEMES

Languages greatly differ in how morphemes are sequenced within a word. As we saw in (6), where the English ordinal marker was shown to be a suffix (as in *ten-th*) but a prefix in Malay, even affixes of the very same meanings may be differently ordered across languages. Here are some examples of crosslinguistic synonyms with differing affix order.

(19) (a) ENGLISH   HUNGARIAN
        im-patient   *türelm-***etlen**   (*türelem* 'patience')
        im-probable   *valószínü-***tlen**   (*valószínü* 'probable')
    (b) ENGLISH   TAGALOG
        *beauti-***ful**   **ma**-*ganda*   (*ganda* 'beauty')
        *oil-***y**   **ma**-*langis*   (*langis* 'oil')
    (c) ENGLISH   KIKUYU
        *teacher-***s**   **a**-*rutani*   (*-rutani* 'teacher')
        *buyer-***s**   **a**-*guri*   (*-guri* 'buyer')

Morpheme order is variable not only across languages but also language-internally: as English shows, the same language may include both prefixes and suffixes; see **im**-*patient*, *child-***less**, **un**-*educat-***ed**.

In addition to placing an affix before or after a stem, there are also other, more complex patterns. In Section 3.3 of Chapter 3, we saw examples of interlocking order in syntax: one of the terms interposed between parts of the other. This pattern also occurs in morpheme order: an affix can occur inside the stem or conversely, an affix may surround the stem. The former, called infixing, is illustrated in (20).

(20) (a) *gap*   'to cut'   *g-***an**-*ap*   'scissors'   Katu
         panh   'to shoot'   *p-***an**-*anh*   'crossbow'
         piih   'to sweep'   *p-***an**-*iih*   'broom'
         (Merrifield 1987, #19)

(b) *gafutan* 'grab'   *g-in-afut* 'grabbed'   Agta
     hulutan 'follow'   *h-in-ulut* 'followed'
     (Merrifield 1987: #18)

An example of circumfixing comes from Chikasaw (21a). Closer to home, Russian also has circumfixing. The form *do-* is normally a perfective prefix (e.g. *do-pivat'* 'to drink up') and *-sja* is the reflexive suffix (e.g. *myt' -sja* 'to wash oneself'); but in example (21b) the two affixes are both needed to convey the word's meaning (Brown 2011: 494).

(21) (a) a. *chokma* 'he is good'   Chikasaw
                ik-chokm-o 'he is not good'
           b. *lakna* 'it is yellow'
                ik-lakn-o 'it is not yellow'
      (b) a. *ždat'* 'to wait'   Russian
                do-*ždat'*-**sja**
                up.to-wait.INF-**REFL**
                'to wait for a long time (with success)'
           b. *do-ždat'*
                up.to-wait.INF
                ždat'-**sja**
                wait.INF-**REFL**

The following German example is unlike Russian in that the affixes *ge-* and *-t* (or *-en*), both required to form the participle of the verb, can never occur without the other to express any meaning.

(22) (c) a. **ge**-*ledig*-**t**   'settled'   German
                ge-*schrieb*-**en**   'written'
           b. **ge-ledig*
                *ge-schrieb
                *ledig-t
                *schrieb-en

A third order pattern of the interlocking kind is even more complex: both the stem and the affix are discontinuous. This pattern, called introfixing (or intercalation), is a hallmark of Semitic languages. Here are examples from Hebrew, where the causative meaning is expressed by the combination of a prefix and the vowel *i* inserted in the stem. The *i*-vowel is not simply infixed: it replaces the two *a*-vowels of the non-causative verb (Merrifield 1987, #20).

(23) *qaraʔ* 'read'   **hi**-*qr*-**i**-*ʔ* 'make read'   Hebrew
      raqad 'dance'   **hi**-*rq*-**i**-*d* 'make dance'
      šaʔal 'borrow'   **hi**-*šʔ*-**i**-*l* 'lend'

In addition to the three linear arrangements of affixes relative to the stem – precede, follow, interlock – there is one more temporal relation in which morphemes may be arranged in a word. To return to the analogy cited in the syntax chapter (Section 3.3 of Chapter 3): in addition to reading the paper before watching the TV news, doing the two in reverse order, and alternating between the two activities, it is also possible, albeit with some effort, to be watching TV while reading the paper at the same time. This kind of simultaneous ordering is not available in syntax: since, by definition, every word has to be independently pronounceable, one word cannot be superimposed upon another. However, this is different for morphemes. Sound features, such as tone or stress, are superimposed on words rather than preceding or following them and if such suprasegmental features change the meaning of a word, they qualify for morphemic status. This results in a non-linear, simultaneous ordering of morphemes.

There are indeed languages where some grammatical meaning is expressed by **suprasegmentals**. In the English examples below, the placement of stress differentiates nominal and verbal meaning. In Kisi, a Niger-Congo language of Tanzania, the low versus high tone on the last syllable of the word signals habitual versus past meaning (Bickel and Nichols 2005: 86).

(24)　(a)　　NOUN:　　VERB:　　　　　　　　　　　　　　English

　　　　　　　tórment　tormént

　　　　　　　áddress　addréss

　　　　　　　púrchase　*purcháse*

　　(b)　a.　Ò　cìmbù.　'She (usually) leaves.'　　　　　Kisi

　　　　　　　3SG　leave.PRES.HABITUAL

　　　　b.　Ò　cìmbú.　'She left.'

　　　　　　　3SG　leave.PST.PFV

The data surveyed above yield a sixth parameter of crosslinguistic morphological variation. The first ((a)) had to do with the combinability of stems and affixes, the next two with multiple meanings of morphemes (cumulative versus separatist exponence ((b)) and monosemy versus polysemy ((c))); the fourth and fifth with multiple forms of morphemes and with affixes lacking form ((d) and (e)). The sixth parameter pertains to the temporal arrangement of morphemes.

　(f)　THE ORDER OF MORPHEMES

　　　In what temporal relations are morphemes arranged?

So far we have seen several types of morphological patterns that differ within and across languages along the six parameters of (a) through (f). What this body of evidence illustrates is what there IS in human languages: things that OCCUR. Based on the examples, we can state existential statements such as that "There are languages where affixes convey more than one meaning element at the same time" or that "There are languages where some affixes are prefixed." But how frequently do these patterns occur across languages and under what conditions? In what follows, we will try to enrich the roster of such existential statements quantitatively and qualitatively. On the one hand, we will search the literature to see if some of the occurring patterns have been found to be more frequent across languages than others. On the other hand, we will search for the conditions under which one or the other pattern occurs – in other words, for unrestricted and implicational universals.

4.2 The choice of morphemes and morpheme forms

4.2.1 Which morphemes?

4.2.1.1 Stems and affixes

The question that we are addressing is this: given that we want to construct a word in a language, what are crosslinguistic constraints on the combination of morphemes?

Of the six parameters of variation set up in the previous section, the first three are relevant here.

(a) STEMS AND AFFIXES
The availability of stems and affixes to form words
(b) SEPARATIST VS. CUMULATIVE AFFIXES
Whether affixes have only one meaning or whether they cumulate multiple meanings
(c) MONOSEMOUS VS. POLYSEMOUS AFFIXES
Whether affixes have only one meaning or whether they have multiple alternative meanings

Regarding (a) STEMS AND AFFIXES: as the examples from Mandarin Chinese and Hmong illustrated above (example (3)), there are languages that have no affixes at all. This means that of the three logically possible word types:

Stem + Stem
Stem + Affix
Affix + Affix,

they cannot have the second and the third. Nonetheless, such analytic (or isolating) languages do have polymorphemic words by the use of the first option above: compounds (Li and Thompson 1981: 47; Whitelock 1982: 40).

(25) (a) *féi-zào*   'soap'   Mandarin
         fat-black
         rù-shén   'fascinated'
         enter-spirit
     (b) *sawv-ntxov*   'morning'   Hmong
         get.up-early
         tsaus-ntuj   'night-time'
         dark-sky

A common type of compounding is noun incorporation: a verb is compounded with one of its nominal arguments, such as in English *baby-sit*. The choice of the nominal argument incorporated in verbs has been found to be non-random. In her sample of a hundred languages, Marianne

Mithun has found the following overwhelmingly valid implications to hold (1984: 875):

> GEN-1: If in a language, intransitive verbs incorporate their Single argument, then transitive verbs incorporate their Patient arguments.
>
> GEN-2: The incorporation of Agents of transitive verbs is almost non-existent.

That is to say, in languages where there are verb forms like "to wind-blow" to mean 'for the wind to blow', there are also verb forms like "to letter-write" meaning 'to write letters'; and there are no, or very few, languages with verb forms like "to teacher-punish" to mean 'for a teacher to punish (e.g. children)'. A language with P-incorporation (but apparently no S-incorporation) is Fijian (Dixon 1988: 227, Aikhenvald 2007: 14; glossing simplified).

(26) (a) P not incorporated: Fijian

        e   '*ani-a* *a*   *uto*

        he eat-it the/some breadfruit

        'He is eating/the/some breadfruit.'

    (b) P incorporated:

        e   '***ana-uto*** '*He is eating breadfruit.*'

        he **eat-breadfruit**

        'He is eating breadfruit (breadfruit-eating).'

A language that has both P- and S-incorporation is Tuscarora; Mithun's examples include 'ice-throw' for the former and 'good-day.be' for the latter (1999: 44–47).

    Since the incorporated noun is generally either a transitive Patient or an intransitive S but not the Agent of a transitive sentence, the pattern is universally ergative. This is another piece of evidence to bear out the comment made in Chapter 3, Section 3.2.2.2: that ergativity is a common pattern of word formation even in otherwise accusative languages.

    Regarding word structures of the Stem + Affix pattern, an implicational generalization emerges if we distinguish two types of affixes illustrated in (27) from English.

(27) (a) derivation: English

           *resource-**ful***

           *child-**less***

           *demonstrat-**ion***

    (b) inflection:

           *resource-**s***

           *pretti-**er***

           *swimm-**ing***

Affixes like *-ful*, *-less*, *-(t)ion* are called derivational: they generally change the word class of the stem such as from noun to adjective, or verb to noun. Inflectional affixes like *-s*, *-er*, or *-ing* in turn introduce less of a meaning change: they add grammatical information such as agreement, comparative degree, or aspect. Not all languages have derivational affixes but languages with inflection have been found to have also derivation.

> GEN-3: If a language has inflection, it always has derivation.
> (Greenberg 1966a: #29)

In other words, it seems more important for languages to use affixes for creating new words than to use them to modify the meanings of existing words.

The third possible word structure noted above: forming a word with the sole combination of affixes, was illustrated from Hungarian above (example (7)); this is a very rare pattern. Historically, it has arisen from a noun-stem plus suffix structure where the independent nominal status of the stem later gave way to affixal status.

4.2.1.2 Affixes: cumulation and syncretism

The distinction made above between derivational and inflectional affixes supports a further crosslinguistic generalization, this having to do with parameter (c) SEPARATIST VS. CUMULATIVE AFFIXES: whether affixes have only one meaning or whether they jointly stand for more than one bit of semantics. Some semantic types of affixes have a greater tendency to cumulate – that is, to be expressed by a single affix – than others. Here are two generalizations proposed by Frans Plank (1999), one about a preference for separatist expression and the other about a preference for cumulation.

> GEN-4: Derivational and inflectional affixes do not have jointly
>   cumulative exponents. (Plank 1999: 290–292)
> GEN-5: Person and number are frequently signaled by cumulative,
>   rather than separatist, affixes. (Plank 1999: 292)

GEN-4 underscores the difference between derivational and inflectional affixes. What it means is that there are no languages where the word for *speaker* would look like it does in English: a stem and a derivational affix, but where the plural form would be *speak-lut*, where the affix *-lut* combines both the deverbal nominalizer '-er' and the plural '-s'.

The force of GEN-5 may be illustrated on Latin and Turkish. As we saw earlier (example (8)), the nominal paradigms of these two languages differ in that Latin cumulates number and case (e.g. *dom-os* 'houses ACC,' where *-os* indicates both plurality and the accusative case), while Turkish has a separate plural affix (*-lar/-ler*) and a separate accusative suffix *-i* (*ev-ler-i* 'houses ACC'). Now compare their verbal paradigms for the past tense of the verb 'go':

(28) LATIN   TURKISH
      S1 *ambula-ba-**m***   *git-ti-m*
      S2 *ambula-ba-**s***   *git-ti-**n***

S3	*ambula-ba-**t***	*git-ti-**0***	
P1	*ambula-ba-**mus***	*git-ti-**k***	
P2	*ambula-ba-**tis***	*git-ti-**niz***	
P3	*ambula-ba-**nt***	*git-ti-**ler***	

While past tense is signaled by a separatist suffix in both languages: *-ba* in Latin and *-ti* in Turkish, neither language separates person and number: the two categories cumulate in joint affixes. This is in spite of the fact that Turkish is generally agglutinating – that is, it has separatist affixes. Plank notes that the very common joint expression of person and number may be due to the fact that the normal sense of additive plurality does not apply to the first and second person: as discussed in Section 2.3.2 of Chapter 2, what 'we' generally refers to is not more than one 'I,' and the plural 'you' is also not necessarily more than one listener.

Let us now turn to the third issue, that of MONOSEMOUS VS. POLYSEMOUS AFFIX EXPONENTS ((c)). Consider the formal distinctions of the German definite article paradigm.

(29)

	SINGULAR			PLURAL			German
	MASC	FEM	NEUT	MASC	FEM	NEUT	
NOM	*der*	*die*	*das*	*die*	*die*	*die*	
ACC	*den*	*die*	*das*	*die*	*die*	*die*	
GEN	*des*	*der*	*des*	*der*	*der*	*der*	
DAT	*dem*	*der*	*dem*	*den*	*den*	*den*	

There are 24 slots defined by the two numbers, three genders (masculine, feminine, neuter) and four cases (nominative, accusative, genitive, dative); yet, there are only one-fourth as many distinct forms: *der*, *die*, *das*, *den*, *des*, and *dem*. With the exception of *des*, all of these forms are multiply employed: they have alternative meanings. Note that each gender, number, and case distinction is formally differentiated in some portion of the chart but no gender, number, and case distinction is formally differentiated in every sub-paradigm. For example, masculine and neuter are differentiated in the singular nominative and accusative but not in the genitive and dative; and genitive and dative are distinct in the singular for masculine and neuter but not for feminine.

Are these multiple uses of the same forms coincidental or do they occur for a reason? This question arises every time a form is found to have alternative meanings: are these forms instances of polysemy or homonymy? The former term applies where the meanings are related, the latter, if the identity of the forms is coincidental. The English word *bear* has two meanings: the animal and the verb to mean 'to carry.' This is accidental – an instance of homonymy. The word *school* also has multiple meanings: it can refer to a building of an educational institution or it can refer to the institution itself. Here the two meanings are clearly related; the word is polysemous rather than homonymous. Is the relationship between the multiple meanings of the five German article forms like those between the meanings of *bear* or like those between the meanings of *school*?

Some of the identical forms seem random, more like *bear* standing for two different meanings. Why should the singular masculine accusative form *den* also be the plural dative? Or why should the singular masculine nominative *der* also serve as the singular feminine dative as well as the plural genitive? These may be accidental coincidences – i.e. homonymies. However, there are also some one-form-more-than-one-meaning patterns in this paradigm that seem less capricious in that they have crosslinguistic parallels. We will discuss two of these.

(30) (a) GENDER POLYSEMY IN ALL PLURAL FORMS
The plural case forms *die*, *der*, and *den* are the same for all three genders even though they have partially different forms in the singular.

(b) CASE POLYSEMY OF NOMINATIVE AND ACCUSATIVE IN FIVE OF THE SIX SUB-PARADIGMS
The nominative and the accusative have the same form in the singular feminine (*die*) and in the singular neuter (*das*) as well as in the plural (*die*); the two cases are differentiated only in the singular masculine (*der* and *den*).

The lack of distinctions within a category, such as gender or case, in certain contexts while they are present in other contexts is known as **syncretism** (cf. Baerman, Brown and Corbett 2005: 34). It is important to pay attention to the proviso that the distinction should show up in some other context in the same language. For example, the lack of gender distinctions in Finnish nouns does not meet the definition of syncretism since grammatical gender distinctions are not made anywhere in the language. Syncretism is thus an instance of paradigmatic asymmetry in the expressions of certain meanings.

Let us take a closer look at the statements in (30). (30a) describes **gender syncretism** in German. We saw this pattern in the case of personal pronouns in Chapter 2, Section 2.3.2: in Russian, the third person singular pronoun has three genders (*on*, *ona*, and *ono*) but in the plural, there is no gender distinction (*oni*). Russian also provides another example of gender syncretism. Singular nouns and their adjectives are case-marked differently depending on gender. In the plural, however, gender distinctions are absent for the noun except for the genitive case and they are completely lacking for the adjective. This is shown in (31). The masculine paradigm is for the phrase 'first class'; the feminine paradigm is of 'first school.'

(31) (a)   SINGULAR   Russian

	MASCULINE	FEMININE
NOM	*perv-yj klass-0*	*perv-aja škol-a*
ACC	*perv-yj klass-0*	*perv-uju škol-u*
GEN	*perv-ovo klass-a*	*perv-oj škol-y*
DAT	*perv-omu klass-u*	*perv-oj škol-e*
INSTR	*perv-ym klass-om*	*perv-oj škol-oj*
PREP	*perv-om klass-e*	*perv-oj škol-e*

(b)   PLURAL

	MASCULINE	FEMININE
NOM	*perv-ye klass-y*	*perv-ye škol-y*
ACC	*perv-ye klass-y*	*perv-ye škol-y*
GEN	*perv-yh klass-ov*	*perv-yh škol-0*
DAT	*perv-ym klass-am*	*perv-ym škol-am*
INSTR	*perv-ymi klass-ami*	*perv-ymi škol-ami*
PREP	*perv-yh klass-ah*	*perv-yh škol-ah*

Gender syncretism in the plural seems to have a plausible rationale: while singular referents have clearly identifiable genders, multitudes of things may include members that differ in gender. Nonetheless, gender syncretism in the plural is not a universal pattern. In Plank and Schellinger's sample of over 300 languages, it was a frequent pattern but about 10% of the languages violated it by having more gender distinctions in non-singular numbers than in the singular (Plank and Schellinger 1997). Their results are nonetheless still consistent with the following frequency statement:

> GEN-6: Crosslinguistically, gender syncretism in the plural is more frequent than in the singular.

(30b) states an instance of case syncretism in the German article paradigm involving the polysemy of nominative-accusative case markers in five of the six sub-paradigms given in (29). Note that the Russian examples in (31) also show the same case syncretism in the plural of both masculine and feminine nouns and in the masculine singular. The syncretism of the two so-called core cases – nominative and accusative, or ergative and absolutive – has been found to be the most common pattern of case syncretism (Baerman et al. 2005).

> GEN-7: Crosslinguistically, case syncretism most frequently involves the two core cases.

The question addressed in this section was this: given that we want to construct a word in a language, what are crosslinguistic constraints on the combination of morphemes available for this purpose? In response, seven crosslinguistic generalizations have been discussed. The first two were about a special type of compounding – incorporation – stating the preference for incorporating objects over intransitive subjects and intransitive subjects over transitive subjects (GEN-1) and the rarity of agent incorporation (GEN-2). The other five generalizations pertain to affixes: the implicational relation between derivation and inflection (GEN-3), the lack of joint cumulation of derivational and inflectional affixes (GEN-4), the frequency of person-number cumulation (GEN-5), the preference for gender syncretism in the plural (GEN-6), and for case syncretism of core cases (GEN-7).

As was seen in Section 4.1, the correct choice of morphemes does not yet guarantee the well-formedness of words: some morphemes have alternative forms and given a particular context, the right variant needs to be chosen. The question we are turning to next is this: what are crosslinguistically valid patterns of morpheme variance?

4.2.2 Which forms of morphemes?

4.2.2.1 Reduplication

As noted above (cf. parameter (d) in Section 4.1), affixes may or may not have alternative exponents. In English, the comparative affix -er (as in pret-tier) has a single pronunciation, while other affixes have multiple variants. One example is the plural affix with allomorphs, such as /s/ as in cats, or /z/ as in dogs or /əz/ as in kisses; another example is the negative prefix which may be im- (as in impossible) or in- (as in intolerable).

If an affix has multiple exponents, the choice among them may be phonologically conditioned. Whether the plural affix in English is pronounced as /s/ or /z/ or /əz/ is determined by the phonological properties of the preceding sound. But this is not always so: the choice between /əz/ and /ən/ in fix-es versus ox-en is unrelated to the phonological environment. The same holds for the choice between un- and in-: as the examples of untenable and intolerable show, either may precede a /t/. The choice in these cases is lexically conditioned.

The three types – invariance, phonologically conditioned variance, and lexically conditioned variance – have many examples in other languages as well. As we saw earlier, case affixes in Finnish are invariant; for example, the genitive is always -n for all nouns. Phonologically-conditioned allomorphy occurs in Turkish: the plural affix is -lar or -ler depending on the vowel of the stem. The Serbo-Croatian case paradigms cited in (11) of Section 4.1 exemplify lexically conditioned allomorphy; for instance, the genitive affix is -i for some nouns and -a for others. Another example is the plural accusative affix of Old English nouns with multiple exponents including those shown by stān-**as** 'stones,' sċip-**u** 'ships,' feld-**a** 'fields,' ēag-**an** 'eyes,' brōþor-**0** 'brothers' (cited in Plank 1999: 305).

Lexically-conditioned allomorphy appears arbitrary: the exponents of the affix differ at random and the relationship between the stem and the particular exponent that it calls for is also arbitrary. Why should the Old English plural accusative affix have such different exponents as -as, -u, -a, -an, and zero; and why should stān 'stone' take -as and sċip 'ship' select -u? While answers to these questions may be found in the history of the declensional paradigms, there are some cases where the choice between non-phonologically conditioned allomorphs follows crosslinguistically recurrent patterns. In the rest of this section and in the next one, we will highlight two instances of this common type of affix variance.

Here are examples of the first type (Schachter and Otanes 1972: 363).

(32) BASE FORM: CONTEMPLATED ASPECT FORM   Tagalog

bigyan	'give to'	**bi**-bigyan	'will give to'
iabot	'hand to'	i-**a**-abot	'will hand to'
ikagalit	'make angry'	ika-**ga**-galit	'will make angry'
makita	'see'	ma-**ki**-kita	'will see'
mangagsikain	'eat(PL)'	mangag-**si**-sikain	'will eat(PL)'

At first blush, it seems that allomorphy is random: the affixes that supply the future-like contemplated aspect: bi-, -a-, -ga-, -ki-, and -si- are very

different from each other. However, a second look reveals that while
the allomorphic exponents do not resemble each other, each resembles the
base that it is added to: the affix is a copy of a portion of the base.
The morphological pattern whereby the base, or some portion of it, is
duplicated is called **reduplication**.

Reduplication is widespread in the world; but what lends special interest to it is that there are recurrent limitations both regarding its formal
properties and the meanings that the construction conveys. Let us see
some examples.

(A) CROSSLINGUISTICALLY RECURRENT FORM PROPERTIES OF REDUPLICATION

Reduplication occurs in European languages as well but the pattern is
somewhat different from the Tagalog examples in (32). First, the European
examples involve the repetition of entire words resulting in compounds or
closely knit phrases, as in English *very very nice, an old old man, many many
thanks,* or *he walked and walked and walked*. In contrast, Tagalog shows partial
reduplication. Second, the English words may be repeated twice or three
times or even more, while in the Tagalog examples, only one duplication is
possible. Third, the meaning of these constructions in English and other
Western languages is almost always emphasis. In other languages, however,
reduplication has various semantic consequences as shown below.

(33) (a) *así*   'hand'   *así-así*   'hand by hand'   Ewe
     (b) *quis* 'who'   *quis-quis* 'whoever'   Latin
     (c) *jang* 'sheet'   *jang-jang* 'every sheet'   Mandarin
     (d) *gapó* 'stone'   *gapó-gapó* 'small stones   Bikol
         (Mattes 2006: 10)   (in rice)'

Total reduplication may be a universal feature; but even if it is not, the
following generalization certainly appears to hold:

> GEN-8: If a language has partial reduplication, it also has total redu-
>   plication.

In some cases, total and partial reduplication are indistinguishable.
Consider the following data from Marshallese (Moravcsik 1978: 306):

(34) (a) *wah*   'canoe'   *wah-**wah**   'go by canoe'   Marshallese
         wit   'flower' *wit-**wit**   'wear a flower'
     (b) *kagir* 'belt'   *kagir-**gir** 'wear a belt'
         takin 'socks'   *takin-**kin** 'wear socks'

The common meaning of all four reduplicated words is 'use X,' where X is
the referent of the base. The examples in (34a) look like total reduplication; however, (34b) shows that there is also partial reduplication to convey the same meaning, involving the duplication of the last CVC portion
of the base. Since the entire bases in (34a) consist of only CVC, these examples are consistent with partial reduplication.

In partial reduplication, three types of constraints are detectable having to do with the phonological make-up of the reduplicated portion of the base, its position in the base, and the number of times it is duplicated.

First, here are examples to show variation in the phonological make-up of duplifixes. C, CV, CVC, and CVCV are all possible duplifix skeleta. A subset of the 12 possibilities (the four skeleta in initial, medial, and final position) is illustrated below (Moravcsik 1978: 308–309).

(35) Initial duplifix
    (a) C-: *gen* 'to sleep'   **g**-*gen* 'to be sleeping'   Shilha
    (b) CV-: *kuna* 'husband'   **ku**-*kuna* 'husbands'   Papago
    (c) CVC-: *woman* 'to bark at' **wom**-*woman* 'to be barking at'   Aztec

(36) Final duplifix
    (a) -CVC: *pwirej* 'dirt'   *pwirej*-**rej** 'to dirty'   Mokilese
    (b) -CVCV: *erasi* 'he is sick'   *erasi*-**rasi** 'he continues   Sirioni
                                         being sick'

(37) Internal duplifix
    (a) -C-: *raʔas* 'to dance' *raʔʔas* 'to make   Syrian Arabic
                             someone dance'
    (b) -V-: *lup*   'dry'   *luʔup* 'it becomes dry'   Coeur d'Alene

Here is a generalization highlighting common patterns:

    GEN-9: Frequent forms of duplifixes are a C, a syllable, or two syllables.

A second point about reduplicative structure has to do with position. The particular CV or V repeated is not freely chosen from any part of the base form: as shown in (35)–(37), in some cases it must be the initial part of the base, in others, it must be a middle part, and in yet others, it must be a final one. For example, the contemplated aspect form of the Tagalog verb *bingyan* must be *bi-bingyan*; it cannot be *bingyan-yan*. Nonetheless, there are sporadic exceptions. In Tagalog, the contemplative aspect of the verb *maipabili* 'be able to have (someone) buy' has alternative forms, such as *mai-pa-pabili* and *maipa-bi-bili* (Schachter and Otanes 1972: 362). In most cases, the duplifix is adjacent to the part of the base that is duplicated.

    GEN-10: Duplifixes are in most cases strictly ordered relative to the
            base. They may be prefixed, suffixed, or infixed; but in each
            case, they are adjacent to the portion of the base that they
            duplicate.

The third aspect of reduplicative structure is how many repetitions it involves.

    GEN-11: Partial reduplication is generally numerically restricted
            and it mostly involves simple doubling.

Total reduplication works somewhat differently. The option of repeating words like *very* or *old* or *many* in English virtually any number of times is present in grammaticalized form in Mokilese (Moravcsik 1978: 312, 313).

(38) *roar* 'to give a shudder'   Mokilese
      roar-roar 'to be shuddering'
      roar-roar-roar 'to continue to shudder'

In rare cases, only triplication is allowed.

(39) *doau* 'to climb'   Mokilese
      doa-doau-doau 'to continue to climb'
      *doau-doau

Let us now turn to semantics.

(B) CROSSLINGUISTICALLY RECURRENT SEMANTIC PROPERTIES OF REDUPLICATION

As noted above, in Western languages, reduplication generally involves emphasis or increased quality, as in *very very* and *old old*. This is also a common meaning of partial reduplication across languages, as is the case in another set of examples from Tagalog (Gleason 1955: 90).

(40) BASIC FORM: REDUPLICATION: Tagalog
      isá 'one'   *i-isá* 'only one'
      dalawá 'two'   *da-dalawá* 'only two'
      tatló 'three'   *ta-tatló* 'only three'
      píso 'peso'   *pi-píso* 'only one peso'

But duplifixes can have other meanings as well. The semantic contributions that they make to the base fit into two broad types: plurality of entities, continuation of action, or intensification of properties on the one hand, and diminution of entities or attenuation of properties on the other. These two semantic effects are at odds with each other: in the first case, the meaning becomes "larger," or stronger, than that of the base; in the second, the meaning becomes "smaller," or weaker. Here are some examples.

(41) Augmentation
      (a) INCREASED QUANTITY
           1. *mōk* 'short'   Atakapa
               mōk-mōk 'short things'
               (Mithun 1999: 344)

           2. *ren* 'man'   Mandarin
               ren-ren 'everybody'

           3. *hiʔ* 'sand'   Tzeltal
               hiʔ-hiʔ-tik 'very much sand'

      (b) REPEATED OR CONTINUED ACTION
           1. *kōl* 'rub'   Atakapa
               kōlkōl 'rub repeatedly'
               (Mithun 1999: 344)

           2. *aló:tkan* 'be full (SING)'   Koasati
               alot-ló:-kan 'be full (PLU)'
               (Mithun 1999: 87)

        3. *mu·tq* 'lop off'   Kyuquot Nootka
        mu-*mu·tq* 'lop off here and there'
        (Mithun 1999: 552)

   (c) INTENSITY
        1. *dana* 'old'   Agta
        da-*dana* 'very old'
        2. *dolu* 'full'   Turkish
        dop-*dolu* 'very full'
        3. *dii* 'to be good'   Thai
        díi-*dii* 'to be extremely good'

(42) Diminution
   (a) SMALLNESS OF ENTITIES
        1. *xóyamac* 'child'   Nez Perce
        xoyamac-**xóyamac** 'small child'
        2. *sqa'xaʔ* 'horse', 'dog'   Thompson
        sqa'-**q**-*xaʔ* 'little horse', 'little dog'
        3. *kwák* 'my thing'   Agta
        kwa-la-kwák 'my little thing'
   (b) DIMINISHED INTENSITY
        1. *lutu* 'to cook'   Tagalog
        mag-**lutu**-*lutu-an* 'to pretend to be cooking',
        'to play cooking'
        (Shkarban and Rachkov 2007: 897)
        2. *duduk* 'to sit'   Indonesian
        duduk-*duduk* 'to sit doing nothing'
        (Ogloblink and Nedjalkov 2007: 1444)
        3. *maji* 'wet'   Swahili
        maji-*maji* 'somewhat wet'
   (c) TONED-DOWN REFERENCE
        1. *jama* 'dress'   Bengali
        jama-**tama** 'dresses and affiliated things'
        2. havlú 'towel'   Turkish
        havlú **mavlú** 'towels and the like'
        (Lewis 1967: 337)
        3. book-**shmuk**   English

Other meanings may not fit squarely into one or the other categories above but may nonetheless be somewhat related. For instance, in Salishan languages, reduplication may signal sudden, accidental occurrence of an action (Mithun 1999: 494); this may be an instance of intensity.

The wide variety of meanings that reduplication is used to express across languages is puzzling since, as noted above, it includes contradictory senses. And it is not only that one language's reduplications have one meaning and the other's the opposite: both meanings may be present among the reduplicative constructions of the very same language and sometimes a single construction is ambiguous between the two interpretations. This is so in Bikol, a Central Philippine language spoken in Southern Luzon (Mattes 2006: 10).

(43) (a) *tumog* 'wet'   *tumog-tumog* 'soaking wet' OR 'wettish' Bikol
     (b) *lugad* 'wounded' *lugad-lugad* 'heavily   OR 'a little
                                            wounded'   wounded'

However, Veronika Mattes suggests that there is a common denominator to the two opposite meanings: change of quantity. In the light of this observation, reduplication may be viewed as a marking device to indicate that the word is to be understood in an out-of-the-ordinary sense: the meaning deviates from the normal sense of the base either by being "more" or by being "less."

Here is a summary generalization:

> GEN-12: The crosslinguistically most common meaning of reduplication is the quantitative or qualitative augmentation of the meaning of the base. Its second most common meaning is the diminution of size or intensity.

Let us take stock. This section has been about the choice of affixal forms: given an affixal meaning, which of the available forms is the proper one to choose? As noted in point (d) (in Section 4.1), one relevant issue is the invariance versus variance of forms: do affixes have a single form or do they have variants? Reduplicative constructions are a case in point: they involve multiple exponents of an affix in that the duplifix takes different phonological forms depending on the form of the material that is copied.

Reduplication is of special interest in that the meaning–form relation is typically iconic: multiplied morphological form stands for multiplied meaning. We will now turn to another morphological pattern that is similarly iconic but in the other direction: reduced morphology stands for reduced meaning.

4.2.2.2 Zero forms

Beyond the issue of choosing the right exponent of an affix from among multiple options, there is also another, more fundamental issue: whether there IS a form available at all to express a given meaning? In other words, when an affixal meaning is in search of a form, it may encounter an *embarras de richesses* by having to choose one from many; or, contrariwise, it may encounter an *embarras de pauvreté*: the lack of any form at all. As we know from everyday life, both the overabundance of choices and the dearth of options can be problematic. The latter issue was formulated above as parameter (e):

(e) OVERT VERSUS ZERO AFFIXES
    What kinds of affixes have overt forms and what kinds can be zero?

Zero forms – the lack of an overt expression of a meaning – may show up in two ways. Consider the following.

> Although in reduplication, the phonological make-up of the duplifix is undoubtedly dependent on the phonological make-up of the base, reduplication is not like phonologically conditioned allomorphy, such as choosing between /t/ and /d/ for the English past morpheme (as in *bake-d* and *love-d*). In phonologically conditioned allomorphy, most of the phonological body is inherent in the affix and is therefore shared by all allomorphs with the form only slightly affected by the base. In contrast, in reduplication, most of the phonological specification comes from the base: the shared form of the allomorphs is a mere template such as a C, or a CV.

(44)　(a)　*lamb-s*　　　　　　　　　　　　　　　　English
　　　　　cow-s
　　　　　sheep_
　　　　　deer_
　　　(b)　*colon-us* 'colonist'　　　　　　　　　　　Latin
　　　　　equ-us 'horse'
　　　　　uxor_ 'wife'
　　　　　consul_ 'consul'

In English, the nominal plural is generally marked by a suffix but for some nouns – such as *sheep* or *deer* – the base form is used both for the singular and for the plural. In this case, zero is invoked as an **allomorph** of the plural affix. The same argument applies to the description of the singular nominative of Latin nouns, which is overtly marked for *colon-us* and *equ-us* but unmarked for *uxor* and *consul*. In these instances, the positing of a zero allomorph is supported by the existence of a synonymous overt analogue.

The following situation is different.

(45)　(a)　PLURAL　　SINGULAR　　　　　　　　　　English
　　　　　lamb-s　　**lamb-_**
　　　　　cow-s　　　**cow-_**
　　　　　school-s　　**school-_**
　　　　　pen-s　　　**pen-_**
　　　(b)　PLURAL　　SINGULAR　　　　　　　　　　French
　　　　　fille-s　　**fille-_** 'daughter'
　　　　　maison-s　**maison-_** 'house'
　　　　　ligne-s　　**ligne-_** 'line'
　　　　　chambre-s　**chambre-_** 'room'

These examples point up an asymmetry of a different kind.

In (44), some nouns have an overt affix for a particular category – plural in English, nominative in Latin – while others do not. The zero is thus a variant – an allomorph – of the plural affix. In (45), variation between overt and non-overt expression is not between different nouns; it is between two values of the category of number: the plural has an affix but the singular does not. As in the case of zero allomorphs, here, too, there is an overt analogue for the zero but it is not synonymous with the zero; rather, it is antonymous to it: it designates the opposite value of a category. Thus, in this case the zero is a **morpheme**, rather than an allomorph.

Why do linguists posit zero allomorphs and zero morphemes? In both cases, our expectations are thwarted by our findings. In the first case, we expect overt affixes for some nouns because other nouns have them; in the second case, we expect overt affixes for one value of a category (the singular) because the other value (the plural) has them. When these expectations are not fulfilled, we posit zero allomorphs or zero morphemes to create balance, or symmetry, where otherwise there would be imbalance, or asymmetry.

While the occurrence of zero allomorphs may well be language-specific, the distribution of zero morphemes shows a widespread pattern across languages. As we will now see, the picture is composed of three mosaic pieces, which will be familiar from our discussion of markedness in connection with antonyms (Chapter 2, Section 2.5.1).

a. Syntagmatic simplicity

First, if we consider the meanings that tend to be represented by zero morphemes, we find that they are "leaner" than the meanings expressed by the corresponding overt affixes. To be more precise: the meaning of the zero-marked affix is less than the meaning of the overtly marked affix. This is clearest in the case of singular versus plural where the plural meaning 'more than one' properly includes the meaning of the singular 'one.'

Consider also other cases of zero marking in English.

(a) The positive degree of adjectives has no marker, as in *bright* or *pretty*, but the **comparative degree** does: *brighter*, *prettier*, and the marked form's meaning implies the meaning of the unmarked one (whoever is brighter must also be bright).

(b) There is no marker for a positive verb but the **negative** is marked (e.g. *he arrived* versus *he did **not** arrive*); and the meaning of a negative verb includes the meaning of the positive verb. For example, 'he didn't arrive' can be paraphrases as 'his arrival did not happen.'

(c) Declarative sentences have simpler structures than **questions**: *He arrived* versus *Did he arrive?* The meaning of questions implies that of the corresponding statements: *Did he arrive?* means 'I am not sure about the truth of the statement 'He arrived'.'

Here are examples from other languages for the constructions just mentioned showing the same patterns of zero versus non-zero marking.

(46) (a) zero singular, overt plural

     a. *lenn* 'lake' – *lenn-**où*** 'lakes'   Breton
       merc'h 'girl' – *mer'c-**ed*** 'girls'

     b. *3ya* 'hand, arm' – *3ya=**tse*** 'hands, arms'   Manange
       4thin 'house' – *4thin=**tse*** 'houses'

  (b) zero positive degree, overt comparative degree

     a. *azkarr* 'clever' – *azkarr-**ago*** 'more clever'   Basque
       ederr 'beautiful' – *ederr-**ago*** 'more beautiful'

     b. *kõrge* 'high' – *'kõrge-**m*** 'higher'   Estonian
       'nūri 'dull' – *'nūri-**m*** 'duller'

  (c) zero affirmative, overt negative

     a. *tika-vaa-aŋ* 'He will eat.'   Chemehuevi
       eat-FUT-he
       kacu-*aŋ tika-vaa-**waʔ*** 'He will not eat.'
       not-he eat-FUT-**NEG**

  (d) zero declarative, overt interrogative

     a. *ken-tze-n ari da* 'is removing'   Basque
       remove-NOM-LOC CONT AUX   (Northern)
       *ken-tze-n ari **dea*** 'is removing?'
       remove-NOM-LOC CONT **AUX.QU**

     b. *gör-mek* 'to see' – *gör-**me**-mek* 'not to see'   Turkish
       git-mek 'to go' – *git-**me**-mek* 'not to go'

b. *Juhani söi omenan.* 'John ate the apple.'   Finnish
John ate the.apple
Söi-kö Juhani omenan? 'Did John eat the apple?'
ate-QU John the.apple

The most literal manifestation of the correlation between more form and more meaning is provided by reduplicative constructions, discussed in Section 4.2.2.1. Let us compare the plural forms of 'chicken' in English and Pangasinan.

(47) (a) English: *chicken*   *chicken-s*
      (b) Pangasinan: *manók manók-*   **manók**

In both languages, the more complex meaning has the more complex form; but while in English, the form increment (the suffix *-s*) is arbitrary, in Pangasinan, the meaning change of adding more of the same meaning already present in the base (at least one other chicken) is mirrored by the addition of more of the same form already present in the base (one other instance of *manók*).

The less specific and thus more inclusive meaning of the zero-marked term is also evident when the zero-marked term is used in a generic sense in reference to the entire semantic dimension. And we saw the same in connection with antonymic adjectives (Chapter 2, Section 2.5.1): in questions like *how wide?*, or *how old?*, the unmarked adjective has a dimensional, rather than polar, interpretation.

However, there are also cases that are counter to the claim that the simpler meaning is zero-marked. As seen before, in Swahili and other Bantu languages, both the singular and the plural are affixed, such as in **m**-*tu* 'man' and **wa**-*tu* 'men.' Likewise, both the affirmative and the negative forms of the verb are complex in Swahili; e.g. *mi-**ru*** 'to see,' *mi-**nai*** 'to not see.' Accordingly, the correlation between the simplicity of form and the simplicity of meaning is best stated as follows.

GEN-13: Given a category with two opposing semantic terms, the form of the simpler value tends to be not more complex than that of the other term.

This statement has to do with the relative syntagmatic simplicity of the morphological expression of the simpler of two opposing values of a category. It is because this value is often – although not always – zero-marked that it is labeled as the **unmarked** term of the opposition, with the other labeled **marked**.

The fact that the unmarked value tends to be crosslinguistically the same – generally the singular and not the plural; the declarative rather than the interrogative, etc. – is interesting all by itself since there is no logical reason why this should be the case. What is even more intriguing is that there are two other properties that tend to cluster with zero expression.

b. Paradigmatic complexity

Consider the expression of lower and higher numbers. As was seen in Chapter 2 (Section 2.4), lower numerals are generally monomorphemic while higher ones are composed of multiple morphemes linked by addition, multiplication, or subtraction. Thus, by the criterion of morphological simplicity, lower numerals are unmarked as opposed to higher ones. Their meaning, too, is simpler. Now consider the gender and case paradigms of some Latin numerals.

(48) (a) 1 SING: Latin
        NOM: *un-us* (M), *un-a* (F), *un-um* (N)
        ACC: *un-um* (M, N), *un-am* (F)
        PLU:
        NOM: *un-i* (M), *un-ae* (F), *un-a* (N)
        ACC: *un-os* (M), *un-as* (F), *un-a* (N)
     2 NOM: *du-o* (M, N), *du-ae* (F)
       ACC: *du-os* (M), *du-as* (F), *du-o* (N)
     3 NOM: *tr-es* (M, F), *tr-ia* (N)
       ACC: *tr-es* (M, F), *tr-ia* (N)
     4 *quatuor*
    11 *un-decim*
    12 *duo-decim*

The lowest numeral – 'one' – has both singular and plural forms and each has distinct gender forms both in the nominative and in the accusative. The numeral 'two' has no forms differentiated for number and it has three distinct gender forms in the accusative and two in the nominative. In 'three,' both the gender and the case distinctions are reduced: only two genders in both cases and no distinct forms for the cases. All higher numbers (with the exception of the hundreds starting with 200) have single forms undifferentiated for gender, number, and case. Although the dividing line between monomorphemic and polymorphemic numerals is not the same as the one between declined and undeclined numerals, it still holds that it is the lower numbers that have both simple, monomorphemic structure and more variability in terms of gender, number, and case. In other words, syntagmatic simplicity is paired with paradigmatic complexity.

Irregularity is a type of paradigmatic complexity. In language after language, the verb 'to be' has a more varied conjugational paradigm than other verbs. In English, it is in fact the only verb that has three person/number forms: *am*, *are*, and *is* in the present and two – *was* and *were* – in the past, while other verbs have only two present-tense forms (zero and *-s* as in *bake*, *bakes*) and a single past form (*baked*).

There is also a third way in which lower and higher numerals tend to differ: how often they occur in texts. This leads us to a third diagnostic of the relationship between unmarked and marked entities.

c. Frequency

According to text counts of English, Spanish, French, and German, numerals between 1 and 9 decrease in frequency the higher they are (Greenberg 1966c: 42–43). Greater frequency tends in general to characterize the unmarked member of a category. The unmarked status of the positive degree of adjective comparison exemplified above is supported by it being more frequent than the comparative and superlative degrees (Greenberg 1966c: 41). Past-tense verb forms generally differ from their present-tense counterparts by including an extra morpheme; and some text counts show that they are less frequent (Greenberg 1966c: 48).

Here is, therefore, an expanded version of GEN-13, echoing GEN-23 in Chapter 2 (Section 2.5.1).

GEN-13': Given a category with two opposing semantic terms, the
form of the semantically simpler term
(a) tends to be no more complex than that of the other term;
(b) tends to have no fewer subtypes than the other term; and
(c) tends to be more frequent.

Why should there be a tendency for semantic and formal simplicity, sub-categorizational variety, and frequency to cluster? Could one of the three factors be seen as the causal attractor of the other two? For example, might structural simplicity invite greater frequency? It is not unreasonable to think that speakers resort to expressions more frequently if they are simpler; but this leaves open the question of why some structures should be more simple in the first place?

The basic engine behind markedness phenomena is undoubtedly the frequency of things in the world that words refer to. Discussing zero form and optional marking, Greenberg says: "The important phenomena of zero and facultative /= optional – EAM/ expression can be understood in terms of frequency phenomena based on the situation in the world with which the users of language must deal.... For example, it is not so much in English that male is in general the unmarked category in relation to female, but the frequency of association of things in the real world" (Greeenberg 1966c: 66). He then compares the words *author* and *nurse*. *Author* is unmarked: it can refer to male or female individuals but most likely to males since most authors are male. *Nurse* in turn is mostly understood as referring to females simply because most nurses are women; the marked form *male nurse* is used for the exceptional meaning.

The primacy of frequency as a causal factor is similarly emphasized by other linguists who have worked on markedness phenomena extensively, among them Martin Haspelmath, who refers to markedness phenomena as frequency effects (Haspelmath 2010: 265–280), and Bernard Comrie. Here is a quote from Comrie: "[There is] a single simple correlation between markedness of situations and markedness in morphological structure: morphological unmarkedness corresponds to greater unmarkedness of the situation while overt morphological marking corresponds to a greater markedness of a (less expected) situation" (Comrie 1986: 97).

Exactly how does frequency bring about the other characteristics of the unmarked? Haspelmath appeals to two factors: ease of pronunciation and memory. Pronunciation preferences have to do with the origins of zero form: frequently used forms are likely to be reduced because of their predictability. Memory in turn has to do with the maintenance of paradigmatic complexity: people remember often-used forms even if they don't fit into a regular paradigm while they would be forgotten if they didn't occur frequently. Frequent use wears away forms; memory preserves their variability.

The fundamental significance of the clustering of markedness phenomena in language is underscored by similar patterns showing up outside language. Of the three factors discussed above, the correlation between lack of marking and frequency is ubiquitous in human social behavior

> This correlation of the three characteristics of the unmarked term – syntagmatic simplicity, paradigmatic complexity, and frequency – is perhaps most evident for the singular–plural opposition. The singular is generally unmarked relative to the plural both by morphological simplicity and by having a richer paradigm than the plural. Thus for example, in the case of the German definite article, the three-way gender distinction collapses completely in the plural. And text counts show that the singular is also more frequent than the plural (Greenberg 1966c: 32, 35–37).

and in the structure of human artifacts. As an example, Haspelmath notes that for dialing local phone numbers, area codes are generally not needed while for long-distance calls they are. This corresponds to the fact that most phone calls are local rather than long-distance.

There will be more discussion about markedness in Chapter 7, Section 7.4.

4.3 The order of morphemes

As noted in the beginning of this chapter, well-formedness of word structure depends on three factors: the choice of morphemes, the choice of forms of morphemes, and the order of morphemes. Having discussed the first two factors, we now turn to linear order (cf. parameter (f) in Section 4.1).

How could the morphemes in a word be sequenced? In the beginning of Section 3.3 of Chapter 3, the same question was asked about the sequencing of words in sentences. In response to that question, we identified five logical possibilities:

1. Precedence regardless of adjacency
2. Adjacency regardless of precedence
3. Both precedence and adjacency (=immediate precedence)
4. Neither adjacency nor precedence ("free order")
5. Interlocking order

We concluded that in syntax, there were crosslinguistic tendencies involving precedence (e.g. Subject before Object) and others involving adjacency (e.g. Object next to Verb), but crosslinguistically valid order patterns involving both precedence and adjacency are rare if occurrent at all, as are also free order and interlocking order. What about morpheme order? Leaving the order in compound words aside, our focus will be the order of affixes relative to the base.

First of all, in Section 4.1 above, one more possible temporal pattern was identified, one that is inapplicable to words but is an option for morphemes: simultaneity. Since the concept morpheme is not defined so as to require independent pronounceability, morphemes may be suprasegmental properties such as stress and pitch which, instead of being linearly sequenced to a word, are simultaneous with it. Here is therefore the complete list of the possible morpheme orders:

1. Precedence regardless of adjacency
2. Adjacency regardless of precedence
3. Both precedence and adjacency (=immediate precedence)
4. Neither adjacency nor precedence ("free order")
5. Interlocking order
6. Simultaneous order (=suprasegmental affixing)

The examples given in Section 4.1 illustrated various patterns of precedence (suffixes, prefixes), of interlocking (infixes, circumfixes, introfixes), and of suprasegmental order (suprafixes). Our task in this section is to

> Additional examples of markedness abound: in making an appointment with somebody, it is not necessary to add the name of the current month but if the appointment is for a different month, it has to be specified. Regular mail does not need to be marked as such; registered mail, and special delivery do. If you expect to be late coming home, you will tell this to your family; but if you expect to be on time, this "goes without saying."

explore the crosslinguistic frequencies of the various order patterns and the conditions under which they occur. There are several relevant generalizations that have been suggested in current research, some pointing up similarities between word order and morpheme order while others showing differences.

First of all, there are two order patterns that are crosslinguistically rare both in syntax and in morphology: free order and interlocking order. In addition, examples of suprasegmental affixing are also few and far between.

> GEN-14: The free order of affixes is rare across languages and if a language has it, it also has fixed affix order.
> GEN-15: Discontinuous affix order (infixing, circumfixing, and introfixing) is rare across languages; and if a language has discontinuous affixing, it also has either prefixing or suffixing or both. (Greenberg 1966a: #26)
> GEN-16: Suprasegmental affixing is rare across languages and if a language has it, it also has segmental affixes.

The statement about free order (GEN-14) is stated probabilistically because there are scattered examples of reversible affix order. One was mentioned in connection with Tagalog reduplication (Section 4.2.2.1); (49) and (50) provide two more examples (Comrie 1980: 81–82).

(49) 'to our house': (a) *kerka-**nim-lan***   Zyrian
                           house-**our-to**
                      (b) *kerka-**lan-nim***
                           house-**to-our**

(50) 'to my forest': (a) *čodra-**m-lan***   Cheremis
                           forest-**my-to**
                      (b) *čodra-**lan-em***
                           forest-**to-my**

Interestingly, variable affix order may also signal different meanings, as in Turkish (Lewis 1967: 40).

(51) (a) *kardeş-**ler-im***   'my brothers'   Turkish
          brother-**PLU-my**
     (b) *kardeş-**im-ler***   'my brother and his family'
          brother-**my-PLU**

The generalizations about discontinuous and suprasegmental affix order (GEN-15 and GEN-16) are similarly statistical rather than absolute. This is due to examples such as those in Section 4.1: infixing in Katu and Agta, circumfixing in Chikasaw, Russian, and German, introfixing in Hebrew, and suprasegmental affixing in English and Kisi. Here are additional examples (as cited in Rubba 2001: 679, 680, 681).

(52) (a) infixing   Bontok

      (i)   *fikas*   'strong'

          *f-**um**-ikas*   'to be/become strong'

      (ii) *bato*   'stone'

          *b-**um**-ato*   'to be/become stone'

  (b) circumfixing   Yucatec Mayan

      (i)   *leti*   'that one'

          maʔ**-leti **ʔi 'not that one'

          NEG-that.one-**NEG**

      (ii) *ʔnkaat*   'I want (it)'

          maʔ**-ʔnkaat-**ʔi 'I don't want it'

          NEG-I.want(.it)-**NEG**

  (c) introfixing   Amharic

      infinitive: *məsbər*

      imperfective: *səbr-*

      perfective: *səbər*

      imperative: *sibər*

  (d) suprafixing   Ancient Greek

      (i)   *potós*   'drunk'

          pótos   'a drink'

      (ii) *leukós*   'white'

          leûkos   'whitefish'

GEN-14, GEN-15, and GEN-16 pertain to the last three of the six possible order patterns in the list above: free order, discontinuity, and suprafixing. Next we will turn to precedence and adjacency relations between affix and base.

a. Suffixing versus prefixing

In his sample of 772 inflecting languages, Dryer (2005i) found that more than half – 382 languages – were predominantly suffixing (e.g. West Greenlandic Eskimo) and a further 114 had a moderate preference for suffixes (e.g. Mokilese). On the prefixing side, there were only 54 languages where this was the predominant pattern (e.g. Hunde, a Bantu language of the Democratic Republic of Congo) and there were 92 with a moderate preference for prefixing (e.g. Mohawk). The number of languages in between – with an approximately equal amount of suffixing and prefixing – was 130 (e.g. Kiribati).

    GEN-17: PRECEDENCE

    Crosslinguistically, suffixing is more frequent than prefixing.

The picture of this overall preference for suffixing becomes more differentiated if two factors are considered. One is the function of individual affixes: whether they express case, subject agreement, object agreement, definiteness, and so forth. The other is the word order types of languages. An observation of the former kind has to do with case affixes. In another of his WALS projects (Dryer 2005f), Dryer found 466 languages where case is affixal. Of these, the overwhelming majority – 431 – have case suffixes;

only 35 have case prefixes. Thus, case affixes show a much greater preference to suffixal position than other affixes.

>GEN-18: Crosslinguistically, case affixes tend to be suffixed.

Here is an example of the rare pattern of case prefixing (cited in Dryer
2005f: 210).

(53) *wakaboola* **a**-*Joni*   'He came along with John.'   Tonga
      he.came   **with**-John

A generalization of the second type, one linking affix position to word
order type, is as follows (cf. Greenberg 1966a: #27).

>GEN-19: Languages that have verb-final sentence order and postposi-
>tions are almost always exclusively suffixing.

What may be the explanation for the general preference for suffixing
over prefixing? Two factors have been explored in the literature: one is a
psychological factor having to do with the processing advantages of suffixing patterns, the other is diachronic involving the historical origins of
affixes. For a direct explanation of the causal sort, only diachrony is available: as John Haiman remarked, "everything is the way it is because it got
that way" (Haiman 2003: 108). But it is psychological factors that in turn
trigger and shape diachronic change and they are the ones to guide the
selective survival of structures.

Christopher Hall's explanatory argument (1988) for the overall preference for suffixing over prefixing (GEN-17 above) combines the two strands:
historical change and processing preferences. His proposal has two components. The first hypothesis is that affixes originate in lexical material:
they start out as free-standing words which, over time, fuse with bases due
to the frequency with which they co-occur with them. These words may
precede or follow the head of the construction that will eventually
become the morphological base and thus, no preference is predicted so far
for either prefixing or suffixing. This is where Hall's second hypothesis
comes in: lexical morphemes that follow stems are more likely to fuse
with them than those preceding stems. This is because, as demonstrated
by Hawkins and Gilligan (1988), from the point of view of word recognition, it is preferable if the identity of the word is revealed immediately in
sequential processing without the prefix getting in the way.

Let us now turn to the proximity of affixes and bases.

b. The Relevance Principle

Based on his 30-language sample, Joseph Greenberg proposed the following crosslinguistic generalization (Greenberg 1966a: #28):

If both the derivation and the inflection follow the root or they both
precede the root, the derivation is always between the root and the
inflection.

Examples abound. In the English word *demonstrate-ion-s*, the derivational
affix *-ion* is placed closer to the stem than the plural *-s* (**demonstrate-s-ion*);
and in *harmon-iz-ing*, *-iz*, a derivational affix, is also next to the base

followed by the inflectional affix *-ing*. Here is an example from prefixing that shows the mirror image of the English order of derivational and inflectional affixes (Kimenyi 1980: 64).

(54) *Úmwáana*   ***y-ii-shyiz-é*-ho**   amabuye   kúrí   we.   Kinyarwanda
     child   **AGR-REFL-**   stones   on   him
               put-ASP-on
     'The child puts stones on himself.'

The derivational affix 'reflexive' is adjacent to the stem; the agreement inflection is on the outside.

However, Greenberg's generalization leaves two questions open. First, what are the orders of multiple derivational affixes relative to each other and the relative orders of multiple inflectional ones? And, second, what might be the reason for derivational affixes placed closer to the stem? Joan Bybee's proposal, labeled the Relevance Principle, suggests an answer to both queries (Bybee 1985: 33–48 *et passim*).

> GEN-20: The varying proximity of an affix from the stem is generally proportionate to how relevant its meaning is to that of the stem.

Consider what this means for derivational affixes.

(55) (a) *possibil-**iti**-**z**-**ation***   English
     (b) *meg-bocsájt-**hat**-**atlan**-**ság***   Hungarian
         ASP-forgive-**able-PRIV-NMLZ**

(55a) is a noun derived by the outermost deverbal nominalizer *-ation*. In order for this affix to apply, a verb is needed: it in turn is derived by *-z*, a denominal verbalizer. It applies to the noun *possibility*, which in turn is derived from *possible* by the deadjectival nominalizer.

(55b) is also a noun: it is derived from an adjective by a privative affix, which in turn is added to a verb that expresses a possibility and that thus directly includes the 'able' affix. In both cases, affix order is in line with semantic scope.

Let us now consider how the Relevance Principle applies to the ordering of inflectional affixes. The examples in (56) are from Kimenyi 1980: 54, 127 (glossing somewhat altered); those in (57) are from Weber 1989: 89.

(56) (a) *Kú-ririimb-a*   ***bi-ra*-kome-ye.**   Kinyarwanda
        INF-sing-ASP **S3-PRES**-be.difficult-ASP
        'To sing is difficult.'
     (b) *Umugóre **y-a**-haa-**w-e***   igitabo n'ûmugabo.
        woman **S3-PAST**-give-**PASS-ASP** book   by.man
        'The woman was given the book by the man.'

(57) *Maqa-**ka-ra-n-mi**.*   Huallaga (Huánuco) Quechua
   hit-**PASS-PAST-3S**
   'He was hit.'

In both Kinyarwanda examples, the tense prefix (present or past) is next to the stem; the agreement morpheme is on the outside. Quechua is suffixing and thus it shows the mirror image of the Kinyarwanda order: the tense suffix is again closer to the stem than the agreement marker. This is as the Relevance Principle predicts it: tense is more relevant to the semantic characterization of the verb; agreement in turn is externally imposed by the syntactic environment.

In the Quechua example, there is also a passive suffix that intervenes between stem and tense: it has a closer semantic relationship to the stem than tense does. There is a passive affix in the second Kinyarwanda example as well but it does not compete with the other affixes for position since it is on the opposite side of the base.

The same relevance-based order can be illustrated for noun affixation. Turkish and Hungarian both have separatist expressions for number and case and in both languages, the number affix is the one adjacent to the stem. Greenberg (1966a: #39) noted: "Where morphemes of both number and case are present and both follow or both precede the noun base, the expression of number almost always comes between the noun base and the expression of case." Number specification adds to the meaning of the noun; case simply signals its role in the sentence.

(58) (a) *ev-**ler**-i*   Turkish
           house-**PLU**-**ACC**

       (b) *ház-**ak**-at*   Hungarian
           house-**PLU**-**ACC**

However, there are also examples of affix order that run counter to the Relevance Principle. The principle would predict that case affixes should always be peripheral and thus on the outer side of possessive affixes but in Finnish the opposite is the case (Comrie 1980: 81).

(59) *ystävä-**lle**-ni*   'to my friend'   Finnish
       friend-**to**-**my**

And of course the sporadic examples of variable affix order that were cited above are also counter to the principle.

The observation, captured by the Relevance Principle, that the proximity of affixes to the stem is governed by semantic coherence has an obvious parallel in syntax: as noted in Chapter 3, Section 3.3, words, phrases, and clauses are generally ordered in terms of Otto Behaghel's principle, according to which semantically coherent elements tend to stand together. This raises the general question of how similar and how different morphological and syntactic structures are.

Let us begin with differences. First, sentences are less tightly structured than words. The number of elements, their choice, the degree of phonological binding among them, and their order show less freedom in morphology than in syntax.

Second, sentences tend to be more compositional than words. That is, the meaning of a sentence tends more to be the sum of the meanings of the words than the meaning of a word is the sum of its morphemes. Word structure is historically more conservative and more idiosyncratic.

What are similarities between syntactic and morphological structure? Beyond the fact that both involve patterns of co-occurrence between certain entities – words or morphemes – and patterns of temporal arrangement, and beyond the parallelism between proximity and semantic cohesion mentioned above, markedness relations – the common clustering of syntagmatic simplicity, paradigmatic complexity, and frequency – are evident both in syntax and in morphology as they are in the lexicon as well. As we will see in the next chapter, phonological structure is even more tightly knit than word structure; and markedness is similarly alive in phonology.

4.4 Morphological categories

In this chapter, a number of crosslinguistic generalizations were cited involving terms like prefix, and suffix, derivational and inflectional affix, and, most centrally, the very term "word." As all scientific statements, these generalizations are of interest only if they are empirically testable: given any language, there must be a way to determining if the statements are true or untrue. Testability in turn crucially depends on a clear definition of the terms involved: exactly what structures do they refer to? Given an affix, we need to have criteria to tell us whether it is a prefix or a suffix; whether it is derivational or inflectional; and, more basically, whether a morpheme is an affix or a word. We need definitions of these terms both for setting up rules for individual languages and also to facilitate crosslinguistic generalizations.

Some of the entities referred to in our generalizations in this chapter can be easily identified. Thus, there is no problem in keeping apart prefixes and suffixes. Differentiating inflectional affixes from derivational ones is somewhat more complex. If we compare suffixes like those in *bake-s*, *bak-ing*, *nic-er* on the one hand, and those in *joy-ful*, *explor-ation*, and *employ-ee* on the other, a difference that leaps to the eye is that the former do not change the word class of the base while the latter do: they change noun to adjective or verb to noun. This is indeed a primary criterion employed in the literature for differentiating inflectional and derivational affixes.

There are also other features that separate the two kinds. For example, inflectional affixes are fully productive: they can be added to all members of a particular word class, while derivational ones have reduced productivity (e.g. there is *explor-ation* but not *postpone-ation*; *joy-ful*, but not *sense-ful*; *employ-ee*, but not *accus-ee*). However, the two characteristics – no change in word class and productivity – do not always go together. While affixes that are inflectional by the criterion of wholesale productivity never change word class, there are affixes that seem to be derivational since they are not fully productive but they are also like inflectional affixes in that they also keep the word class of the base, such as *child-less*, *ideal-ism*, or *kitchen-ette*. In other words, preserving the word class of the base is a necessary feature of inflections but not a sufficient one.

Another example of the misalignment of various criteria is compositionality. Many derived words have non-compositional interpretations – such as *mouth-ful* or *child-hood* – as opposed to inflected words, which are always compositional. But there are compositional derivations as well, such as *nice-ly* or *speak-er*.

Similar problems arise in attempting to draw clear boundaries around the other concepts mentioned in the crosslinguistic generalizations of this chapter. How exactly do we differentiate affixes from words? An obvious answer may be that affixes are bound forms: they cannot stand by themselves, while words can. But certain morphemes that appear to be affixes when they are closely attached to the base may, under different conditions, stand by themselves. Are the English verb particles affixes or words? They form a stress unit with verbs as in *He gave **up** the fight*, and they form a single prosodic and orthographic unit in nominalizations such as ***up**take*; but they can also be separated from the base as in *He gave it **up***. For these borderline cases, the term clitic has been used in the literature, but some other linguists, such as Brian Joseph in his account of Modern Greek morphology (2002), simply accept the scalar nature of the criteria of wordhood, as well as the mismatch among the different criteria for word.

While words are in some cases difficult to distinguish from affixes, there is also a similarly somewhat fluid facet of words: how to tell them apart from phrases. When it comes to compounds, English orthography is ambivalent: some compounds are spelled in one word (such as *blackboard* or *uptick*) while others are separated (*high school, apple pie*).

How the concept of word should be defined in any one language is problematic; and the problems increase manifoldly when we try to formulate a universally valid definition of this notion so that it is set apart both from affixes and from phrases. The enormous amount of literature on the topic is a testimony to the complexity of the problem (Di Sciullo and Williams 1987 and Dixon and Aikhenvald 2002 are some of the most extensive discussions). This is so even though the concept of word is fundamental to linguistic analysis: the division between morphology and syntax is based on the division between word and phrase. The word is also a crucial domain in phonology.

The problem is the same as discussed in Section 3.4 of the syntax chapter (Chapter 3). For crosslinguistic generalizations about subjects – or about any other syntactic category – to remain vulnerable to empirical testing, the terms involved need to be defined. As we saw, subjects have multiple characteristics and while some may cluster – that is, mutually imply each other – this is not always the case: subject properties may be distributed over different noun phrases both within and across languages and so far no morphosyntactic property has been identified for a universally valid definition of subjects.

Given that we do need clear definitions of the basic concepts in order to lend empirical force to our generalizations, the question is what is to be done? As noted in the syntax chapter, some of today's leading typologists, such as William Croft and Martin Haspelmath, have concluded either that there are NO crosslinguistically applicable grammatical categories (Croft 2001) or, if there are any, they have to be defined in ways very different from the traditionally assumed definitions (Haspelmath 2010). A less radical approach is just to accept the fact that most – or all – grammatical categories are not amenable to strict definitions in terms of necessary and sufficient properties: instead, they are prototype-based, having typical core members that have many properties in common and peripheral ones that are more thinly characterized.

This is the approach advocated by Newmeyer when, talking about the overall research methods of language typologists, he says: "[The typologist's] strategy is to have some idea of the prototypical subject, dative, ergative, and so on in mind (which are generally defined in semantic terms) and then look for instantiations of that construct in the languages that constitute their sample" (Newmeyer 2010: 692). He continues to note that in case of several entities each manifesting only some of the assumed properties, the analyst has to make a decision as to which structures to label as subject, or affix, or whatever category is at stake. To guarantee the empirical testability of our generalizations, we choose one particular set of definitional criteria for our terms, state the definition explicitly, and then, adopting that definition as a hypothesis, attempt to look for patterns within and across languages guided by our definitions. The more instrumental a provisional definition is in formulating generalizations, the more it is confirmed.

It is worth recognizing that the problem of the proper definitions of concepts is by no means restricted to linguistics. What is the definition of the concept school? How is it defined within our culture and what is a cross-culturally applicable definition? In American culture, kindergarten falls within the category of schools and so do colleges and universities. In German usage, however, only elementary and high schools are labeled as schools, nothing below or beyond. Or what is the proper definition of religion that could encompass its instances even just within a single culture? And how is the notion definable cross-culturally? As in all other domains, definitions are hypotheses that are used as tools for representing the natural joints of the structure of reality. They are justified to the extent that they allow for generalizations in the respective domains.

Summary

Six parameters of morphological variation have been explored.

(a) STEMS AND AFFIXES
What combinations of stems and affixes are possible in a language?

(b) SEPARATIST VS. CUMULATIVE AFFIX EXPONENTS
Does an affix have only one meaning or more than one meaning at the same time?

(c) MONOSEMOUS VS. POLYSEMOUS AFFIX EXPONENTS
Does an affix have only one meaning or more than one alternative meaning?

(d) INVARIANCE VERSUS VARIANCE OF AFFIXES
Do affixes have a single form or do they have variants?

(e) OVERT VERSUS ZERO AFFIXES

What kinds of affixes have overt forms and what kinds can be <u>zero</u>?

(f) THE ORDER OF MORPHEMES

In what <u>temporal relations</u> are morphemes arranged?

In response, 20 crosslinguistic generalizations – frequency statements and implicational universals – have been cited and discussed.

Activities

1. The Latin examples of (9) in Section 4.1 were used to illustrate the monosemy and polysemy of affixes. Are there cases of cumulativity in these examples as well?

2. Consider the following crosslinguistic regularity (Hawkins 1983: 119–120; cf. also Rijkhoff 2002: 273–276):

When any or all of the items – demonstrative, numeral, and descriptive adjective – precede the noun, they (i.e., those that do precede) are always found in that order. For those that follow, no predictions are made, although the most frequent order is the mirror image of the preceding modifiers.

Examples of the two common orders are English (*these three red apples*) and Yoruba ("apples red three these"). Could the Relevance Principle (GEN-20 above) and Behaghel's Law discussed in the Syntax chapter help explain these orders?

3. The following is a set of Swahili words.
   (a) Identify the morphemes and their allomorphs.
   (b) In (5)–(9), it seems the plural is less marked than the singular. Can you find an alternative analysis by considering the initial sounds of these stems?
   (c) What might be a historical explanation of the plural prefix in (10)–(14)?

	SINGULAR		PLURAL	
1.	*ubao*	'plank'	*mbao*	'planks'
2.	*ubawa*	'wing'	*mbawa*	'wings'
3.	*udevu*	'hair'	*ndevu*	'hairs'
4.	*ugwe*	'string'	*ŋgwe*	'strings'
5.	*ufuŋguo*	'key'	*fuŋguo*	'keys'
6.	*ufagio*	'broom'	*fagio*	'brooms'
7.	*ufizi*	'gum'	*fizi*	'gums'
8.	*usiku*	'night'	*siku*	'nights'
9.	*ušaŋga*	'bead'	*šaŋga*	'beads'
10.	*wakati*	'season'	*ñakati*	'seasons'
11.	*wavu*	'net'	*ñavu*	'nets'
12.	*wayo*	'footprint'	*ñayo*	'footprints'
13.	*wembe*	'razor'	*ñembe*	'razors'
14.	*wimbo*	'song'	*ñimbo*	'songs'

4. Identify the derivational affixes in the following data from Agta (Merrifield *et al.* 1987: ##94, 95)

1	*adanuk*	'long'	*adadanuk*	'very long'
2	*addu*	'many'	*adaddu*	'very many'
3	*apisi*	'small'	*apapisi*	'very small'
4	*uffu*	'thigh'	*ufuffu*	'thighs'
5	*labaŋ*	'patch'	*lablabaŋ*	'patches'
6	*furab*	'afternoon'	*fufurab*	'late afternoon'
7	*wer*	'creek'	*walawer*	'small creek'
8	*pirak*	'money'	*palapirak*	'a little money'
9	*pesuk*	'peso'	*palapesuk*	'a mere peso'

5. (a) Find the morphemes in the following data from Cheyenne (from Merrifield *et al.* 1987, #33)
   (b) Are all affixes continuous?
   (c) Does affix order support or weaken the Relevance Principle?

1.	*namesehe*	'I eat.'
2.	*emesehe*	'He eats.'
3.	*naešemesehe*	'I already ate.'
4.	*esaamesehehe*	'He doesn't eat.'
5.	*emeomesehe*	'He ate this morning.'
6.	*eohkemesehe*	'He always eats.'
7.	*epevemesehe*	'He eats well.'
8.	*eohkepevemesehe*	'He always eats well.'
9.	*eohkesaapevemesehehe*	'He never eats well.'
10.	*esaaešemesehehe*	'He has not eaten yet.'
11.	*nameoešemesehe*	'I already ate this morning.'
12.	*naohkepevenemene*	'I always sing well.'

Further reading

- For comprehensive surveys of morphological typology, see the excellent textbooks by Jae Jung Song (2001: especially 119–132) and by Martin Haspelmath and Andre D. Sims (2010), as well as articles in handbooks such as Brown 2011, Haspelmath *et al.* 2001, Spencer and Zwicky 1998, Booij *et al.* 2000, and Malchukov and Spencer 2009. On noun incorporation, see also Baker 1996, Chapter 7.

- For a detailed evaluation of the various attempts to explain the suffixing preference, see Song 2001: 119–132.

- On markedness, see Croft 2003, especially Chapter 4.

- On linguistic categorization, see Taylor 2003, Aarts 2007.

5 The sounds of languages
Phonological typology

CHAPTER OUTLINE

The chapter presents crosslinguistic generalizations about the sounds that languages use, how the sounds take on variant forms depending on the phonological context, how they are ordered relative to each other, and what the basic phonological terms are that crosslinguistic generalizations are couched in. Recurrent properties of visual forms of language – writing systems and sign languages – are also discussed.

5.1 Introduction

As we saw in the preceding syntax and morphology chapters, the well-formedness of a linguistic object depends on the choice and arrangement of its parts. In syntax, it is the proper choice of words and word forms and their ordering that make up well-formed sentences. In morphology in turn, words are the wholes and morphemes are the parts: words are well-formed if the morphemes, their forms, and their sequences are the way grammatical conventions require them to be.

However, syntactic and morphological well-formedness doesn't guarantee that a linguistic utterance is fully grammatical. In addition to words and morphemes, there is a third type of element whose choice and arrangement are crucial for grammaticality. For an illustration, consider three alternative pronunciations of the sentence *Spring is here*. In (1c), /y/ is a high front rounded vowel.

(1)   (a)   /sprɪŋ   ɪz   hiːr/
       (b)   */ʃprɪŋ   ɪz   hiːr/
       (c)   */spryŋ   ɪz   hiːr/

All three variants comply with English syntax and morphology but only (1a) is "real English"; (1b) and (1c) sound heavily accented at best. The problems lie in the sound forms of the first word *spring*. In (1b), /ʃprɪŋ/ starts with a sequence of consonants – /ʃpr/ – that no English word can start with (in the standard dialect). In (1c) in turn, it is the occurrence of a single sound – the high front rounded vowel /y/ – that is anomalous.

(1b) and (1c) are examples of two kinds of phonological deviance. (1b) starts with three sound segments each of which is available in English – /ʃ/ as in <u>sh</u>ark, /p/ as in <u>p</u>lane, and /r/ as in <u>r</u>ig – but they cannot be combined word-initially. (1c) illustrates a more drastic departure from English: it includes a sound – the high front rounded vowel /y/ – that is not available in the language at all: in English, high front vowels are pronounced without lip-rounding.

Languages greatly differ both in which sounds are allowed to co-occur with each other and also in what sounds are individually available to begin with: what is phonologically ill-formed in one language may be the rule in another. English does not combine the palatal fricative /ʃ/ with /p/ and /r/ word-initially in any order but German does; for example in *Sprache* /ʃpraχə/ 'language.' And while English high front vowels must be unrounded, German has both the unrounded and the rounded varieties, as in *biegen* /biːgən/ 'to bend' and *Bücher* /byːçər/ 'books.'

These two kinds of crosslinguistic differences – the availability of constituents and their proper choice in a given context – are familiar from both syntax and morphology. Recall that the verb of existence – 'be' – may occur in two languages but its distribution may be different: to say 'I am a student,' English and Serbo-Croatian use this word but Russian and Arabic do not (cf. Chapter 3, Section 3.1). Another such example from syntax is the use of resumptive pronouns in relative clauses: pronouns are available in all languages but not all languages use them resumptively in relative clauses (cf. Chapter 3, Section 3.2.1.1). Similarly, case affixes may be available but it depends on the language which nouns and pronouns they are used with. The crosslinguistically varying use of the segment /ʃ/ in word-initial consonant clusters is an analogous example from phonology: languages make different choices from among their inventories of elements for use in a given context.

The other kind of constraint is more basic: a type of constituent may not be available at all in a language. As discussed in the syntax chapter (Section 3.1), indefinite articles and classifiers are not part of the inventory of syntactic constituent types in all languages; and similarly, inflectional affixes are not in the morphological inventory of some languages (Section 4.1). These examples are paralleled by the front high rounded vowel, whose very availability also varies with the language.

In syntax and morphology, we witnessed a further twist in choosing the right constituents: they have to take on a form appropriate to a given context. Words have to carry the inflection required by agreement and government and morphemes have to appear in their proper allomorphic form as dictated by the environment. For example, German adjectives must have gender and number forms as controlled by their nouns (see Chapter 3, Section 3.2.2.1); and the Turkish plural morpheme *l*-VOWEL-*r* has to have the right allomorph containing either /a/ or /e/ depending on the vowels of the stem (cf. Chapter 4, Section 4.1).

The same holds in phonology: just as words and morphemes, sounds, too, are chameleon-like: they have different variants and the choice among them depends on the context. For an example, consider two pronunciations of the English word *peer* in (2).

(2)   (a)   [pʰir]
      (b)   *[pir]

In both forms, the voiceless bilabial plosive occurs word-initially; yet, only (2a) is well-formed. This sound has two varieties in English: aspirated and unaspirated. When it occurs syllable-initially directly followed by a stressed vowel, it is aspirated: the correct allophone is [pʰ] (as in *peer* and *appeal*). Otherwise – as in *preen*, *pecan*, *spear*, and *hop* – it appears in its unaspirated form. The same holds for the aspirated and unaspirated versions of /t/, /k/, and /č/; compare *tin* [tʰɪn] and *train* [treyn]; *kin* [kʰɪn] and *crane* [kreyn], and the two /č/-s of *church*: [čʰərč]. It is this distributional pattern of the allophones of the English voiceless plosives and affricates that is violated in (2b).

However, this pattern is not universal. In Thai, Hindi, and Burmese, for instance, the two kinds of plosives are separate phonemes rather than allophones of the same phone: either can occur word-initially resulting in different word meanings. In Burmese, the distinction has morphemic status all by itself in that for some verbs, it makes the difference between transitivity and intransitivity.

(3) (a) /taa/   'eye'   Thai
     (b) /tʰaa/   'to daub'

(4) (a) /pal/   'want'   Hindi
     (b) /pʰal/   'fruit'

(5) (a) /pjè/   'to lessen'   (intransitive verb)   Burmese
     (b) /pʰjè/   'to lessen'   (transitive verb)

In addition to what is available in a language, which of the available items are chosen in a particular context and in what form, in syntax and morphology we identified one more condition of well-formedness: the correct temporal arrangement of constituents. Once again, there is a parallel requirement in phonology. In English, a word-initial consonant cluster may include /s/ and /p/, but not in either order: there are words that start with /sp/, such as **sp**ot or **sp**oof, but none that start with /ps/. Note that if a word is spelled with initial *ps*, e.g. *psychology*, it is pronounced without the /p/. In German, the ordering options of /p/ and /s/ are the opposite: /ps/ is allowed – the beginning of the word *Psychologie* is pronounced as /ps/ – but word-initial /sp/ does not occur.

So far we have seen that the phonological systems of languages show differences in all four basic parameters parallels of which were identified in syntax and in morphology: what sounds languages have available, which sounds can co-occur in a particular construction, what are their variant forms, and how they are ordered. Our concern is whether these crosslinguistic differences are unbounded or there are limits to them.

In their textbook *Understanding phonology*, authors Carlos Gussenhoven and Haike Jacobs invite the reader to imagine what it would be like for languages to vary in their phonologies without any limits (1998: 19–21). This would mean that any sound produceable by the human articulatory mechanism could occur in any language, and any sound could be freely chosen to pair up with any other sound in any of their variant forms and in any order. For example, click sounds could be part of the segmental inventory of all languages; and all 24 possible permutations of sounds like /k/, /f/, /p/, and /i/ – such as /kfli/, /iklf/, etc. – could form entire words without any context-induced adjustment.

The actual state of affairs could not be any farther from this imaginary situation: languages do not enjoy this kind of unbridled freedom. In what follows, we will explore some of the crosslinguistic resemblances in sound patterns: what sound segments can occur in a language, what sounds can co-occur, what are contextual variants of sounds, and what are constraints on their linear order. Here are the schemata of the generalizations that we are seeking. "Sound pattern" refers to the occurrence of an individual sound segment, or the co-occurrence of sound segments, or the context-induced variation of segments, or the order of segments.

1.   EXISTENTIAL GENERALIZATIONS
      Sound pattern SP is a possible pattern: it is attested in at least one language.

2. UNIVERSAL GENERALIZATIONS
   A. CONDITIONAL (IMPLICATIONAL) STATEMENTS
      If condition C holds, sound pattern SP occurs either universally or with such-and-such frequency across languages.
   B. UNCONDITIONAL (UNRESTRICTED) STATEMENTS
      Under any condition, sound pattern SP occurs either universally or with such-and-such frequency across languages.

Section 5.2.1 is about the choice of sounds; 5.2.2 takes up the choice of variants of sounds; Section 5.3 discusses the sequencing of sounds; and Section 5.4 turns to the issue of the basic phonological categories that are instrumental in stating crosslinguistic generalizations. Section 5.5 will probe into visual forms of language.

5.2 The choice of sounds and sound forms

5.2.1 Which sounds?

Given the inventory of speech sounds in a language, what are the principles that determine how they may co-occur? Two of the domains where selectional patterns of sound segments are evident are the word and the syllable. We will consider each in turn.

(A) THE CHOICE OF SOUNDS WITHIN WORDS

The most general word-level constraint on the choice of sounds follows from the very definition of word: words must be pronounceable. Since sequences containing only pure consonants, such as [kptčsm] or [rʃtlks], cannot be pronounced, all words must include at least one vowel or vowel-like (vocalic, syllabic) sound segment.

> GEN-1: In all languages, all words must include at least one vocalic segment.

Other principles limiting the choice of sounds highlight the tendency for co-occurring sounds to be of the same ilk. In some cases, all consonants within a word have to be of the same kind; in other cases, all vowels have to be similar. Word-domain **consonant harmony** is rare among the languages of the world (but it is more common in child language; cf. Levelt 2011). One of the few examples is the American Indian language Chumash, which has sibilant harmony: sibilants occurring in a stem are either all produced at the alveolar ridge or all produced at the palate. Here are some examples (Mithun 1999: 28–29):

(6) (a) words with alveolar sibilants: Chumash
        /sqoyis/   'kelp'

        /swoʔs/   'feather ornament'
    (b) words with palatal sibilants:
        /šošo/   'flying squirrel'
        /čʰumaš/   'Santa Cruz islander'

This means that Chumash could not have a word like *slash*, which has both an alveolar and a palatal sibilant; it would have to be either *slas* or *shlash*. Although sibilant harmony is very rare across languages, the difficulty of pronouncing alveolar and palatal sibilants in quick succession is reflected in tongue-twisters of different languages. Here are examples from English and Hungarian. In English, *s* stands for an alveolar sibilant ([s] or [z]) while *sh* stands for a palatal. In the Hungarian transcription, [s] is an alveolar sibilant, [ʃ] and [č] are palatals, ([c] is also palatal but a plosive rather than a sibilant).

(7) (a) *I ṣaw S̲u̲ṣie ṣitting in a ṣhoe ṣhine ṣhop.*   English
          Where ṣhe ṣits ṣhe ṣhineṣ, and where ṣhe ṣhineṣ ṣhe ṣitṣ.
     (b) *Mit   s̲ütsz,   kiṣ   szücs? S̲ós   húṣt ṣütsz, kiṣ szücs?* Hungarian
          /mit   ʃyc   kiʃ   s̲y̲č   ʃoːʃ   huʃt ʃyc   kiʃ s̲y̲č/
          'What are you roasting, little fur-maker? Are you roasting salty meat, little fur-maker?'

Another indication of languages' reluctance to combine alveolar and palatal sibilants is that in a sample of 104 languages, Joseph Greenberg found none with a word-final [ʃs] cluster (1978b: 257).

In contrast to the sparseness of consonant harmony across languages, harmony constraints on vowels are widely documented cropping up in different parts of the world albeit taking different forms. In languages with vowel harmony, only vowels that share certain phonetic features may occur within a word.

An example is Turkish. As was discussed in the morphology chapter (Chapter 4, Section 4.1), some suffixes of this language have allomorphs that differ in whether the vowel is front or back, with the choice depending on the last vowel of the stem: if it is front, the suffix takes the front-vowel form, if it is back, the suffix will have the back vowel. Here are examples of the plural suffix.

(8) *çocuk-lar*   'children'   Turkish
     köpek-ler   'dogs'

The preference for not mixing front and back vowels holds not only across morpheme boundaries: it is the prevalent pattern even in monomorphemic words. Notice that in (8), the root *çocuk* 'child' contains vowels that are both back and in *köpek* 'dog,' both are front. Here are some more examples to show root-internal vowel harmony in Turkish.

(9) *köyüm*   'village'   Turkish
     resim   'photo'
     doğru   'straight'
     lokanta 'restaurant'

Nonetheless, the rule has exceptions. Loan words are a prime example: they often have mixed vowels; e.g. *otobüs* 'bus' (from French?), or *insan* 'person' (from Arabic?). Another common type of exception to vowel harmony rules is compounds. In Hungarian, which is another vowel-harmony language, the components of compound words keep their vowels; e.g. *baba-cipö* 'baby-shoe,' *cseresznye-fa* 'cherry-tree.' On the assumption that vowel harmony's domain is the word, compounds are an exception; alternatively, we may define the concept of word for purposes of vowel harmony in a special way so that compounds count as multiple words.

Other languages related to Turkish are also known to have vowel harmony based on the front–back distinction (labeled in the literature as palatal harmony) and beyond the Turkic group, Finno-Ugric languages such as Hungarian and Finnish, and some Caucasian ones (e.g. Hinalug) also follow the same pattern. However, Maddieson (2011: 543) has found that front–back (palatal) harmony is much less common around the world than other varieties such as one based on vowel-height occurring in some African languages, in Itelmen (Chukotko-Kamchatkan), and in the American Indian language Nez Perce.

Nez Perce has five vowels: /i/, /e/, /a/, /o/, and /u/ (Mithun 1999: 26–27). From the point of view of their word-internal co-occurrence possibilities, the vowels fall into two groups defined roughly by height. There is a "dominant" series consisting of /a/ and /o/, and a "recessive" one containing /e/ and /u/. The vowel /i/ straddles the line: it is a member of both sets. Within a word, all vowels are either of the dominant or of the recessive series. If a dominant vowel occurs anywhere in the word, the rest of the vowels need to be of the dominant kind as well. Thus, consider the root *wé.yik* 'go across,' which contains the recessive vowel /e/. In (10a), the suffix *-sene* is added, which also has a recessive vowel structure; but in (10b), the suffix is *-saqa* containing dominant /a/. As a result, the first root vowel also has to be /a/ (/i/ is no problem since it is consistent with dominance).

(10) (a) *wé.yik-sene*   '(I) went across long ago.'   Nez Perce

    (b) *wá.yik-saqa*   '(I) went across recently.'

In addition to exemplifying the relatively common pattern of vowel-height harmony, Nez Perce also serves to document an unusual aspect of vowel harmony. Crosslinguistically, in the case of inflected words, it is generally the stem vowels that call the shots: the affix vowels need to conform. However, as seen in (10), in Nez Perce (as well as in some other languages, such as Warlpiri), the affix may control harmony in the root (Maddieson 2011: 543–544).

From the point of view of how vowels are classified for harmony, we have seen two scenarios thus far: front versus back, and higher versus lower. A third feature by which vowels can be harmonized in languages is lip rounding, but this is a crosslinguistically much less frequent scenario (van der Hulst and van de Weijer 1995: 523). For an example, consider the shapes of the suffix 'on' in Hungarian.

(11) (a) *kalap-on*   'on hat'   Hungarian
    (b) *keret-en*   'on frame'
    (c) *füv-ön*   'on grass'

(11a) and (11b) show palatal harmony: in (11a), the stem has back vowels calling for the suffix vowel /o/ and in (11b), the suffix has the front vowel /e/ in accordance with front vowels of the stem. But note (11c): just as in (11b), the root has a front vowel /ü/, but the suffix vowel is /ö/, rather than /e/. The reason is that while in (11b), the stem's front vowel /e/ is unrounded, in (11c), /ö/ is rounded and the vowel of the suffix is sensitive to this difference in lip shape. Hungarian labial harmony, however, does not apply within roots; e.g. *öreg* 'old,' *üres* 'empty': thus, it is a morphologically-conditioned rather than purely phonological phenomenon.

In sum, the following statistical statements may be stated regarding the word-internal choice of phonological segments:

> GEN-2: Vowel harmony is more frequent across languages than consonant harmony.
>
> GEN-3: Vowel-height harmony is more frequent across languages than palatal harmony.
>
> GEN-4: Most languages that have labial harmony also have another kind.

The co-occurrence of sounds within words is further constrained by the structure of subparts of words known as syllables – a pattern that we will turn to next.

(B) THE CHOICE OF SOUNDS WITHIN SYLLABLES

Just as words, syllables are also defined as pronounceable portions of speech. Since a syllable containing only pure consonants is not pronounceable, we would expect that all syllables in all languages include a vowel. However, this is not so: in some languages – including English – there are syllables that do not contain vowels; in their place, vowel-like – syllabic – consonants occur. Here are some examples (Maddieson 2011: 546). Consonants with dots underneath are syllabic.

(12) (a) *bitten*   /bɪtn̩/   English

           little   /lɪtl̩/

      (b) /sedm̩/   'seven'   Czech

           /vl̩k/   'wolf'

           /kr̩k/   'neck'

The syllabic consonants of these examples are of the typical kind: liquids and nasals. However, these are not the only attested syllabic consonants. In Imdlawn Tashlhiyt Berber, there are syllables and even words with a complete absence of any audible vowel or even a liquid or a nasal (transcription simplified).

(13) /ḳkst   tšštt/   Imdlawn Tashlhiyt Berber
      remove.it eat.it
      'remove it (and) eat it'

In this language, any consonant, including plosives and fricatives, can serve as a syllabic nucleus (Dell and Elmedlaoui 2002: 73).

Plosives and fricatives do not commonly form syllabic centers. In a survey of 85 languages, Alan Bell (1978) found strong crosslinguistic preferences for syllabicity among the various types of consonants. Here are some of these paradigmatic generalizations.

> GEN-5: (a) The occurrence of syllabic liquids in a language almost always implies that of syllabic nasals.
>
> (b) The occurrence of syllabic stops in a language always implies the occurrence of syllabic fricatives.
>
> (c) The occurrence of syllabic voiceless stops in a language always implies the occurrence of syllabic voiced stops.

In other words, syllabic nasals are preferred over syllabic liquids; syllabic fricatives over syllabic stops; and voiced stops over voiceless ones.

Given that every syllable must be pronounceable, we would expect that the simplest imaginable syllable type that fulfils the pronounceability requirement – a single vowel – would be universal across languages. However, V is not a universal syllable type: the only near-universal syllable structure includes a consonant as well. The interesting fact is that the order of these two segments matters: VC is not present in all languages but CV is nearly universal. The preferential ordering of C and V will be discussed in Section 5.3.

An additional pattern of contextually-determined sound selection will be given in the next section under the label of neutralization.

5.2.2 Which forms of sounds?

Here is a set of words from Spanish (simplified from Luraghi, Thornton and Voghera 2003: 42). How are the alveolar voiced stop [d] and the interdental voiced fricative [ð] distributed? The left column shows orthography; forms in square brackets are the pronunciations.

(14) (a) *dedo*   [deðo]   'finger'   Spanish
     (b) *Madrid*   [maðrið]   'Madrid'
     (c) *andar*   [andar]   'to go'
     (d) *padre*   [paðre]   'father'
     (e) *dos*   [dos]   'two'
     (f) *alcalde*   [alkalde]   'mayor'
     (g) *sed*   [seð]   'thirst'
     (h) *aduana*   [aðwana]   'customs'

The two sounds are in complementary distribution: each occurs in a context where the other does not. In particular, [ð] appears only right after a vowel; [d] in turn never shows up postvocalically: it occurs in other contexts, such as following a consonant or in the beginning of the word. Since both [d] and [ð] are voiced obstruents formed roughly in the same area of the mouth, we can take them to be the very same sound in two different "guises": their small phonetic difference is attributable to the context where each occurs. Given that the mouth is relatively open when forming a vowel, it makes sense that a sound immediately following a vowel would be pronounced with only a partial closure – i.e., as the fricative version [ð] of the dental-alveolar obstruent rather than the stop version [d]. [d] and [ð] are thus analyzed as variants of the same sound with their difference attributable to their environment. They are **allophones** of the same phoneme.

This example of allophonic variation illustrates a very common type of contextual modification: a sound becomes somewhat like a neighboring one. This pattern is labeled **assimilation**.

In the Spanish example, it is the **manner of articulation** of the dental-alveolar obstruent that is at issue. Assimilation may also affect various other properties of sounds, such as voicing, place of articulation, and oral versus nasal articulation.

The example given in the first section of this chapter (5.1) is of **voice assimilation**. As we saw, English word-initial pre-tonic voiceless stops and affricates are aspirated (as in *put* [pʰUt]). Although it may not look like it, this is actually an instance of assimilation: the voicelessness of the plosive preceding the vowel spreads to the beginning of the following vowel. The delayed voice onset time – the late start of the vibration of the vocal cords – results in the devoicing of the initial portion of the vowel, which is perceived as a puff of air and heard as the aspiration of the voiceless stop. Since aspirated and unaspirated voiceless stops and affricates occur under distinct conditions – they are in complementary distribution – the aspirated-unaspirated pairs, such as [p] and [pʰ], and [č] and [čʰ], etc., may be analyzed as contextually altered variants of the same sound, or allophones of the same phoneme.

This example shows how the voice status of a vowel may be affected by a neighboring consonant. The opposite also occurs: the voice status of a consonant may depend on the presence or absence of vowels in its neighborhood. In several languages, all stops and fricatives are voiced between vowels. Korean is an example. (15a) illustrates lax stops and affricates occurring word-initially as voiceless. In (15b), these sounds are in intervocalic position and they are voiced. The voiceless and voiced varieties are in complementary distribution everywhere in the language: they are allophones of the same phoneme.

> Intervocalic voicing is somewhat similar to what we saw for Spanish above ((14)), where the phonetic form of a consonant was similarly affected by the presence of an adjacent vowel. Both are instances of assimilation. But whereas in the Spanish example it is the manner of articulation of the consonant that varies, in Korean, the voicing of the consonant does.

(15) (a) voiceless obstruent   (b) voiced obstruent: Korean

[pɛ]	'pear'		[cibɛ]	'domination'
[pan]	'half'		[kiban]	'base'
[ton]	'money'		[sadon]	'in-law(s)'
[kɛ]	'crab'		[cogɛ]	'shellfish'
[ča]	'measuring ruler'		[iǰa]	'interest (financial)'
[čoŋ]	'bell'		[keǰoŋ]	'conversion'

Thirdly, in addition to assimilation in manner of articulation and in voice, context may affect the place where a sound is articulated in the mouth. (16) is an example of assimilation in **place of articulation**: in Korean, the voiceless sibilant is alveolar ([s]) in all contexts except immediately preceding /i/, where it takes on the palatality of the following vowel result-ing in [š].

(16) alveolar [s]:   palatal [š]:   Korean

[say]	'bird'	[ši]	'poem'
[sul]	'alcohol'	[šil]	'thread'
[sucun]	'level'	[šido]	'trial'
[somang]	'hope'	[šiksa]	'supper'
[sesang]	'world'	[šin]	'new'
[seron]	'introduction'	[šinggepta]	'to be unsalted'

In Korean, a neighboring vowel affects the place of articulation of a consonant. In the Spanish example below, it is an adjacent consonant that influences the place of articulation of a consonant. Note the distribution of the four nasals: bilabial /m/, alveolar /n/, palatal /ɲ/, and velar /ŋ/.

(17) *tambor*   /ta<u>mb</u>or/   'drum'   Spanish

      puente   /pue<u>nt</u>e/   'bridge'

      enfermo   /e<u>mf</u>ermo/   'sick'

      rancho   /ra<u>nč</u>o/   'ranch'

      mangas   /ma<u>ŋg</u>as/   'sleeves'

As these examples show, the nasal and the following obstruent agree in their place of articulation: both are bilabial, or both are alveolar, or both are palatal, or both are velar. Using standard terminology, the nasals are **homorganic** with the following obstruents.

This particular pattern, illustrated in (17) with Spanish with word-internal clusters, is crosslinguistically widespread. In his study of nasal-obstruent clusters in word-final positions, Greenberg found the following (1978b: 253):

> GEN-6: "In final systems, the existence of at least one sequence consisting of a nasal (voiced or unvoiced) followed by a het-erorganic obstruent implies the existence of at least one sequence consisting of a nasal (voiced or unvoiced) fol-lowed by a homorganic obstruent."

Of the 61 languages that Greenberg based this observation on, 33 have both homorganic and heterorganic nasals before obstruents, 20 have only homor-ganic ones, and 8 had neither kind. The fourth possibility – languages with only heterorganic nasal-obstruent sequences – is not attested in his sample.

One of the 33 languages that Greenberg lists as having both types of clusters is English. The examples in (18) show homorganic word-final nasal-stop clusters.

(18) *li<u>mp</u>*   English

      sla<u>nt</u>

      ki<u>nd</u>

      tank   /tæ<u>ŋk</u>/

While the English homorganicity pattern holds in monomorphemic words, such as those in (18), it does not hold across morpheme boundaries. For example, in *screamed* /skri:mt/, the morpheme-final /m/ is bilabial even though the suffix is an alveolar stop; and in *hanged* /hæŋd/, the morpheme-final /ŋ/ is velar preceding the alveolar suffix. Thus, English has both homorganic and heterorganic nasal-obstruent clusters word-finally.

A language listed by Greenberg – one among 20 – as having only homorganic nasal-obstruent clusters at the ends of words is Hindi. Here are a few examples (cf. M. Ohala 1975: 318).

(19) [čand]   'moon'   Hindi
      [mənč]   'platform'
      [siŋg]   'horn'

Greenberg's statement above pertains to word-final nasal-obstruent clusters. He also studied such clusters in word-initial position and concluded as follows (1978b: 253).

> GEN-7: "A similar statement for initial systems holds in almost all cases, but a number of Slavic languages (e.g. Russian, Polish, Czech) are conspicuous exceptions in that they contain initial heterorganic combinations such as /mg/ without having homorganic sequences."

A Russian example of the initial heterorganic cluster /mg/ is /mgla/ 'fog.'

John Ohala offers an explanation for the crosslinguistically predominant homorganicity of nasal-obstruent clusters. He suggests that nasal consonants that differ only in place of articulation – [m], [n], [ɲ], and [ŋ] – are acoustically very similar and the resulting auditory ambiguity makes them subject to articulatory re-interpretation under the influence of the adjacent obstruent (J. Ohala 1975: 196).

The conformity of nasals to following obstruents has much in common with the patterns that we saw above: fricativization in Spanish, aspiration in English, intervocalic voicing and palatalization in Korean. In all five instances a sound is assimilated to a neighboring sound. However, there is also a difference. In Spanish fricativization, English aspiration, and Korean intervocalic voicing and palatalization, the alternative forms – plosive versus fricative forms of voiced obstruents in Spanish, aspirated and unaspirated voiceless stops in English, voiced and voiceless lax stops in Korean, and alveolar and palatal fricatives in Korean – occur in complementary distribution everywhere in the language. In other words, there is a perfect "division of labor": members of these pairs of sounds occur in different environments with no overlap at all. Given a context, only one member of the set can occur. It is for this reason that they may be viewed as being the very same sound in different "clothing": **allophones** of the same phoneme.

This is not so for the nasals in Spanish and English. They, too, exhibit complementary distribution but only under certain conditions: preceding obstruents (see (17) and (18). Otherwise, each nasal can occur in any environment. In English, for example, the three nasals /m/, /n/, and /ŋ/ all occur word-finally in *Tom*, *son*, and *song* /soŋ/; it is only preceding an obstruent that the nasals are willing to give up their own place of articulation in favor of that of the following sound. In Spanish, too, /m/ and /n/ are independent phonemes; cf. *mi* 'mine' and *ni* 'neither.' This kind of restricted complementary distribution is labeled **neutralization**: the difference between the bilabial, alveolar, (palatal in Spanish) and velar nasal phonemes is said to be neutralized, or suspended, in front of an obstruent: preceding an obstruent, only one of the nasals – the homorganic one – can occur. Thus, what is involved is not a choice between alternative forms of a single phoneme but a choice between different phonemes, such as in the cases discussed in Section 5.2.1.

The difference between allophony and neutralization can be clearly seen if we compare the Korean data in (16) with the Japanese data in (20a) and (20b).

(20) (a) alveolar [s]:   palatal [š]:   Japanese

[kasu]	'lend'	[šinu]	'die'
[isogu]	'hurry'	[muši]	'insect'
[arimasu]	'is'	[booši]	'hat'
[isu]	'chair'	[hikidaši]	'drawer'
[sara]	'saucer'	[omoširoi]	'interesting'
[sensei]	'teacher'	[širu]	'juice'

At first blush, the two patterns seem to be the same: palatal sibilant preceding /i/ and alveolar sibilant elsewhere. But here is additional data from Japanese.

(20) (b) alveolar [s]:   palatal [š]:   Japanese

[sakai]	'boundary'	[šakai]	'society'
[soːkai]	'general meeting'	[šoːkai]	'introduction'
[suːkai]	'several times'	[šuːkai]	'assembly'

As seen in (20b), the palatal fricative is not restricted to occurrence before /i/: it occurs in front of other vowels as well. The constraint has to do only with the alveolar sibilants: they cannot precede /i/. That is to say, the difference between alveolar and palatal place of articulation is neutralized before /i/ in favor of palatality. In Korean in turn, there are no such minimal pairs: the occurrence of [s] versus [š] is contextually conditioned throughout the language: they are allophones.

Another crosslinguistically common neutralization pattern has to do with the voice status of word-final (and more generally, syllable-final) obstruents. Consider German alveolar stops, of which German has both the voiced and the voiceless variety: /d/ and /t/. They are separate phonemes of full rights: each can occur in most environments. (21) shows that they both occur word-initially and word-medially.

(21) *die*   'the'   German
      Tier   'animal'
      Bünde   'societies'
      bunte   'colored'

However, word-final position is a different story: /t/ occurs but /d/ does not. Thus, the singular form of *Bünde* 'societies,' spelled *Bund*, is pronounced as /bunt/. This neutralization pattern, referred to in the literature as **terminal devoicing**, also holds for the other German obstruents and it is a pervasive pattern in Slavic languages as well as in languages as genetically different as Catalan, Turkish, and Thai. Word-final terminal devoicing may perhaps be viewed as an instance of regressive assimilation: the obstruent takes on the voicelessness of the pause that follows the word when it is pronounced in isolation.

Allophony and neutralization are diagrammed below. The squares enclose the sets of all phonological environments in the language; the rectangles are different environments. On the left, [t] and [d] are allophones: they occur in mutually exclusive environments (e.g. [t] before consonants and [d] before vowels). On the right, /t/ and /d/ are neutralizing phonemes: normally, they can occur in any environment but in some contexts (e.g. syllable-finally in German) only /t/ occurs.

(22)

Allophones: Neutralizing phonemes:

t	*t
*d	d

t	t
d	*d

> The two patterns may be illustrated from outside language. An amphibious vehicle is like a phoneme with its two "allo-shapes" in complementary distribution: in water, it glides on its smooth underside but on land, it sprouts wheels. Motorbikes and bicycles in turn are like neutralizing phonemes: two distinct vehicles of which either may be used for city driving but for freeways, the choice is eliminated: the motorbike is the only option.

In addition to manner of articulation, voice, and place of articulation, a fourth phonetic property type that may spread from one sound to another is **orality versus nasality**. English exemplifies a very common subtype of this: the nasalization of vowels preceding a nasal consonant.

(23) *boot* [buːt]   *boom* [bûːm]   English
      bead [biːd]   *bean* [bîːn]
      bore [boːr]   *bong* [bõːŋ]

The nasalization of vowels next to, and especially before, nasals has been found to be a universal feature of languages (Ferguson 1975: 181).

In this section, we considered the ways in which sounds take on different shapes depending on their environment, whether as allophones of a phoneme or as separate phonemes in a neutralization pattern. In all of the examples considered, the influence of the context was assimilatory: the different shapes that sounds take on mimic adjacent sounds. As was seen above, assimilation may involve various types of sounds and various types of properties, and the spread may go "forward," from left to right (called progressive assimilation) or "backwards," from right to left (regressive assimilation). Here is the summary of eight of the examples sorted by the assimilation feature, by direction, and by the distribution pattern involved (allophonic or neutralizing).

PATTERN	FEATURE	DIRECTION	ALLOPHONIC OR NEUTRALIZING
English aspiration	voice	progressive	allophonic
Spanish fricativization	manner of articulation	progressive	allophonic
Korean palatalization	place of articulation	regressive	allophonic
Japanese palatalization	place of articulation	regressive	neutralization
Spanish and English homorganic nasals	place of articulation	regressive	neutralization
German terminal devoicing	voice	regressive	neutralization
English vowel nasalization	nasality	regressive	allophonic

In sum, here is a set of crosslinguistic generalizations to complement GEN-1 through GEN-7 stated above:

GEN-8: Assimilation may involve consonant–vowel pairs or consonant–consonant pairs.

GEN-9: In assimilation involving consonant–vowel pairs, the consonant may affect the vowel or the vowel may affect the consonant.

GEN-10: The features involved in assimilation include place of articulation, manner of articulation, voice, and nasality.

GEN-11: Assimilation may be progressive or regressive.

GEN-12: Vowel nasalization is predominantly regressive.

GEN-13: Nasal homorganicity is predominantly regressive.

GEN-14: The devoicing of obstruents at the edge of words or syllables is generally word-final or syllable-final. Word-initial or syllable-initial obstruent devoicing has not been observed in any language.

GEN-15: The conditions for allophonic assimilation and phonemic neutralization are of the same kinds.

5.3 The order of sounds

Speech happens in time. The linear progression of speech boils down to one thing: the sequencing of sounds, one pronounced after the other with co-articulation somewhat blurring the boundaries. But what determines the linear order of sounds? There are multiple answers to this question. For an example, take the English phrase in (24).

(24) *two sleepy cats*   English
      /tuːsliːpiːkæts/

A non-English speaker, coming to this phrase cold, might wonder why the /uː/ of /tuː/ precedes the /s/ of /sliːpiː/. Why not the opposite order: /sːuː/, as in *Sue*? The answer is a **syntactic** order rule, according to which given a numeral and an adjective, the numeral must precede the adjective. Since the /uː/ is the last sound of the numeral and /s/ is the first segment of the adjective, the /uː/ ends up preceding the /s/. The immediate precedence of the final /iː/ of /sliːpiː/ before the initial /k/ of /kæts/ is also the result of a syntactic rule. The reverse order, /kiː/, is possible in English, as in *key*; but a rule requires the adjective to precede its noun. These syntactic rules make no direct reference to sound segments: the phonemes receive their order indirectly through their carriers.

A second portion of this phrase that a non-English speaker may wonder about is why in /kæts/, the /s/ follows /t/, rather than /t/ following /s/ as in *list*. This order is dictated by a **morphological** rule that requires inflectional affixes to follow the stems. Since the /t/ is the last segment of the noun stem and the /s/ is a suffix, the morphological rule defines their order indirectly, with the rule making no reference to the phonological segments themselves. The order of the last two segments of /slipi/ – /p/ before /i/ – is also due to morphology: the final /i/ is a denominal adjectivalizer which is required to follow the stem and therefore all its phonological segments.

Thirdly, here is /kæt/ itself. Why are these three sounds ordered the way they are as opposed to any of the other five possible arrangements? All six are shown in (25).

(25) (a) /kæt/
      (b) /tæk/
      (c) /ækt/
      (d) /ktæ/
      (e) /ætk/
      (f) /tkæ/

(25a) is the correct order for 'cat.' (25b) and (25c) are not the right orders because they stand for other meanings: (25b) names a *tack* and (25c) names an *act*. It is the **lexicon** of English that requires the order of /k/ before /æ/ before /t/ in /kæt/.

This leaves (25d), (25e), and (25f). The ungrammaticality of these orders has nothing to do with syntax since the sequences are word-internal, nor with morphology since they are morpheme-internal; and there is no competing lexical item that would rule out these forms as inappropriate for 'cat.' But it is not a coincidence that there are no such lexical items: the sequences /ktæ/, /ætk/, and /tkæ/ are simply "unpronounceable," or, more precisely, they clash with normal English pronunciation habits. The problem is the sequence of the two consonants /t/ and /k/: /kt/ can occur at the end of a word (as in the word *act*) but not in the beginning; and /tk/ cannot occur either word-initially or word-finally. Thus, the reason is **phonological**. A similar case is the order of the /s/ and /l/ in /sliːpiː/ the opposite order – /lsiːpiː/ – would yield a phonologically impermissible word in English.

In sum: there are four different types of linearization constraints that yield the order of sounds in (24): syntactic, morphological, lexical, and phonological. The basic idea is that linear order may be imposed on phonetic segments either by rules that make direct reference to these segments or indirectly by ordering the larger wholes – morphemes, words, and phrases – that the sounds are parts of.

There are parallels for these options in domains outside language as well. Take music. Like language, music is also linear: sounds and chords are laid out in sequence and this temporal sequencing has diverse reasons. An example that is analogous to syntactic order is the order of two songs performed at a concert: all the notes of the first will precede all the notes of the second. Within a given song, the sequence of notes is in part due to the sequence of the lines of the song: all the notes of the first line will precede all the notes of the second. This is somewhat like morphological ordering. Thirdly, the notes of a musical motif – as in a Wagner opera – are sequenced in a particular way for "lexical reasons" – that is, to convey the special meaning that is assigned to that motif. And, fourthly, some musical genres have their own sequential constraints on notes and chords. In certain styles of twelve-tone music, once a note has sounded, it cannot occur again before all the other eleven notes of the scale have occurred. Violating this rule is unacceptable, just as /tk/ is unacceptable in the beginning of an English word.

(25d), (25e), and (25f) illustrate that English has phonological constraints on the linear ordering of sound segments. In Section 5.1, we saw that other languages also have such constraints and at least some of them are different from English (recall that word-initial *ps*-clusters are not possible in English but they are in German). Our question in this chapter is whether, in spite of such differences, there are also crosslinguistically recurrent order constraints on sounds. To explore this topic, we will first consider linearization patterns of consonants and vowels; secondly, the order of consonants in clusters; and finally, stress placement.

(A) CONSONANT–VOWEL ORDER IN SYLLABLES

As mentioned above (Section 5.2.1), syllables, by definition, have to be individually pronounceable. Since syllables that consist only of pure consonants cannot meet this requirement but syllables containing only a single vowel do, we might expect that syllables consisting of a single vowel are present in every language. Nonetheless, as also noted above, while such minimal syllables are frequent across languages, they are not universal. The only syllable structure that has been found in almost all languages consists of a vowel and a consonant. However, the linear order of these two elements is crucial: VC is not a universal syllable type but CV (almost) is. Thus, the English word *on* does not represent a universal syllable skeleton but the word *no* does.

Some languages have only CV syllables; one of them is Mba, a Niger-Congo language of the Democratic Republic of Congo (Maddieson 2005e: 54). In a sample of 484 languages, Maddieson documented a tendency for languages with simpler syllable structures – that is, syllables containing few consonants – to have fewer consonants in their segment inventory, while more complex syllables correlate somewhat with larger consonantal

There is only one mention in the literature of a language where there is some doubt as to the occurrence of CV syllables: Arrente, an Arandic language of Central Australia has been reported to have no syllable-initial consonants (Breen and Pensalfini 1999).

inventories (Maddieson 2005e: 55). While the correlation between consonantal inventory and complexity of consonant clusters would seem natural, it is by no means logically necessary. For example, one can imagine a
language that has only six consonants but has a very large number of complex clusters consisting of 3, 4, 5, and 6 consonants without allowing any
simple clusters.

English is very different from an only-CV-syllable-type language such as
Mba. In addition to having both the universal CV structure (as in *to*) and
the reverse VC (as in *an*), English has many other syllable types including
some with long sequences of consonants. The word *strengths* /strɛnkθs/
illustrates the longest English syllable: CCCVCCCC. The possibility of such
poly-consonantal sequences raises the question of whether the order of
the consonants within clusters is completely random in a language and if
not, whether there are any overarching crosslinguistic tendencies in this
regard. This is the topic we are turning to next.

(B) CONSONANT–CONSONANT ORDER IN SYLLABLES

The most extensive crosslinguistic study to date of the linear structure of
consonant clusters is Joseph H. Greenberg's (1978b). Based on a study of
104 languages, Greenberg proposed 40 crosslinguistic generalizations
about initial and final consonantal sequences. Drawing from his work and
from subsequent research, two regularities will be discussed below: the
Sonority Hierarchy, and Resolvability.

a. The Sonority Hierarchy

In Section 5.2.2, Greenberg's generalization was cited (GEN-6) according to
which in word-final position, clusters of a nasal and an obstruent tend to
be homorganic. Notice now that the clusters Greenberg talked about had
a specific order: nasal before obstruent. This was so because this is the
more common sequencing of these two sound types across languages: for
example, /nt/# preferred over /tn/#.

The preference for nasal & obstruent order over obstruent & nasal order
word-finally is part of a more general pattern of how consonants are
ordered within clusters. Here are some other regularities that Greenberg
noted (1978b): they are mosaic pieces that, as we will see, jointly form an
overarching picture. The statements below come in pairs, one pertaining
to (word- or syllable-) initial clusters and the other to final clusters: they
state preferences for mirror-image clusters in the two positions.

(26a) and 26(b) say that the preferred position of LIQUIDS relative to
OBSTRUENTS is liquids occurring on the inner side of obstruents; e.g. /#kl/
over /#lk/ in initial clusters and /lk#/ over /kl#/ for final ones.

(26) (a) "In initial systems, the existence of at least one sequence
            containing a liquid, whether voiced or unvoiced, immediately
            followed by an obstruent implies the existence of at least one
            sequence containing an obstruent immediately followed by a
            liquid." (257–258)

   (b)   "In final systems, the existence of at least one sequence containing /an obstruent/ immediately followed by a liquid implies the presence of at least one sequence containing a liquid followed by /an obstruent/." (258)

(27a) and (27b) are about LIQUID and NASAL order: once again, the preferred position for liquids is on the inner side, e.g. /#nl/ over /#ln/ and the reverse word-finally.

(27) (a) "In initial systems, the existence of at least one sequence consisting of a voiced liquid followed by a nasal implies the existence of at least one combination consisting of a nasal followed by a liquid." (261)

     (b) "In final systems, the existence of at least one sequence consisting of a nasal followed by a liquid… implies the existence of at least one sequence consisting of a liquid followed by a nasal." (262)

(28a) and (28b) state the preferred order of STOPS and FRICATIVES with the latter inside; e.g. /#pf/ over /#tp/ and /fp#/ over /tp#/.

(28) (a) "In initial systems, the presence of at least one combination of stop + stop implies the presence of at least one combination of stop + fricative." (254)

     (b) "In final systems, the presence of at least one combination of stop + stop implies the presence of at least one combination of fricative + stop." (254)

(29) states a preference for VOICED sounds to precede VOICELESS ones: e.g. /aps#/ but not /apz#/.

(29) "In final systems, except for unvoiced obstruents followed by a voiced nasal, an unvoiced consonant or sequence of unvoiced consonants following a vowel is not followed by one or more voiced consonants." (261)

Here is the roster of preferences pieced together from (26) through (29). Also, given that Greenberg cites many languages with final nasal & obstruent clusters, we can cautiously conclude that there is a preference for this order in final clusters.

Initial clusters:	Final clusters:
Obstruent & Liquid (e.g. #kl)	Liquid & Obstruent (e.g. lk#)
?	Nasal & Obstruent (e.g. nt#)
Nasal & Liquid (e.g. #nl)	Liquid & Nasal (e.g. ln#)
Stop & Fricative (e.g. #ks)	Fricative & Stop (e.g. sk#)
?	Voiced & Voiceless (e.g. nt#)

This yields an approximate picture of preferred syllable structure given in (30).

(30)

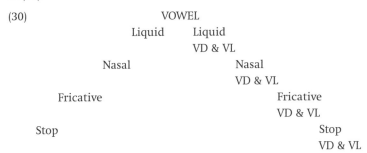

How can we make sense of these order preferences? It is worth considering the phonetic similarities and differences between vowels and the four consonant types: liquids, nasals, fricatives, and stops. First of all, since vowels are normally voiced, any consonant formed with vocal cord vibration is more vowel-like than those without it. Since nasals and liquids are normally voiced, they are more similar to vowels than obstruents that may be voiced or voiceless. Between nasals and liquids, liquids are more vowel-like: nasals involve an occlusion in the mouth (e.g. the closing of the lips for [m]) while for liquids, the air flow is uninterrupted, just as it is for vowels. And in the same way, fricatives are more like vowels than stops since fricatives do not involve complete occlusion. Thus, by and large, it seems that more vowel-like consonants are closer to the vocalic peak of the syllable than less vowel-like ones.

The observation that the increasing proximity of the various consonant types to the vowel of the syllable reflects their increasing degree of similarity to vowels is supported in part by what is known about consonants that can themselves serve as syllabic centers taking the place of vowels. As stated in Section 5.2.1 (GEN-5), nasals are more likely to be syllabic than liquids, liquids are more likely to be syllabic than fricatives, and fricatives tend to be syllabic more than stops. Since it makes sense to hypothesize that this ranking has to do with how similar these sound types are to vowels, it supports the idea that the intra-syllabic ordering of liquids, nasals, and obstruents has to do with how vocalic these segments are. The only discrepancy between Bell's syllabicity hierarchy (GEN-5) and the syllable structure hierarchy in (30) is that while nasals are more likely to be syllabic than liquids, liquids tend to be closer to the vowel peak of the syllable than nasals.

Subsequent research following in the steps of Greenberg's ground-breaking work has borne out this picture. The set of regularities depicted in (30) is known as the **Sonority Hierarchy**. Sonority is definable as the perceptual salience of sounds, or a sound's "loudness relative to other sounds produced with the same input energy, such as length, stress, pitch, velocity of airflow, muscular tension etc." (Blevins 1995: 207, 211). Thus, vowels are the most sonorous, followed by liquids, nasals, and fricatives, with stops having the least sonority. Here is the principle by first approximation:

GEN-16: First version
> Between any member of a syllable and the syllable peak,
> sonority must rise.

Nonetheless, it does not take a thorough search to find exceptions to the Sonority Hierarchy. First, notice that, in stating the homorganicity tendency for obstruents and nasals, Greenberg talks about initial nasal & obstruent clusters; e.g. Russian /mgla/ 'fog' (see Section 5.2.2 above). If this word were to comply with the Sonority Hierarchy, it would have to be /gmla/ with the stop preceding rather than following the nasal. Some Russian initial clusters are in conformity, e.g. /gnev/ 'anger,' but not all of them are. Thus, Russian initial clusters of nasal & stop violate the hierarchy.

Exceptions to the Sonority Hierarchy can also be found closer to home. Consider the word-initial three- and two-consonant clusters of English that contain /s/ (those including the glides /j/ and /w/ are omitted here).

(31) (a) /sp-/   (e.g. *spit*)   English
           /st-/   (e.g. *stand*)
           /sk-/   (e.g. *skew*)
           /sf-/   (e.g. *sphere*)
           /sv-/   (e.g. *svelte*)
           /sm-/   (e.g. *smile*)
           /sn-/   (e.g. *snare*)
           /sl-/   (e.g. *slick*)
      (b) /spl-/   (e.g. *spleen*)
           /spr-/   (e.g. *sprain*)
           /str-/   (e.g. *street*)
           /skr/   (e.g. *screen*)

Some of these clusters do comply with the Sonority Hierarchy but others do not. Starting with the bi-consonantal clusters in (31a), we see that /sv-/ reflects the voiceless-before-voiced portion of the hierarchy, /sm-/, /sn-/ illustrate the fricative-before-nasal segment, and /sl-/ has fricative-before-liquid. But other clusters are problematic: /sp-/, /st-/, /sk-/. If sonority were at work, they would have to be /ps-/, /ts-/, and /ks-/ instead, with the stop preceding the fricative – clusters that are alien to English phonotactics.

Let us now inspect the sequences in (31b). These three-consonants clusters are in compliance as far as the sequencing of their second and third segments is concerned: stop before liquid. However, the initial /s/ preceding the stop goes against the hierarchy, which would require /psl-/, /psr-/, /tsr-/, and /ksr-/ instead, but these do not occur in English at all.

There is one biconsonantal cluster in English that we have not yet evaluated from the point of view of the hierarchy: /sf-/ having a voiceless fricative followed by another voiceless fricative. It would be in violation if the requirement were for sonority to steadily increase towards the vowel peak. This does not hold for /sf-/ since both consonants are fricatives; but at least it does not show a decrease in sonority. In view of this and other such clusters in other languages, the following more relaxed version of the Sonority Hierarchy has been proposed, which condones clusters like /sf-/ (Blevins 1995: 210):

GEN-16: Second version

"Between any member of a syllable and the syllable peak, a sonority rise **or plateau** must occur."

While this version accommodates fricative–fricative sequences, there is still the problem of the initial nasal & obstruent clusters of Russian mentioned above and of the initial fricative & nasal and fricative & liquid sequences of English also noted. Additional problems are supplied by Georgian, a language of the Caucasus that is famous for its deviant consonant clusters.

Georgian has clusters up to six consonants long – among the longest ever attested in a language. Here are two examples (Butskhrikidze 2010: 24). /x/ is a voiceless velar fricative; /c/ is a palatal-alveolar stop; the period separates syllables.

(32) (a) **msxvre**.va   'to brake'   Georgian
      (b) **prckvn**a   'to peel'

In (32a), the /sxvr/ sub-portion of the cluster is in accordance with the Sonority Hierarchy but the initial nasal is not: Sonority would require it to come between the /v/ and the /r/. In (32b), the problem is the /rc/ portion: a liquid followed by a stop rather than in reverse. In search for an explanation of these unusual clusters, Butskhrikidze (2010) traces the historical path that led to them and appeals, among others, to vowel deletion between consonants; but the unusual synchronic facts remain as they are.

In sum, Blevins' statement cited above must be softened into a tendency.

GEN-16: Final version

Generally, between any member of a syllable and the syllable peak, a sonority rise or plateau occurs.

Note that all the phonological patterns that we have seen involving the choice of sounds, the choice of forms of sounds, and the sequencing of sounds are, on the final analysis, instances of assimilation: neighboring sounds tending to share phonetic characteristics. It should be noted, however, that dissimilatory patterns are also evidenced although they are less common across languages. Consider the Latin derivational affix that forms adjectives out of nouns. While in general, the form is *-alis*, as in *nav-alis* 'naval,' or *crimin-alis* 'criminal,' if the last syllable of the stem includes an /l/, the allomorph *-aris* shows up; e.g. *milit-aris* 'military,' *sol-aris* 'solar.' This is best interpreted as the liquid of the suffix dissimilating from the liquid of the stem-final syllable.

b. Resolvability

The Sonority Hierarchy is primarily a **syntagmatic** constraint: it holds over consonants co-occurring in the same cluster. There is also a **paradigmatic** regularity that holds for consonant clusters: it makes predictions from the occurrence of one consonant cluster type to the occurrence of another in the same language. Consider again the set of English initial clusters cited in (31) above.

(31) (repeated) English
    (a) /sp-/   (e.g. *spit*)
          /st-/   (e.g. *stand*)
          /sk-/   (e.g. *skew*)
          /sf-/   (e.g. *sphere*)
          /sv-/   (e.g. *svelte*)
          /sm-/   (e.g. *smile*)
          /sn-/   (e.g. *snare*)
          /sl-/   (e.g. *slick*)
    (b) /spl-/ (e.g. *spleen*)
          /spr-/ (e.g. *sprain*)
          /str-/ (e.g. *street*)
          /skr/   (e.g. *screen*)

Notice that there is a close relationship between the shorter and the longer clusters: it is as if the longer ones were constructed out of the shorter ones. The tri-consonantal clusters can be analyzed into these parts:

(33) /spl/:   /sp/   and   /pl/
      /spr/: /sp/   and   /pr/
      /str/:   /st/   and   /tr/
      /skr/: /sk/   and   /kr/

Each of these binary sequences occurs as an initial cluster all by itself: /sp/ as in *spit*, /st/ as in *stand*, /sk/ as in *scheme*, /pl-/ as in *plane*, /pr-/ as in *pride*, /tr-/ as in *try*, and /kr-/ as in *cry*.

Greenberg has found this regularity to hold for almost all of his 104-language sample. The exceptions involve a few larger clusters in some languages which do not fully resolve into smaller ones; but he found no language where all longer clusters were unresolvable. To accommodate the exceptions, he proposed the following **Principle of Partial Resolvability** (Greenberg 1978b: 250):

> GEN-17:
> "Every initial or final sequence of length m contains at least one continuous subsequence of length m − 1."

He also added that in all of the languages in his sample, the number of completely resolvable clusters was always larger than those that were not completely resolvable.

The explanation Greenberg suggests for resolvability is that initial and final clusters are often bimorphemic in origin: a consonantal prefix or suffix is added to a root which can also form a word by itself.

So far we have considered two patterns in the linear relations between sounds in words and syllables: the order of consonants and vowels and the order of consonants. We will now turn to a third aspect of the temporal relations among phonological units.

The Resolvability Principle makes predictions from the occurrence of four-consonant clusters for the occurrence of three-consonant and two-consonant ones; and from the occurrence of tri-consonantal clusters for the occurrence of bi-consonantal ones. What prediction does this principle make from bi-consonantal clusters? What it says is that clusters cannot include consonants that do not occur by themselves in the same position in the word. Thus, if a language has words starting with /sp/ as English does, the principle predicts that it should also have words starting with a lone /s/ and words starting with a lone /p/. This is true for English; cf. *sane* and *pipe*.

(C) STRESS PLACEMENT

Stress has to do with the amount of acoustic strength imposed on a sound. Based on a sample of 500 languages, Goedemans and van der Hulst (2005) report on how the various stress positions in a word stack up in terms of crosslinguistic frequency. About half of their sample languages have fixed stress positions regarding the place of the syllables on which stress falls; the others have no such fixed positions. Among the languages with fixed stress position, the largest number (110) have penultimate stress – i.e., stress on the next-to-the-last syllable of the word. The next most common pattern was found to be initial stress – i.e., stress on the first syllable of the word (92 languages); third in line was word-final stress (50 languages).

> GEN-18: If in a language, stress consistently falls on a syllable of a particular position in the word, this syllable is most frequently penultimate.

English has penultimate stress in some words such as *di-SCU-ssion* and *re-so-LU-tion* but it is not prevalent throughout the language. A better example of a penultimate-stress language is Latin. In two-syllable words, stress is on the penultimate syllable; e.g. *HOmo* 'man' and *ACer* 'sharp.' The same holds for trisyllabic words if the penultima is long, as in *paLUSter* 'swampy,' or *oNUStus* 'burdened'; but if it is short, stress shifts to the left to the antepenultima, as in *ARbores* 'trees' or *GLOmero* 'I wind.'

* * * *

This chapter and the two before explored crosslinguistically common patterns of three aspects of language structure: syntax, morphology, and phonology. How are the three domains similar and how are they different? A conspicuous difference has to do with **temporal relations**; a subtle similarity is the presence of **markedness relations**.

(A) TEMPORAL RELATIONS

The arrangement of syntactic constituents is sequential: it involves adjacency and precedence (see Section 3 of Chapter 3). Both of these relations are evident in the arrangement of morphemes as well (see Section 3 of Chapter 4); but, while words by definition cannot be superimposed on each other, morphemes may be suprasegmental and thus may be simultaneous with other morphemes. In phonological structure, both sequentiality and simultaneity are central: sound segments are linearly ordered (with considerable overlap) and their phonetic features correspond to simultaneously performed articulatory gestures.

Let us take a closer look at adjacency and precedence in syntax, morphology, and phonology. **Adjacency** is a very basic relation underlying much of the arrangement patterns of words, morphemes, and sounds. As noted in the syntax chapter (Section 3.2, Chapter 3), semantically coherent constituents tend to be adjacent both within words and within sentences. There are also several syntactic patterns which are strictly "local":

they pertain to adjacent or proximal elements. Thus, the verb normally agrees with the subject of its own clause and complements governed by the verb are generally next to their governors. Semantically-based proximity relations are also prevalent in morphology as stated in the Relevance Principle for affix order. A similar pattern is evident in phonology: assimilation generally affects adjacent sounds (e.g. a nasal is homorganic to an obstruent that is adjacent to it) and neutralization is also conditioned by immediate environments.

Beyond adjacency, linear precedence is also constrained in syntax, morphology, and phonology but there is an important difference: the constraints vary in strength. The order of syntactic constituents – especially longer, more complex ones – tends to be less tightly defined than the order of morphemes and the order of sound segments; and the order of sentences in a discourse is even less constrained than the sequence of sentence-internal parts. "Free word order" may possibly occur in the syntax of some languages; but "free morpheme order" is very rare and so is "free segment order" (cf. English *relevant* sometimes pronounced as *revelant*).

There are also differences in the details of the particular linear precedence relations in the three domains. As we saw in this chapter, initial and final positions in syllables and words make a difference; and for stress assignment, penultimate – second from the end – position is criterial. While initial and final positions in sentences may play a role in syntactic order, penultimate position never does. Second position, however, is a significant factor in the ordering of words in some languages, while in morphology and phonology, it does not appear to play a role.

(B) MARKEDNESS RELATIONS

In Chapter 4, Section 4.2.2.2, three overall characteristics of markedness were identified: the unmarked member of an opposition is syntagmatically simpler (or at least not more complex), paradigmatically more complex (or at least not less so), and more frequent within and across languages. In syntax, declarative sentences versus questions, and affirmative versus negative sentences tend to show this clustering of properties. In morphology, singular versus plural and present tense versus past are similar examples. Vocabulary also shows markedness relations as discussed in Chapter 2 for body-part terms, kinship terms, personal pronouns, numerals, and antonymic adjectives.

In phonology, too, there is often a correlation between simplicity, variability, and frequency. Greenberg's classic monograph of markedness offers many examples (Greenberg 1966c: 13–24): voiceless stops are both simpler and more frequent than voiced ones across languages and within some languages such as Klamath; and in cases of neutralization between voiced and voiceless obstruents, such as in German and Sanskrit, it is the simpler, voiceless variety that prevails. Similarly, in sign languages, some hand shapes are both simpler and more frequent.

As noted before, the correlation between simplicity and variability of structure and frequency is evident outside language as well. There are traffic signs to make cars stop at intersections but if cars are free to cross, there is no sign to tell them so. In talking about a close friend Brian, there is no need to add his last name but if you are talking about a Brian who is barely known to speaker and hearer, last name or some other descriptor is called for. There is a general tendency for humans to keep frequent entities simpler and more variegated than less frequent ones.

* * * *

So far in this chapter, 18 crosslinguistic generalizations have been discussed concerning the choice of sounds, their forms, and their temporal arrangement. As in syntax and morphology, a nagging issue arises: how are the basic terms of these statements defined? This is the topic of the next section.

5.4 Phonological categories

Throughout this chapter, the generalizations cited have made crucial use of terms such as word, syllable, sound segment, vowel, consonant, obstruent, nasal, and others. Does this mean that these entities are present in all languages? As an example, let us take a closer look at a portion of the Sonority Hierarchy (Section 5.3 above).

(34) Within syllables, stops tend to precede fricatives in pre-vocalic position; post-vocalically, fricatives tend to precede stops.

This statement can be interpreted in two ways.

(35) (a) **All** languages have syllables, stops, and fricatives; and in **all** languages, within syllables, stops tend to precede fricatives in pre-vocalic position; post-vocalically, fricatives tend to precede stops.
      (b) **Some** languages have syllables, stops, and fricatives; and in **those** languages, within syllables, stops tend to precede fricatives in pre-vocalic position; post-vocalically, fricatives tend to precede stops.

Which of (35a) and (35b) is the correct interpretation of (34)? The issue is the crosslinguistically applicable definition of phonological categories. These categories include not only syllable, stop, and fricative as in (34) but also other categories that figure in other crosslinguistic generalizations, such as consonant, vowel, high vowel, nasal vowel, and many others. The definition of concepts like stop, fricative, or nasal vowel is less problematic: these are articulatory classes whose defining properties are part of the physical "hardware" of language. Concepts such as word or syllable are less clearly definable.

In our discussions above, the concept of the word cropped up several times: as a domain within which the devoicing of obstruents and the composition of consonant clusters can be stated and with respect to which stress assignment patterns can be identified. As we saw earlier, the word is also central to both syntactic and morphological analysis. In syntax, the word is a part in terms of which sentences can be analyzed; in morphology in turn, the word is a whole rather than a part and it is analyzed in terms of morphemic composition. However, the morphosyntactic and phonological concepts of the word are not congruent: morphosyntactic words are not necessarily phonological words nor is the reverse the case.

Take for example articles such as in *the sparrow*. Is this one word or two? Syntactically, *the* is a separate word – a clitic – since other words may be placed between it and the noun, such as in *the two small sparrows*. But from the point of view of stress, the article forms a single unit with the following word. Or take prepositions. Here is a Russian example; *s mal'číkom* 'with (the) boy.' The preposition *s* is a separate word in syntax (again, additional elements can intervene between it and the noun), but it is pronounced as a single word with what follows.

Similar ambiguities arise in connection with the syllable even though it is predominantly only a phonological constituent, not a morphosyntactic one. It is a useful domain for stress assignment, as well as – as will be seen in the next section – for the analysis of some writing systems. However, there are ambisyllabic segments: phonemes that straddle the line between syllables. Also, phonological and phonetic syllables may be different (cf. Blevins 1995: 232–234).

The identification of **sound segments** is also fraught with problems. Both types of problems, basic to definitions of any kind, arise: the partonomic one – how to delimit one sound segment from another – and a taxonomic one: once identified as separate segments, how are they to be classified? Are affricates and diphthongs two segments or just one? Are geminate consonants and long vowels one segment or two? Are glides consonants or vowels? (For discussion, see Greenberg 1978b: 245–247, Maddieson 2005a, 2005b.)

In what follows, we will nonetheless assume that most segments can be delimited from each other and that they can be classified in articulatory phonetic terms as it is generally done in the literature; and we will turn to the question of the extent to which they occur crosslinguistically. Below are 14 crosslinguistic generalizations, some unconditional, others conditional (implicational). Unless noted otherwise, they are selected from the much larger number offered by Maddieson (2005a, 2005b, 2011). As stated by him (2011: 545), almost none of these are fully exceptionless even within the samples that have been studied. They will be listed by topic: those pertaining to consonant–vowel inventories, vowels, consonants, and suprasegmentals.

Consonants and vowels

GEN-19:
>   All languages have both consonants and vowels.

GEN-20:
>   A minimal inventory consists of only 11 sound segments (Rotokas has 6 consonants and 5 vowels); a very large one consists of more than 100 sounds (e.g. !Xóõ) (Maddieson 2011: 540)

Vowels

GEN-21:
>   The smallest basic vowel inventory found consists of 2 vowels (e.g. Yimas, a Sepik language of Papua New Guinea); the largest has 14 vowels (German).

GEN-22:

> The most common vowel inventory is /i, e, a, o, u/; e.g. Spanish.

GEN-23:

> All languages have contrast in vowel height.

GEN-24:

> No language has a rounding contrast for vowels without also having front-back contrast.

Consonants

GEN-25:

> All languages have plosives but not all languages have fricatives.

GEN-26:

> Most, but not all, languages have nasal consonants.

GEN-27:

> Voiceless obstruents are more common than voiced ones: all languages have voiceless plosives and if a language has voiced fricatives, it also has voiceless ones.

GEN-28:

> Voiced nasals and liquids are more common than voiceless ones.

GEN-29:

> Dental-alveolar point of articulation is more common than others. (Greenberg 1978b: 170)

GEN-30:

> Large inventories may include consonants that are inherently more complex (such as clicks, lateral fricatives, or glottalized consonants); small inventories generally do not have these.

Suprasegmentals

GEN-31:

> In close to half of the world's languages, stress is predictable.

GEN-32:

> About 40% of the world's languages are tone languages.

The discussion so far in this chapter had to do with the sound structures of spoken languages. However, there are forms of language – writing and signed languages – that are visual rather than auditory. Writing is a secondary, visual reflection of spoken language; the signed languages of the deaf are in turn fundamentally visual without any attempt to reflect spoken forms. These are the forms of language we will turn to next.

5.5 Visual forms of language

5.5.1 Writing systems

Suppose you see a man and his cow walking by the river under a starry sky. How could this view be preserved and communicated to others who are not present? A visual rendition would be best, either a photo or a drawing, such as in (36) (Figure 5.1).

(36)

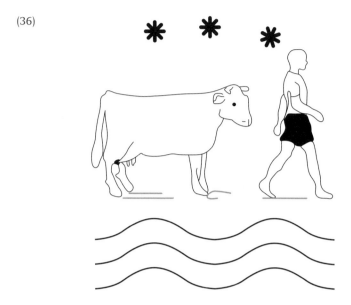

Figure 5.1
The man and the cow are walking near the water under the starry sky.

Pictures that convey messages are all around us. **Pictograms** are pressed into service for road signs such as announcing eating facilities, deer crossings, or restrooms (Figure 5.2).

(37)

Figure 5.2
Road signs.

The obvious idea of pictorially representing ideas has been fundamental to the invention of writing and has given rise to many, if not all, writing systems of the world. Over and above drawing pictures on the spur of the moment, two novel ideas have been crucial: to break down images into components so that they can be recombined in different ways, and to assign conventional shapes to these parts that can be uniformly produced and unambiguously recognized.

A writing system whose pictographic origins are still fairly apparent is that of Chinese. Here is the sentence 'The man and the cow are walking near the water under the starry sky' written in Chinese, along with the meaning of each character.

(38)   Chinese

在	星	空	下	人	跟	牛	在	水	邊	走
at	star	sky	under	man	and	ox	at	water	side	walk

In such word-writing systems, called **logographic**, the symbols represent meanings rather than sound forms. For this reason, the Chinese system, which took shape around 1200 BCE, constitutes a great unifying force linking the various Chinese languages. The words are pronounced differently depending on the language – such as in Mandarin and Amoy shown in (39) – but they can be written the same way as in (38).

(39) (a) *zài xīng kōng xià rén gēn niú zài shuǐ biān zǒu*   Mandarin
      (b) *di xing kong ha lang kap gu di sui bing giang*   Amoy

The image-like nature of contemporary Chinese characters is not readily apparent; but in Figure 5.3 there is a set of them alongside their earlier, pictographic shapes. You'll recognize two – 'man' and 'water' – that occur in (38).

(40) Earlier pictogram   Contemporary logogram   Meaning

Earlier pictogram	Contemporary logogram	Meaning
ᨑ	山	mountain
川	水	water
林	林	tree
⊙	日	sun
	月	moon
	馬	horse
	鳥	bird
	魚	fish
	手	hand
	目	eye
	耳	ear
	刀	knife
門	門	door
	車	car
	雨	rain
	人	man

Figure 5.3
Chinese pictograms and logograms.

In pictographic and logographic systems, it is the intended meanings that are analyzed into parts and represented by symbols regardless of how they are pronounced. A diametrically opposite stab at the problem of conveying thoughts visually is to focus on sound form rather than meaning by breaking pronunciation into smaller bits of sound and using signs to represent these sound segments. Here is the description of the image in figure 5.1 in Finnish.

(41)   Finnish

Mies   ja   lehmä kävelevät lähellä vettä   tähtitaivaan alla.
man and ox   walk   close   water starry.sky   under
'The man and the cow are walking near the water under the
starry sky.'

While in Chinese writing, every symbol is a conventionalized shape for a word-size meaning, in the Finnish alphabet, every symbol is a conventionalized shape for a sound. Finnish has a nearly pure phonetic writing system: unlike in English, every letter is pronounced individually and invariantly. There are no silent letters or combinations of letters to stand for a single sound, and each letter can be pronounced in only one way.

As mentioned above, pictographic and logographic systems preceded sound-based, phonographic systems in history. The revolutionary leap from writing meanings to writing sounds is documented in Egyptian hieroglyphs. Attested since around 3,250 BCA, this writing system is one of the oldest, second only to Sumerian. Here is the cow-sentence as it might be written in hieroglyphs (Figure 5.4):

(42)

Figure 5.4
Egyptian hieroglyphs.

The sentence contains some obvious pictures: the second sign is the image of an owl, the third shows two walking legs; in the middle there is a cow, next to it there is an extended arm; the next to the last character is a leg and the last one is a star. Four of these images – the walking legs, the cow, the water, and the star – relate to the meaning of the sentence but the presence of some of the other pictures is puzzling. Why the image of an owl? And why the outstretched arm and the leg?

The owl figure is employed here not for the animal that it depicts; instead, it stands for the sound /m/, which is the initial sound of the Egyptian word for 'owl': *muloch*. Along with the first symbol, which stands for the sound /ʃ/, it spells the consonants of the word *ʃem* 'walk.' In the same way, the shape of the outstretched arm stands for the sound /a/ and the leg stands for /b/. While Egyptian hieroglyphs started out as pictograms, with the passing of time the signs came to stand for the sounds of words rather than their meanings.

(43) presents the sentence again, this time with the sound values of the symbols and the approximate pronunciations underneath (Figure 5.5). The fourth line has the meanings of the symbols.

(43)

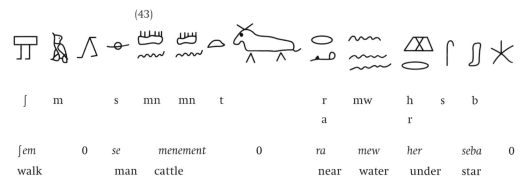

ʃ	m	s	mn	mn	t		r	mw	h	s	b
							a		r		

ʃem	0	se	menement	0		ra	mew	her	seba	0
walk		man	cattle			near	water	under	star	

Figure 5.5
Egyptian hieroglyphs with pronunciation and meaning.

The images of the two legs, the cattle, and the star are not pronounced (indicated by 0-s in (43)). Called determinatives, they have a function similar to illustrations in a book, or classifiers in languages such as Chinese or Korean: they serve to underscore the content spelled out in the preceding words.

The idea of using the image of an object to represent not its referent but a sound form of the word is called the Rebus Principle. If I want to pictorially represent the sentence "The room was bare," I can use the picture of a bear to stand for "bare." Or to represent "belief," I can use the picture of a bee followed by the picture of a leaf. In order to get the intended meaning, the reader has to alter his view: he has to make a leap from picture to sound, just as it happened in the evolution of Egyptian writing.

Given a phonographic writing system with content conveyed by sounds, there are still several options as to what portions of the sound form the symbols should stand for. In Finnish (as seen in (41)), as well as in many other languages including English, the letters stand for individual sound segments: the system is **alphabetic**. Two other options are representing units larger than single sound segments and units smaller than entire sounds.

A phonetic unit larger than individual segments that some writing systems are based on is the **syllable**. Consider the cow-sentence written in Japanese: 'Under the starry sky, near the water the man and the cow are walking.' (The numbers are added for reference.)

(44)   Japanese

　　　　星 空 の 下 水 ┌ を 男 と 牛 が ┌ い て い る。

　　　　1　2　3　4　5　6　7　8　9　10　11　12　13　14　15　16

(45) has the pronunciations and word meanings (PART = particle, GER = gerundival affix, TNS = tense).

(45) Japanese

1	2	3	4	5	6	7	8	9	10	11
hoʃi	*zora*	*no*	*ʃita*	*mizu*	*be*	*o*	*otoko*	*to*	*uʃi*	*ga*
star	sky	PRT	under	water	side	PRT	man	and	cow	PRT

12	13	14	15	16
aru	*i*	*te*	*i*	*ru*
walk	GER	PRT	be	TNS

The sentence contains two kinds of signs called *kanji* and *hiragana*. *Kanji* symbols spell nouns, verbs, and other semantically contentful concepts. They have been borrowed from Chinese as shown by the striking similarity between the Chinese symbols for 'star,' 'water,' and 'cow' in (38) and the Japanese equivalents (#1, #5, #10 in (44)). These are logographs although they are now linked to the pronunciation of specific Japanese lexical items. The other symbols are from the *hiragana* syllabary: they are generally grammatical particles that consist of single syllables (*no, o,* and *to* above) or suffixes (*-i, -te,* and *-ru*).

As noted above, in addition to syllabic writing, a further alternative to alphabetic representations is to analyze segments into **phonetic features**. While German has an alphabetic system, there is one feature of German letters that correlates with a phonetic feature: the use of the "Umlaut": two dots over a vowel. It is used on three non-front vowels: ö, ü, and ä; in each case, the umlauted letter stands for a corresponding front vowel [œ}, [y], and [e].

(46) (a) *offen* 'open' *öffentlich* 'public' German
         /offƏn/   /œffƏntliç/
     (b) *Buch* 'book' *Bücher* 'books'
         /buχ/   /byçƏr/
     (c) *Macht* 'power' *mächtig* 'powerful'
         /maχt/   /meçtik/

A language that makes more extensive use of feature spelling is Korean. Consider (47) (SBJ = subject marker; OBJ = object marker):

(47) Korean

별아래   남자와   소가   물가를   걷고   있다
pyel-alay *namca-wa* *so-ka* *mul-ka-lul* *ket-ko* *iss-ta*
star-under man-and cow-SBJ water-near-OBJ walk-and stay-DC
'The man and the cow are walking near the water under the stars.'

Designed by King Sejung in the fifteenth century, the Korean *han'gul* system has 19 consonantal and 21 vocalic and diphthongal letters. Perhaps under Japanese influence, the symbols are grouped into syllabic blocks. The outstanding characteristic of this system is that the shapes of some of the consonantal symbols are constructed out of components that correspond to articulatory features. As pointed out by Gnanadesikan (2009: 297), this system uses a kind of pictogram except that the pictures correspond not to the shapes of the objects that the words refer to but to the shapes of the articulatory organs involved in pronunciation!

Consider, for example, the letters for alveolar and velar consonants in the above text: /n/, /t/, and /k/. In each case, a horizontal line stands for the body of the tongue and the vertical one indicates the tongue's raised portion. The two alveolar consonants are /n/ on the top of the first syllable of the second word and /t/ in the lower part of the first syllable of the fifth word and in the second syllable of the last word. Both shapes include ∟ suggesting the front of the tongue touching the alveolar ridge. The letter /k/ in turn (in the third and fifth words) has the reverse shape ㄱ depicting the back of the tongue raised against the velic. This pictorial representation of place of articulation differentiates *han'gul* from the German Umlaut. The two dots over German vowels do correlate with a phonetic feature – front articulation – but they do not provide an iconic representation of the articulatory positions involved.

Given a writing system that is alphabetic rather than syllable-based or feature-based, there is still a further possible parameter of variation: which of the phonological segments that make up the sentence are represented by symbols? As was seen in (43), Egyptian hieroglyphs spell mostly consonants, with the vowels left for the reader to complete. Other Semitic languages, such as Arabic and Hebrew, are also predominantly consonantal. This is shown in (48) for Hebrew. The sentence is familiar: 'The man and the ox are walking near the water under the stars.'

(48) הרפ הולכים דיל המימ תחת הכוביס שיאה הו   Hebrew

The line consists of seven words separated by spaces, to be read from right to left. (49) provides letter-by-letter transliteration, word-for-word pronunciation, and word-for-word translation of (48) but, for ease of reading, the order is left-to-right.

(49)

h-a-i-sh	v-h-p-r-h	h-v-l-ch-i-m	l-i-d	h-m-i-m
haish	vehapara	holchim	leyad	hamayim
the.man	and.the.cow	walk	near	the.water

t-ch-t	h-k-v-ch-v-i-m
tachat	hakochavim
under	the.stars

So far we have seen that writing systems differ in whether they are meaning-based or sound-based. Within the latter, the sound units may represent single segments, syllables, or phonetic features and if they are single segments, there is a choice regarding which ones should be present. Hebrew brings up yet another parameter of variation: the direction of writing. European languages write from left to right; Semitic languages write from right to left; Chinese and Japanese may be written horizontally left to right or vertically top to bottom; Egyptian hieroglyphic writing also shows variable direction; and in some ancient Greek inscriptions, the lines alternate between left-to-right and right-to-left. The etymology of the Greek term for this style of writing – *boustrophedon* – refers to the route an ox follows when pulling a plough back and forth on a piece of land.

In sum: we have seen examples of variation along the following four parameters:

(a) the nature of the units that written symbols represent: pictographic/logographic versus phonetic

(b) the size of the sound units represented: syllables, segments, phonetic features

(c) the kinds of sound units represented: consonants and vowels or only consonants

(d) the direction of writing: left to right, right to left, top to bottom, bottom to top, *boustrophedon*

Given this wide range of variation, the obvious question is whether there are any overarching, cross-systemic properties of the writing systems of the world. There appears to have been little research in this area; but here are five tentative generalizations.

> GEN-1 Sound-based writing systems are employed in more languages than meaning-based ones.
>
> GEN-2 Among sound-based writing systems, alphabetic writing systems are more frequent than syllabaries. (Comrie 2005b: 568–569)

These two patterns make sense: the smaller the size of the units that the signs stand for, the fewer signs are needed in the inventory since smaller-size signs can be made more use of in writing words and sentences. Logographies require more characters but they also have their own advantages: sentences take up less space to write and they can be understood by speakers of languages that would pronounce the words differently. Here is a comparison of the number of signs needed in the various systems. In Egyptian logography, there were about 500 hieroglyphic signs used at any one time. If a Chinese speaker wants to be able to read newspapers and magazines, he needs to be familiar with about 3,000 characters. In Japanese, there are about 2,000 logographic *kanji* signs but only 46 basic syllabic *hiragana* signs; and the Finnish phonetic alphabet has only 28 letters.

> GEN-3 Among alphabetic systems, while there are some that are purely or mostly consonant-based, none are known that represent only vowels.

The reason is clear: most words in most languages contain more consonants than vowels and thus the missing vowels of a word are easier to guess than the missing consonants would be. For example, *e..o..a..io* does not suggest the word *demonstration* but *d..m..nstr..t..n* does.

> GEN-4 While there are writing systems that are wholly alphabetic or wholly syllabic, there are no writing systems where all signs are composed of representations of individual phonetic features.

This may reflect the fact that sound articulation is something that speakers are not readily aware of. King Sejung, who designed the Korean *han'gul* system, stands unmatched among other engineers of writing systems in that he, or his advisors, analyzed the way sounds are formed in the mouth.

> GEN-5 The left-to-right writing direction is more frequent than right-to-left or top-to-bottom.

If true, this may have to do with the predominant right-handedness of humans. If writing proceeds from right to left, the moving right hand blocks and possibly smears what has been written, while in writing from the left, the moving right hand does not cover the existing text.

5.5.2 Sign languages

Compare the following representations of the word for 'father' (Figure 5.6):

(50) (a) *father*

(b)

Figure 5.6
The sign for 'father' in American Sign Language.

(50a) is the spelling of the word in English; (50b) is the picture of its signed form in American Sign Language (ASL) (Klima and Bellugi 1979: 134). Both are visual representations of a concept but there is an important difference between the two. (50a) is a rendition of the spoken-language form of the word while the hand position in (50b) IS the language itself: there is no audible form that it tries to represent. In (50a), the relationship between concept and visual form is indirect: sound is intermediate between the two, while the gesture in (50b) directly conveys the concept. In this sense, (50b) is like a logogram; but note that it is not iconic.

ASL is only one of many sign languages (also known as signed languages) that serve as first-learnt, primary languages used mostly among deaf people. Zeshan's crosslinguistic survey lists 39 sign languages from around the world (2005a: 558). While they are natural languages just as spoken languages are, sign languages form a distinctive subclass of human languages due to the medium of expression employed: not body sounds but body gestures. Thus, from a language-typological point of view, two questions arise:

1. What are shared properties of the sign languages of the world?
2. What are shared properties of sign languages and spoken languages?

(A) SHARED PROPERTIES OF SIGN LANGUAGES

Sign languages around the world have so far been sparsely documented. Nonetheless, there are three characteristics that have been found to be universal among them: the use of space, the use of simultaneous expression, and iconicity (Sandler and Lillo-Martin 2006: 478). The use of space means that the signer assigns a unique place in the given situational context to each entity referred to. For example, the pronominal distinctions of 'I,' 'you,' and 'he/she' are conveyed by pointing at the speaker and the hearer and at distinct locations for the other referents involved (Sandler & Lillo-Martin 2006: 481–482, 487). The use of **simultaneous expression** means that aspects of the message can be signaled at the same time by different parts of the body. For example, basic sentence content may be signed manually with the interrogative intent conveyed concurrently by facial expression.

The use of space and of simultaneous signals are actually instances of **iconicity**. When the signer points at himself to say 'I,' he is presenting the referent. Similarly, the simultaneous expression of meaning elements iconically signals that the various semantic components apply at the very same time. A further example of iconicity in sign languages is the use of reduplication: the repetition of a sign can indicate plurality and other aspects of meaning. Here are examples of iconic signs for 'paws' and 'claws' (Supalla 1986: 209).

(51)

"paws"

"claws"

Figure 5.7
The signs for 'paws' and 'claws' in American Sign Language.

However, the sign for 'father' ((50)) and many signs are not at all iconic.

The communicative use of space, simultaneous expression, and iconicity is made possible by the medium of sign languages: hands can move in three dimensions and hand movements and facial expression can be controlled independently of each other. However, not all shared properties of sign language are "modality effects" of this sort (Emmorey 2002: 13–71). A modality-independent property of sign language is the existence of multiple levels of structure: signed sentences consist of words, words consist of morphemes, and morphemes can be analyzed into smaller units which, just as sounds, do not carry meaning by themselves.

Beyond these four general characteristics, more specific grammatical features have also been found to be widespread in sign languages, such as how negation and interrogation are expressed. Negation is generally signaled by negative particles placed after the predicate or at the end of the clause and they are accompanied by a special head movement (Zeshan 2004a: 51–54, Zeshan 2005b: 560). Question particles are not frequently used but if a sign language has them, they occur in polar – yes/no – questions more commonly than in content (*wh-*) questions, they are accompanied by non-manual signs, and they are never obligatory (Zeshan 2004b; 2005c: 564).

(B) SHARED PROPERTIES OF SIGN LANGUAGES AND SPOKEN LANGUAGES

All four of the general sign language characteristics mentioned above are present in spoken languages as well, although the first three to a much lesser extent. Both sign languages and spoken languages are based on multiple levels of structure: both can be analyzed into sentences, words, morphemes, and smaller units – syllables and segments – that are not independently meaningful. Similarly, the spatial identification of referents is employed in spoken languages as well: deictic elements such as demonstratives (*this*, *that*) point at different things in space and may even be accompanied by hand or head gestures. The availability of stress and intonation makes it possible in spoken languages to separate the message into parts that are expressed simultaneously, some segmentally and others suprasegmentally; such as when a statement is made into a question purely by intonation, as in *We are leaving?*

The fourth sign-language pattern, iconicity, is also a feature of spoken languages. It is interesting that some iconic expressions have the same meanings in sign language and in spoken language. As was discussed in the morphology chapter above (Chapter 4, Section 4.2.2.1), reduplication is frequently used in spoken languages to express plurality, continuity, and iteration. The same meaning elements are signaled by reduplication in sign languages (Aronoff *et al.* 2005: 336–337). It is important to note that iconic expressions are nonetheless highly conventionalized in both spoken and sign languages (Zeshan 2004a, 2004b) and that originally iconic signs may become fully schematized, or grammaticalized, with their mimetic features becoming barely apparent (Sandler & Lillo-Martin 2006: 497). As has been remarked in the literature, languages are as iconic as they can be. The concepts of 'paws' and 'claws' could not possibly be named iconically by sound but the availability of hand shapes in sign languages makes this possible.

A further overarching structural feature common to sign languages and spoken languages is **markedness relations**. Throughout the preceding chapters (especially in Chapter 4, Section 4.2.2.2), we identified three basic criteria that differentiate unmarked members from the marked ones in spoken languages: syntagmatic simplicity, paradigmatic variability, and frequency. They apply to sign languages as well (cf. Sandler 1996: 124–131, Sandler & Lillo-Martin 2006: 160–166). Some hand shapes – such as an extended pointing finger or an extended thumb – are both most frequent and most simple in form. Paradigmatic variability as related to frequency is illustrated by negation: irregular expressions of negation tend to occur with frequent verbs such as 'know,' 'understand,' 'want,' 'be able,' 'be possible,' and 'have' (Zeshan 2004a: 50). This is analogous to irregular past tense forms in English that are most common with frequent verbs such as *be*, *have*, *come*, and *go*.

Beyond the five general characteristics of hierarchical organization, deixis, simultaneous expression, iconicity, and markedness relations, construction-specific features of sign languages also have parallels in spoken languages. Examples include verb agreement and classifier constructions. Negative particles, too, are equally employed in spoken and sign languages and so are question particles.

One kind of question particle used in sign languages has the X-NOT-X structure: "This is an apple IS NOT IS?" Question markers of the structure "X (OR) NOT-X" are common in spoken languages as well; for example Finnish *menetkö, tai et?* "you.are.going, or not" 'Are you going?' Among sign languages, this type of question marking is most common in Asia and thus it is likely to be the result of contact with Sinitic languages such as Mandarin, where this construction is very frequent (Zeshan 2004b: 33–36; Zeshan 2005c: 565).

Another construction-specific similarity between sign languages and spoken language has to do with question words such as 'who' or 'why.' In sign languages, they are often related to indefinite pronouns: the sign for 'who' is also used for 'someone,' etc. (Zeshan 2004b: 25–26; 2005c). This is so in some spoken languages as well, such as Latin: compare *quis* 'who?' and *aliquis* 'somebody.' The semantic relation is obvious: a question is about a person or thing that the questioner does not know the identity of.

In conclusion: many distinctive properties of sign languages are directly related to the visual medium employed and many differences between sign languages and spoken languages are due to their differing means of expression: auditory versus visual. Here is a set of summary generalizations.

GEN-1

Common patterns of forming questions **across sign languages** are the following (cf. Zeshan 2004a, 2004b, Zeshan 2005c):

(a) All sign languages employ non-manual marking for polar questions, such as eyebrow raise or forward body posture.

(b) Question particles are never obligatory.

(c) Question particles used in polar questions and in content-questions never differ in form.

(d) Question particles are almost always predicate-final or clause-final.

GEN-2

Some shared patterns of **sign languages and spoken languages** are as follows:

(a) Question words such as for 'who' or 'where' are often formally related to the corresponding indefinite pronouns ('someone,' 'somewhere').

(b) Both language types have multi-level structure: syntax, morphology, and phonology.

(c) Both types utilize deixis for identifying referents but sign languages use it to a larger extent.

(d) Both types utilize simultaneous expression but sign languages do this to a larger extent.

(e) Both types have iconic expressions but sign languages have them to a larger extent.

(f) Both types exhibit markedness relations between members of oppositions.

Summary

This chapter probed into universal properties of human languages as related to the choice and arrangement of sound segments and their visual representations. First, 32 crosslinguistic generalizations were presented about phonological systems. The first four stated recurrent harmony patterns; GEN-5 characterized syllabic consonants; GEN-6–GEN-15 pertained to assimilation; GEN-16 formulated the Sonority Hierarchy; GEN-17 was about Resolvability; GEN-18 pointed out a frequent stress pattern; and GEN-19–GEN-32 characterized frequencies of various sound types. These were followed by five statements about writing systems and two sets about how sign languages are similar to each other and what features they share with spoken languages.

Activities

1. Describe the distribution of the voiceless and voiced stops in the following data from Mohawk. (Halle and Clements 1983: 59)

(a)	oli:deʔ	'pigeon'	(h)	oya:gala	'shirt'
(b)	zahset	'hide it! (sg.)'	(i)	ohyotsah	'chin'
(c)	ga:lis	'stocking'	(j)	labahbet	'catfish'
(d)	odahsa	'tail'	(k)	sdu:ha	'a little bit'
(e)	wisk	'five'	(l)	ǰiks	'fly'
(f)	degeni	'two'	(m)	desdaʔn	'stand up! (sg.)'
(g)	aplam	'Abram, Abraham'	(n)	de:zekw	'pick it up! (sg.)'

2. Assess the validity of the Sonority Hierarchy for the following word-initial consonant clusters of Russian.

(a)	bl-	e.g.	/bliz/	'close to'
	br-	e.g.	/brat/	'brother'
(b)	vd-	e.g.	/vdova/	'widow'
	vz-	e.g.	/vzad/	'backwards'
	vž-	e.g.	/vžive/	'alive'
	vk-	e.g.	/vklad/	'donation'
	vl-	e.g.	/vlaga/	'moisture'
	vm-	e.g.	/vmeste/	'together'
	vs-	e.g.	/vsje/	'all'
	vt-	e.g.	/vtora/	'second voice'
	vč-	e.g.	/včera/	'yesterday'
	vh-	e.g.	/vhod/	'entrance'
	vš-	e.g.	/všivyj/	'lousy'
	vr-	e.g.	/vremja/	'time'
	vsk-	e.g.	/vskok/	'at a gallop'
	vsl-	e.g.	/vsled/	'immediately behind'
	vsp-	e.g.	/vspol'e/	'ridge'
	vskl-	e.g.	/vskloživat'/	'to tangle'
	vskr-	e.g.	/vskryvat'/	'to uncover'
	vstr-	e.g.	/vstrečat'/	'to meet'
(c)	gr-	e.g.	/gran'/	'border'
(d)	dv-	e.g.	/dve/	'two'
	dr-	e.g.	/drat'/	'to tear'
(e)	žb-	e.g.	/žban/	'can'
	žv-	e.g.	/žvačka/	'rumination'
	žg-	e.g.	/žgut/	'torch'
	žr-	e.g.	/žrebyj/	'fate'
(f)	kr-	e.g.	/krest'/	'cross'
(g)	sp-	e.g.	/sputn'ik/	'satellite'
	st-	e.g.	/stat'/	'to stand'
	sh-	e.g.	/shodka/	'meeting'
	sč-	e.g.	/sčitat'/	'to count'
	str-	e.g.	/strana/	'home land'
	stv-	e.g.	/stvor/	'leaf of a door'

3. Compare the Arabic and Roman ways of writing numerals. What are the underlying principles?

1	I	11	XI	90	XC	
2	II	12	XII	100	C	
3	III	13	XIII	200	CC	
4	IV	15	XV	210	CCX	
5	V	20	XX	500	D	
6	VI	21	XXI	502	DII	
7	VII	30	XXX	600	DC	
8	VIII	40	XL	900	CM	
9	IX	50	L	1000	M	
10	X	60	LX	1010	MX	

4. Here is a set of data from Akan, a Kwa language of Ghana and the Ivory
    Coast (Roca and Johnson 1999: 21)
    (i)   Most of the words show vowel harmony. What is the phonetic
          feature by which vowels are harmonized?
    (ii) There are words that do not show vowel harmony. What may be the
          reason?

Here is the Akan vowel inventory. In each pair of vowels, the one on the left
is tense and the one on the right is lax.

i ɪ   u ʊ
e ɛ   o ɔ
      a

(a) *o-fiti-i*   'he pierced it'

(b) *ɔ-tsɪrɛ-ɪ*   'he showed it'

(c) *e-bu-o*   'nest'

(d) *ɛ-bʊ-ɔ*   'stone'

(e) *ɔ-bɛ-jɛ-ɪ*   'he came and did it'

(f) *o-be-je-i*   'he came and removed it'

(g) *o-bisa-ɪ*   'he asked it'

(h) *ɔ-kari-i*   'he weighed it'

5. In Ulwa, a language of Nicaragua, the affix indicating possession is *ka*.
    The data below show that this affix is prefixed in some cases and infixed
    in others. Can you find a single condition that determines the placement
    of this affix? (Roca and Johnson 1999: 124–125)

(a) UNSUFFIXED   POSSESSED:
     ál   *ál-ka* 'man'
     bás   *bás-ka* 'hair'
     kí: *kí:-ka* 'stone'
     saná   *saná-ka* 'deer'
     amák   *amák-ka* 'bee'
     sapá: *sapá:-ka* 'forehead'
(b) *sú:lu*   *sú:-ka-lu* 'dog'
     kúhbil   *kúh-ka-bil* 'knife'
     báskarna   *bás-ka-karna* 'comb'
     siwának   *siwá-ka-nak* 'root'
     aná:laaka   *aná:-ka-laaka* 'chin'
     karásmak   *karás-ka-mak* 'knee'

Further reading

*   This chapter presupposes a basic knowledge of articulatory phonetics and of phonology. For an
    introduction to phonetics, see for example Ashby and Maidment 2005. For an introduction to phonology,
    see for example Nathan 2008, Odden 2005.

*   On terminal devoicing, see Nathan 2008: 88–93; Blevins 2004: 103–106.

- For a comprehensive summary of vowel harmony phenomena across languages, see van der Hulst and van de Weijer 1995 and Nevins 2010.

- On the syllable and problems regarding its identification, see Blevins 1995. Recent comprehensive accounts of the syllable are Hulst and Ritter (ed.) 1999 and Charles E. Cairns and Eric Raimy's handbook (2011).

- On phonological units other than the word, syllable, and segment (e.g. foot, mora), see for example Nathan 2008: 43–58 and Lahiri 2001.

- For surveys of the sounds of the world's languages, see Ladefoged and Maddieson 1996 and the UCLA Phonetic Segment Inventory (UPSID) on the Internet.

- Written in a lively and highly reader-friendly style, Gnanadesikan 2009 offers a comprehensive account of writing systems and their development. See also Daniels and Bright 1996, Rogers 2005. An engaging account of how the Linear B script was deciphered is given by Chadwick 1970.

- On the phonological structure of American Sign Language, see Brentari 1995. On sign language morphology, see Aronoff *et al*. 2005. A comprehensive introduction to sign languages is Emmorey 2002. On classifiers in ASL, see Supalla 1986; Emmorey 2002: 73–91; Aronoff *et al*. 2005: esp. 324–326; on verb agreement in ASL, see Aronoff *et al*. 2005: esp. 315–324.

6 Language in flux

Typologies of language change

CHAPTER OUTLINE

Languages change on three levels: in acquisition, in use, and in the course of history. In this chapter, crosslinguistically recurrent patterns of these three processes will be discussed. How do articles come about in history? How does word order change? How are antonyms and spatial terms acquired by children? What characterizes the interlanguages of second-language learners? And what processes are evident in language use?

6.1 Introduction

So far in this book, we searched for crosslinguistically recurrent patterns in synchronic structure. However, languages keep evolving. Take, for instance, the phonemic inventory of today's English. It has gaps: it does not contain certain sounds that other languages have. An example comes from fricatives: English has labiodentals (as the /Θ/ in *thick*), alveolars (as the /s/ in *seal*), and palatals (as /ʃ/ in *sheen*) but velar fricatives (as /χ/ in the German word *lachen* 'laugh') do not occur. This was not always the case: Old English did have velar fricatives; their traces are preserved in the silent *gh*-s of the spelling of *night* or *light*. This shows that there has been a process of phonological loss spanning the centuries as Old English gradually morphed into the modern variety.

But if languages change, this means that their synchronic state is not the only possible locus of crosslinguistic convergences. In addition to synchronic structure, **historical change** is another area where crosslinguistically recurrent patterns may be sought. Have other languages also lost velar fricatives? What kinds of sound do languages lose? Do languages gain sounds? What are other changes that can take place in a language? And, crucially, how do changes happen and why?

Historical change affects an entire community. In addition, we also find small changes happening within a single individual's lifetime. As a child, each of us has acquired a language and we constantly draw upon this acquired knowledge for comprehending and speaking. Language acquisition is a process of going from no language to language, or from one language to a second one; language use in turn takes us from knowing to doing. The processes of **language acquisition** and **language use** are two additional areas where crosslinguistic similarities may be sought.

The descriptive study of any process – in language or in any other domain – involves four components: initial stages, final stages, intermediate stages, and conditions for the changes to occur. Accordingly, in this chapter we will keep in mind four types of questions for each process. A and B refer to structures.

(A) QUESTION ABOUT INITIAL STAGES

Given B as a final stage, what are crosslinguistically recurrent A-s that B can (or must) come from?

(B) QUESTION ABOUT FINAL STAGES

Given A as an initial stage, what are crosslinguistically recurrent B-s that A may (or must) turn into?

(C) QUESTION ABOUT INTERMEDIATE STAGE(S)

Given that A changes to B, what are crosslinguistically recurrent intermediate stage(s) C (if any) that can (or must) occur between A and B?

(D) QUESTION ABOUT CONDITIONS

What are crosslinguistically recurrent conditions under which A may (or must) change into B with (or without) the mediation of C?

> The three dimensions of change can be illustrated from behavior patterns outside language, such as how we dress or what we eat. Take clothing. The kind of attire that people wear nowadays is not the same as what they wore five hundred years ago: there have been changes affecting the entire culture. But the way a person dresses depends on two additional factors: how he has internalized the societal dressing habits and how he may have modified these conventions in his daily practice.

For an example, take SVO order. One question is what other orders (if any) can SVO come from? ((A) above) Second, what other orders (if any) can SVO change into? ((B) above) Third, given that SVO morphs into VSO, what orders (if any) mediate this process? ((C) above) And fourth, what conditions favor this change? ((D) above)

Before we turn to such questions, there are three points to make about these issues. First, the terms "initial stage" and "final stage" are used here in a relative sense: the demarcation of the beginning and the end of a process depends on our focus of interest. For example, if we want to explore the history of English auxiliary verbs such as *must* or *will*, the final stage will be their existence, and the initial stage is where these auxiliaries did not exist but some other structures did to which we are able to trace them back. But auxiliaries themselves may further evolve into something else and conversely, their source structures may have been the outcome of an earlier change.

Second, things may change but then again, they may remain what they are, at least on the short run. Thus, we will be interested not only in what can change to what but also in what grammatical patterns are resistant to change in history, in acquisition, and in language use. After all, the very concept of language universals is based on the **invariance** of some grammatical properties.

Third, for an entire language to change in the course of history, a novel form cannot remain isolated within the speech of a single individual: it must spread throughout the entire speech community. Thus, an additional question asks about the conditions under which a novel structure **propagates**.

Sections 6.2, 6.3, and 6.4 will discuss crosslinguistic generalizations about language change, language acquisition, and language use in this order.

6.2 As the centuries pass ... historical change

In this section, we will consider two instances of diachronic change where languages follow similar evolutionary paths.

6.2.1 The genesis of articles

Surveying the crosslinguistic distribution of definite and indefinite articles, Roman Jakobson's remark cited earlier (in Section 2.5.2 of Chapter 2) comes to mind: "Languages differ essentially in what they must convey and not in what they may convey." One of the meaning contrasts that speakers of English must express is whether they talk about something that is familiar to the hearers or something whose referent is unknown to them. In (1a), the car is not a known entity to the hearer but in (1b) it is one that has been identified before or is obvious from the situational context. Since the difference must be signaled in English by the use of the definite and indefinite articles (at least for singular count nouns), (1c), which has neither article, is ungrammatical.

(1) (a) *Bill* *is* *fixing* ***a*** *car.*   English
     (b) *Bill* *is* *fixing* ***the*** *car.*
     (c) **Bill* *is* *fixing* ___ *car.*

Jakobson's insight is borne out by the fact that many languages do not require that this distinction be made: they have no articles at all. Russian and Korean are examples:

(2) *Eva* *jest* ___ *jabloko.*   Russian
     Eva   eats   apple
     'Eva is eating an apple.' or '…the apple.'

(3) *Eva-ka*   *sagwa-lul*   *mek-ko*   ___   *iss-ta.*   Korean
     Eva-NOM   apple-ACC   eat-INF   PRES-DC
     'Eva is eating an apple.' or '…the apple.'

Not only is the presence of articles crosslinguistically variant, they are not overwhelmingly frequent, either. In Dryer's sample of 566 languages, somewhat more than half – 337 – have words or affixes functioning as definite articles and in a sample of 473 languages, less than half – 204 – have indefinite article words or affixes (Dryer 2005g, 2005h). There is no implicational relationship between the existence and lack of definite and indefinite articles across languages: either article can be present in a language without the other. Out of Dryer's 566 languages, 41 have definite but no indefinite articles (e.g. Egyptian Arabic) and out of 473 languages, 81 have indefinite articles and no definite ones (e.g. Tauya, a language of Papua New Guinea).

While the crosslinguistic distribution of articles does not allow either for unconditional statements (e.g. "All – or most – languages have definite articles") or for implications (e.g. "All – or most – languages that have definite articles also have indefinite ones"), a striking convergence emerges regarding their historical origins. *The world lexicon of grammaticalization* (Heine and Kuteva 2002) – a unique treasure trove of information about the crosslinguistically attested origins of grammatical elements – indicates a single historical source for definite articles and similarly a single ancestor for indefinite articles. Although alternative sources for definite articles are noted by Jan Rijkhoff (2002: 186), it is safe to say that definite articles almost always arise from demonstratives and indefinite articles come from the numeral 'one' (with demonstratives and the numeral 'one' remaining as categories in the language).

While the formal and semantic relationship between articles and their historical sources is evident, the two structures are generally not quite the same. However, the differences are not random: they fall into crosslinguistically uniform patterns. Let us start with the form relationship between articles and their historical ancestors. In some languages, they have exactly the same segmental form, as in Bizkayan Basque (Heine and Kuteva 2002: 109).

(4) (a) *gizon*   ***a***   'that man'   Bizkayan Basque
      man   **that**
  (b) *gizon-**a*** 'the man'
      man-**the**

In English, however, demonstratives and definite articles are similar but not identical.

(5) (a) ***that***   *man*   English
  (b) ***the***   *man*

The same two scenarios are attested for indefinite articles and the numeral 'one.' In Turkish, the two consist of the same segments (Heine and Kuteva 2002: 220), but in English, the similarity is minimal.

(6) (a) ***bir***   *büyük*   *tarla*   'one large field'   Turkish
      one   large   field
  (b) *büyük*   ***bir***   *tarla*   'a large field'
      large   **one**   field

(7) (a) ***one***   *pear*   English
  (b) ***a***   *pear*

In those cases where the ancestral form and the article are not exactly the same, the difference is predominantly quantitative: both the definite and the indefinite article have diminished phonological shapes in comparison to their historical sources.

Beyond the loss of segments, phonological erosion is shown in other ways as well. Articles are generally stressless even though their ancestral forms carried stress. Also, related to their diminished suprasegmental marking, articles generally become clitics or even suffixes, as seen in Bizkayan Basque in (4). Note that demonstratives and 'one' can form noun phrases all by themselves and even if they occur with a noun, they retain their separate word status. Articles, however, cannot be noun phrases by themselves and in construction with a noun, they are not separate words. The lack of non-phrasal status of articles is shown in (8) and (9) for English.

(8) (a) *I*   *don't*   *want*   *this,*   *I*   *want*   ***that**.*   English
  (b) **I*   *don't*   *want*   *this,*   *I*   *want*   ***the**.*

(9) (a) *These*   *are*   *nice*   *apples;*   *I*   *want*   ***one***   *of*   *them.*   English
  (b) **These*   *are*   *nice*   *apples;*   *I*   *want*   ***an***   *of*   *them.*

Beyond Basque, further examples of suffixed articles come from languages on the Balkan Peninsula, where they are an areal feature; see (10), (11), and (12) (from Bynon 1977: 246). In (11) and (12), the article has allomorphic variants.

(10) *trup-**at***   'the body'   Bulgarian
     *konj-**at***   'the horse'

(11) *mik-**u***   'the friend'   Albanian
      *djal-**i***   'the boy'

(12) *om-**ul***   'the man'   Rumanian
      *munte-**le*** 'the mountain'

Beyond the reduction of **phonological form**, articles may also lose the **inflections** of their ancestors. In Hungarian, the adnominal demonstrative has number and case suffixes in agreement with the head noun but the definite article derived from it does not. This is shown in (13); note that in this language, the demonstrative obligatorily co-occurs with the definite article.

(13) (a) *ez-**t***   *az*___   *almá-t*   Hungarian
               this-**ACC**   the   apple-ACC
               'this apple (ACC)'
      (b) *ez-**ek-et***   *az*___   *almá-k-at*
               this-**PLU-ACC**   the   apple-PLU-ACC
               'these apples (ACC)'

The same holds for Maltese Arabic: the demonstrative agrees with the noun in gender and number but the definite article does not inflect for either category.

So far we have seen that the form differences between articles and their historical sources are due to the loss of phonological and morphological substance. In addition, articles and their historical sources are also somewhat different in their meaning. A demonstrative, just as the definite article, refers to something whose referent is evident to both speaker and hearer. The difference is that demonstratives identify the referent by pointing (e.g. when saying *this book* or *that day*). Definite articles also point but in a more abstract way: they single out something that is known because it was mentioned before in the discourse or due to its familiarity in the speaker's and hearer's world. In some uses, there is no pointing involved at all: the non-deictic aspect of the definite article's semantics is particularly clear when it refers to an abstract noun or when it is an invariant part of a proper name.

(14) (a) *They were impressed by **the** honesty of this man.*   English
      (b) ***The** Hague is one of my favorite cities.*

The numeral 'one' and the indefinite article show a comparable semantic difference: both refer to a single entity but the indefinite article does it less emphatically. This is shown by the fact that the numeral *two* contrasts with *one* but not with *a*.

(15) (a) *I don't want **two** apples, I want only **one** apple.*   English
      (b) *?I don't want **two** apples, I want only **an** apple.*

In some languages, the original quantitative meaning of 'one' has faded out completely to the extent that the indefinite article has plural forms, such as Spanish *unos* and *unas*. The plural forms of the indefinite article are in direct conflict with the original singular meaning.

Thus, in the course of historical change, meaning is diminished just as form is: demonstratives turning into definite articles lose the semantic property of spatial deixis and in the course of the numeral 'one' turning into indefinite articles, the quantity feature is weakened or lost entirely.

The processes of phonological, morphological, and semantic reduction have been documented for the genesis of articles all over the world. The indefinite article has arisen from the numeral 'one' in Mandarin, Sherpa, Hungarian, Neo-Aramaic, Persian, Turkish, Hebrew, Germanic languages, Romance languages, and various Amerindian and Austronesian languages (Givón 1981: 35). Crosslinguistic support for the demonstrative-to-definite-article route comes from Romance and Germanic languages, Hungarian, Vai, Haitian Creole, Grand Ronde Chinook Jargon, and many others (Heine and Kuteva 2002).

There are two more aspects to note of these processes. First, they do not happen all at once. Let us take the Romance definite articles, such as French *le* and *la*, or Spanish *el* and *la*. They are derived by gradual phonological reduction from *ille* and *illa* – the masculine and feminine forms of demonstratives in Latin, the ancestor of Romance languages. The semantic bleaching was also gradual: in Old French, the incipient definite article was first used with nouns whose referent was uniquely identifiable (as in English *I have bought a house.* **The** *house is spacious*) before its use was extended to nouns in a generic sense (as in English **The** *polar bear is an endangered animal*). (For detail, see Epstein 1994). In the same way, the incipient indefinite article *xad* in colloquial Hebrew, derived from *exád* 'one,' is used primarily with referential nouns but its use has not yet spread to generic nouns as it has in French and English (e.g. *Joe would like to live in* **a** *big house*) (Givón 1981).

The second point to add about the processes described above has to do with the conditions under which these developments take place. In their book about areal effects among European languages, Bernd Heine and Tania Kuteva show how both definite and indefinite articles are currently emerging in a number of languages with the process triggered or at least accelerated by the influence of neighboring languages (2006: 97–139). Some of the European languages with the most developed articles are German, Italian, and Greek; and languages that are now developing article systems – e.g. Serbian or Finnish – are exactly those that have had the closest contact with them.

The interesting point is that these languages are not borrowing articles directly from another language. Straight borrowing would consist of taking over the very words lock, stock and barrel – say, *der*, *die*, *das* from German – just as words like *television*, *pizza*, or *politics* are borrowed by one language from another. In this case, however, what the recipient languages are copying is the method of "growing" their own articles from the same sources as their model languages did a long time ago: from demonstratives and from the numeral 'one.' In other words, it is the evolutionary path that is being replicated. Contact-induced article-creation is known

> The pattern is similar to calques: languages often do not borrow a word but replicate its composition in terms of their own resources; such as English *sky-scraper* giving rise to German *Wolkenkratzer* "cloud-scratcher" and French *gratte-ciel* "scrape-sky".

also from outside Europe: Pipil, an Aztecan language of El Salvador, seems to have gotten the idea from Spanish (Heine and Kuteva 2006: 137).

As we have just seen, the general characteristics of the article-making process are phonological and morphological erosion and semantic bleaching. This process is widely documented in historical change far beyond the development of articles. Labeled grammaticalization, it is evidenced in many – although not all – grammatical changes.

As an example, take the English auxiliary form *'ll* as in *He'll arrive late*. It is a variant of *will*, which is derived from the Germanic verb for 'want' (cf. German *wollen*). The form *'ll* is clearly reduced and the meaning is bleached: both wanting to do something and doing something in the future refer to future action but the latter does not include the intentionality component (cf. *If you feed spinach to the baby, she **will** throw up*). The auxiliary *will* is morphologically diminished as well: unlike main verbs, it does not show agreement with the subject.

Another future auxiliary which is undergoing grammaticalization right in front of our eyes is *going to*, as in *He is going to sleep*. When used as an auxiliary, it has abandoned the semantic component of motion and its form is frequently reduced to *gonna*. The same grammaticalization process that turns lexical verbs into auxiliaries has yielded auxiliaries in many other languages as well. French *aller* 'to go,' *venir* 'to come,' and *avoir* 'to have' are all main verbs that are now also used as auxiliaries to indicate the tense of the main verb. In Germanic languages, the verb originally referring to ownership (*have* in English, *haben* in German) has turned into a tense-and-aspect-marking auxiliary; and in Georgian, the auxiliary for necessity, obligation, and intention has arisen from the main verb 'to want.'

Here is a summary of the crosslinguistically recurrent patterns of the evolution of articles.

> GEN-1
> (A) INITIAL STAGES
>   (a) Given a definite article, it is likely to have arisen from a demonstrative.
>   (b) Given an indefinite article, it is likely to have arisen from the numeral 'one.'
> (B) FINAL STAGES
>   (a) Given a demonstrative, it may change into a definite article.
>   (b) Given the numeral 'one,' it may change into an indefinite article.
> (C) INTERMEDIATE STAGES
>   Both changes are instances of grammaticalization – a gradual phonological, semantic, and, if applicable, morphological reduction.
> (D) CONDITIONS
>   Language contact may trigger or accelerate the development of articles.

Note that GEN-1 is stated in probabilistic terms. This is for two reasons. First, we can never be sure that a historical process WILL take place. We may state the direction that the change would take IF it were to occur but we cannot vouch for its actual occurrence. Second, while demonstratives and the numeral 'one' are almost unique sources for definite and indefinite articles, demonstratives do not necessarily turn into articles: they may be ancestors of complementizers (such as in English *I told you **that** it was going to rain*), or of third person pronouns (such as in Lezgian, a language of the Caucasus). Similarly, the numeral 'one' can evolve into the word 'alone' (as in Albanian) or an indefinite pronoun (as in German) (Heine and Kuteva 2002).

As mentioned earlier, the concepts of initial and final stages are relative to the researcher's interest: the structures labeled initial may have arisen from a more remote source and those labeled final may in turn evolve into something else. This raises the question of whether the sources of articles – demonstratives and the numeral 'one' – have historical ancestors themselves and whether articles can undergo further changes.

It is not clear whether the numeral 'one' has any ancestors and if it does, whether these ancestors are the same across languages. Similarly, there is no indication that demonstratives have evolved from other words: they are universally present in all known languages. Their cognitive primacy is also shown by the fact that they are among the first words acquired by children (Diessel 1999: 150–153).

What about the afterlife of articles? Do they turn into something else? Definite articles do: with their semantics further bleached, they may begin to be used on all nouns and turn into gender markers before they disappear completely. These further developments are additional outcomes of the grammaticalization process. Turkana provides examples of the definite article shedding its definiteness feature and simply marking nouns for their gender (cited in Diessel 1999: 129). M, F, and N stand for masculine, feminine, and neuter genders.

(16)   Turkana

                 Demonstratives: Nouns:

masculine:	*ye'*	'that(M)'	*(n)e-kìle*	"M-man"	'man'
feminine:	*ya'*	'that(F)'	*(n)a-ber-ɔ`*	"F-woman"	'woman'
neuter:	*yi'*	'that(N)'	*(n)i-iŋok*	"N-dog"	'dog'

Why is grammaticalization such a widespread engine behind historical change? This question will be discussed in Chapter 7, Section 7.4.

6.2.2 Word order change

Earlier in this book, a number of crosslinguistic regularities of word order were discussed (see Section 1.1 of Chapter 1 and Section 3.3 of Chapter 3). One of them has to do with the frequency of individual order patterns.

(17) THE ORDER OF S, O, AND V
    Among the six logically possible linearizations of Subject,

Object, and Verb, SOV, SVO are the most common, with VSO a distant third.

Other generalizations stated implicational relations between the order of major sentence-internal and phrase-internal constituents.

(18)   CORRELATION PAIRS
    (a)   Most OV languages show the following patterns:
         – Noun Phrase & Adposition
         – Possessor & Possessum
         – Head Noun & Relative Clause
    (b)   Most VO languages show the mirror image of (a):
         – Adposition & Noun Phrase
         – Possessum & Possessor
         – Relative Clause & Head Noun

Where do we go from here? Upon noticing something about the world, the human mind is prompted to ask: why is it the way it is? The most convincing answer has to do with the history of the observed facts: things are what they are because of how they evolved. Ice on a winter road is what it is because it started out as water and when the temperature dipped below freezing, the water turned into ice. Cats are what they are because of how they have evolved from feral felines through domestication.

Supplying causes for facts calls for raising two specific queries: **how did things evolve** and **why did they evolve the way they did**. Explaining ice on the road requires describing the process of water turning into ice and then finding the causes that underlie this transformation. Explaining what cats are like involves describing the domestication process and why that process has had the effect it has. Similarly, explaining crosslinguistic order patterns calls for answering the how-question: how have they evolved? and then addressing the why-question: why has the evolution taken place as it has?

In the previous section, we dealt with the **how-question** about the genesis of articles. In this section, we will take up the how-question about the evolution of some word order patterns. The **why-questions** about the causes behind these evolutions will be addressed in the last chapter (Chapter 7, Section 7.3).

(A) THE EVOLUTION OF THE ORDER OF S, O, AND V

As a first stab at the problem of the historical origins of the various orderings of S, O, and V, one might hypothesize that each has been historically invariant and thus each of the six order types originated from one of six different proto-languages. However, historical facts do not support this scenario: we have evidence that constituent order changes over time.

One example of word order change emerges from the history of English. In Old English, the order of Subject, Object, and Verb in main declarative sentences was mostly free (cf. Section 3.3 of Chapter 3) except for a few constraints, such as that object pronouns always preceded the verb. It was during the Middle-English period (between 1100 CE and 1500 CE) that the SVO order – today's pattern – became solidified. But the change from relatively free order to a rigid SVO structure was only one small time segment of a much longer evolutionary process. English ultimately derives from the ancestor of all Germanic languages, which linguists call Proto-Germanic. This language, spoken in Northern Europe before 1000 BCE, is reconstructed as having been an SOV language. Thus, the entire sequence of word order changes that English has been part of is this:

(19) Proto-Germanic: SOV
      Old English: SOV
                           SVO
                           VOS
                           VSO
                           OSV
                           OVS
      Modern English: SVO

The ancient OV order is replicated in an English compounding pattern still productive today, as in *letter-opener*, *baby-sitting*, *shoe-shining*, *mail-carrier*, and even in terms as recent as *lawn-mower*, and *word-processor*.

Other languages in the Germanic family have also moved in the same direction. In today's German, the verb is normally second in a main sentence just as in English but it may be preceded not only by the subject but also by other constituents; and most subordinate clauses have kept the original SOV structure.

From such evidence, we can deduce that SVO did not have to be the order in an original first language of mankind: it could have evolved from SOV.

Are there any other attested changes among the six possible major-constituent orders? Given that each of the six fixed orders could in principle change into any of the five other orders, there are 30 logically possible paths of change. Of these, only 9 have been documented. (20) shows the 30 logical possibilities with YES marking the documented changes and 0 marking those not documented (Gell-Mann and Ruhlen 2011).

(20) FROM: TO: →

↓	SOV	SVO	VSO	VOS	OSV	OVS
SOV	–	YES	0	0	YES	YES
SVO	0	–	YES	YES	0	0
VSO	0	YES	–	YES	0	0
VOS	0	YES	YES	–	0	0
OSV	0	0	0	0	–	0
OVS	0	0	0	0	0	–

These changes have taken place gradually through stages of mixed order, with a new order beginning to be used simultaneously with the older one and gradually gaining more ground. The nine attested changes are dia-grammed in (21) (Figure 6.1) (Gell-Mann and Ruhlen 2011: 17291).

(21)

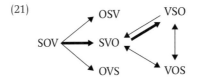

Figure 6.1
Changes in word order.

Several things are worth noting in (21). First, the two bold lines show that SOV to SVO and SVO to VSO are the most frequent changes. Second, in each step in the documented processes, there is just a single constituent changing place. In other words, one-step mirror-image changes do not occur: SOV does not directly develop into VOS and SVO does not turn into OVS. Third, all three OV orders (SOV, OVS, OSV) are connected by pathways of change and so are the three VO orders (SVO, VSO, VOS); but the only pathway between the two basic types – OV and VO – is SOV changing to SVO. Fourth, the very rare orders – OSV and OVS – have just a single chance to evolve: only from SOV, while the other orders have multiple alternative origins: VSO and VOS have two possible sources and SVO has three. The reasons for these major-constituent order changes may be diverse and are disputed; for a survey, see Harris and Campbell 1995: 215–220.

The only order without any source to evolve from is SOV. This is because, according to Gell-Mann and Ruhlen and some other researchers such as Talmy Givón, SOV is likely to have been the order of the ancestral language of mankind spoken around 50,000 BCE.

However, there is some indication that the SOV → SVO change is not necessarily unidirectional: VO, under certain conditions, may change into OV. There are two conditions under which this change has been shown to occur: borrowing and grammaticalization. A well-known case of **borrowing** is the Semitic languages of Ethiopia (Harris and Campbell 1995: 137–138).

Two of the language groups spoken in Ethiopia are Semitic and Cushitic. While they are distantly related – both belong to the Afro-Asiatic language family – they are structurally different: Semitic languages are of the VO type while Cushitic languages are of the OV type. Nonetheless, some of the Semitic languages, such as Amharic and Harari, have taken on some un-Semitic order patterns and this is attributed to Cushitic influence. Here are orders from Arabic, a Semitic language, Galla (also known as Oromo) of the Cushitic branch, and Amharic, with the structures borrowed from Cushitic in bold:

(22) | Arabic (Semitic) | Prepositions | Noun & Gen |
|---|---|---|
| Galla (Cushitic) | **Postpositions** and Prepositions | **Gen & Noun** |
| Amharic (Semitic) | Prepositions, **Postpositions,** and Ambipositions | **Gen & Noun** |

The second way in which the SVO to SOV route has arisen is by a change which does not at all involve the transposition of words. How is this possible? For a simple analogy, imagine play-dough figures of a boy and of a bear on the boy's right. Suppose you want to change the order of the two figures so that the bear is on the left. One way to do that is by moving around the figures. There is, however, also another way: you can re-mould the play-dough making the boy into a bear and the bear into a boy. The result is the same even though the two figures did not actually change position.

Something like this happened in Mandarin Chinese (Li and Thompson 1974, 1975; Sun 1996: 10–11, 59–78, 180–187). In the contemporary language, certain kinds of direct objects are marked with the preposition *bă*. The historical source of this preposition is a verb *bă* meaning 'to grab' as used in Old Chinese (500 BCE–200 CE). The word frequently occurred as the first member of serial verb constructions. In such constructions, the verb of the first clause is often a semantically light element that does not contribute much to the meaning, such as in English ***Try*** *and call your brother* or ***Go*** *(and) get the hammer*. Given that the meaning of the verb *bă* was immaterial to the semantics of the sentence, *bă* underwent grammaticalization: its semantics thinned and it turned into an object-marking preposition. Here is the schema of the historical process:

(23)　　　　　　　　　　　　　　　　　　　　　　　　　　Mandarin

    (a) INITIAL STAGE: COORDINATION OF TWO FULL SVO CLAUSES
        [Subj & ***bă***$_V$ & Obj] & [Subj & V & Obj]
        (E.g. "Jack **grabbed** the book and he burnt it.")

    (b) INTERMEDIATE STAGE: COORDINATION OF A FULL SVO
        CLAUSE AND AN ELLIPTED CLAUSE
        [Subj & ***bă***$_V$ & Obj] & [___ & V & ___]
        (e.g. "Jack **grabbed** the book and burnt.")

    (c) FINAL STAGE: THE TWO CLAUSES MERGED INTO A SINGLE
        CLAUSE WITH ***bă*** REINTERPRETED AS AN OBJECT-MARKER
        [Subj & ***bă***$_{OM}$ & Obj & V]
        (E.g. "Jack **OM** the book burnt.")

Notice that this process resulted in the merger of two SVO clauses into a single SOV clause – and this without Verb and Object actually changing positions! While this change did not affect the entire language, it added to Mandarin's already existing inventory of SOV structures.

A similar example, also showing a change of SVO to SOV through reinterpretation rather than repositioning, comes from Mande languages, a West-Atlantic subgroup of the Niger-Congo family (Claudi 1994). Here are examples from Kono, one of the Mande languages, to show the change (Claudi 1994: 202–203).

(24) (a) *m̀bé*   *tí*   *mìn-dà*   Kono
         1S.be.at tea drink-LOC

    (b) *m̀bé*   *tí*   *mìn-dà*
         1S.PRG   tea drink-PRG

Both sentences mean 'I am drinking tea.' Even though the word forms are exactly the same, the structural skeleta are different. What (24a) says is 'I am at tea's drinking'; in other words, it consists of an auxiliary verb 'I am at' and the direct object noun phrase of the auxiliary that consists of the unmarked genitive modifier 'tea's' and the noun 'drinking' in the locative – a VO structure.

(25)   Verb$_{AUX}$ & [GEN & Noun]$_O$

There are two crucial signs of reinterpretation evident in (24b). First, the auxiliary verb of (24a) has lost its verbal character and has turned into a marker of the progressive aspect – a common process exemplified by the English future marker *will*, originally a lexical verb meaning 'want' (cf. Section 2.1 above). The second change has to do with the word for 'drinking.' In (24a), it is a noun suffixed for location; in (24b), the locative suffix is re-interpreted as an additional marker of the progressive aspect (also a common process, cf. Heine and Kuteva 2002: 202–203), which shows that the word is now a verb rather than a noun. The word for 'tea,' originally a genitive modifier, has been reanalyzed as the direct object of the newly emerged verb 'drink.' Here is the schema of the change (bold-faced V-s and O-s highlight the change from VO to OV).

(26)   V$_{AUX}$ & [GEN & Noun]$_O$ → ASPECT & O & V

Once again, grammaticalization is at work here: the auxiliary grammaticalized into a tense marker. In addition, what facilitated the VO-to-OV change is that possessors are unmarked in Kono and thus can pass for objects, and that nouns and verbs have interchangeable forms.

In sum: in both Mandarin and Mande, it is a structural change that has resulted in the switch from SVO to SOV, without the constituents switching positions. In both cases, the crucial instrument of the change is a grammaticalization process (cf. Section 6.2.1 above).

Here is the summary of the historical paths of the order of major sentence constituents discussed in this section.

GEN-2
(A)   INITIAL STAGE
    (a)   The most common word order change in major sentence constituents starts with SOV.
    (b)   Object-initial orders are not initial stages.
(B)   INTERMEDIATE STAGES
    (a)   SVO is a necessary intermediate stage to V-initial orders.
    (b)   SOV is an infrequent intermediate stage.
(C)   FINAL STAGE
    (a)   OVS and OSV may be final stages in a change from SOV.

  (b) VSO and VOS may or may not be final stages from the change from SOV mediated by SVO.

  (c) SOV is an infrequent final stage.

(D) CONDITIONS

   SOV may be a final stage in a change from SVO if SOV is either borrowed from another language or if it is the result of grammaticalization.

Having considered possible changes in the order of major sentence constituents, let us turn to changes in the order of phrase-internal constituents such as adpositions and genitives.

(B) THE EVOLUTION OF CORRELATION PAIRS

Let us now assume that a language undergoes the common change from OV to VO. As shown in (18), a number of phrase-internal order patterns tend to correlate with OV versus VO crosslinguistically. Here are again three of the correlation pairs.

(27) S & O & V	V & S & O
Possessor & Possessum (GN)	Possessum & Possessor (NG)
NounPhrase & Adposition	Adposition & NounPhrase
(e.g. Hindi, Japanese, and Turkish)	(e.g. Arabic and Rapa Nui)

In other words, OV languages tend to have the genitive before the possessum and to have postpositions, while VO languages tend to have the opposite orders.

   But how would such correlations be maintained when the order of verb and object changes? Suppose a language changes OV to VO (that is, from *the book read* to *read the book*) and it also changes the linearization of possessive constructions from GN to NG (*the boy's book* to *the book of the boy*). Given that the synchronic clusters tend to be invariant across languages, adpositions must somehow scramble to keep up with this change by relinquishing their post-nominal position ("London in") and turning into prepositions ("in London"). How does this happen?

   In their encyclopedic work on the crosslinguistic tendencies of syntactic change, Alice Harris and Lyle Campbell identify two ways in which phrase-internal constituents may keep in lock-step with order changes in other aspects of grammar (1995: 210–215). They are labeled harmony by reanalysis and harmony by extension.

   An example of harmony by extension (analogy) is provided by German. The language has undergone a change from the OV to VO. In accordance with the original OV order, most adpositions were postpositions although, for reasons unknown, there must have been some prepositions as well to begin with. In today's German, most adpositions are prepositions, others are postpositions, and a third group of adpositions can occur in either order.

(28) (a) Only prepositions: German

       in (e.g. **in** *der Stadt* 'in the city')

       um (e.g. **um** *die Stadt* 'around the city')

   (b) Only postpositions:

       willen 'for the sake of' (e.g. *einer Sache* **willen** 'for

         the sake of something')

   (c) May be either prepositions or postpositions:

       wegen 'because of' (e.g. *des Vaters* **wegen** or **wegen** *des*

         Vaters 'because of the father')

       gegenüber 'across' (e.g. *dem Bahnhof* **gegenüber** or

         gegenüber *dem Bahnhof* 'across the station')

       gemäss 'according to' (e.g. *den Vorschriften* **gemäss** or

         gemäss *den Vorschriften* 'according to the rules')

The forms in (28c), which can be either preposed or postposed, have an interesting distribution across styles, which tells a tale about their history. For *wegen* 'because of,' the prepositional use is normal; the postpositional version occurs in literary style only. *Gegenüber* and *gemäss* in turn are normally postposed; the preposed versions occur only in low colloquial register. Since colloquial style is generally more innovative, these facts suggest that the prepositional use is the newer one. Another piece of evidence comes from petrified pronominal forms such as *meinet***wegen** 'because of me,' *seinet***willen** 'for his sake,' *wo***von** 'from where?' and *wor***über** 'about what?,' which include postpositions. Since pronouns generally lag behind in historical change, this shows again that postpositional order is older. Given some already existing prepositions in the language, some of the postpositions simply joined the ranks of the rest of the adpositional inventory of the language: they switched to the new prepositional order.

Besides such examples of harmony by extension, where adpositions change position in conformity with other adpositions, the other process that facilitates the preservation of uniform order among correlation pairs is **harmony by reanalysis** – that is, the evolution of new adpositions in conformity with the new order pattern of the language. Adpositions generally arise from the possessed noun of possessive constructions, e.g. English *in front of the house*, and from verbs, as English *concerning*, *behind* (from *be* and *hindan* 'back part'), or *ago* (from *agone* 'passed away'). German has also replenished its roster of adpositions from both sources. Some prepositions arose from the new VO order itself, as *ungeachtet des Wetter* 'regardless of the weather.' Other prepositions evolved from the new NG order that developed in the course of the OV-to-VO process: **jenseits** *der Donau* 'beyond the Danube,' **ausserhalb** *der Stadt* 'outside the city,' and **zufolge** *ihres Wunsches* 'in accordance with your wishes.' In such cases, harmony is attained by the grammaticalization of certain word classes – nouns and verbs – into adpositions.

Here is a summary of the harmonization of adpositions in concert with changes from OV and GN.

GEN-3

(A) INITIAL STAGE

OV, GN, Postpositions

(B) INTERMEDIATE STAGES

When OV changes to VO and GN changes to NG,

– erstwhile postpositions may switch their position by **analogy** to already existing prepositions; and

– new prepositions may evolve from the new NG and VO orders by **grammaticalization**.

(C) FINAL STAGE:

VO, NG, Prepositions

6.3 As the weeks pass … developmental change

6.3.1 From the mouth of babes. First-language acquisition

6.3.1.1 Antonyms

As children are acquiring their first language, they need to be able to segment continuous speech into units and figure out the relationships among them. There are several such relationships crucial to the comprehension and production of sentences: partonomic (which portions of speech form a significant unit?), taxonomic (which units form a category?), dependency-related (which units depend on other units for their occurrence and form?), and linear relations (which units follow which other units?). How do children figure out all of this?

The answer is: initially, they do not. Early language shows that children deviate from the ambient language by lacking the relevant concepts. For example, incipient child utterances show **partonomic** deviances labeled "chunking": units that in the ambient language are separate words are construed as a single chunk, such as *allgone* (for *all gone*), *gimmi* (for *give me*), or *ohboy* (for *oh boy*). The opposite pattern is also documented: words of the ambient language are dissembled by the child into multiple segments. An example is the phrase *lead us not into temptation* heard by a child as *lead us not into Penn Station* (Peters 1983: 64). Peters also reports on a child learning Hebrew, who took the word *zebra* to be the sentence *Ze bra* "this (is a) zebra" and used the non-existent word *bra* as the name of the animal (48).

The early **taxonomic** hypotheses that children form also tend to deviate from the ambient language. Categorization errors – that is, mismatches between the child's categories and those of the ambient language – point in two directions. On the one hand, the child may use a word less generally than the language would allow; such as when a common noun like *dog* is interpreted as referring to a particular dog only. This parallels the segmentation error discussed above, where a single word is taken to be more than one word by the child. On the other hand – analogously to chunking discussed above – children often overshoot the target by extending the applicability of a word beyond the boundaries dictated by the ambient language. Here are some examples from English, French, and Serbian (Clark 2003: 89).

(29) | Child's word: | First referent: | Extensions: |
|---|---|---|
| *mooi* | moon | > cakes > round marks on windows > writing on windows and in books > round shapes in books > tooling on leather book > covers > round postmarks > letter O |
| *mum* | horse | > cow > calf > pig > moose > all four-legged animals |
| *nénin* (French) | breast | > button on garment > point of bare elbow > eye in portrait > face in portrait > face in photo |
| *buti* (Serbian) | ball | > radish > stone spheres on park gates |
| *kutija* (Serbian) | cardboard | > matchbox > drawer > bedside table |

Semantic overextensions of this kind are not random. In the examples above, it is clear that the child generalizes by shape. There is a striking similarity between the significance of shape in children's overextensions of word meanings and the way nouns are categorized in some classifier systems (cf. Chapter 3, Section 3.2.1.2).

An additional pattern governing semantic overextension is evidenced in children learning the meanings of antonyms. In this section, three studies will be reported on about the acquisition of antonyms in English. The following points will emerge.

a. In acquiring antonyms, children frequently overextend the meaning of one of the two terms.
b. Overextension is consistently unidirectional across examples and across subjects.
c. The asymmetry between the two terms is not entirely due to the differential frequency of the use of the terms in the ambient language.

We will now take up these points in order.

a. Overextension

Several researchers have noted that in the course of acquiring the meanings of antonyms, English-speaking children learn to understand and use one of the two terms before they understand and use the other and that they overextend the first-learnt term's meaning to the other. At the initial stage, studies show that children do not understand either member of oppositions such as *before* and *after*. Next, the word *before* was acquired by nursery-school-age subjects before the word *after* was and *after* was used as if it meant *before* (Clark 1971). Similarly, *more* is learnt before *less*, and the word *less* is used as a synonym of *more*. The same holds for other antonymic pairs, such as *tall* – *short*, *big* – *small*, etc. (Donaldson and Wales 1970). In each case, one of the two terms is privileged: it is acquired before the other and, in some cases, it has its meaning extended to the other term so that the latter is used as a synonym of the former.

Why do children overextend the meaning of one term to the other member of the same opposition rather than, say, to a different word? Why is the meaning of *more* assigned to *less* and not to a member of another antonymic pair, such as *thick*, or to some other word such as *red*? This is explained by hypothesizing that children learn word meanings piecemeal: they first learn the general semantic properties of the words before getting the more specific ones. Thus, for *more* and *less*, they notice that both have to do with quantity without realizing that they stand for two opposing poles of the dimension. Similarly, for *before* and *after*, they learn that they both have to do with temporal sequence without recognizing that they refer to opposite poles of the dimension.

b. The asymmetry of overextensions

A second observation made by these studies is more intriguing. Across all pairs of antonyms, the direction of overextension has been uniform: it is always the meaning of the term that refers to a larger extension that is generalized to the other term. Thus, *more*'s meaning is adopted by *less* but *more* is not used to mean *less*; *tall* lends its meaning to *short* but *tall* is not used to mean *short*; and so forth. Semantic overextensions are thus asymmetric and consistently so by favoring always the term expressing the larger extension along the dimension.

What might be the reason for the asymmetry of overextensions?

c. The effect of frequency

Asymmetric patterns of overextensions are also documented in other aspects of child language, such as morphology. Well-known examples are regularized past tenses of English verbs – such as *comed* or *goed* – and regularized plurals of English nouns (*foots*, *sheeps*). While undergeneralization has been found to be more frequent than overextension (Bates *et al.* 2001: 379–380), morphological overextensions are common and are not limited to English. Dan Slobin's survey (1985a: 1222–1231) provides rich evidence. In Polish, the plural genitive is zero for feminine and neutral nouns but the plural masculine genitive is *-ov* and this suffix is commonly used by children on feminine and neutral nouns as well.

> Another example of overextension comes from Kaluli, a language of Papua New Guinea. The language has two word orders: SOV and OSV, the latter expressing focus on the object. In adult language the ergative marker on the subject is used only in OSV sentences but children commonly use it on subjects of SOV sentences as well.

In morphological overgeneralization, children overuse the regular forms at the expense of the irregular ones. For example, while English children will use *foots* for *feet*, they will not apply the *foot–feet* pattern to the plural of *root* resulting in *reet*. The reason seems clear: there are more nouns with the regular plural than nouns that are irregular and thus children hear the regular plural more frequently. Another factor may be that the regular plural is compositional: the past tense marker is a separate affix and thus more telling than a vowel change in the irregular forms.

If frequency of use in the ambient language is a factor in explaining the asymmetry of overextension in morphology, perhaps this explanation applies to semantic overextensions as well. In other words, could it be the greater frequency of the positive antonym that causes its meaning to be overextended to the negative pole?

This hypothesis has some support. As was discussed in Chapter 2, Section 2.5.1, frequency counts show the positive members of antonymic pairs to be more frequent in discourse. This may be in part because the member that refers to a greater extension along the dimension can be used not only in a polar sense but also in a neutral way in reference to the entire dimension, as in the question: *How tall is Grumpy the Dwarf?*

If the frequency difference between members of antonymic pairs is indeed the correct explanation for the asymmetry of the semantic extension of antonyms by children, this would mean that children's brains somehow manage to keep frequency counts of what they are hearing. That is to say, the language environment would be shown to play a significant role in language acquisition not just in the obvious sense of children learning the very language that they are surrounded by but also through their sensitivity to frequency. This would be an important argument regarding the balance of "nature" and "nurture" – the long-debated issue of whether language grows out of children's minds with little environmental influence or whether it is instilled into children's mind by the environment. If frequency counts in the ambient language could be shown to crucially influence children's language, this would tip the scale in the direction of nurture.

Nonetheless, there is also an alternative explanation for children's semantic overextension in antonymic pairs: one that draws upon nature – i.e., on children's internal cognitive resources. Perhaps the asymmetry of antonymic meanings is innately carved into the human mind. In order to test this hypothesis, an experiment is called for that cancels out frequency effects. This was the idea that prompted a study by Klatzky, Clark, and Macken (1973).

The experiment involved 24 children ranging from the ages 3;9 to 4;8. In order to eliminate the possible frequency effect of English words, the children were taught a "new language": made-up words for antonymic adjectives. If frequency of exposure were a crucial factor in children learning antonyms of English, they should show no differences in processing the newly learnt words since these words did not occur in their linguistic input before the experiment.

Adjectives pertaining to four dimensions were tested: size, height, length, and thickness. Examples of the nonsense words are *ruk* 'long' and *dax* 'short'; *hiz* 'thick' and *gep* 'thin.' In the comprehension part of the study, the experimenter displayed objects that differed along each of these scales. For size, the children saw orange cardboard cubes of differing size; for height, there were drawings of doors of various heights; for length, the children saw various strips of balsa wood; and for thickness, they were given blue wooden dowels that varied in thickness. The children were then asked questions like "Show me the one that is *ruk*?," where the answers required the understanding of the adjectives' meanings.

Results were derived from two measures for each pair of antonyms: Which of the two members was acquired sooner? And if one member was incorrectly used for the other, which member had the extended meaning? The results showed that the member referring to the larger extension – 'tall' rather than 'short,' 'big' rather than 'small' – was acquired before the other member; and in incorrect substitutions, the member with the smaller extension was used for the other member but never in reverse (e.g. the adjective for 'short' to mean 'long' but not the one meaning 'long' to mean 'short').

As the authors point out, the frequency of the corresponding English words may still have played a role: perhaps the children unconsciously translated the new words into the familiar English ones and thus frequency differences in the adult language could have crept in. To explore this option, the experimenters also tested children on the English words. If in the original test, children unconsciously translated the nonsense labels into English words, there should be no difference between their performance with the nonsense words and the English ones. However, it turned out that their performance was much better when they were prompted with English words. Thus, the children's performance with the nonsense words must have had to do with the conceptual priority of the larger-extension concepts. This in turn may be due to the greater perceptual salience of the positive terms: a thick object or a wide one is more conspicuous than a thin one or a narrow one and thus, objects with larger extension are better representatives of the dimension than objects with lesser extent. This fact may lie behind the markedness relationship between members of antonymic pairs in the adult language as well (cf. Chapter 2, Section 2.5.1).

However, this does not mean that frequency in the ambient language is irrelevant. Since, as noted above, in the test employing English words, where children did much better than when nonsense words were used, prior exposure to data did make a difference. Thus, both "nature" and "nurture" seem to have an influence on how children understand and use antonyms.

The process of acquiring antonyms in English can thus be schematized as follows (cf. Clark 1971):

GEN-4
(A) INITIAL STAGE:
　　Children do not understand or use either member of an
　　antonymous pair.
(B) INTERMEDIATE STAGES:
　　(a) The term referring to greater extension has been acquired;
　　　　 the opposite term has not yet been.
　　(b) Both terms are used but the one referring to the smaller
　　　　 extension is used in the sense of the other term.
(C) FINAL STAGE:
　　Both terms are understood and used as in the ambient
　　language.

As we have just seen, studies probing into the acquisition of antonyms indicate that frequency of exposure – that is, the effect of the environment – plays a role; but there is also indication that children have innate biases regarding which of the two poles of an opposition they construe as basic. Note, however, that these studies involved only one language: English. Crosslinguistic studies about the acquisition of antonyms are yet to be undertaken.

Returning to the issue of "nature versus nurture" (that of the "initial stage"): the most convincing way of gauging the effect of the ambient language on the acquisition process is by taking languages that differ in a particular way and see how children acquire the different constructions. As we saw above, two measures that can be used in assessing the acquisition process are the order in which grammatical patterns are acquired and the errors in children's speech – i.e. the number of deviations from the adult language. If children acquire languages at the same rate no matter how different they are and they make the same kinds of errors irrespective of the ambient language, that indicates an inborn bias. If the rate of acquisition and the errors differ according to the ambient language, this underscores the significance of the linguistic environment. This is the area of research we will turn to next.

6.3.1.2 Spatial terms

Finding out how children acquire words in one semantic area: space has been the purpose of a number of studies by Melissa Bowerman and her co-workers. Spatial distinctions – such as 'close' and 'far,' 'up' and 'down' – seem to be intuitively obvious: given how things are in the world, one would assume that spatial terminology reflects the same distinctions in all languages. However, as it turns out, this is not so: languages greatly differ in how they construe space. Even genetically related languages show surprising differences. Do you get your tan in the sun? Yes, if you are an English or German speaker; but you get it *on* the sun if you speak Hungarian. Both English and Dutch use the preposition *in* for an apple being in a bowl and both languages use the same preposition (*on* in English and *aan* in Dutch) for the handle being on the pan and a picture hanging on the wall; but English uses *on* for a ring being on the finger and a fly being on the door, while Dutch uses distinct prepositions for these relations: *om* for the ring on the finger and *op* for the fly on the door. Finnish in turn uses the same case suffix *-ssa* for an apple in the bowl and the fly on the door (Bowerman 1996: 151–158).

Two languages that show extensive differences in how spatial relations are construed are English and Korean. In English, the basic difference between *in* and *on* has to do with containment versus support: we put something *in* a place when we move an object inside a receptacle but when the object is to be supported by a surface, we put it *on* that surface, whether horizontal like a table or vertical like the wall. In Korean, spatial relations between objects are partitioned in a different way in terms of verbs. One of the differences does have to do with containment versus support; thus, as shown in (30), putting an apple into a bowl requires the verb *nehta* but putting a cup on the table requires *nohta*.

(30) (a)   *Sagwa-lul rulus-e* **nehta**   Korean

            apple-ACC bowl-in **put.in**

            'put the apple in a bowl'

       (b)   *cup-eul table-e* **nohta**

            cup-ACC table-on **put.on**

            'put the cup on the table'

In both of these situations, the objects have a loose contact with each other. However, if there is a close fit between the two objects, the opposition between containment and support is suspended: the verb *kkita* is used both for placing an object into something and onto something with a close fit between the two, such as putting Lego pieces together, ear plugs into ears, or fitting a ring on a finger. This is shown in (31).

(31) (a)   *caseteu-reul sangja-e* **kkita**   Korean

            cassette-ACC box-into **put**

            'put the cassette in the box'

       (b)   *pyung-e ttukkyeong-eul* **kkita**

            jar-onto lid-ACC **put**

            'put the lid on the jar'

These differences between English and Korean are illustrated in Figure 6.2

(Bowerman 1996: 152–153).

(32)

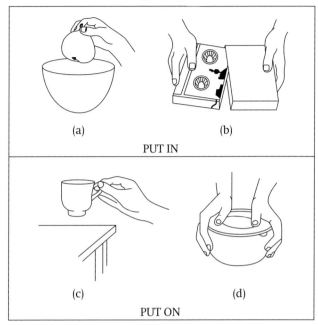

Semantic classification of four actions in English

Semantic classification of four actions in Korean

Figure 6.2
The semantic classification
of four actions in English
and in Korean.

Of course it is possible in English, too, to use verbs for putting objects together in a tight fit, such as by saying **sliding** *the cassette into the box* and **forcing** *the top on the jar*. However, conveying the idea that there is a close fit between the two objects is only an option in English: the verbs *put in* and *put on* can also be used regardless of the closeness of fit. But in Korean, the distinction between loose connection and close fit must be expressed by using different verbs. Roman Jakobson's observation cited in Section 6.2.1 is borne out again: languages differ not that much in what they can express but in what they must express.

Even though languages differ in how they analyze space, it is still possible that there is a more basic, cognitively-rooted construal of space and that children approach the acquisition of their first language with this in-built bias. Given the crosslinguistic differences in spatial vocabulary, the acquisition of spatial terms provides a test of the nature versus nurture issue: what concepts do children start out with? What is the initial stage of the process of language acquisition? On the nature side: if children are born with in-built biases for construing space, their incipient language will initially show the same spatial categories in all languages before frequency of exposure takes over guiding them towards the spatial schemata of the ambient language. If, however, children's earliest spatial terminology already reflects that of the ambient language, this weakens the argument for "nature" and strengthens the case for the significance of "nurture."

Bowerman (1996) has found that both English and Korean children start talking about spatial relations at 14–16 months and they tend to talk about similar events, such as sitting down, climbing on a chair, and handling objects. If one or the other of the two distinctions observed in English and Korean vocabulary – containment versus support, and loose fit versus close fit – corresponded to a spatial primitive that children were hard-wired for, two predictions would follow, one regarding the relative timing of acquisition in the two languages and the other regarding errors. Suppose it is the containment versus support distinction that is part of the children's cognitive endowment. First, it would then be expected that English children acquire the proper use of *put in* and *put on* sooner than Korean children did because for the English kids the structure of the ambient language matches their inborn concept, whereas for Korean children the ambient language neutralizes this distinction for close-fitting objects. Second, the errors made by Korean children would be in the direction of the containment–support distinction: they might use *kkita* not only for putting things together in a close fit, such as a cassette into a box, but also for putting an apple in a bowl. If in turn the close-fit–loose-fit distinction were given cognitively, we would expect the opposite: Korean children would acquire the spatial expressions of their language sooner than the English kids and the English kids' errors would reflect a Korean-like bias.

Bowerman reports (1996: 166) that English-speaking children acquired the containment–support distinction – that is, the proper use of *put in* and *put on, take out* and *take off* – by the time they were 18–20-month old. Similarly, the Korean children acquired the verbs *nehta* and *nohta*, which differ along the containment–support dimension, also around the same age. But when it came to verbs having to do with a close fit between objects, the Korean children's speech gave no evidence of the container-support distinction: they acquired *kkita* for fitting something closely into a tight space without regard to whether the action involved a container or a surface. English children, too, simply acquired the distinction of their ambient language.

The results were the same regarding another distinction that English and Korean differ on (Bowerman 1996: 166–167). In English, *up* and *down* are parts of various different vertical motion verbs such as *sit down*, *lie down*, *stand up*, and *pick up something*. In Korean in turn, there is no shared morpheme for 'down' in the verbs for sitting down and lying down (e.g. *ancta* 'sit down' and *nwupta* 'lie down'); nor is there a morpheme for 'up' in the verbs for standing up and picking something up. English-speaking children acquire the use of *up* and *down* by the age of 16 to 20 months: they use them for any vertical motion: *down* for sitting down, lying down, putting something down, and *up* for being picked up and picking up objects. If the up-down distinction were a conceptual primitive, we would expect Korean children to overextend one downward-motion verb to another, such as 'sit down' for 'lie down,' and we would expect a similar overextension of verbs of upward motions. However, Bowerman has found no instances of such overextensions. Examples of overextensions had to do merely with details within the categories of the language, such as that English-speaking children were observed to use *open* for pulling pop-beads apart and using *in* for putting a ping-pong ball between the knees (Bowerman 1996: 168) but the overextensions did not cross the boundaries defined by the ambient language.

Are these results to be interpreted as showing that Korean children are not clear about the difference between containment and support, or up and down; and that English children are blind to the difference between two objects having a close fit or a loose fit? This conclusion does not follow: the way we use language to partition the world does not necessarily reveal our conceptualization of the world. As discussed earlier (Chapter 2, Section 2.5.2), Dan Slobin has pointed out that "thinking" and "thinking for speaking" are two different levels of cognition (Slobin 2003: 158–161). "Thinking for speaking" involves segmenting and categorizing the world as dictated by the structure of the language that we use; beneath it, there may be a different structuring of the world free of words. In some cases, the two may coincide: we can differentiate one person from another just as language provides for this distinction but in other cases, the two systems of segmentation and categorization may not be the same. Every Hungarian knows that people have two eyes and two gloves; yet, speakers will re-structure their categories in compliance with what the language suggests. They will use 'eye' and 'glove' in the singular even though they mean both eyes or both gloves; and they will use "half-eye" and "half-glove" in reference to only one of the two objects.

Since the studies reported above show that children are sensitive to the spatial distinctions of the ambient language, the question is whether anything could be said about the acquisition of spatial terms that cuts across these crosslinguistic differences and holds for children regardless of the intricacies of the language they are learning? Several conditions have been noted as recurrent factors shaping the language-acquisition process across languages (cf. Bowerman and Choi 2001: 498). One such condition is the frequency of forms in the ambient language: frequent exposure facilitates learning. Second, children show a preference for one-to-one relationships between form and meaning. If a word is polysemous (e.g. English *bank*) or if the language has words whose meanings either overlap (e.g. English *cake* and *pastry*) or are identical (i.e. they are synonyms, such as *doctor* and *physician*), zeroing in on the proper use of the word is more difficult for the child.

Here is the summary of the process of acquiring spatial terms by children as evidenced by the above studies on English and Korean.

> GEN-5
> (A) INITIAL STAGE:
>   Children do not understand or use spatial terms. There does not appear to be an inborn bias either for containment versus support or the close-fit versus loose-fit distinction.
> (B) INTERMEDIATE STAGES:
>   Children extend and possibly overextend words but these extensions still stay within the basic categories of the ambient language.
> (C) FINAL STAGE:
>   Terms are understood and used as in the ambient language.
> (D) CONDITIONS:
>   Frequency of exposure and biunique relationships between word forms and word meanings facilitate acquisition.

6.3.2 Two systems in one head. Second-language acquisition

The task of a second-language learner is somewhat different from that of a child acquiring his first language. First-language acquisition involves starting with no language and arriving at knowledge of a language. Second-language acquisition in turn involves adding a language to one's already-existing repertoire. Nonetheless, there are parallels between the two acquisition processes.

From the point of view of the analyst, the problem is the same: there is a discrepancy between the language input that the learners are exposed to and what they are able to comprehend and produce: model and replica are mismatched. If the learners simply imitated the input, their production would consist of error-free replicas of what they have heard and nothing else. This, however, is not what actually happens:

(a)   PRODUCTION BELOW THE INPUT (selectivity) Learners do not produce all that they have heard: their production is selective of the input.

(b)   PRODUCTION BEYOND THE INPUT (creativity) Learners do not only produce what they heard: their production includes novel forms as well.

The question is how to account for selective imitation and creativity in learners' production. Since acquiring a language is a process, the selectivity issue boils down to the order in which various aspects of the target-language structures are gradually absorbed by the learner. The creativity issue in turn involves finding the sources of errors: forms that deviate from the target language, and noting the changes in these deviant structures over time.

To begin with, it is helpful to think about how we acquire other skills in life. Learning something new involves a change in the mental set of the learner and thus it is generally a difficult and stressful process. It is therefore likely that learners will unconsciously or consciously try to reduce the task by making it as easy for themselves as possible. This can be achieved in two ways.

First, learners are likely to want to minimize the difference between the target skill and what they already know by trying to apply their existing skills to the new area. In other words, they hope that the new skill is more or less the same as the old one and when this expectation is not borne out, they will make mistakes. For example, when tennis players first try their hand at ping-pong, they are likely to overshoot the table. Similarly, if you know how to play the piano and are learning to play the organ, your organ performance is likely to have a "piano accent." Thus, when it comes to second-language acquisition, it is a plausible hypothesis that the L1 – the language the learner already knows – would have an effect on how the L2 (the target language) is acquired.

A second way in which learners may try to reduce the task of learning a new skill is by "cutting corners" – that is, by substituting simpler structures for more complex ones. Simplification may involve abbreviation: rather than memorizing long phrases such as *American Telephone and Telegraph*, *Acquired Immune Deficiency Syndrome*, *et cetera*, and *ante meridiem*, we opt for acronyms: *AT&T*, *AIDS*, *etc.* and *a.m.* The two tendencies – **using the familiar for the unfamiliar** and **using the simple for the complex** – both alleviate the burden of acquiring new skills and thus can reasonably be expected to play a role in L2 acquisition as well. In this section, we will test this hypothesis on two examples: learning to pronounce the target language and acquiring relative-clause structure.

6.3.2.1 Accents

The famous Russian linguist Roman Jakobson (mentioned in Section 6.2.1) was a prominent expert in phonetics; nevertheless, he had a heavy Russian accent. When he was about to deliver a lecture at Indiana University in the 1960s, the chair of the event introduced him by saying: "Here is Professor Roman Jakobson, who speaks six languages – all of them in Russian."

Why do L2-learners tend to pronounce their target language with an accent? Why do beginning-level German learners of English say *What is dis*? Why do English speakers pronounce the composer Bach's name as [bak] rather than [baχ] as it is said in German and why do they pronounce French *tu* 'you' as [tu] rather than [ty]? And why do Spanish learners of English tend to announce their native language with *I əspeak əSpanish*?

Foreign accents reflect the language-learner's brave attempts to imitate the pronunciation of the speakers of the target language. Here are the two questions stated before re-formulated for accents.

(a)　PRODUCTION BELOW THE INPUT (selectivity) Why does the learner not pronounce the target language exactly the way native speakers do?

(b)　PRODUCTION BEYOND THE INPUT (creativity) Given that the learner's pronunciation deviates from the phonology of the target language, what is the nature of the deviations?

The first question is easier to answer, at least on a superficial level. Pronouncing words in L2 requires learning new skills and, as in all learning processes in and outside language, progress is gradual. The learner absorbs the new knowledge piecemeal: it is easier to take several small steps than one big stride. But this raises another question: what are aspects of the new skill that are learnt before other aspects? In other words, what is the order of acquisition?

The second question is more complex. Exactly how do L2-learners mispronounce the target language and why? From research carried out in the last half-century addressing the problem of the order of L2 acquisition and of the nature of the learners' errors, three comprehensive hypotheses stand out. In his highly influential book of 1957, Robert Lado proposed that the learner's difficulties with the target language depended on how different his L1 was from the L2 (Lado 1957). According to his theory, known in the literature as the **Contrastive Analysis Hypothesis**, it will be more difficult for the learner to acquire aspects of the L2 that are different from L1 than to acquire those properties of L2 that are the same as in the L1. Thus, matching features will be acquired before differing features and learner's errors will occur in the areas of mismatches. Lado's hypothesis accounts for the examples of foreign accents given above: they are due to the fact that the L2-sounds involved – English interdental fricatives such as /ð/, the German velar fricative /χ/, the French front rounded high vowel /y/ – are missing in the L1 of the learner; and even if the individual sounds are shared by L1 and L2, their clusterings – such as the English word-initial /sp/ cluster – may not be part of the L1, e.g. Spanish.

While according to Lado's claim, differences between L1 and L2 are both necessary and sufficient to predict both the order of L2 acquisition and the areas of errors, the empirical facts have not always turned out as predicted. In particular, some learners have no problem with features of L2 even though they are unfamiliar to them from their L1; and some learners have trouble learning aspects of the L2 even though they are the same in their L1.

Twenty years later, a new proposal was put forward by Fred Eckman (1977). Whereas according to the Contrastive Analysis Hypothesis, differences between two languages would cause problems for the learner regardless of which is the L1 and which is the L2, Eckman proposed that the direction of the difficulty was not symmetrical. His Markedness Differential Hypothesis states that while comparing L1 and L2 structures is needed for predicting the order of acquisition and learners' errors, it is not sufficient in and of itself: in addition, considering the markedness relations between L1 and L2 structures is necessary as well. If the L2 has structures that are more marked than the corresponding structures in L1, the learners will have difficulties; but if the L2 structures are less marked, acquisition will be easier. The difficulty in learning a new language is thus directional: given a structural difference between two languages, acquiring the target structure may be easy when coming from one of the two languages but it may be difficult in the other direction. It is predicted that learners will not make many errors if they have to learn unmarked structures in L2 and they will make more errors if the L2 structures are marked. In other words, "stepping down" toward the unmarked pole of the markedness scale in the course of the learning process is predicted to be easier than having to "step up" toward the marked pole.

Diagnostics of the markedness relation were discussed in Chapter 2, Section 2.5.1 in connection with antonymic adjectives, in Chapter 4, Section 4.2.2.2 in reference to zero forms, and in Chapter 5, Section 5.3 in phonology. The notion of markedness that Eckman adopts is based on one of these diagnostics: frequency; in particular, crosslinguistic distribution. Structure B is considered unmarked relative to structure A if the occurrence of A in a language implies the occurrence of B but not vice versa. So for example, the unrounded front vowel /i/ is unmarked relative to its rounded counterpart /y/ because languages that have /y/ also have /i/.

One of Eckman's studies testing the Markedness Differential Hypothesis investigated how German and English subjects acquired the voicing status of word-final obstruents (Eckman 1977). While in English, both voiced and voiceless obstruents occur at the ends of words (e.g. in *lack* and *lag*) in German, word-final obstruents must be voiceless (cf. Chapter 5, Section 5.2.2). It was found that English L1 learners of German had no trouble learning that obstruents must be devoiced at the ends of words but German L1 learners of English had trouble getting the word-final voice contrast. The terminal (word-final) devoicing of obstruents is an unmarked structure in that the absence of a word-medial voice contrast between obstruents in a language implies the absence of a word-final voice contrast. In other words, if a language has no words like *lacking* and *lagging*, where /k/ and /g/ contrast in the middle of word, it will also have no words like *lack* and *lag*, where /k/ and /g/ contrast word-finally. Thus, the English L1 learners of German had to acquire an unmarked structure and the German L1 learners English had to cope with a marked structure. As predicted by the Markedness Differential Hypothesis, the English L1 learners were found to have less difficulty than the German L1 learners.

While the Markedness Differential Hypothesis explains some data in L2 acquisition, there are also facts that are beyond its pale. For example, it has been observed that some Spanish and Hungarian learners of English de-voice word-final obstruents even though both their L1 and their L2 languages have voiced and voiceless obstruents word-finally. These learners opted for the unmarked structure even though neither their L1 nor their L2 prompted them in that direction.

Such evidence suggests that the L2 learners' tendency to use unmarked structures is present regardless of whether their L1 and L2 have them or not: there is an overall preference for using unmarked structures. This means that in trying to predict the order of acquisition and the nature of learners' errors, comparing L1 and L2 is not only insufficient – as the Markedness Differential Hypothesis proposed – but also unnecessary: learners may simply opt for unmarked structures regardless of what their L1 and L2 have.

But given that unmarked structures are considered unmarked because they are preferred by primary languages over their marked counterparts, the tendency in learners' languages to use unmarked structures sheds new light on interlanguages. Rather than being largely accidental upshots of the L2 learner's fumbling efforts to navigate their way between L1 and L2, interlanguages appear to be like primary languages in their shared preference for unmarked structures. This recognition has given rise to a third hypothesis regarding the nature of learners' languages. Dubbed the **Structural Conformity Hypothesis**, it proposes that crosslinguistic tendencies that hold for primary languages also characterize interlanguages (Eckman *et al.* 1989). This hypothesis makes predictions both for the order of acquisition and for the nature of learners' errors. Its prediction for the order of acquisition is the same as that of the Markedness Differential Hypothesis: if the L2 has unmarked structures, these will be acquired sooner than L2's marked structures. However, in its prediction of learners' errors, it differs from the Markedness Differential Hypothesis (MDH). The MDH predicts that if L2 has a marked pattern, it will be difficult for learners to acquire it but it does not predict the specific nature of their errors. The Structural Conformity Hypothesis, however, predicts that these learners will resort to the unmarked pattern.

By way of evidence concerning the Structural Conformity Hypothesis, we will next review two additional studies of the acquisition of L2 phonology. Both studies are reported in Eckman 1991. The purpose of these studies was the testing of two crosslinguistic phonological patterns on L2 learners to see if their interlanguages were in conformity with the Structural Conformity Hypothesis by evidencing the patterns of primary languages. The two Greenbergian universals are familiar from the phonology chapter (Chapter 5, Section 5.3).

The first study took up a generalization about word-final consonant clusters. Greenberg has found that in such clusters, the presence of at least one stop & stop sequence (as in *apt*) implies the occurrence of at least one fricative & stop sequence in that language (as in *list*). The second study was based on Greenberg's Resolvability Principle, according to which if a language has a particular consonant cluster in either word-initial or word-final position, at least one continuous subsequence of that cluster will also occur in the same position. That is, if a language has word-initial *str* (as in **string**), either *st* or *tr* – or perhaps both – will also occur word-initially (as in **stain** and **train**).

Both studies involved 11 subjects: 4 Japanese, 4 Korean, and 3 Cantonese Chinese learners of English with an age range of 25–32. None of these L1-s allow consonant clusters in either word-initial or word-final position. The tasks involved reading word lists, describing pictures, reading continuous texts, and engaging in free conversation with the interviewer. Data were elicited in four or five sessions over a period of 2–3 weeks.

Given that both universals are implicational, test results were considered confirmatory of the generalization if both the implicans and the implicatum were found to be present in the interlanguages. For the Fricative-Stop principle, this meant that both word-final stop & stop and fricative & stop sequences had to occur; and for Resolvability to hold, both a larger cluster and at least one subset of it had to be present. If only the implicatum (fricative-stop sequences and subset clusters) occurred, this would also have been confirming evidence. However, if the implicans was present but the implicatum was not, that showed that the generalization did not hold for the learners' languages. Thus, if subjects had word-final stop & stop sequences but no fricative & stop sequences, or if they had a larger cluster but not any of its subpart, this falsified the claim that interlanguages were like primary languages in these respects.

The actual results showed overwhelmingly that the two generalizations held for the learners' languages. For the Fricative-before-Stop principle, there were 524 relevant test cases; out of them only 5 ran counter to the generalization. Resolvability was borne out in 147 cases (74%) out of 200 test cases. There were subjects who had mastered the implicatum only – fricative & stop, and a shorter consonant cluster – but not the implicans; but there were few subjects that had mastered the implicans without having mastered the implicatum. These results are by and large consistent with both the Markedness Differential Hypothesis and the Structural Conformity Hypothesis.

Here is a summary of what emerges from these studies regarding phonological acquisition.

> GEN-6
> (A) INITIAL STAGE
>   No knowledge of the phonological system of the target
>   language.
> (B) INTERMEDIATE STAGES
>   Both the order of acquisition and deviations from the target
>   are affected by two factors:
>   (a) Structures shared by L1 and L2 are acquired earlier in the
>   course of learning L2 than those that are different.
>   (b) Errors in acquiring marked structures tend to show
>   preference for the unmarked structures.

(C) FINAL STAGE

(Near-)perfect comprehension and production of the target-language system.

(D) CONDITIONS

Several factors may play a role including frequency of exposure to the L2, type of exposure, and learners' motivation and attitudes toward the L2.

6.3.2.2 Resumptive pronouns

In an influential study, the Swedish linguist Kenneth Hyltenstam reported on native speakers of Persian learning Swedish (Hyltenstam 1984). The target structure was relative clauses of the kinds exemplified in (33) (data from Veronika Lundbåck). The relative clause structures are between square brackets.

(33) (a) SUBJECT RELATIVIZATION   Swedish

  mannen [som kom från Iran]

  the:man [that came from Iran]

  'the man that came from Iran'

  (b) DIRECT-OBJECT RELATIVIZATION

  mannen [som jag slog]

  the:man [that I hit]

  'the man that I hit'

  (c) INDIRECT-OBJECT RELATIVIZATION

  mannen [som jag gav mjölk (till)]

  the:man [that I gave milk (to)]

  'the man that I gave milk to'

In Persian, the native language of the students, these phrases would be formulated somewhat differently as shown in (34), with the crucial parts in bold (data from Shigekazu Hasegawa).

(34) (a) SUBJECT RELATIVIZATION   Persian

  mardi   [ke   az]   Irân]   âmad]

  man   [that   from   Iran   came:S3]

  'the man that came from Iran'

  (b) DIRECT-OBJECT RELATIVIZATION

  *mardi   [ke   man   (**u-ra**)   zadam]*

  man   [that   I   (**him-OBJ**) hit:S1]

  'the man that I hit'

  (c) INDIRECT-OBJECT RELATIVIZATION

  *mardi   [ke   man   shir-râ   **be**   **u**]   dadâm*

  man   [that   I   milk-OBJ   **to**   **him**   gave:S1]

  'the man that I gave milk to'

As discussed in the syntax chapter (Chapter 3, Section 3.2.1.1), Persian has resumptive pronouns in non-subject relative clauses: they are optional in direct-object relatives and obligatory in indirect-object relatives. Swedish, however, is like English: relative clauses contain no resumptive pronouns.

The task that Hyltenstam's Persian subjects faced was two-fold. On the one hand, they had to notice that subject relatives in Swedish were like those in Persian: no resumptive pronouns. On the other hand, they needed to observe that Swedish direct-object and indirect-object relatives were unlike the Persian ones: these clauses did not include resumptive pronouns just as subject relatives did not.

A sample of the Persian students' Swedish constructions is given in (35). (These are hypothetical examples constructed on the basis of Hyltenstam's report.)

(35) (a) SUBJECT RELATIVIZATION   Persian L1, Swedish L2

    mannen   [som   kom   från   Iran]

    the:man [that came from Iran]

    'the man that came from Iran'

(b) DIRECT-OBJECT RELATIVIZATION

    *mannen   [som   jag   slog   **honom**]*

    the:man [that I   hit   **him**]

    'the man that I hit'

(c) INDIRECT-OBJECT RELATIVIZATION

    *mannen   [som   jag   gav   mjölk   till   **honom**]*

    the:man [that I   gave milk   to   **him**]

    'the man that I gave milk to'

The phrases in (35) reflect "speaking Swedish in Persian." The distribution of the resumptive pronouns mirrors Persian: no pronoun in subject relatives but pronouns in direct-object and indirect-object relatives. The fact that in subject relatives, the subjects did not use the pronouns may be explained either by the effect of the target language or by the effect of the native language. That is to say, the students may already have noticed that Swedish did not have resumptive pronouns in subject relatives; or they may have simply transferred this pattern from Persian. But the presence of resumptive pronouns in direct-object and indirect-objects relatives is not target-like: it seems to be transfer of the native construction.

The likely effect of the native language is also shown by the differential frequency with which the Persian subjects used resumptive pronouns in their Swedish relatives. As noted above, the use of resumptive pronouns in Persian is optional in direct-object relatives but required in indirect-object relatives. This frequency difference is directly reflected in the Persian students' productions: out of the 12 students, 10 used the pronouns in all of their indirect-object relatives while in direct-object relatives, the pronouns were used less often.

The influence of native language is also shown by Hyltenstam's data from learners of Swedish with L1-s other than Persian. Some were speakers of Finnish. This language is like Swedish: no resumptive pronouns in relative clauses. Correspondingly, the Finnish speakers did not use them in their Swedish sentences, either. There were also subjects with L1 Spanish and Greek. Both Spanish and Greek, just as Persian, have resumptive pronouns in non-subject relative clauses and these students followed this pattern in their Swedish.

However, there is also evidence that the erroneous use of resumptive pronouns in relative clauses is not always the result of transfer from the native language. There are three strands of research to show this.

First, Stephen Matthews and Virginia Yip (2003) tested the developing English-L2 of two Cantonese-speaking children between the ages of 2 and 5 and found that they tended to use resumptive pronouns in their relative clauses, as in (36).

(36) (a) *I got that red-flower dress that Jan gave *it* to me.
      (b) *This is the homework that I did *it*.

Since Cantonese has resumptive pronouns in non-subject relatives, this might seem like a case of transfer. However, two facts speak against this. First, the children did not use resumptive pronouns in their Cantonese relative clauses. Second, they used resumptive pronouns in their English sentences only when the clauses followed the English order: head preceding relative clause. When they were sticking to the Cantonese pattern by placing the relative clause before the head, they did not use resumptive pronouns. Both of these observations suggest that the use of resumptive pronouns in adult Cantonese and their use in the incipient English of the children were independent phenomena.

In the case of these Cantonese children, the primary language has resumptive pronouns; nonetheless, the use of these pronouns in the English sentences by the children seems highly unlikely to go back to the influence of the native language. A second set of data in turn completely excludes the influence of the primary language.

Fernando Tarallo and John Myhill (1983, especially 63–64, 70–72) elicited grammaticality judgments from 99 English-speaking university students studying different foreign languages including German, Portuguese, Mandarin Chinese, and Japanese. None of these languages have resumptive pronouns in relative clauses, nor does English of course, the primary language of the students. Yet, when students were given relative clauses in their respective target languages that had resumptive pronouns, some students rated them as grammatical. This was clearly not due to L1-transfer.

Third, there is also startling evidence from first-language acquisition studies. Ana Teresa Pérez-Leroux (1995: 121) surveys the occurrence of resumptive pronouns in relative clauses in the speech of children acquiring English and French as their native language. Here are English examples of the children's productions containing resumptive pronouns.

(37) (a) *I hurt my finger that Thomas stepped on **it**.*   English
      (b) *Smoky is an engine that **he** pulls the train*

Transfer from a primary language is out of the question in these cases since there is no primary language involved at all.

Let us take stock. While the use of resumptive pronouns in the Swedish speech of Hyltenstam's Persian, Spanish, and Greek subjects may be explained by transfer from the primary language, other instances of the use of resumptive pronouns in deviation from the target language must have alternative explanations. This is so in the cases of Matthews and Yip's Cantonese children, of the grammaticality judgments by English speakers learning German, Portuguese, Mandarin, and Japanese in Tarallo and Myhill's study and, needless to say, in the case of the speech of French-speaking and English-speaking children acquiring their first language. How can these data be explained?

A possible explanation arises if we interpret the concept of transfer in an extended sense. The underlying motivation behind transfer from the primary language is the unconscious attempt to use familiar structures for unfamiliar ones. But familiarity does not have to come from the L1: it may come from structures already acquired in the L2. Compare the following relative-clause structures with the corresponding main sentences.

(38) (a) *the doll [that I played with]*   English
      (b) **I played with.*
      (c) **the doll [that I played with **it**]*
      (d) *I played with **it**.*

(38c) is a deviant structure but notice that it has a possible advantage over (38a) for the learner of English: the relative clause is an exact replica of the corresponding main clause. If learners rely on what is already known to them from the target language, they are likely to favor resumptive pronouns in relative clauses. Thus, familiarity with main-sentence constructions in the target language resulting in internal transfer (internal because a structure is transferred from the L2 rather than from the L1) would explain why the Cantonese kids used resumptive pronouns in some of their English relative clauses. It would also explain why children acquiring English as their first language would use resumptive pronouns in their relative clauses.

However, internal transfer does not explain all of Tarallo and Myhill's subjects. As noted above, they were native English speakers studying German, Portuguese, Mandarin, and Japanese and some of them judged relative clauses with resumptive pronouns in their target language as grammatical. Since in main sentences of German, pronominal arguments are obligatory, the subjects whose target language was German could have drawn upon main sentence structure when they accepted relative clauses with resumptive pronouns. In Portuguese, however, subject pronouns are optional and in Mandarin, and Japanese pronouns are generally omitted in all argument positions. Thus, subjects studying Portuguese, Mandarin, or Japanese would not have been exposed to large numbers of main sentence structures complete with pronouns, which means relative clauses with resumptive pronouns would not have been judged correct on the basis of already familiar main sentence structures. How can their judgments be explained?

As mentioned in the beginning of this section, substituting familiar structures for unfamiliar ones – that is, external or internal transfer – is only one of the ways in which language learners may make the task more manageable. Another plausible route is to use simpler structures instead of the more complex ones; that is, simplifying the target structures. If it could be shown that relative clauses with resumptive pronouns are simpler than those that do not include them, this would account for the appeal of pronoun-ful relative clauses to language learners.

On the face of it, pronoun-ful relative clauses are more complex than pronoun-less ones since the former include one more constituent: the pronoun. Nonetheless, there is one respect in which the pronouns add simplicity to clause structure. As seen in (38) and as noted in Section 3.2.1.1 of Chapter 3, if relative clauses include resumptive pronouns, the otherwise truncated construction becomes compositional since all verb arguments are formally represented. In other words, they "make more sense." The semantically explicit, compositional structure of pronoun-ful relative clauses may explain why language learners opt for it even if their primary language does not have this structure nor do simple main clauses of the target language provide a model for it.

The hypothesis that the use of resumptive pronouns makes relative clause structure simpler suggests that resumptive pronouns would be preferentially used when the overall task is more difficult. This prediction is supported. As noted above, Matthews and Yip's Cantonese-speaking children used resumptive pronouns only when they placed the relative clauses into the target position, i.e. after the head, but not when they used the Cantonese order of relative clause before the head. Since the English order must have created an added difficulty, the use of resumptive pronouns in post-head relative clauses is explained by the hypothesis that resumptive pronouns provide a crutch when the going gets tough.

The following schema summarizes the acquisitional process of relative clauses of an L2 that has no resumptive pronouns by speakers whose L1 has such pronouns.

GEN-7
(A) INITIAL STAGE:
Use of resumptive pronouns in some or all positions.
(B) INTERMEDIATE STAGES:
The order of acquisition and the errors in the use of resumptive pronouns may show the effects of the following factors:
– external transfer (transferring the distribution of pronouns in L1 relative clauses)

- internal transfer (transferring the distribution of pronouns in L2 main clauses)
- complexity of relative clause constructions (use of the pronouns in more complex constructions)

(C) FINAL STAGE:

No use of resumptive pronouns.

How do these findings relate to the Structural Conformity Hypothesis discussed in Section 6.3.2.1: the idea that interlanguages reflect the same tendencies as primary languages do by prioritizing unmarked structures over marked ones? We have seen a tendency for interlanguage speakers to use resumptive pronouns even if neither the L1 nor the L2 has them. This is in line with the Structural Conformity Hypothesis if resumptive pronouns are an unmarked option but not if they are marked structures. Are pronoun-ful relative clauses marked or unmarked? On the one hand, they are structurally more complex since they include an extra constituent: the pronoun. But, on the other hand, if as noted above, we consider the congruence of form and meaning, they are simpler due to their compositional structure. Also, by the criterion of crosslinguistic distribution, pronoun-ful relative clauses down the Accessibility Hierarchy are unmarked because they form implicata: if a language has resumptive pronouns in subject relatives, it also has them in direct-object relatives; and so forth. On this analysis, the presence of resumptive pronouns in interlanguages amounts to the presence of unmarked structures and thus the pattern is in line with the Structural Conformity Hypothesis.

* * * *

In closing, let us return to our initial thoughts regarding the nature of learners' languages. Based on what seemed to characterize learning processes in general, we hypothesized that some aspects of interlanguages would reflect what is familiar to the learners and other aspects would be the result of simplification. In the data discussed above about the acquisition of L2 pronunciation and the acquisition of L2 relative-clause structures, we have indeed found a preference for the familiar over the unfamiliar in external and internal transfer: learners transferring constructions from their L1 and from already-acquired parts of the L2.

Evidence was also found for the preference for simple over complex. The tendency for final devoicing may be analyzed as an instance of simplification: lack of action on the part of the vocal cords reduces the amount of articulatory effort. Also, the fact that learners acquire subsequences of consonant clusters before they acquire the longer ones – such as learning to pronounce *st-* and *tr-* before acquiring *str-* – is a clear preference for simplicity. And since, as pointed out above, resumptive pronouns render relative clauses compositional, their use also simplifies the task of acquiring these structures.

So far in this book, we have discussed relative clauses in two contexts: in primary languages (Section 3.2.1.1 of Chapter 3) and in language acquisition just above. The next section will complement these discussions by reporting on how speakers of a language actually process relative-clause structures in real time.

6.4 From knowing to doing. Linguistic performance

6.4.1 Relative clauses

Historical change and acquisitional development are two of the temporal processes that shape language. There is also a third relevant process: one leading from knowledge to action.

In considering historical change and acquisition, it was relatively easy to set up an initial stage for the process. Establishing the initial stage behind performance is more difficult. We cannot tap into knowledge directly by circumventing performance: what people know is shown only by what they do. What form might our internalized knowledge of language take? Clearly, it must include a list: the inventory of the sound–meaning relations that make up the lexicon of the language. But what about the patterns of combining sounds, morphemes, words, phrases, and clauses? Do we have a list of permissible combinations? Or does our competence take the shape of rules that yield the combinations? There are no agreed-upon answers to these questions in the field. In what follows, we will simply assume what is beyond doubt: that the elements and patterns of our language are present in some form in our brain and in using language, we draw upon this knowledge. The studies to be reported on below probe into the question of exactly how linguistic knowledge is implemented in linguistic performance.

There are three principal measures of linguistic performance. One is preferential use: if there is a meaning that may be expressed in more than one way, which expression is more frequently resorted to? The second one is reaction time: how long does it take for speakers to produce or comprehend a construction? The third measure is error rates: if comprehension or production goes awry, how many errors do people make and what is the nature of the errors?

In the present section, we explore psychological evidence on how people process relative clauses of different kinds. This discussion will lead us to a second topic: the competition between conflicting motivations in linguistic performance (Section 6.4.2).

In our discussions of resumptive pronouns in the syntax chapter (Chapter 3, Section 3.2.1.1) and in Section 6.3.2.2 of the present chapter, we saw that both in the grammars of primary languages and in first- and second-language acquisition processes, preference for using resumptive pronouns increases with level of difficulty. In primary languages, their use increases to the right on the Accessibility Hierarchy, repeated in (39).

(39) SU > DO > IO > OBL > GEN > OCOMP

A similar process applies to all areas of human competence and performance. Having internalized a skill is one thing; implementing this knowledge in behavior is another. Jury members at a piano competition are likely to know how to play a piano; but could they do it themselves? Theater critics have knowledge about good acting but this does not mean they would make good actors. The same way, knowing a language does not mean that we can speak and comprehend every bit of it with equal ease.

Since the insertion of resumptive pronouns changes a truncated clausal skeleton to a main-clause structure – *that [I saw ___]* is changed to *that [I saw **him**]* – we hypothesized that resumptive pronouns were invoked to help with otherwise difficult constructions by turning them into well-known main-clause structures. But, as discussed in the syntax chapter, the only evidence we had for assuming that relative clause structures to the right on the Accessibility Hierarchy were more difficult was crosslinguistic distribution. Some languages do not have clause types to the right and we attributed this fact to complexity. However, in order to bolster the guess that the reason why resumptive pronouns are preferentially used in relative clause structure toward the lower end of the hierarchy is that these structures are more difficult, we need independent support to show that difficulty increases to the right of the hierarchy. In what follows, we will see that there is actual experimental evidence to show this.

Here are first three studies testing the relative difficulty of the first two positions of the Accessibility Hierarchy: subject relatives and direct-object relatives. Wanner and Maratsos (1978) probed into the psychological process underlying the comprehension of English relative clauses of these two types. In one of the experiments, subjects were given sentences with relative clauses projected on the screen, such as (40).

(40) (a)   subject relative   English

       *The witch **who ___ despised the sorcerers** frightened
       little children.*

   (b)   direct-object relative

       *The witch **who the sorcerers despised ___** frightened
       little children.*

The presentation of these sentences was interrupted at varying points by lists of five names (such as *Peter, Charles*, etc.). The subjects' task was two-fold: recalling the names and comprehending the sentences. Comprehension was measured by the subjects' answers to various wh-questions (such as *Who frightened the children?*). The final scores were a combination of the accuracy of recalling the names and of understanding the sentences.

The results showed that subject relatives were generally better understood than object relatives. Wanner and Maratsos explained this by pointing out that the head of the relative clause – *witch* in (40) – had to be held in memory until the gap in the relative clause was located. That is to say, hearing *The witch who*, the listener would know that a relative clause was to follow but would not know the grammatical role of the witch in the clause until he has found the gap. Since the gap shows up later in object relatives than in subject relatives, there is an increased memory load involved in processing object relatives and this may explain their difficulty over subject relatives.

Two further studies also took up subject and object relative clauses but the language was different: French. In one of the experiments (Frauenfelder,

Segui, and Mehler 1980), 30 Parisian university students heard sentences with subject relatives and object relatives. They were told to pay close attention to the meanings of the sentences and to push a button when they heard a particular sound. For example, they were given sentences like in (41).

(41) (a) subject relative   French
      Le savant   **qui ___ connaît** *le docteur* *travaille dans une*
      the scholar **who ___ knows** **the doctor** works   in   a
         université   moderne.
         university modern
      'The scholar who knows the doctor works at a modern
      university.'

      (b) direct-object relative
      Le savant   **que connaît le docteur ___** *travaille dans une*
      the scholar **who knows** **the doctor ___** works   in   a
         université   moderne.
         university modern
      'The scholar who the doctor knows works at a modern
      university.'

In the sentences of (41), subjects were told to spot the /t/ phoneme, which occurs at the beginning of the first word after the relative clause (*travaille*). The subjects' comprehension of the sentences was assessed by their answers to questions about the content immediately after the presentation of each sentence. What was measured was reaction time: how fast did subjects push the button showing that they have both understood the sentence and detected the target sound. It turned out that reaction time was longer if the sound occurred after an object relative than if it occurred after a subject relative. A possible interpretation suggested by the researchers is that this is because the comprehension of object relatives involves more neural work than getting the meaning of a subject relative.

In a second study on French relative clauses (Holmes and O'Regan 1981), an additional novel measure was employed. Subjects were given sentences like in (42).

(42) (a) subject relative   French
      L'auteur   **qui ___ connaît l'éditeur** *a rencontré mon ami.*
      the author **who ___ knows** **the editor** has met   my friend
      'The author who knows the editor met with my friend.'
      (b) direct-object relative
      L'auteur   **que** **connaît l'éditeur ___** *a rencontré mon ami.*
      the author **whom knows** **the editor ___** has met   my friend
      'The author whom the editor knows met with my friend.'

In addition to error rates in comprehension, the other measure used was eye movement activity. Two of the relevant results showed that

subjects made more errors in comprehending object relatives than subject relatives; and that eye movement measurements registered more
regressive eye behavior – i.e. "re-looks" – in object relatives than in subject
relatives. These data suggest once again that direct-object relatives are
more difficult to comprehend than subject relatives.

The three studies described above tested the psychological reality of
the Accessibility Hierarchy's top segment: subject and direct-object relatives. A classic experiment gauging the differing difficulty of the various
English relative clause types took up a larger portion of the hierarchy all
the way down to genitive relatives. In Edward Keenan and Sarah Hawkins'
study (1987), 40 adults and 40 children served as subjects; the experimental task was the repetition of relative-clause sentences. Examples:

(43) (a) subject relative   English
           *I know that the girl **who got the answer right** is clever.*
      (b) indirect-object relative
           *He remembered that the dog **which Mary taught the trick** to
           was clever.*

The testing procedure consisted of subjects hearing the sentences with
each followed by a set of digits; afterwards, they were asked to write down
both the sentences and the numbers that they had heard.

From among the various results that emerged, two are of particular
interest. They have to do with the number of errors and with the nature
of errors.

(44) (a) NUMBER OF ERRORS
           Accuracy of performance correlated with the order of relative
           clauses on the Accessibility Hierarchy: the number of errors
           increased to the right of the scale of SU > DO > IO > OBL > GEN
      (b) NATURE OF ERRORS
           If subjects replaced a type of relative clause that they had heard
           with another type, in 74%–80% of the cases, the relative clause
           they substituted was higher on the Accessibility Hierarchy than
           the stimulus.

(44a) says that there were more errors made in, say, indirect-object
relatives than in direct-object relatives. (44b) states that if an indirect-object
relative clause was replaced by another type, it was almost always a direct-
object relative or a subject-relative but not an oblique-relative or a
genitive-relative. Both results show a preference for relative clauses to the
left on the hierarchy.

While all of these studies have shown that people have more trouble
processing relative clauses toward the right end of the hierarchy, there is
more than one possible explanation for this observation. One reason may
simply be **familiarity**. If there are frequency differences among the various relative clause types in the language so that people hear and use more
subject relatives than, say, direct-object or indirect-object relatives, they
may process subject relatives better due to constant practice.

The other reason may be differences in **complexity**. As we saw above, this is the reason that Wanner and Maratsos, and Frauenfelder *et al.* suggested. Wanner and Maratsos proposed that identifying the gap into which the referent of the head noun fits calls for a longer memory span the farther down the clause is on the Accessibility Hierarchy.

This basic idea has been expanded and elaborated on by John Hawkins as he has proposed that it is indeed increased filler–gap distance that causes processing difficulties. The clearest cases of this explanation are SVO or VSO languages with head-initial relatives as in (45) (N stands for the head of the relative clause).

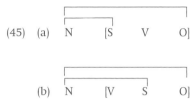

(45) (a)   N   [S   V   O]

(b)   N   [V   S   O]

In subject relatives, the gap (the subject position of the relative clause) is closer to the filler (the head noun) than it is in object relatives. Distance between filler and gap continues to increase down the hierarchy. (For a detailed explanation and more illustration, see Hawkins 1999 and Hawkins 2004: 169–221, especially 177–180.)

All four of these studies show that the processing of relative clause types becomes more difficult proceeding down the Accessibility Hierarchy and that a plausible reason is increasing filler–gap distance. This evidence provides the missing argument for explaining why resumptive pronouns are used preferentially at lower points in the hierarchy: we now have psychological evidence that relative clause types to the right of the Accessibility Hierarchy are indeed more difficult to process. These pronouns occur where otherwise there would be gaps. The pronouns provide a partial representation of the head and therefore the head, which is at increasing distance as we proceed down the hierarchy, does not need to be consulted for full interpretation.

But if resumptive pronouns are so helpful, why are they not used in all relative clauses including even subject relatives? Since the filler–gap distance is short in such cases, they may not be necessary but they would help and would certainly not do any harm. Hawkins' answer is that the distribution of resumptive pronouns in relative clauses along the Accessibility Hierarchy is the result of a compromise between two general principles (Hawkins 2004: 31–44). On the one hand, the principle labeled **Minimize Domains** favors the insertion of resumptive pronouns in difficult relative clauses so that grammatically yet-uninterpreted material – the head of a relative clause – does not need to be stored in memory very long. But, on the other hand, there is also another principle labeled **Minimize Form** that counteracts Minimize Domains: it discourages the use of more form than necessary, such as redundant pronouns. Languages differ in how they strike a balance between the two principles. Arabic and Gilbertese require resumptive pronouns in direct-object relatives and farther down the hierarchy; Hebrew and Persian have optional resumptive pronouns in direct-object relatives and obligatory ones farther below; and Korean and Turkish have them only in genitive relatives. Finally, some languages such as English and Swedish, assign absolute priority to the Minimal Form principle over Minimize Domain: they do not use resumptive pronouns in any of their relative clauses (Hawkins 1999: 159).

Here is the summary of the results of the psycholinguistic studies surveyed above for English and French. Initial stage here refers to the presumed internal competence in the language; final stage refers to speakers' performance in the experiments. There is no evidence of intermediate stages.

GEN-8
(A) INITIAL STAGE
Speakers are familiar with relative-clause structures in English and French although to varying degrees depending on frequency of exposure.
(B) FINAL STAGE
In processing relative-clause structures, speakers' comprehension and recall decrease to the right on the Accessibility Hierarchy.
(C) CONDITIONS
These observations were made in experimental settings.

As noted above, the distribution of resumptive pronouns in relative clauses across languages and in acquisitional sequences can be viewed as a compromise between two conflicting principles. As Hawkins put it: "We have a competing motivation…between (reduced) form processing and explicit dependency marking, with structural complexity increasingly requiring the latter" (Hawkins 1999: 260). Similar competitions may be observed in other areas of linguistic performance. This will be illustrated next.

6.4.2 Competing motivations

Most of us living in a human society are constrained by the rules of conduct set by our community. In applying for a loan, we go through the steps set by the bank; when invited to a party, we take along a present appropriate to the occasion; and when driving, we make sure we obey the traffic rules. However, even though societal standards have been designed or have evolved to be helpful, there are situations where individual needs conflict with them. I may need a loan in a hurry and thus would try to circumvent the rules; I may not have enough money to get the proper gift for the host; or I may be rushed to get to some place so that traffic rules are a hindrance. In such instances, there is a conflict between the rules and my needs and I have to make a choice.

This is true for verbal behavior as well. Consider the following utterances (Fox *et al.* 1996: 187, 189).

(46) (a) *I don't know but it's /PAUSE/ it's going to cost quite a bit.*   English

    (b) *But it- it does work out if you have just the common*
        dena- denominator here

    (c) *And I haf /PAUSE/ my class starts at two.*

Any speaker of English would recognize that these structures do not conform to the grammar of the language. (46a) contains an ungrammatical repetition: *it's* occurs twice in a row. (46b) also includes a repetition (*it*) and it also contains the form *dena* – not an English word at all. In (46c), *And I haf* is not interpretable by itself nor does it connect with what follows. Yet, these utterances have been produced by English speakers.

What these examples show is that speakers may need to pause in the middle of a sentence to plan the rest of the expression and they may even change their mind about what to say or how to say it. In (46a), it seems the speaker needed a bit of time to decide what he really wanted to say. In (46b), the repetition of *it* may be due to the same reason; and *dena-* is a false start for *denominator*, which was then canceled and replaced. And in (46c), the speaker may have wanted to say *I have to be in class at two* but then aborted the structure and re-cast the intended message in a different way. Such verbal patterns are labeled self-repairs. A self-repair is an act by the speaker either to correct something that he has said, or to cut short a construction in favor of a new one, or just to pause for further planning. The moves may involve repetition, substitution, insertion, or deletion.

Self-repairs are based on speakers monitoring their own speech and making adjustments to suit their communicative needs. But, as shown above, they yield ungrammatical utterances: they clash with the grammatical standards of the language. Repairs can thus be analyzed as compromises between two competing motivations: to behave according to the rules of the language and at the same time to attend to current interactional needs. Or, as Martin Pfeiffer (to appear) puts it, the conflict is between formal (morphosyntactic) and functional (cognitive and interactional) motivations.

Barbara Fox and her co-authors (2012) analyzed self-repair structures in two languages, with 500 repairs in an English corpus and 225 in a Japanese one. From among the many different insights of this paper, two are particularly relevant here. The first is a similarity between repair structures in the two languages: both English and Japanese speakers strike a balance between responding to current needs while staying within the bounds of grammatical conventions. The second observation is about a difference between the two sets of speakers: repair structure reflects the special grammatical properties of the speakers' language.

This latter point is richly documented in the paper by Fox *et al.*; here is just one example. Japanese speakers may repair an affix by replacing it with another while this kind of morphological repair has not been observed in English. Here is a Japanese example (Fox *et al.* 1996: 202).

(47) *ja   nani   goro   ni kurida**shi-soo***   Japanese
     then what.time about OBL go.out
     'Then about what time (shall we) go out?'

The verb has the suffix *shi*, a form which is generally followed by auxiliaries or particles. In this context, however, there is no such subsequent material and thus the speaker replaces -*shi* with -*soo*, a so-called cohortative suffix. Fox *et al.* attribute the occurrence of suffix repairs in Japanese and its dearth in English to factors having to do with the greater phonological and grammatical independence of the Japanese suffixes. Japanese suffixes are full syllables, while the English suffixes -*s* and -*ed* are generally pronounced as lone consonants. Also, Japanese verbal suffixes do not mark a close connection with the subject by verb agreement as English -*s* does (e.g. *he sit-s*): they indicate tense and aspect. The relative independence of Japanese suffixes may render them better candidates for replacement in repair structures.

Similar observations about crosslinguistic differences in repair structure have been made by Martin Pfeiffer (to appear) in his analysis of German self-repairs that involve semantic elaboration, with the repairing segment providing more information than the repaired one. From a corpus of 2000 self-repairs in German dialogues, he analyzed 58 instances involving substitutions of nouns within prepositional phrases. The question he addressed was this: If the speaker wants to substitute the noun of a prepositional phrase, is he going to utter the new noun only or is he going to retrace his steps to the entire prepositional phrase?

Here is an example. One of the interlocutors asked the other person where he had done his apprenticeship. The answer was (48).

(48) hh   *auf_m **Ring auf_m Hohenstaufenring***   German
      hm   on_the **boulevard on_the Hohenstaufen.boulevard**
      'Hm. On the Boulevard; on Hohenstaufen Boulevard.'

Hohenstaufenring is a street in Cologne, colloquially referred to as the Ring. In this case, what the speaker replaced was the noun of the prepositional phrase but in doing so he repeated the preposition and the article as well. Compare (48) with the English example in (49) (Fox and Jasperson 1995: 102).

(49) *They get their g- teeth keep growing round from the **fron** – **back***   English
      to the front.

Here the speaker wants to replace *front* with *back* and in doing so he does not repeat the entire prepositional phrase *from the front* but simply replaces the noun: *front*.

Pfeiffer has found this to be a common pattern in the two languages. While in English, it is not common to recycle back to the beginning of the prepositional phrase (cf. Fox *et al.* 2009: 285), in German the entire prepositional phrase tends to be repeated. Pfeiffer explains this by a syntactic difference between the two languages. In German, the definite article is often cliticized to the preposition (e.g. *aufm* for *auf dem*) and the preposition-and-article unit is more closely bound to the following noun in that the article varies in shape depending on the gender and number of the noun and depending on the case that the preposition governs. In English in turn, prepositions do not cliticize to the article, they do not govern different cases of the article nor does the noun affect the article's gender and number. Thus, in English, the article does not form as close a unit either with the preposition or with the noun as it does in German.

This is once again evidence for how the grammar of the language is implicated in repair patterns. Speakers engaged in self-repair do not back up to a random segment of the utterance: it is a relatively independent unit that is being reviewed by them and that gets repeated. The resolution between the competing formal and functional desiderata consists in the speaker attending to his current communicative needs of making a repair while at the same time observing a formal, grammatical factor: the boundedness of grammatical elements.

Here is a summary of repair strategies in English, Japanese, and German based on a portion of the results reported in Fox *et al.* (1996) and Pfeiffer (to appear).

> This is similar to how we resolve similar conflicts outside language. If I have to drive to a place and I am in a great hurry, I may drive at the very top of the speed limit posted – but not beyond; or I may exceed the speed limit but will stop short of taking an illegal left turn.

GEN-9

(A) INITIAL STAGE
   An intended utterance.

(B) INTERMEDIATE STAGES
   (a) What is uttered is an unintended form or unintended meaning, or merely a part of the intended utterance followed by pause.
   (b) Repair is made by either correcting a mistaken form, or by re-casting an already-expressed meaning, or by simply picking up the aborted sentence. The repaired segments conform, at least in part, to the morphosyntactic segmentation of the language.

(C) FINAL STAGE
   A revised utterance.

(D) CONDITIONS
   Interactive language use.

Summary

In this chapter, crosslinguistic patterns of language change were discussed: evolutional paths that affect an entire community of speakers, successions of stages in acquiring first and second languages, and the process of implementing knowledge in action. Nine generalizations (GEN-1–GEN-9) have been proposed although based only on the limited crosslinguistic evidence available to date in the literature. The first three pertained to diachrony: the genesis of articles, changes in the ordering of major sentence constituents and of adpositions. GEN-4 and GEN-5 stated regularities in how children acquire antonyms and spatial terms. GEN-6 and GEN-7 presented recurring patterns in second-language acquisition; GEN-8 and GEN-9 had to do with processing relative clauses and making "repairs" in live discourse.

The next chapter will show how the three processes of historical change, acquisition, and processing line up into a single explanatory argument as we explore why languages are the way they are.

Activities

1. Consider the various uses of the verb *do* in English. Is there any indication for grammaticalization to be involved?

2. Back in the 1950s, the orthographic dictionary issued by the Hungarian Academy of Sciences recommended that the word for 'bread and butter' – *vajaskenyér*, literally "buttered bread" – be spelled in one word but *zsiros kenyér* "larded bread" 'bread and lard' should be written as two words. What might explain the differential recommendation for these two compounds?

3. Has grammaticalization played a role in the evolution of writing systems? (Cf. Section 5.5.1 in Chapter 5.)

4. Bambi B. Schieffelin reports the following errors of a Kaluli child's early language (1985: 566, 580). Kaluli is a language of Papua New Guinea. For both A and B, determine what it is that the child has already learnt and what is it that she has not.
   A. The child wants to tell her mother to give some sugar cane to a child named Babi. Since the mother does not respond to the first two attempts, the child provides a third version.
   (a) Child's versions:
       (i)   Hono Babi-mɔ dimina.
       (ii) Babi-mɔ hono dimina.
       (iii) Babi-mɔ hono-mɔ dimina.
   (b) Adult sentence: *Babi hono-mɔ dimina.*
                       Babi that-DAT give.IMP
                       'Give to that Babi over there.'
   B. The verb *fagema* means 'to untie.' The child uses it for the following meanings: 'untwist,' 'pick off tree bark,' 'tie up,' and 'open up (a door).'

5. Here is a passage from the New Testament of the Bible in English and translated into Hawaii Creole English (Hawaii) and Tok Pisin (Papua New Guinea). Both creoles have derived from English and indigenous languages.
   a. How are these two languages similar in phonology, morphosyntax, and vocabulary?
   b. What are some historical processes that account for the differences between the source language English and the two creoles?

   (a) English
       1. *Our Father, who are in heaven,*
       2. *your name be honored.*

3. *Your kingdom come,*
4. *your will be done in heaven*
5. *as it is on earth.*
6. *Give us today our daily bread*
7. *and forgive us our sins*
8. *just as we forgive*
9. *all those who sinned against us.*
10. *And do not lead us into temptation*
11. *but deliver us from evil.*

(b) Hawaii Creole English
Note: *jalike* 'just like'
1. *God, you our Fadda, you stay inside da sky,*
2. *we like all da peopo know fo shua how you stay, an dat you stay good an spesho, an we like dem give you plenny respeck.*
3. *We like you come King fo everybody now,*
4. *we like everybody make jalike you like,*
5. *ova hea inside da world, jalike da angel guys up inside da sky make jalike you like.*
6. *Give us da food we need fo today an every day,*
7. *hemmo our shame, an let us go fo all da kine bad stuff we do to you,*
8. *jalike us guys let da odda guys go awready, and we no stay huhu wit dem*
9. *fo all da kine bad stuff dey do to us.*
10. *No let us get chance fo do bad kine stuff,*
11. *but take us outa dea, so da Bad Guy no can hurt us.*

(c) Tok Pisin
Notes: *mipela* ("me fellow") 'me'
      mas 'must'
      bihainim ("behind him") 'to follow'
      long (from *along*) – a general-purpose preposition
      laik ("like") 'will'
      kaikai 'food'
      samting nogut ("something not good") 'evil'
      -im ("him") is a suffix of transitive verbs
1. *Papa bilong mipela, yu i stap long heven,*
2. *nem bilong yu i mas i stap holi.*
3. *Kingdom bilong yu i mas i kam,*
4. *laik bilong yu ol i bihainim long heven*
5. *olsem tasol mipela bihainim long graun tu.*
6. *Nau yu givim mipela kaikai inap long dispela de*
7. *na yu lusim ol sin bilong mipela*
8. *olsem mipela tu i lusim pinis sin bilong*
9. *ol man i bin rongim mipela.*
10. *Na yu no bringim mipela long samting bilong traim mipela,*
11. *tasol tekewe mipela long samting nogut.*

Further reading

- On historical change, see Deutscher 2005: a delightful book on language change that is erudite, engrossing, and highly entertaining.

- For a crosslinguistic survey of articles, see Krámský 1972. On the change of definite articles to gender markers, see Greenberg 1978c.

- On grammaticalization, see for example Pagliuca (ed.) 1994, Lehmann 1995, Hopper and Traugott 2003.

- On language contact, see Thomason 2001.

- For a clear and concise statement on word order change in English, see Traugott 1972: 106–109, 160–161, 185–187, 200.

- For comprehensive accounts of language change and the origins of human language, see Davis and Iverson 1992, Dixon 1997, Hurford *et al.* 1998, Croft 2000, Givón 2002, and Kinsella 2009.

- The Child Language Data Exchange System (CHILDES) (childes.psy.cmu.edu) provides child language data from over 20 languages. It is part of TalkBank (talkbank.org), which also includes extensive data from second-language acquisition, conversations, and aphasic language, among others.

- For crosslinguistic studies in first-language acquisition, see the monumental five-volume collection of Dan I. Slobin (ed.) 1985, and especially Slobin's article in volume V, 1–39 on the universal, the typological, and the particular in acquisition.

- For additional literature on the relationship between second-language acquisition and crosslinguistic generalizations, see the papers in Giacalone Ramat (ed.) 2003.

- Comprehensive discussions of L2 phonology are found in Archibald 1998 and Major 2001. Eckman 2011 provides a very informative and clear overall review of the relevant research; the brief survey in Section 6.3.2.1 above is largely based on this work.

- For crosslinguistic studies on sentence processing, see MacWhinney and Bates 1989.

- For a comprehensive survey of competing motivations in grammar, language acquisition, and language use, see MacWhinney *et al.* to appear.

CHAPTER OUTLINE

KEY TERMS

permissive, probabilistic, and nomological explanations

structural, historical, and functional explanation

synchrony

diachrony

function

domain-general properties

domain-specific properties

Universal Grammar

The concept of explanation is illustrated by explaining the structure of an English sentence. The three-step process is then applied to the explanation of crosslinguistically recurrent patterns. The postscript adds a few general comments about the study of language typology.

7.1 Introduction

Why are crosslinguistically recurrent patterns the way they are? In the preceding chapters, a few explanatory comments have already been made about some of them. The genesis of articles was explained by the general process of grammaticalization (Chapter 6, Section 6.2.1). The distribution of resumptive pronouns in relative clauses was accounted for by reference to the varying degrees of difficulty of relative clause constructions, which in turn stem from processing problems (Chapter 6, Section 6.3.2.2 and 6.4.1, Chapter 3, Section 3.2.1.1). The preference for homorganic consonant clusters was explained by auditory similarity among nasal consonants (Chapter 5, Section 5.2.1). The reason for the predominance of suffixing over prefixing was given by the history of affixation and by processing preferences (Chapter 4, Section 4.3). The predominance of the accusative and ergative alignment patterns over the other logical possibilities was explained by the need for clarity and economy (Chapter 3, Section 3.2.2.2). The crosslinguistic frequency of certain color terms was causally linked to cultural factors (Chapter 2, Section 2.5.2). And markedness was invoked for explaining a variety of patterns, such as asymmetries in body-part terms, kinship terminology, personal pronouns, number words, and antonymic adjectives (Chapter 2, Section 2.2–2.5), the distribution of zero forms (Chapter 4, Section 4.2.2.2), and some phonological patterns (Chapter 5, Section 5.3).

However, the general question of how crosslinguistic tendencies may be explained and what it really means to explain something are issues that have not yet been addressed head-on. The purpose of this present chapter is to turn to these issues. We will see how the three kinds of processes discussed in Chapter 6: historical change, developmental change, and usage processes link up to explain properties of synchronic structure including crosslinguistic preferences.

7.1.1 What are explanations?

One of the most pervasive characteristics of human thought is a quest for explaining things. Medical researchers, doctors, economists, physicists, geologists, meteorologists, politicians, news commentators, and all of us engaged in daily existence are trying to figure out reasons for things around us and based on these theories, to predict the future.

What exactly does it mean to look for an explanation and what is it like to have found one? The search for explanations is spawned by a discrepancy between what there is and what we think there could be or should be. Suppose an experimental aircraft has crashed. Our first reaction is to ask why it has happened. We ask this question because we can conceive of two possibilities: the plane crashing or staying in the air. Yet, reality came down hard on one side: the plane did crash. The question is why, of the two imaginable scenarios, one happened rather than the other.

In this example, the two imagined possibilities are pretty much on a par: for an experimental plane on its maiden flight, flying and crashing seem equally possible. In other scenarios, one outcome is not only possible but more likely. In the case of commercial planes, we generally assume that they fly without any problem. Thus, when a crash happens, the mismatch between expectation and fact is wider: what happened was considered possible but unlikely. In a third scenario, the gap between expectation and reality is maximal: if the plane was thought to be "uncrashable" – just as the Titanic was considered unsinkable – and the crash nonetheless did happen, the event confronts us with the reality of the "impossible."

How could the mismatch between what is expected and what is "out there" be eliminated? If the ensuing investigation of the plane crash shows that there was a small mechanical fault that made it likely for the disaster to happen, or that there was a crucial mechanical problem that inevitably doomed the plane, this forces us to retroactively revise our expectations: of the two scenarios, the one that took place needs to be considered more probable or even necessary. We explain the crash by re-conceptualizing what is possible, probable, and necessary so that fact and expectation are aligned.

The history of science is full of examples of "impossible" things happening, which called for the re-construal of some basic laws. In his fascinating book *Physics of the Impossible*, Michio Kaku cites a number of physical phenomena that even the greatest minds considered impossible; yet they did happen. It was noted for a long time that the coastlines of South America and Africa showed a close fit; yet, former geological theories excluded the possibility that the two continents could have once been a single piece of land before they drifted apart. When this possibility began to be taken seriously, it led to the theory of plate tectonics, which brought this idea into the realm of the possible (2008: xi–xii). Black holes in the universe used to be considered an astronomical impossibility; Albert Einstein stated that they could not be formed by natural means. Yet, the Hubble Space Telescope has provided evidence for the existence of these dark stars – perhaps billions of them all over the universe – which has caused physicists to re-consider their theories (Kaku 2008: 298-299). Kaku remarks: "As a physicist, I have learned that the 'impossible' is often a relative term … The point is that things that are impossible today violate the known laws of physics, but the laws of physics, as we know them, can change" (2008: xi, 285). The impossibility of these scenarios followed from certain theoretical assumptions that ruled them out. As evidence for their reality accumulated, a gap opened up between theory and fact and theory had to yield.

Structural patterns previously thought unlikely if not impossible have been identified in crosslinguistic research as well. Examples are the expression of negation without negators and numeral systems with gaps (cf. Wohlgemuth and Cysouw 2010a, 2010b and the Rara et Rarissima website (http://typo.uni-konstanz.de/rara)). One of the recent discoveries of unusual grammatical patterns that have been widely discussed in the popular media is Daniel Everett's work on the Pirahã language of Brazil. It revealed surprising grammatical features, such as the lack of numerals, lack of color terms, and no recursive constructions – findings whose validity and significance are still debated in the literature. As in physics, such

Here is another example. In 1982, Dan Shechtman announced the discovery of a new crystalline chemical structure which at the time seemed to violate the laws of physics and thus considered to be impossible by most physicists. Five years later, his proposal was experimentally verified and in 2011, he was given a Nobel Prize for his discovery.

findings may call for revisions of grammatical theories. Infrequent phenomena are a puzzle: if they are so odd, why do they occur at all? and if
they do occur, why are they rare?

Here is a recap.

(1) An explanation is a generalization that serves to close or narrow a
     gap between expectation and reality. An explanation may restruc-
     ture our thinking in one of three ways:
     (a) **Permissive explanations** bring an event from the realm of the
          impossible into that of the **possible** by stating that it **may**
          happen.
     (b) **Probabilistic explanations** bring an event from the realm of
          the impossible or from the realm of the possible into the realm
          of the **probable** by stating that it is **likely** to happen.
     (c) **Nomological explanations** bring an event from the realm of
          the impossible, or from that of the possible, or from that of
          the probable into the realm of the **necessary** by stating that it
          must happen.

An indispensable ingredient of explanations is generalizations: facts
cannot be explained by individual stories. Something can be seen as
the cause of an event only if the effect is multiply documented. A plane
crash may be attributed to a malfunction of the wing flaps only if there
is independent evidence for this kind of mechanical problem causing
crashes.

All of this so far had to do with explaining things in general in any
domain of science and life. Let us now turn to explaining language structure. Exactly what needs to be explained and what kinds of explanations
are called for?

7.1.2 Explaining language structure

We will start with a basic grass-root-level phenomenon: an English sentence. Joe says to his friend:

(2)   *Let's go downtown to see a movie.*

Why is this sentence formulated the way it is? Why not, for example, (3a)
or (3b)?

(3)   (a) *Let's go downtown to see **movie a**.*
      (b) *Let's go downtown **a movie to see**.*

The answer is complex but straightforward. One component of the explanation is that ENGLISH GRAMMAR requires the indefinite article to precede the noun and the direct object to follow the verb. Another component is that Joe has ACQUIRED English grammar including these rules;
and a third one is that in saying this sentence, Joe USES this acquired
knowledge in a particular way.

The explanation thus relies on three factors: the grammar of English,
language acquisition, and language use. This is, however, not an ultimate
explanation since it in turn raises three additional questions.

(4) (a) ENGLISH GRAMMAR

Why does English require the indefinite article to precede the noun and the direct object to follow the verb?

(b) ACQUISITION

How and why has Joe acquired these order patterns of English?

(c) USE

How and why has Joe used the acquired knowledge to formulate the sentence in this way?

Let us begin with question (4b): it probes into the acquisition process. Why did Joe learn the ambient language as his L1 or as an L2? And in either case, how did the acquisition take place: what exactly was learnt about English and by what mental processes? To answer these questions, information about the general processes of first- and second-language acquisition needs to be invoked.

The question in (4c) is also about a process, one linking knowledge to action. However Joe learnt English, how does this knowledge translate into the formulation of the sentence? The answer calls for an understanding of language use.

Finally, (4a) is about the system that has been learnt and has been used: the conventions of English grammar. The answer to why *a movie* is correct in English but *movie a* is not may be answered by rules of English of varying generality, such as in (5).

(5) (a) The indefinite article must precede the noun.

(b) All articles (indefinite and definite) must precede the noun.

(c) All determiners (articles, demonstratives) must precede the noun.

(d) All single-word dependents (articles, demonstratives, numerals, single-word adjectives) must precede the noun.

Similar rules may be formulated about the order of verb and object that rule out *a movie to see* in this sentence. Such rules provide structural explanations of various levels of generality. However, these rules do not provide **causes** for the indefinite article preceding the noun and the object following the verb. How could these structural patterns be causally explained?

John Haiman has remarked: "Everything is what it is because it got that way" (Haiman 2003: 108, originally in D'Arcy Wentworth Thompson's book *On Growth and Form*, 1917). Indeed, this holds for everything in the world including grammar. The only possible causal explanation for synchronic structures is historical: how and why the current patterns changed (or did not change) from an earlier stage. Here is the description of **how** the position of the indefinite article in (1) evolved (cf. Chapter 6, Section 6.2.1, GEN-1).

(6) (A) INITIAL STAGE

Centuries ago, the indefinite article was the unstressed numeral 'one' which preceded the noun.

(B) PROCESS

>In the course of centuries, the numerical interpretation of the unstressed numeral 'one' was backgrounded and its form was reduced to a single vowel through grammaticalization, while its position relative to the noun remained the same.

But **why** did this change take place? As noted by Joan Bybee (1988: 370, 374), "[these changes] are themselves in need of explanation. Why do certain lexical items undergo these related semantic changes and develop grammatical characteristics? To answer this question, we are drawn back to the synchronic plane to investigate how language is used … We must ask what cognitive processes are behind the historical changes." Change happens either because children or second-language learners acquire the ambient language in a somewhat altered form; or because form and/or meaning change in the course of use. Given the appropriate social conditions, these changes are then propagated across the entire speech community resulting in a change of the language itself. These acquisitional and usage-based changes and their spread must in turn be motivated by **function**: the goals of linguistic expression whose attainment is both enabled and limited by the physical and conceptual tools that humans are endowed with.

We have sketched a route to follow for explaining the form of one specific utterance of a speaker in (2). It is explained by the speaker having acquired the language, by his using the acquired knowledge, and by the grammar of the language that has been acquired and used. The grammar in turn is explained by history; historical change is explained by acquisition and use, which are ultimately motivated by the functions of language.

However, as noted above, in order for an explanation to be fully convincing, it cannot just be a specific "story" pertaining to that individual case: instead, the principles invoked have to be true as broadly as possible. For an analogy, consider the "historical" explanation of why the cup that I dropped broke. The explanation cannot just refer to how the cup slipped out of my hands. It also needs to include general laws of gravity and of what happens inside an object made of china when it crashes against a particular kind of surface. As was shown in (5), linguistic generalizations differ in scope and the most useful ones are the most comprehensive ones: those that apply not only within a language (as those in (5)) but also across languages. Thus, to explain how Joe has acquired English syntax, it is not enough to know how English-speaking children internalize syntax and how they use this knowledge; we would like to know how children in general acquire their language and how people use language around the world. Similarly, to explain how the indefinite article evolved historically, it is not enough to present the actual story of the specific English case: once again, we need crosslinguistic generalizations from which the particular English process falls out.

The formulation of such crosslinguistic generalization has been the very subject matter of this book. For example, we know that children tend to acquire the unmarked member of antonymic pairs (at least in English); we know that subject relatives are preferred in linguistic performance across languages; and we know that articles evolve through a crosslinguistically widespread process of grammaticalization.

The remaining question is: why are these crosslinguistically recurrent patterns the way they are? Unmarked members of antonymic adjectives are acquired by children sooner than the marked members; but why? Subject relatives are preferred by speakers over object relatives in various languages; but why this general preference? Grammaticalization explains articles; but why is there grammaticalization to begin with? Crosslinguistic generalizations explain facts about individual languages but they themselves are also in need of explanations.

In what follows, we will take up a small set of crosslinguistic generalizations. Adopting the explanatory schema laid out above, we will first attempt to explain crosslinguistic tendencies in synchronic structure by exploring crosslinguistically recurrent processes of history (Section 7.2). Second, we will focus on how crosslinguistically recurrent historical processes may be derived from crosslinguistic patterns of acquisition and use (Section 7.3). Third, we probe into how crosslinguistic patterns of acquisition and use may in turn fall out of general features of language function (Section 7.4). The final section is a summary followed by a Postscript that offers a few closing comments.

7.2 Synchrony is explained by diachrony

In Chapter 6, Section 6.2, the crosslinguistically attested evolution of articles and changes of certain word order patterns were discussed. The engine behind the genesis of articles was shown to be grammaticalization. The driving force behind harmonization – the maintenance of correlation pairs in the course of change – was also grammaticalization in some instances and analogy in others. Here are summaries of the two explanatory arguments.

(7) Articles
    (a) EXPLANANDUM: the crosslinguistically recurrent **synchronic** pattern of formal and semantic similarities between some demonstratives and definite articles, and between the numeral 'one' and indefinite articles
    (b) EXPLANANS: the crosslinguistically recurrent **historical** process of **grammaticalization**
        (i) INITIAL STAGE
           There are demonstratives and there is the numeral 'one.'
        (ii) PROCESS
           Demonstratives and the numeral 'one' may evolve into articles by grammaticalization. In the course of this process, the lexical elements are formally and semantically reduced but they still retain some of their phonological makeup and meaning properties.

(8)   A word order correlation
   (a) EXPLANANDUM: the crosslinguistically recurrent **synchronic** pattern of VO languages having prepositions
   (b) EXPLANANS: the crosslinguistically recurrent **historical** process of **harmonization**
       (i)   INITIAL STAGE
            OV, postpositions, perhaps some prepositions
       (ii) PROCESS
            When OV changes to VO, adpositions harmonize in one of two ways: erstwhile postpositions may change their position by **analogy** to already existing prepositions; or new prepositions may evolve from the new NG and VO orders by **grammaticalization**.

Let us now consider a third general synchronic pattern to see if there is a historical process that provides a causal explanation for it.

In our discussions of syntactic and morphological linearization (Section 3.3 in Chapter 3 and Section 4.3 in Chapter 4), it was noted that interlocking order – that is, the discontinuity of constituents – is infrequent across languages. In morphology, this means that affixes tend to be either prefixed or suffixed: discontinuous affixes (i.e. circumfixes) and discontinuous stems (infixation) are not common. In syntax, split constituents, such as in French negatives *Je* **ne** *sais* **pas** "I not know not" 'I don't know,' are similarly exceptional. All of these examples point at a general tendency for semantically related elements to be adjacent rather than separated. The same principle also accounts for why adjectives tend to be next to their nouns, why objects tend to be next to their verbs, and so forth. It is also manifested in the Relevance Principle about the order of affixes relative to each other (see Section 4.3 of Chapter 4).

What is the historical source of the strong preference for the adjacency of semantically coherent elements? One possible answer is that there is no historical process behind this pattern: this is "how it has always been." This would mean that the earliest form of human language already favored adjacency. While this may be true, there is also evidence for historical processes that actually create adjacency where it did not exist before.

In their extensive study of universals of diachronic syntax, Alice Harris and Lyle Campbell provide a number of examples of emergent adjacency patterns (1995: 220–228). One involves main verbs and auxiliaries. Corresponding to their close semantic relationship, these two constituents are generally adjacent, with the auxiliary either directly preceding or directly following the main verb. In English, as in German and French, the perfective auxiliary *have* (*haben*, *avoir*) has arisen from a main verb 'to own.' In the original biclausal structure, 'have' and the participial form of the lexical verb were separated by the direct object. As 'have' grammaticalized into an auxiliary, the participle abandoned its original position and moved next to the auxiliary. In English, both structures still occur: (9a) reflects the original order with non-adjacent *have* and participle, while (9b) shows the new grammaticalized structure.

(9) (a) *Sarah* **has** *the report* **finished**.   English
    (b) *Sarah* **has finished** *the report*.

This is an instance where a language is caught in the act of creating adjacency for semantically related constituents. We will label the process **proximization**. Here is the explanatory argument.

(10) (a) EXPLANANDUM: the crosslinguistic recurrent **synchronic** adjacency of auxiliaries and verbs
     (b) EXPLANANS: the crosslinguistically recurrent **historical** process of **proximization**
         (i) INITIAL STAGE
             Structures like *Sarah* **has** *the report* **finished**.
         (ii) PROCESS
             The main verb is grammaticalized to an auxiliary and the participle moves next to the newly minted auxiliary.

This process has been observed for only a handful of languages; nonetheless, it forms a possible path toward the adjacency of auxiliaries and verbs, although perhaps not a probable path and even less a necessary one.

In the three examples above – articles, prepositions, and auxiliaries – we invoked the three crosslinguistically recurrent historical processes of grammaticalization, harmonization, and proximization to explain crosslinguistically recurrent synchronic patterns. But what explains these historical processes themselves? As we saw in Section 7.1, for the explanation of historical processes we have to turn to acquisition and use.

7.3 Diachrony is explained by acquisition and use

Why do grammaticalization, harmonization, and proximization take place? As shown in Section 7.1, synchrony is explained by diachrony and for diachronic change in turn, possible causes are acquisition and use: how people acquire a language and how they use it. Changes may emerge from children or second-language learners not acquiring the input language exactly as it is; or even if they have acquired it as it is, forms of expressions may be altered in the course of language use.

Is **children's language** a plausible source of historical change? There is evidence that some of the errors children make do parallel the directions in which languages evolve. For example, children regularize exceptions, such as the irregular past tenses of English verbs, e.g. *came* → *comed*, or *went* → *goed*. The same has happened to some irregular verbs in the history of English, such as *dived* gradually edging out *dove*. Also, the spatial use of adpositions precedes their more abstract use in child language; for example, a child used *behind* to mean *after* in *Can I have any reading behind the dinner?* (cited in Diessel 2012). This sequence of spatial-to-temporal use is paralleled in the semantic change of adpositions in language history (e.g. *The table is* **behind** *me* → *The exam is* **behind** *me*).

But there are also differences: consonant harmony is common in child language but rare across the languages of the world (cf. Chapter 5, Section 5.2.1). However, the main argument against child language playing a crucial role in historical change is that children's tendencies are fleeting and short-lived and they are unlikely to propagate across entire speech communities. It is children who yield to the force of the ambient language rather than the other way around. The similarities must be due to the fact that children have the same perceptual and cognitive apparatus as adult speakers and they respond to the same external factors, such as frequency (Diessel 2012, Bybee 2010: 114–119).

Interlanguage (the language of the L2-learner) is another matter. The speech patterns of people acquiring second languages have been widely documented to affect language change: they may lead to borrowing and other manifestations of language contact (cf. e.g. Thomason 2001, esp. 128–156).

This leaves us with **usage**, which is the principal source of language change: the frequent discrepancy between what speakers have acquired and how they actually employ that knowledge in their linguistic performance. In what follows, we will see evidence that speakers' preferences for one or another alternative structure actually parallel crosslinguistic frequencies. As examples of usage-based explanations of historical change, we will take up the three processes discussed in Section 7.2: grammaticalization, harmonization, and proximization starting with the last-mentioned one.

(A) WHY PROXIMIZATION?

John Hawkins' explanation of the crosslinguistic predominance of adjacency among semantically cohesive elements is that adjacency favors ease of processing (Hawkins 2004: 103–146). He proposes that this preference in actual linguistic behavior is the engine behind the genesis of crosslinguistically frequent adjacent structures. Here is Hawkins' general principle (Hawkins 2004: 3).

(11) Performance-Grammar Correspondence Hypothesis
      Grammars have conventionalized syntactic structures in proportion
      to their degree of preference in performance, as evidenced by
      patterns of selection in corpora and by ease of processing in
      psycholinguistic experiments.

In other words, the prediction is that whatever pattern is preferred, more frequently used, and more easily processed by users of languages will be more frequent in the grammars of languages.

In order to be able to invoke this hypothesis for explaining the preference for adjacent structures across languages, we need two kinds of data. On the one hand, we need to establish the explanandum: that the adjacency of two particular semantically related constituents is indeed more frequent across languages than their non-adjacency. On the other hand, we need to have evidence for the explanans: that given the same two constituents, their adjacency is favored in actual language use over a structure where the two are separated. In what follows, we will see three examples where crosslinguistic frequency and preferential use by speakers run in tandem.

a. Verb and direct object

As noted in Chapter 3, Section 3.3, the two most common major-constituent orders are SOV and SVO, in both of which the direct object is adjacent to the verb. This establishes our explanandum.

If the crosslinguistically prevalent adjacency of verb and object is the result of the process of proximization that creates adjacency from non-adjacent structures, the question is how this process comes about? Hawkins' answer is that it is the accumulation of individual users' preferences. In order for this to hold, it would have to be shown that if in a language, speakers have a choice between placing the object next to the verb or apart from it, they prefer the former. Such evidence is indeed cited by Hawkins. Consider the Japanese sentences below, both meaning 'Tanaka bought that book from Hanako' (Hawkins 2004: 109, 118–119).

(12)   Japanese

   (a) *Tanaka ga*   [[*Hanako kara*]$_{pp}$ [*sono hon o*]$_o$ *katta*$_v$.]$_{vp}$
         Tanaka SUBJ   Hanako from   that book ACC   bought.

   (b) *Tanaka ga*   [[*sono hon o*]$_o$ [*Hanako kara*]$_{pp}$ *katta*$_v$.]$_{vp}$
         Tanaka SUBJ   that book ACC   Hanako from   bought.

The difference between the two versions is that in (12a), the direct object is adjacent to the verb while in (12b), it is separated from it by the postpositional phrase. Hawkins' prediction is that sentences like (12a), where verb and direct object are adjacent, are more frequent than those in (12b). This is indeed the case: Hawkins reports that of 244 sentences of these two types, 69% were of type (12a). Thus, preference for the O-V adjacency in usage provides an explanans for the preference for O-V adjacency in crosslinguistic distribution.

b. Verb and adposition

Another set of data discussed by Hawkins has to do with adjacency relations between verb and adposition. Depending on the order of verb and its complement and of the adposition and the noun phrase it pertains to, in some languages the verb ends up adjacent to the adposition while in others the two are separated by the noun phrase that the adposition goes with. Here are the two logically possible structures in VO-type languages.

(13) VO-type languages

    (a) V & PP and preposition
        [V [P NP]$_{pp}$]$_{vp}$
        e.g. "**live in** Paris"

    (b) V & PP and postposition
        [V [NP P]$_{pp}$]$_{vp}$
        e.g. "**live** Paris **in**"

A large language sample shows that there are eight times more languages with V & PP order and prepositions, as in (13a), than V & PP languages with postpositions, as in (13b). Thus, the adjacency of verb and adposition is a greatly preferred option across languages. This is what we want to explain.

Once again, Hawkins addresses this issue by referring to processing ease. He proposes that upon receiving a sentence, the hearer's interest is to have the entire blueprint of the sentence available to him as soon as possible. What this means is that those words that announce the presence of the main sentence parts – such as the presence of a verb phrase or a prepositional phrase – should follow in close proximity, possibly adjacently. In other words, the constituent recognition domain (the distance between those constituents diagnostic of the highest phrasal structure of the sentence) should be minimal.

There is experimental evidence to show that speakers indeed opt for structures where the constituent recognition domain for the verb phrase and the prepositional phrase is small. Evidence pertains to sentences like in (14) (Hawkins 2004: 50).

(14) (a) *John **went to** London **in** the late afternoon.*   English
      (b) *John **went in** the late afternoon **to** London.*

Of these two structures, (14a) was found to be preferred. Notice that in the short-before-long construction of (14a), the hearer gets the overall structure of the sentence sooner than in (14b) because the crucial elements – the verb *went* and the two prepositions *to* and *in* – follow in closer sequence than in (14b), where the long phrase *the late afternoon* delays the appearance of the second preposition *to*.

Let us now see how this explanation applies to the structures in (13). In a verb phrase like *live in Paris* (as in (13a)), the two diagnostic constituents are the verb *live*, which signals the verb phrase, and the adposition *in*, which heralds the prepositional phrase. Given the English order, the verb and the adposition are adjacent: the hearer receives the adposition right after the verb. However, if English had postpositions rather than prepositions (as in (13b)), the construction would be *live Paris **in***. In this case, the hearer would have to wait until the noun – *Paris* – is over to find out that the next constituent was a prepositional phrase. Thus, as predicted, greater crosslinguistic frequency is indeed paralleled here by preference in processing with the latter – language use – giving rise to the former: crosslinguistic frequency.

(13) has to do with VO languages. What does Hawkins' adjacency principle predict for adposition order in OV languages? Here are the logical possibilities.

(15) OV-type languages
      (a) PP & V with preposition
           $[[\text{P NP}]_{pp} \text{ V}]_{vp}$
           e.g. "**in** Paris **live**"
      (b) PP & V with postposition
           $[[\text{NP P}]_{pp} \text{ V}]_{vp}$
           e.g. "Paris **in live**"

What needs to be explained is that, as a sample of languages shows, there are 34 times more languages following the (15b) pattern than those having (15a).

Hawkins' theory, according to which processing ease favors the adjacency of verb and adposition and this in turn translates into crosslinguistic frequency, is borne out once again. The predicted pattern is (15b), the crosslinguistically more common one. This is because here, as in (13a), the verb and the adposition – the two constituents that announce the basic sentence structure – follow in close sequence and thus benefit the hearer while in (15a) they are separated. These data provide further indication of the parallelism between crosslinguistic and usage-based preferences and the explanatory significance of the latter.

c. Possessed noun and adposition

Crosslinguistic preference for constructions where the identifiers of the dominating phrases are adjacent is also evident in the position of adpositions in possessive constructions, such as *in Peter's book*. The four logically possible configurations are given in (16). The phrase-identifiers are the adposition signaling the prepositional phrase and, by Hawkins' analysis, the possessed noun indicating the noun phrase.

(16) (a)   NG with preposition
        $[P[N\ G]_{np}]_{pp}$
        e.g. ***in book*** *Peter's*

     (b)   NG with postposition
        $[[N\ G]_{np}\ P]_{pp}$
        e.g. "***book*** *Peter's* ***in***"

     (c)   GN with preposition
        $[P[G\ N]_{np}]_{pp}$
        e.g. ***in*** *Peter's* ***book***

     (d)   GN with postposition
        $[[G\ N]_{np}\ P]_{pp}$
        e.g. "*Peter's* ***book in***"

The two phrase indicators – adposition and possessed noun – are adjacent in (16a) and (16d) and separated in the other two structures. Language samples have once again borne out the statistical preference for the adjacency of the two structurally crucial constituents: (16a) occurs in about twelve times as many languages as (16b), and (16d) is over twelve times more frequent than (16c).

The general preference for adjacent structures in sentence processing supplies an answer to the question we started out with: why is there a historical tendency for proximization – that is, for certain constituents to occur adjacently, as we saw happening in the case of auxiliaries and main verbs? Here is the summary.

(17) (a)   EXPLANANDUM: the crosslinguistic recurrent **historical** process of **proximization**
        Semantically and syntactically relevant words may be made adjacent over time by re-ordering.

(b)   EXPLANANS: a crosslinguistically recurrent **performance** process
Speakers seek ease and efficiency of processing. Thus, if
there is a choice for expressing a meaning, they prefer structures where semantically and syntactically relevant words are
adjacent rather than separated. This preference then translates
into historical processes that change languages in the preferred directions.

(B) WHY HARMONIZATION?

Our second question is why, in the course of time, languages show a tendency to maintain correlation pairs such as VO, NG, and AdpNP versus OV,
GN, and NPAdp. The German examples that we saw in Chapter 6,
Section 6.2.2 had to do with adpositions either moving to a new place
when the basic system changes, or the language developing new adpositions in harmony with the new system. But why do languages tend to keep
these three orders in harmony in the course of historical change?

The problem is that verb, adposition, and possessed nouns are very different kinds of syntactic constituents and it is therefore puzzling to see
that they are ordered uniformly relative to the direct object, the noun
phrase, and the possessor, respectively. To explain this, a common denominator must be found for the constituents that have uniform order across
languages so that they can be shown to form a single class.

One explanation presented in the literature has focused on the distinction between heads and dependents. As noted in Chapter 3, Section 3.3,
according to this analysis, languages tend to order syntactic constituents
uniformly depending on whether they are heads or dependents
(Vennemann 1973). VO languages opt for the head-before-dependent order,
while OV languages go with the dependent-before-head sequence: in each
case, a single pattern would cover all the relevant constituents. According
to an alternative view, the common denominator is whether a constituent
is just a single word or whether it is branching – i.e. consisting of multiple
words (Dryer 1992). In both cases, the rationale behind the explanation is
that paradigmatic simplicity is a good thing: it is easier to acquire and use
a language if there is a single pattern from which the order of the various
constituent types falls out than if separate rules need to be internalized
for each pair of constituents.

While both the head-dependent and the branching-direction theories
account for much of the linearization patterns of languages, they do not
cover everything: in both approaches, there are order-relevant subdistinctions among constituent types that fall below their radar. For
example, according to the head-dependent theory, single-word adjectives,
multi-word adjectival phrases, and (multi-word) relative clauses should all
be ordered the same way since they are all dependents of the head noun.
Yet, they often have distinct patterns; cf. English *a* **good** *girl* versus *a girl*
good in math and *a girl* **that is good in math**. The branching theory tops
the head-dependent theory here by predicting that single-word adjectives
and multi-word phrases or clauses have different positions. But two phrases

that are both branching may not be linearized the same way, either: both *very good* and *good in math* are multi-word, branching structures, yet, *very good* precedes the noun head in English but *good in math* follows it.

A third explanation emerges from Hawkins' adjacency principle described above. As we saw above, in this theory, adpositions and verbs are preferably adjacent and so are adpositions and possessed nouns because these orders ensure quick and efficient sentence processing. The predicted patterns seen above are as follows:

(18) (a) VO structures:

   V Prep NP   ("**live in** Paris")
   Prep N G   ("**in book** Peter's")

   (b) OV structures:

   NP **Postp V**   ("Paris **in live**")
   G **N Postp**   ("Peter's **book in**")

In other words, VO languages with NG order are predicted to be prepositional and OV languages with GN order are predicted to be postpositional. Notice now that these are exactly the correlation pairs known to be crosslinguistically prevalent (Hawkins 2004: 123–127)! Thus, the drive toward adjacency provides an explanation for a crosslinguistic historical tendency towards at least some of the common harmonic order patterns. In this view, the motivation for VO languages being prepositional and having the genitive after the possessed noun is not that verb, adposition, and the possessed noun are heads or that they share non-branching structure. Instead, the motivation is that these order patterns allow the verb to be adjacent to the adposition and the possessed noun to be next to the adposition. In each case, the constituents that are diagnostic of the higher phrase that they belong to and thus of the overall blueprint of the sentence are next to each other and thus provide the hearer with an immediate map of the sentence.

(19) (a) EXPLANANDUM: the crosslinguistic recurrent **historical** process of **harmonization**

   There is a tendency for languages to maintain over time either a system with VO, NG and prepositions, or one with OV, GN and postpositions.

   (b) EXPLANANS: one or both of the following crosslinguistically recurrent **performance** processes:
   (i) Speakers prefer a single order pattern applying to the various constituent types by classifying them either as heads versus dependents, or as branching versus non-branching types.
   (ii) Speakers seek easy and efficient processing. If they have a choice, they prefer structures where functionally-related words are adjacent rather than separated. Since verb, adposition, and possessed noun share the role of announcing the overall structure of sentences, their preferred arrangement is adjacency.

So far, we have probed into explanations of two kinds of historical changes: proximization and harmonization. In our search for explanations of crosslinguistically common historical changes, we will now turn to the third process discussed in Section 7.2: grammaticalization.

(C) WHY GRAMMATICALIZATION?

Section 7.2 illustrated the way the historical process of grammaticalization explains synchronic facts. But why does grammaticalization take place at all and why is it so widespread across diverse parts of grammar and across languages?

As discussed above, grammaticalization involves the gradual re-analysis of some lexical items into more formal elements and some formal grammatical elements into others that have even less meaning and even less form. Common examples are the genesis of the English future markers: *will* or *'ll* having evolved from a verb meaning 'want'; *going to* or *gonna* coming from the verb *go* designating locomotion; and the origin of definite and indefinite articles from demonstratives and the numeral 'one.' Compounds may also result from grammaticalization. The English words *girlfriend* and *boyfriend* come from the phrases *girl friend* and *boy friend*, which originally referred to only young people. In today's usage, the phrases have been compressed into compounds and they can be used without reference to age.

The four main steps in the grammaticalization process are **chunking**, whereby originally multi-word phrases are lumped together into a single word (also called univerbation); **semantic bleaching**, whereby meanings are thinned out; **phonological reduction** – that is, the diminution of phonological form; and **automatization**, which means that the use of the formally collapsed and semantically simplified new form morphs into a single habitual act. The process is the result of frequent use. The naturalness of this process is indicated by the fact that similar processes take place outside language as well.

Here is an example. In early twentieth-century Eastern Europe, men of some social standing greeted each other with the formula *Servus humillimus* – the Latin phrase for 'most humble servant' – and, as a gestural symbol of humility, they took off their hats and bowed, presumably to make themselves look shorter. By the middle of the century or so, both the phrase and the gestures had been simplified: men merely tipped or touched their hat and used the abbreviated phrase *servus* 'servant' whose use broadened from initial greeting to general salutation. This reduced phrase is still in use in Austria and Hungary but its literal meaning and its associated self-humbling connotation are completely gone. In Hungarian, phonological shape has also been reduced: first /sevas/ (with the consonant cluster *rv* lost) and later /sia/ have become the going forms, the latter perhaps influenced by English *see you*. And hats and bowing are not at all involved in the greeting ritual anymore.

John Haiman presents a comprehensive broad-brushed picture of a wide variety of social conventions (extending even to animal behavior) that parallel grammaticalization (1994). The key component is the frequent repetition of an act, in the course of which it is liberated of its original significance and becomes a ritual. Religious practices are prime examples. Baptism, originally an act of cleansing by submersion, is now performed in most denominations with just a few drops of water sprinkled on a child, which stands for acceptance into the church community. Similarly, Holy Communion is a replica of Christ's Last Supper in a simplified and stylized form. Analogous processes are apparent in personal behavior as well. We learn phone numbers digit by digit but later the meanings of the individual numbers fade out: we remember the number holistically, shown by the fact that bilinguals are often hard-put to translate a phone number from one language to the other. This explains why it is difficult to pronounce a well-rehearsed phone number or other sequence slowly, part by part.

Chunking all by itself – sequences of individual items turning into larger, fluid wholes that resist analysis into component parts – is common behavior. For example, ballet dance routines are first learnt step by step, motif by motif but the final product is a unified flowing movement with seams barely discernible. We learn driving in terms of its components: foot work, hand movements, watching the rear-view mirrors and so forth; but once we have acquired the skill, the whole act is performed holistically and automatically with the ingredient parts barely separable. The same holds for morning routines – brushing teeth, taking a shower, combing hair – where the separate portions, originally assembled piece by piece, tend to blend together into a continuous whole.

Thus, grammaticalization is the linguistic reflection of a more general cognitive process of routinization, in the course of which originally compositional sequences turn into unanalyzable wholes by frequent repetition.

(20) (a) EXPLANANDUM: The crosslinguistically recurrent historical process of **grammaticalization**.

(b) EXPLANANS: Frequently repeated acts tend to lose some of their original meaning and to reduce their form. Grammaticalization is an instance of this general process.

> The same holds in reading: we learn how to read letter by letter but later we recognize words as gestalts. Personal signatures, too, start out as series of letters but later they tend to become gestalts with the letters blurred and some completely gone.

7.4 Acquisition and use are explained by function

In Section 7.3, we invoked general preferences in linguistic use that, when expanded and propagated within a speech community, result in crosslinguistically recurrent historical changes that in turn shape the synchronic structures of languages. These are a preference for speed and efficiency of processing (underlying the historical processes of proximization and harmonization), preference for a few general rules rather than several more specific ones (possibly underlying harmonization), and preference for chunking and ritualizations (underlying grammaticalization). These concepts, which help explain crosslinguistically prevalent historical changes, are in need of an explanation themselves. Why does human behavior show these preferences?

According to Niko Tinbergen, a researcher of animal behavior, there are four questions that can be asked about the behavior of animals. One is about the **mechanism** underlying the behavior: what are the physiological and cognitive structures involved? A second question is about **phylogeny**: what is the ancestral history of the behavior? A third question is about **ontogeny**: what factors influence individual development that gives rise to the behavior? And the fourth one is about **function**.

Daniel Nettle, who cites Tinbergen's questions known as the 'four why-s,' notes that they boil down to three 'how'-s and a single 'why' (Nettle 1998: 458–460). The real **why**-question is the fourth one about function. Once function has been identified, the rest of the questions are mere **how**-questions: how function motivates historical and individual change and, by way of these changes, how it motivates the resulting structures.

The same applies to language as well. Thus, having considered structural, historical, and developmental explanations for syntactic structures in the preceding sections, we will now turn to exploring the ultimate explanatory factor for language structure: function.

Note first that language function cannot be used to explain synchronic grammar directly. The fact that it is easier to pronounce words that have both consonants and vowels than if they only had consonants does not directly explain why English has both consonants and vowels since there is no causal trajectory between the virtues of having both consonants and vowels and English having both. Causal links must be temporal processes and therefore it is only through history and through the factors that shape it – acquisition and use – that function can emerge as an explanatory concept. Consider an analogy. The fact that knives have blades is not directly explained by the fact that blades are necessary for knives to perform the function of cutting. What this function explains is why knives are manufactured so that they have blades.

Function in language involves two factors: the **goals** that people are after when using language and the **means** that they have at their disposal to attain those goals. It is easy to see that considering goals without the available means for achieving them is not going to lead to functional explanations of any artifact. Humans, beavers, and birds all build shelters for protection; yet, bird nests, beaver dens, and people's homes look very different. This may in part be due to differences in secondary goals; but differences in capabilities must be the dominant factors.

Simon Kirby cites an example of Stephen Gould's that further shows how the means available to an organism will bear on its ways of achieving its goals (Kirby 1999: 104–105). While locomotion is an important goal for animals of all kinds, no animal is known to have evolved wheels for moving around. The explanation given by Gould is that wheels must spin freely and thus they cannot be fused to the object that they move. But animals need to have all parts of their bodies physically connected so that nutrients can flow everywhere. This physical limitation constrains the range of the devices animal bodies can develop for purposes of locomotion.

For language, it might appear easy to construct functional explanations: we just select a grammatical phenomenon and then show that it is dictated by language function – i.e., by the goals of the speaker–hearer coupled with his cognitive and physical powers and constraints. However, there are several reasons why this is not quite so simple, three of which are as follows.

First, we cannot expect **all grammatical phenomena** to be equally determined by language function. In thinking about functional explanations of instrumental objects in general, Gerald Sanders takes knives as an example (Sanders 1977). He first notes that while all structural properties of a knife have to be compatible with its function, not all of them are necessary for it: structure is not fully determined by function. For example, a carved geometric pattern on the knife's shaft is **compatible** with its cutting function but immaterial to it. Second, a knife may have properties that are **conducive** to its function but still not necessary, such as a convenient length and shape of the shaft. And, thirdly, there are certain features – such as having a handle at all that is not made of cotton candy – that are **determined** by the knife's function.

This means that functional explanations cannot all be nomological; in some cases they are only probabilistic or permissive (cf. Section 7.1.1 of this chapter). All properties of instruments can be given a permissive functional explanation by showing that they are compatible with the instrument's function. Some of the properties may be open to probabilistic explanations if we can show that they favor the optimal use of the instruments. And some instrument properties are indispensable for function and thus can be accounted for nomologically.

The second factor that complicates functional explanations is that language serves **more than one function**. Functions are benefits that users derive from tools but these benefits may be manifold, subject to change, and altogether difficult to pin down. We use language for imparting ideas but also for making contact with others or simply for thinking. Cognition, communication, and socialization are all part of language use whether singly or jointly. Noam Chomsky designates conceptualization as the primary goal of language (2002: 76).

Language is not properly regarded as a system of communication. It is a system for expressing thought, something quite different. It can of course be used for communication, as can anything people do – manner of walking or style of clothes or hair, for example. But in any useful sense of the term, communication is not the function of language, and may even be of no unique significance for understanding the functions and nature of language.

Other linguists opt for communication as a central goal; for example those adopting the user-based approach to language as represented in the papers in Barlow and Kemmer 2000. Additional purposes may be socially based such as making an impression and showing off by using a prestigious expression, a newly acquired word, or a witty phrase. Martin Haspelmath terms such efforts extravagance.

The third factor that makes it difficult to construct functional explanations for language is that **the multiple functions may be in conflict**. One such potential conflict is that language must serve the goals of both the speaker (encoder) and those of the hearer (decoder). The speaker is concerned with ease of expression; the hearer is interested in ease of comprehension. But comprehensibility often requires redundancy while ease of expression calls for economy, which is the opposite of redundancy.

In addition to the basic conflict between encoder's and decoder's interests, there are also other conflicting functions. While the speaker's and hearer's communicative preferences shape the development of novel structures, the propagation of new structures is often influenced by social factors which may be at cross-purposes to these desiderata. People often prefer structures that are used by prestigious speakers even if they are less communicatively or cognitively effective.

In addition to **goals**, the second factor in a functional explanation is the **means** available for achieving those goals. In human language, the means available are our physical and cognitive endowments. While our bodily tools are observable and thus less subject to controversy, it is more difficult to establish what the relevant cognitive tools might be for acquiring and using language.

To begin with, let us consider those aspects of our cognitive apparatus that most linguists and psychologists agree are crucially engaged in the use of language. These are the same instruments that underlie any aspect of human behavior whether driving a car, learning math, playing an instrument, or cooking. Here are ten examples of these domain-general cognitive tools that appear to play a strong role in language as well. They may have shaped the proto-language(s) of all mankind or they could have surfaced to channel language structures in the course of time; or perhaps both.

a. Wholes and parts
Sentence structure falls into phrases which in turn generally contain other phrases and ultimately words, morphemes, syllables, and sounds. This kind of partonomic complexity is part and parcel of our everyday activities, as well as of scientific analysis. On the one hand, we dissemble things: children love to pick objects apart – just as physicists do when they search for the smallest components of matter. Since it is easier to remember several smaller items than one large one, we divide telephone numbers and credit card codes into groups of three or four digits. But, on the other hand, given a long number, we may not cut it into individual digits: we memorize it as a chunk. As seen in the discussion about grammaticalization above, we build large structures from little pieces and automatize certain sequences of bits of behavior into large units with the original parts barely perceptible. Attention to the components often vanishes as shown by the fact that people involved in physical exercise routines have

to be given refresher courses where the automatized wholes are picked apart to make sure every move is performed correctly.

Sorting things into parts and wholes is ubiquitous and highly useful. In his classic article on complex systems, Herbert A. Simon notes that complex systems often take the form of a partonomic hierarchy consisting of successive sets of subsystems (1962). Families are parts of neighborhoods, which in turn are parts of cities; cities form counties and ultimately countries. Animal bodies have parts on multiple levels and so do books and musical compositions. To illustrate the utility of multi-level partonomic structures, Simon offers his now-famous example of the two watchmakers Hora and Tempus. Tempus makes watches where all pieces are immediate parts of the whole, while in Hora's watches, parts belong to sub-assemblies. When Tempus had to run to pick up the phone while working on his watch, the whole mechanism fell apart, while for Hora, only one sub-assembly collapsed. Simon then shows the evolutionary advantages of systems that consist of multiple partonomic levels over systems where all parts are on a par.

b. Heads and dependents

The parts that sentences can be analyzed into are not all on a par: even those that appear on the same level of structure, such as a verb and an adverb (e.g. *to run fast*) are asymmetrically related, with the verb being the obligatory part of the phrase with the adverb optional. This kind of head–dependent relation is evident also outside language. In a family consisting of the parents and their children, one of the parents may stand for the family but a child cannot. Or, given a committee consisting of a chair and several members, the chair may represent the whole committee more appropriately than any one of the members.

c. Types and tokens

In addition to its **partonomic** structure, another fundamental property of sentence structure is that certain parts behave alike: they form categories and subcategories. **Taxonomic** analysis – lumping similar things into a single category – is basic to every moment of life. The very basis of our existence is the ability to generalize from one thing to another thing that we judge to be of the same kind. This happens when we taste an unfamiliar kind of fruit, we like it, and then assume that any other fruit of the same kind will also be tasty. Categorization is also the basis of constructing stereotypes of men versus women, Italians versus Norwegians, and so forth. Subcategorization is also prominent in our thinking: we perceive differences among the members of a class such as that even though both the Korean war and the Vietnam war were wars, they were "not the same thing"; and even though both June and July are summer months, they may differ in weather conditions.

In conceptualizing our experiences, we have a broad range of choices as to categorizing things and in particular, how much we want to stick to the observed facts as opposed to generalizing from them. Suppose you buy an HP computer from a store that turns out to work well. What conclusion would you draw from this experience? Would you simply note that the particular computer you bought was a good buy? Or would you generalize to the entire brand of HP computers? Or to all HP products, computers and others? Or to all computers sold in that store regardless of brand? The following anecdote illustrates the variety of possible choices that we have in construing our experiences by different degrees of generalization. It is told by the young autistic British boy in Mark Haddon's novel (2001: 143).

There are three men on a train. One of them is an economist and one of them is a logician and one of them is a mathematician. And they have just crossed the border into Scotland … and they see a brown cow standing in a field from the window of the train … .

And the economist says, 'Look, the cows in Scotland are brown.'

And the logician says, 'No. There are cows in Scotland of which one at least is brown.'

And the mathematician says, 'No. There is at least one cow in Scotland, of which one side appears to be brown.'

The boy then comments:

And it is funny because economists are not real scientists, and because logicians think more clearly, but mathematicians are best.

Indeed, the mathematician's statement has a better claim on truth than those of the others that venture beyond the actual observation. However, from a narrowly factual statement there is nowhere else to go.

d. Marked and unmarked

The categories that we place our experiences into show certain recurrent characteristics. In his book *The Hedgehog, the Fox, and the Magister's Pox; Mending the Gap between Science and the Humanities* (2011: 81), the famous biologist and science writer Stephen Jay Gould notes the human propensity to dichotomize: people tend to sort things into opposite poles of a dimension. In his view, this strong predilection cannot just be the result of a societal convention, nor does it reflect an inherently "correct" division forced upon us by reality. Some dichotomies such as night and day or male and female are strongly supported by how the world is but other dichotomies, such as raw and cooked or matter and spirit, are much less reality-based. "Nature does not dictate dualities" – he says and he concludes "I strongly suspect that our propensity for dichotomy lies deeply within our basic mental architecture as an evolved property of the human brain . . ."

Superimposed on the **dichotomies** that our minds create is the relation of **asymmetry**: we often view one of the opposing poles as more basic than the other. This is the taxonomic analogy of head–dependent structure: just as of two parts of a whole, one (the head) is construed as more dominant than the other (the dependent), of two tokens of a type, one (the unmarked) is treated as more dominant than the other (the marked). We saw various manifestations of this marked–unmarked opposition in linguistic structure: the unmarked poles of a given dimension as more frequent, syntagmatically simpler (that is, simpler in structural composition), and paradigmatically more complex (that is, having more subdistinctions). As noted before, such markedness relations also crop up outside language.

First, there is a common relationship between **frequency and paradig-matic complexity** – that is, the degree of our familiarity with things and the distinctions that we perceive among them. Just as trees all look alike if viewed from a distance, songs of various birds will sound all the same to somebody who is not familiar with them. Yet, at close range, we can differentiate the various tree types and with frequent listening, bird songs take on distinguishing characteristics.

The same asymmetry – frequency linked to paradigmatic complexity – holds not only in how we perceive things but also in how we construct them. Think of greeting cards: the most common kind is for birthdays and there is a greater variety of them than of graduation cards or sympathy cards. Or take dressing patterns. Everyday clothing is the most common kind and it comes in a greater variety than, say, wedding attire. The same holds for food: everyday recipes are more frequently used and are more varied than recipes for special occasions, such as religious holidays or birthdays.

Second, **frequency and simplicity of structure** are also commonly associated outside language as well. Everyday clothing is more frequently worn than, say, wedding dresses and, besides coming in greater variety, the individual pieces are simpler. Similarly, everyday food and basic-purpose buildings are more common than festive meals and special-purpose architecture and they are not only more varied in type but are also simpler in design.

Thus, dichotomy and markedness relations superimposed on it are yet another domain-general conceptual tool of the human mind which is multiply manifested both in language and outside it.

e. Linearization

Sounds, morphemes, words, phrases, clauses, and sentences are all arranged in linear order in spoken language with one following the other. The same preference for linear arrangement is apparent in our human world outside language. Books are lined up on shelves as are cans in kitchen cabinets; buildings follow straight lines along streets. We organize our activities in temporal order and our calendars into days, weeks, months, and years all in a strict temporal lineup. In a classic paper on serial behavior, K. S. Lashley remarks (1951: 113, 121): "Not only speech, but all skilled acts seem to involve the same problems of serial ordering … Temporal integration is not found exclusively in language; the coordination of leg movements in insects, the song of birds, the control of trotting and pacing in a gaited horse, the rat running the maze, the architect designing a house, and a carpenter sawing a board present a problem of sequences of action which cannot be explained in terms of successions of external stimuli." The crucial significance of serial order in all corners of behavior is shown by egregious mistakes that can ensue when actions are performed out of sequence; such as mixing unbeaten egg-white with flour and then beating the mixture; or trying to fit a roof over a house when only two of the four walls have been erected.

f. Symbolism

Language consists of symbols: forms associated with meanings. But symbols are present in every nook and cranny of our individual and social lives even when language is not implicated. Body language – facial expressions, body postures and movements – powerfully convey social messages. A lock of hair from a long-gone ancestor stands for that person and our relationship to him or her. Presents are symbols of love: the gift of a box of chocolates may not be to the recipient's taste but it may still be appreciated for its symbolic value. Red and green traffic lights symbolize instructions for drivers and walkers. Flags are symbols of countries: burning a flag is taken to be an insult to the nation that it symbolizes.

g. Iconicity

Linguistic symbols are predominantly arbitrary in that the forms of words do not directly depict their meanings. However, as we saw in the section on reduplication (Chapter 4, Section 4.2.2.1), there are cases where form imitates meaning, such as when plurality is expressed by the reiteration of a word or a subpart of it. Syntax, too, is iconic at times, such as when in a coordinate structure we mention an earlier event before a later one (e.g. *Joe went home and had dinner*); and iconicity is an important modality effect of sign languages (cf. Chapter 5, Section 5.5.2). Instances of markedness relations are also iconic, such as when singular is expressed by a zero morpheme but the plural marker has phonological body.

The drive after iconic representations is fundamental to human nature. We are surrounded by pictures everywhere. Artists paint, sculpt, or photograph people and objects; music often replicates sounds of nature. Computer-screen icons tend to live up to their name, such as the image of a paint brush indicating painting capability and the icon showing two overlapping pages standing for the copying function. Books that contain illustrations are easier to read than those consisting of solid text. That "a picture is worth a thousand words" is shown also by the incomparably larger effect on us of TV pictures than radio or print reports. Visualization is a prominent therapeutic tool used in psychiatry: rather than just talking about what we want to achieve, it is more useful to form mental images of the desired situations.

h. Imitation

Iconicity involves form imitating referent. Imitation plays a large role in other aspects of grammar as well. Analogy – making novel or irregular forms conform to existing ones – involves imitation. And, beyond iconicity and analogy, imitation of a different kind is a decisive factor in language acquisition and use: we act like the people around us do. Imitative behavior is crucial to any instance of learning. Body language, social rituals, political views, religious beliefs may all be adopted by imitating others.

Here are examples of how social rituals often begin with individual preferences that subsequently become communal conventions. Whenever the first few bars of George F. Handel's choral piece *Hallelujah* are heard by an audience, people jump to their feet. How did this convention begin? Very likely, a few individuals that were inspired by the music felt like expressing their enthusiasm by standing up. Others, perhaps moved by the same sentiment or just imitating those around them, followed suit. When this happened repeatedly on several occasions, it evolved into a worldwide convention.

Another example is the post-funeral repast. Once the ritual part of a funeral is over, it is common practice for the family to offer a meal to the people in attendance. It may have arisen from a need to relax, to socialize, and to quench actual hunger after an emotionally draining event. It has then become a convention so that people participate in it even if they are not hungry and don't experience the various needs that originally gave rise to this convention.

A third example of imitative behavior and the resulting conventionalization is what is German is called a *Trumpelpfad* – a 'trample path.' Grassy areas are often diagonally bisected by a narrow footpath initially barely visible and over time turning more and more conspicuous. It starts out with just a few people in a hurry cutting across the lawn; others then follow even if they would have the time to take the longer route; and the grass gradually withers under the frequent pounding of feet until a visible trail emerges. The linguist Rudi Keller used this analogy to explain how linguistic structures emerge by the moves of an "invisible hand." People create these paths involuntarily with their individual preferences gradually adding up to a communal tool. Social institutions in general may come about as "the causal consequence of individual intentional actions which are based on at least partially similar intentions" (Keller 1994: 70–71).

i. Making things easier
We have seen two manifestations of the tendency to make things easier in acquisition and in historical change: "choosing the familiar for the unfamiliar" and "choosing the simple for the complex." Both of these tendencies are apparent in non-linguistic behavior as well.

Opting for the **familiar** is a force that retards change: sticking with the "tried and true" often seems safer. Acting by convention is often more attractive than striking out on our own. Habits are based on this principle: having the same food for breakfast every day, following the same route when going to work, listening to the same radio station, or voting for the same political party.

Trying to **simplify** our tasks is a very common tendency as well. Cutting across the lawn rather than taking the roundabout way, heating up frozen food for dinner rather than preparing the meal from scratch, buying a stack of the same birthday cards to send to various friends rather than picking a special one for each, or taking care of all shopping at the same time rather than doing it piecemeal: these are all simplifying measures.

j. Conflict resolution

The analysis of language structure reveals how grammars may opt for different resolutions of competing desiderata. As mentioned earlier, one of the basic conflicts is whether the speaker's or the hearer's interest be given priority. Other conflicts emerge from the different weights of the various aspects of grammar, such as phonology and morphology, or morphology and syntax. Infixes in some languages arise as a compromise between phonological and morphological desiderata. As discussed in Chapter 4, Section 4.3, Bontok is a prefixing language and thus the verbalizing affix *um-* would be expected to precede stems. However, this would create consonant clusters between the prefix and consonant-initial clusters, such as in *um-fikas* 'to be/become strong,' but these clusters are ruled out by the phonology of the language. The solution is to split the stem and place the affix as close to the beginning of the stem as possible without violating phonotactics – that is, right after the initial consonant: *f-um-ikas*. In the theoretical frameworks of Natural Morphology, Natural Phonology, and Natural Syntax, three factors are posited as in potential conflict: universal tendencies, the preferences of the particular language type, and the conventions of the individual language (e.g. Dressler 1995, 2003).

Language use, too, presents constant choices: should I say things as others would or should I strike out on my own and employ an unusual expression? Any learning process is also fraught with conflicts between habit and change.

Grappling with competing priorities is part and parcel of everyday life outside language as well. Should I arrange my books in alphabetic order for easy retrieval or by topic so that I am reminded of other books of similar content? Should I spend my extra money on a new car or on a vacation trip? Should I have a piece of pie for taste or an apple for health? The conflict-laden nature of human thought is captured in the psychological construct of cognitive dissonance. Neuroscientist David Eagleman (2011) characterizes the architecture of the human brain in terms of a "team of rivals." "Just like a good drama, the human brain runs on conflict" (107) and "Behavior is the outcome of the battle among internal systems" (149), with two of the major conflicting factors being emotions and rationality. Others are short-term benefits versus long-term consequences; me and others; clinging to the past and stepping out into the future.

We have just seen ten general tendencies of human cognition that apply both in and outside language. While most linguists and psychologists recognize the role that these concepts play in language, there is nonetheless one issue where there is disagreement: whether these general cognitive tools wired into human brains are **sufficient** to explain language or whether, in addition, there is also a **specific segment of cognition** which only pertains to language. Noam Chomsky's proposal for a Universal Grammar represents this second view. According to his hypothesis, there is a separate "language organ" in the brain that is innate to all humans and that has specifically evolved to make language possible.

In Chomsky's view, there are three factors that are crucial to language acquisition. External linguistic input is one of them; genetic endowment "which sets limits on the attainable languages, thereby making language acquisition possible" is the second; and "principles not specific to FL (faculty of language) is the third. Some of the third-factor principles have the flavor of the constraints that enter into all facets of growth and evolution" (2007: 3). The first factor is the availability of an ambient language; the second factor is a domain-specific endowment pertaining to language only (the locus of Universal Grammar); the third factor is domain-general cognitive capabilities.

Views on what exactly is the content of Universal Grammar (the second factor above) have changed over the years. In an influential approach, UG's structure has been construed as consisting of principles and parameters, with the principles reflecting absolute universals and the parameters offering limited options for languages to choose from (for a review and criticism of this approach, see Newmeyer 1998). Here are three examples of what have been proposed as innate principles of the domain-specific kind.

(21) (a) Subjacency
          A noun phrase cannot be moved in a single step across more than one major constituent boundary.

For example, given the sentence *Bill* **claims** *[that he fired Joe]*$_s$, the corresponding question *Who does Bill* **claim** *[that he fired ___]*$_s$,? is grammatical. However, the question derived from *Bill* **makes** *[the claim [that he fired Joe]*$_s$*]*$_{NP}$ is ungrammatical: *Who does Bill* **make** *[the claim [that he fired ___]*$_s$*]*$_{NP}$? In each case, the question word *who* is analyzed as having moved from the blank to the beginning of the sentence, but there is a crucial difference: in the first instance, *who* steps across only one boundary (S), while in the ungrammatical question, it moves over two boundaries: S and NP.

(21) (b) Structure-dependence
          Syntactic rules are structure-dependent.

E.g. in yes-no questions of English, the verb is analyzed as moving from being second in the clause to being initial. From simple sentences having one-word subjects, such as *Has John ___ arrived?*, it would seem that the verb switches position with the first word of the sentence. However, sentences with multi-word subjects – such as *Has the boy that you met last week ___ arrived?* – show that the inversion rule applies to the entire multi-word structural unit.

(21) (c) Syntax and phonology
          Syntax is blind to segmental phonology.

This principle excludes syntactic rules that would say: "Consonant-initial adjectives follow the noun but vowel-initial adjectives precede it."

Since these principles have been found to be consistent with grammatical phenomena in English, there is the possibility that they may indeed be universal. However, no large-scale study has been carried out to show the probability of their crosslinguistic validity, let alone their necessity.

Over the decades, the hypothesized content of Universal Grammar has been reduced. More recently it has been proposed that the only structural principle present in Universal Grammar is recursion (Hauser, Chomsky and Fitch 2002). Recursion is a special type of partonomic structure, where a structure includes another structure of the same kind.

In contrast with a theory that posits **specific language-structural properties** for the content of Universal Grammar, such as those above, there is an alternative view according to which Universal Grammar is not a compendium of universals but rather a **toolkit**. This means that structures are not built **from** these principles but **with** them: they are learning aids specific to language acquisition (e.g. Pinker and Jackendoff 2009).

The most important argument that has been offered in favor of assuming a set of domain-specific structures or learning tools is "poverty of stimulus." Children acquiring their first language are exposed to linguistic data; but what they end up knowing is more than what has been present in their linguistic environment. How is it that they end up knowing so much from such limited input? The answer is in part that children generalize from the data; but this raises another question: how is it that they generalize in certain directions but not in others? How is it that their generalizations tend to remain within the existing bounds of the ambient language system? The explanation in terms of Universal Grammar holds that the generalizations are channeled and limited by universal principles of language structure. For example, out of the statement *Bill ate a hamburger **with** fries*, we can formulate the question *What did Bill eat a hamburger **with** ___?* However, the question formed from *Bill ate a hamburger **and** fries* would be ungrammatical (**What did Bill eat a hamburger **and** ___?*). This has been found to be the case not only in English but apparently in other languages as well; nor do children stray into this kind of construction. The UG hypothesis explains this fact by saying that the ill-formedness of this structure is innately given.

There are, however, arguments on the other side, against the need for positing domain-specific endowments. First, as we have seen in the preceding chapters of this book, there are few if any structural properties of languages that are exceptionless universals. This means there is very little linguistic knowledge that can be assumed to be innately given to humans. Second, children acquire not only the crosslinguistically recurrent features of the ambient language: they also acquire strictly language-specific patterns. For example, English children have to learn that the sentence *Ann is likely to be late* is grammatical but *Ann is probable to be late* is not. In other words, the so-called raising construction is possible with *likely* but not with its synonym *probable*. One could say that children will not say *Ann is probable to be late* because, while they have heard such constructions with *likely*, they have not heard any with *probable*. But children are capable of saying a lot of things that they have not heard simply by generalizing ambient structures; so why don't they generalize from *likely* to *probable* as well? To explain facts of this sort, a powerful learning mechanism must be assumed that helps children internalize the specific features of their language, which of course cannot be part of Universal Grammar. But if so, perhaps children use the same learning mechanism for acquiring the crosslinguistically invariant parts as well, in which case there is no need to posit an innate Universal Grammar (cf. Hawkins 1988: 8, 2004: 10–11, Tomasello 2003: 321–322). For such reasons and others, many linguists tend to adopt the view that – with possible exceptions, such as the auditory processing of speech (Bybee 2010: 136) – the acquisition and use of language is underlain by domain-general, rather than domain-specific endowments: that is, by general cognitive abilities.

The hypothesis of an **innate Universal Grammar** is often thought to be a distinct approach orthogonal to the so-called **functional approach** that attempts to "derive language from non-language" (Lindblom *et al.* 1984: 187) by hypothesizing that general cognitive tools are all that are needed to explain language. However, the two approaches are not that far apart. They have two things in common: they both assume certain goals for language and they both assume the importance of a number of domain-general conceptual tools, such as the ten items listed above. Where they differ is only whether **in addition**, the "initial stage" of the processes of language acquisition and language use also contains some special domain-specific cognitive constructs.

But this assumption does not exclude the UG approach from the domain of functional explanations. Let us adopt the following definition.

(22) Functional explanations
     An object is explained functionally if the explanation makes reference to the goals of the users of that object and the tools that the users have available to them for achieving these goals.

By this definition, both the UG approach and the functional one offer functional explanations since they both assume some goals – cognition and/or communication – and also some tools. They differ only regarding the nature of the tool they posit: whether all of them are domain-general or whether some are domain-specific.

A final question that has been left open has to do with function – the ultimate explainer in our framework. Where does function come from – the goals that people have in using language and the means that they have available to them to achieve these goals? Linguistic goals and means must be related to the general goals that humans pursue in life and to their physical and psychological makeup. Ultimately, it is our genetic endowment that must underlie all of language as it shapes everything else in how we perceive, interpret, and affect the world on our own specifically human terms.

Summary

The goal of this chapter has been to explain crosslinguistically common grammatical patterns. Here is the synopsis of the chapter.

In Section 7.1, the concept of explanation was first discussed, its three basic types – permissive, probabilistic, and nomological – defined and a three-stage explanatory argument of linguistic structures was exemplified. Applied to the explanation of crosslinguistic patterns, it is as follows.

(23) (a) Crosslinguistically common structural patterns are explainable by crosslinguistically common historical changes.
     (b) Crosslinguistically common historical changes are explainable by crosslinguistic patterns of language acquisition and language use.
     (c) Crosslinguistic patterns of language acquisition and language use are explainable by language function: the goals of language use and the conceptual tools that are conducive or necessary for it.

Section 7.2 took up the first stage: how crosslinguistically recurrent synchronic patterns may be explained historically. The three diachronic trends invoked were grammaticalization, harmonization, and proximization.

Section 7.3 turned to the second step of explaining crosslinguistically common diachronic processes (grammaticalization, harmonization, and proximization) by acquisition and, mainly, use. Performance preferences such as efficiency of processing, generalization, and routinization served in our user-based explanations. The substance of functional explanations of language structure is summarized in John DuBois' oft-cited pithy remark: "Grammars do best what speakers do most" (1985: 363).

Section 7.4 took up the third stage of the explanatory argument by searching for the functional roots of these tendencies manifested in performance. Functional explanations were defined as making reference to goals and tools. While the exact nature of the tools speakers use in language is subject to debate in the field, most linguists would agree that – additionally or exclusively – certain domain-general preferences do play a role in language, ten of which were briefly described.

Postscript

The generalizations discussed in this chapter and throughout the book have all been of the permissive or probabilistic kind. The adjacency of semantically related constituents is preferred but there are also examples where a language moves in the opposite direction, such as English verbal particles separating from the verb (e.g. **Check** it **out!** (Harris and Campbell 1995: 225–228)). Correlation pairs generally show uniform order but not always: there are OV languages with prepositions (such as Persian) and VO languages with postpositions (e.g. Arawak). Grammaticalization is also not without exceptions: normally it is unidirectional but there are instances where affixes become clitics or even lexical items. The possessive marker in English historically started out as an affix but it is now a clitic as shown by the fact that it is attached to entire phrases; e.g. *The girl who called me's sister is sick* (as opposed to **The girl's who called me sister is sick*).

Physicist Lisa Randall noted (2011): "an important part of science is understanding uncertainty." In linguistics, too, there are many large questions to which answers are tentative. Why is there language to begin with? How and why did it arise? How does language shape our perception and interpretation of the world? How is language anchored in the brain? How is language similar and different from other communication systems including those of animals? As we compare languages among themselves, is it the similarities that need to be identified and explained? Or, as Nicholas Evans and Stephen Levison have argued recently (2009), is it the diversity of human languages that cries out for explanations?

It was mentioned above that the force of functional explanations for language structures is limited by three factors: multiple functions, conflicting functions, and functionally unexplainable facts. These factors are present in linguistic explanations in general. One hardship is the **multitude of factors** and the fact that, while they may be acting in concert, they may also be **in conflict**. William Croft recalls Joseph Greenberg saying on one occasion: "A speaker is like a lousy auto mechanic: every time he fixes something in the language, he screws up something else" (Croft 2002: 5). And, while in some cases, possible causes come in multiples, in other instances, there is **no apparent cause at all**: a structure may evolve by chance. In her analysis of some rare morphosyntactic patterns (e.g. in the Caucasian language Batsbi, a verb may contain multiple copies of the same agreement marker), Alice Harris addresses the question of why such patterns are rare and if they are, why do they exist at all and why do they survive. Her answer is that such structures arise from a set of common diachronic processes which, however, come into play in an unlikely combination (2010).

In addition, a fundamental factor that stands in the way of achieving certainty in our explanatory endeavors in any field is our tenuous grasp of reality both in language and outside it. The Danish physicist Niels Bohr said: "It is wrong to think that the task of physics is to find out how nature **is**. Physics concerns only what we can **say** about nature" (Gregory 1988: 95; emphasis original). In other words, the language that we use to describe things may easily fall short of capturing true reality. This view is echoed by the prominent linguist Ray Jackendoff: "We can understand things in the world as belonging to categories only because we (or our minds) construct the categories" (2012: 132).

In their recent analysis of linguistic theorizing, András Kertész and Csilla Rákosi (2012) point at two sources of uncertainty. One is the fleeting and variable status of the data: rather than solid, rock-bottom entities, they are theory-dependent themselves. The other is that our argumentation processes are necessarily prismatic: just as the appearance of an object changes depending on how we hold the prism and the view always remains fractured, linguistic arguments provide merely partial accounts of facts and they are not static but constantly evolving. According to Paul the Apostle's metaphor, what we perceive is fragmented images of things reflected in a blurry mirror. Or, in Anaïs Nin's words, "We don't see things as they are; we see things as we are."

Activities

1. The French negative construction as in *Je ne sais pas* "I not know not" 'I don't know' originated from the negator *ne* paired with *pas* meaning 'step'. In its genesis, it expressed emphatic negation, similar to English *I shall not go **one step** further*, or *I haven't heard **a peep** from her*. In today's colloquial French, *ne* is often dropped as in *Je sais pas*. How and why do you think this change happened?

2. One of Joseph Greenberg's universal hypotheses is this: "If the pronominal object follows the verb, so does the nominal object" (1966a: #25). This is borne out in French, where the major constituent order pattern is SVO if the object is a noun but SOV if the object is a pronoun; e.g. *J'ai vu Bill.* "I've seen Bill" 'I have seen Bill' but *Je t'ai vu.* "I you've seen" 'I have seen you.' What might be the reason for this discrepancy between nominal and pronominal objects? Note that French has evolved from Latin, which was primarily SOV.

3. How are the words *come* and *go* used in English? Normally, *come* is used for motion toward the speaker but I can say *When are you coming to my office?* even if I am not in my office. Consider also such metaphoric uses as *His temperature is going up; when the going is hard*, etc. Do these expressions translate into other languages the same way?

4. English has some "plurale tantum" words: nouns that are used only in the plural: *pants, scissors*, etc. Find more English examples and then see if in other languages the same words would also be pluralia tantum.

5. As noted in this chapter (also in Chapter 2), two conceptual tools that play a role in naming things are partonomy and taxonomy. Partonomy is based on spatial or functional coherence, taxonomy is based on similarity. The way merchandise is arranged in a food market is also based on one or the other of these principles. For example, cork screws may be displayed along with other kitchen appliances due to their similarities or they may be placed next to the wine racks. Find other examples for each of the two organizational principles in other domains of everyday life.

Further reading

- For a general overview of explanations in linguistics, see Moore and Polinsky 2003. For explaining language universals, see Butterworth *et al.* (eds.) 1984, Hawkins (ed.) 1988, Moravcsik 2007, 2010.

- On typological research in the generative framework, see Cinque and Kayne 2005. A survey of different approaches to typology is provided in Shibatani and Bynon 1995. For Hansjakob Seiler's UNITYP approach, see Seiler 2000.

- For competing motivations in morphosyntax, see Malchukov 2011.

- On what may be possible, probable and necessary in language structure, see Newmeyer 2005.

- For Daniel Everett's work on the Pirahã language, see Everett 2008 and 2012. On the ensuing controversy, see Tom Bartlett's article in *The Chronicle of Higher Education*, March 21, 2012.

- On how phonological structure can change in the course of language use, see Blevins 2004: 31–44.

- On functional and formalistic explanations, see Nettle 1998.

- On domain-general cognitive abilities relevant to language, see Slobin 1985b, MacWhinney 1999, Tomasello 2003, Bybee 2010: 6–8, 34–37.

- About partonomy in syntax and beyond, see Moravcsik 2009.

- On iconicity, see Haiman (ed.) 1985 and Simone 1995.

- On competing motivations, see Du Bois 1985, Dressler 1995. A recent contribution is the volume of papers edited by MacWhinney *et al.* to appear.

- For sources and discussion of Subjacency and Structure dependency, see Newmeyer 1998: 51–52 and 85–86.

- On the mechanisms by which processing preferences create crosslinguistic consistencies of grammar, see Kirby 1999.

- For an excellent comparative assessment of the nativist and constructivist hypotheses about how children acquire their language, see Ambridge and Lieven 2011.

Languages mentioned

Genetic and areal information comes mostly from Ethnologue.com. Language family is mentioned first and (in some cases) the name of the sub-family. Following the semicolon, the main area(s) is/are named where the language is spoken.

Agta: Austronesian, Malay-Polynesian; Philippines
Ainu: isolate; Japan
Akan: Niger-Congo, Kwa; Ghana and Ivory Coast
Albanian: Indo-European; Albania
American Sign Language (ASL): USA
Amharic: Afro-Asiatic, Semitic; Ethiopia
Anindilyakwa: Australian; Northern Australia
Arabic: Afro-Asiatic, Semitic; Saudi Arabia and other Near-Eastern countries
Aramaic: Afro-Asiatic, Semitic; West Asia
Arawak: Caribbean, Maipuran; Suriname
Arrente: Pama-Nyungan, Arandic; Central Australia
Atakapa: isolate; Louisiana, Texas (extinct)
Aztec: Uto-Aztecan; Mexico
Basque: isolate; Spain
Batsbi: North-Caucasian; Georgia
Bengali: Indo-European, Indo-Iranian; India
Berber Imdlawn Tashlhiyt: Afro-Asiatic, Berber; Morocco
Bikol: Austronesian, Malayo-Polynesian; Philippines
Bontok: Austronesian, Malayo-Polynesian; Philippines
Breton: Indo-European, Celtic; France
Bulgarian: Indo-European, Slavic; Bulgaria
Burmese: Sino-Tibetan, Tibeto-Burman; Myanmar
Catalan: Indo-European, Romance; Spain
Cebuano: Austronesian, Malayo-Polynesian; Philippines
Chemehuevi: Uto-Aztecan, Numic; California
Cheremis (=Mari): Uralic, Mari; Russian Federation
Cheyenne: Algonquian; Montana, Ontario
Chikasaw: Muskogean; Mississippi, Alabama
Chinese: Sino-Tibetan, Sinitic; China
Chukchi: Chukotko-Kamchatkan; Russian Federation
Chumash: Hokan; S. California (extinct)
Coeur d'Alene: Salishan; N. Idaho
Czech: Indo-European, Slavic; Czech Republic
Dakota: Siouan; North and South Dakota, Nebraska
Dutch: Indo-European, Germanic; the Netherlands
Dyirbal: Pama-Nyungan; Queensland (Australia)
Estonian: Uralic, Finnic; Estonia
Ewe: Niger-Congo, Kwa; Ghana
Fijian: Austronesian, Malayo-Polynesian; Fiji

Finnish: Uralic, Finnic; Finland
French: Indo-European, Romance; France
Galla (=Oromo): Afro-Asiatic, Cushitic; Ethiopia, Kenya
Gêgbĕ: Niger-Congo, Kwa; West Africa
Georgian: Kartvelian (=South Caucasian); Georgia
German: Indo-European, Germanic; Germany
Gilbertese (=Kiribati): Austronesian, Malayo-Polynesian; Kiribati
Grand Ronde Chinook Jargon: pidgin, Chinook-based; Oregon
Greek: Indo-European; Greece
Greenlandic Eskimo: Eskimo-Aleut; Greenland
Guana: Arawakan (extinct)
Guugu Yimidhir: Pama-Nyungan; Australia
Haitian: Creole, French-based; Haiti
Harari: Afro-Asiatic, Semitic; Ethiopia
Hausa: Afro-Asiatic, Chadic; Nigeria
Hawaiian: Austronesian, Malayo-Polynesian; Hawaii (Ni'ihau Island)
Hawaii Creole English: creole, English-based; Hawaii
Hebrew: Afro-Asiatic, Semitic; Israel
Hinalug: Dagestanian, Lezgian; Azerbaijan
Hindi: Indo-European, Indo-Iranian; India
Hmong: Hmong-Mien; Vietnam
Hunde: Niger-Congo, Bantu; Democratic Republic of Congo
Hungarian: Uralic, Finno-Ugric; Hungary
Ibibio: Niger-Congo, Benue-Congo; Nigeria
Ibo: Niger-Congo, Benue-Congo; Nigeria
Indonesian: Austronesian, Malayo-Polynesian; Java, Bali
Italian: Indo-European, Romance; Italy
Itelmen: Chukotko-Kamchatkan; Russian Federation
Jahai: Austro-Asiatic, Mon-Khmer; Malaya
Jalé: Trans-New-Guinea; New Guinea
Japanese: Japonic; Japan
Kaluli: Trans-New-Guinea, Bosavi; Papua New Guinea
Katu: Mon-Khmer; Vietnam, Laos
Kayardild: Pama-Nyungan; Queensland (Australia)
Kikuyu: Niger-Congo, Bantu; Kenya
Kinyarwanda: Niger-Congo, Bantu; Rwanda
Kiribati: see Gilbertese
Kisi: Niger-Congo, Bantu; Tanzania
Klamath: Penutian; Oregon
Koasati: Muskogean; Louisiana, Texas
Kono: Niger-Congo, West Atlantic, Mande; West Africa
Korean: isolate; Korea
Kyuguot Nootka: Wakashan; British Columbia
Lahu: Sino-Tibetan, Tibeto-Burman; China
Latin: Indo-European, Italic; used in the Catholic Church worldwide
Lavukaleve: Papuan, Central Solomons; Solomon Islands
Lezgian: Northeast-Caucasian (=Dagestanian); Dagestan
Lonwolwol: Austronesian, Malayo-Polynesian; Ambrym Island

Luiseño: Uto-Aztecan; Southern California
Lunda: Niger-Congo, Bantu; Zambia
Malay: Austronesian, Malayo-Polynesian; Malaysia
Maltese (Arabic): Afro-Asiatic, Semitic; Malta
Manange: Sino-Tibetan, Tibeto-Burman; Nepal
Mandarin: Sino-Tibetan, Sinitic; China
Mande: Niger-Congo, West Atlantic; West Africa
Maranao: Austronesian, Malayo-Polynesian; Philippines
Marshallese: Austronesian, Malayo-Polynesian; Marshall Island
Mba: Niger-Congo, Ubangian; Democratic Republic of Congo
Meithei: Tibeto-Burman; India, Myanmar
Mohawk: Iroquoian; Quebec
Mokilese: Austronesian, Malayo-Polynesian; Micronesia
Neo-Aramaic: see under Aramaic
Nepali: Indo-European, Indo-Iranian; Nepal
Nez Perce: Penutian, Sahaptin; N. Idaho
Ngawon: Pama-Nyungan (extinct)
Nootka: Wakashan; British Columbia
Oksapmin: Trans-New Guinea; Papua New Guinea
O'odham (=Papago): Uto-Aztecan; Arizona
Old English: Indo-European, Germanic; British Isles (about 500 CE through 1100 CE)
Oromo: see Galla
Panara: Macro-Gé; Brazil
Pangasinan: Austronesian, Malayo-Polynesian; Philippines
Papago: see O'odham
Persian: Indo-European, Indo-Iranian; Iran
Pipil: Uto-Aztecan, Aztecan; El Salvador
Pirahã: Mura; Brazil
Polish: Indo-European, Slavic; Poland
Proto-Indo-European: Indo-European (reconstructed language)
Quechua (Huallaga Huánuco): Andean-Equatorial, Quechuan; Peru
Rapa Nui (=Easter Island): Austronesian, Malayo-Polynesian; Easter Island
Rotokas: North Bougainville, Rotokas; Papua New Guinea
Rumanian: Indo-European, Romance; Rumania
Russian: Indo-European, Slavic; Russian Federation
Salish: Salishan, Central Salish; State of Washington
Sanskrit: Indo-European, Indo-Iranian; India
Samoan: Austronesian, Malayo-Polynesian; Samoa
Serbian: Indo-European, Slavic; Serbia
Serbo-Croatian: Indo-European, Slavic; Serbia, Croatia
Sherpa: Sino-Tibetan, Tibeto-Burman; Nepal
Shilha: Afro-Asiatic, Berber; Morocco
Sierra Popoluca: Mixe-Zoque; Mexico
Siriono: Tucanoan; Columbia
Southern Barasano: Tucanoan; Colombia
Spanish: Indo-European, Romance; Spain
Swahili: Niger-Congo, Bantu; Tanzania
Swedish: Indo-European, Germanic: Sweden

Tagalog: Austronesian, Malayo-Polynesian; Philippines
Tamil: Dravidian; India
Tauya: Trans-New Guinea; Papua New Guinea
Thai: Tai-Kadai, Kam-Tai; Thailand
Thompson: Salishan; British Columbia
Tiv: Niger-Congo, Benue-Congo; Nigeria
Tlingit: Na-Dene; Alaska, Canada
Tok Pisin: Creole, English-based; Papua New Guinea
Tonga: Niger-Congo, Bantu; Zambia
Tongan: Austronesian, Malayo-Polynesian; Tonga
Tsakhur: North-Caucasian, Lezgian; Azerbaijan
Tsimshian: Penutian; British Columbia
Turkana: Nilo-Saharan, Eastern Sudanic; Kenya
Turkish: Altaic, Turkic; Turkey
Tuscarora: Iroquoian; Ontario
Tümpisha Shoshone: Uto-Aztecan; Nevada, Idaho
Tzeltal: Mayan; Mexico
Ulwa: Misumalpan; Nicaragua
Vai: Niger-Congo, Mane; Liberia
Vietnamese: Austro-Asiatic, Mon-Khmer; Viet Nam
Walmatjari: Pama-Nyungan; Australia
Warlpiri: Pama-Nyungan; Australia
West Greenlandic Eskimo: Eskimo-Aleut; Greenland
Yoruba: Niger-Congo, Benue-Congo; Nigeria
Yucatec Mayan: Mayan; Yucatán Peninsula
Yumas: Sepik; Papua New Guinea
Zyrian (=Komi): Uralic, Finno-Permic; Russian Federation
!Xóõ: Khoisan; Botswana

Glossary

Many of the terms below are specific to language-typological research. For other grammatical terms, see for example Robert L. Trask 1993, *A dictionary of grammatical terms*, London: Routledge, James R. Hurford 1994, *Grammar. A student's guide*. Cambridge University Press, and Silvia Luraghi and Claudia Parodi 2008, *Key terms in syntax and syntactic theory*, New York: Continuum. For phonetic terminology, see Michael Ashby and John Maidment 2005, *Introducing phonetic science*, Cambridge University Press.

Accessibility Hierarchy: A set of implicational generalizations stating that particular syntactic patterns preferentially involve certain sentence constituents (e.g. Subjects over Direct Objects).

adjunct: See under **complement**.

adposition: A cover term for prepositions, postpositions, intrapositions, and ambipositions.

agglutination: A morphological pattern where each morpheme of a word can be clearly separated from the others and each carries a single meaning element.

agreement: A syntactic pattern where the inflection of one constituent repeats some of the properties of another constituent, such as when the verb expresses the person and number of the subject or the adjective carries an inflection that indicates the gender and number of the noun. The constituent that is source of the properties is called the **agreement controller**, the constituent that carries the corresponding inflection is called the **agreement target**; the properties involved are the **agreement features**.

alienable possession: The relationship between two entities where one happens to possess the other, as in *Jill's school*. It contrasts with **inalienable possession**, where the relationship is unalterable and permanent, as in *Jill's arm* or *Jill's mother*.

alignment: A pattern of like morphosyntactic behavior between two of three constituents: the Agent of a two-argument verb (A), the Patient of a two-argument verb (P), and the Single argument of a one-argument verb (S).

ambiposition: An adposition that may stand either before or after a noun phrase.

Animacy Hierarchy: A set of implicational generalizations stating that particular syntactic patterns preferentially involve certain sentence constituents depending on how human-like and/or definite they are (e.g. Pronouns over Nouns).

argument: A noun phrase designating a semantic participant of a predicate.

complement: A non-subject noun phrase that obligatorily co-occurs with a predicate (as in *The painting resembles **a flower***). Complements contrast with **adjuncts**, which are noun phrases that are optional (as in *The painting was stolen **from the museum***).

compositionality: A construction is compositional if the total meaning equals the sum of the meanings of the parts and of their relationships.

constituent: A unit within a grammatical construction, such as a sound, a syllable, a word, a phrase, or a clause.

dependent: An optional constituent of a phrase. It contrasts with **head**, which is an indispensable, obligatory constituent. For example, in *blue herons*, *herons* is the head and *blue* is a dependent.

diachrony: This is a synonym for history. It contrasts with **synchrony**, which refers to a single stage of evolution.

duplifix: An affix that duplicates part of the stem (as in Agta **da**-*dana* 'very old').

head: See under **dependent**.

homorganicity: Two sounds are homorganic if they are formed in the same place of articulation, as /m/ and /p/ both being bilabial.

inalienable possession: See under **alienable possession**.

linearization: Placing items in temporal order.

logograph: A writing system where every written symbol stands for a word without its parts corresponding to parts of the meaning of the word.

monomorphemic words: Words that consist of a single morpheme only, such as *bird*. **Polymorphemic words** in turn consist of more than one morpheme, such as *bird-s*.

monosemy: A word is monosemous if it has only a single meaning, such as *fail*. A word is **polysemous** if it has more than one meaning, such as *nail*.

neutralization: A pattern where a contrast between two phonemes disappears in a given context so that only one of the two can occur; such as that at the end of German words, only voiceless obstruents and no voiced ones can occur.

paradigmatic relation: The relationship between related forms such that in a given context, only one or the other can occur but not both; e.g. two demonstratives: *this* and *that*. A **syntagmatic relation** in turn holds between forms that occur together in a construction, such as a demonstrative and a noun in *this book*.

partonomy: Also called mereonomy, it is the relationship between parts and wholes, such as a table and its legs.

phonotactic constraints: Constraints on the sequences of speech sounds; such as that in English, there is word-initial /st/ (e.g. *stain*) but no /ts/ (*tsain*).

pictograph: An element of a symbol system that forms a picture of the referent that it stands for (such as a road sign for deer crossing depicting a deer head).

plosive: An alternative term for stop consonants.

polymorphemic words: See under **monomorphemic words**.

polysemy: See under **monosemy**.

possessor: In a possessive construction such as *Jill's house*, *Jill* is the possessor; *house* is the **possessum**.

possessum: See under **possessor**.

resumptive pronoun: A pronoun that occurs in a relative clause referring back to the head of the clause.

syllabary: A writing system where each written symbol stands for a syllable.

symbol systems: A set of forms with each having a meaning; such as road signs, traffic lights, or languages.

synchrony: See under **diachrony**.

syntagmatic relation: See under **paradigmatic relation**.

taxonomy: A taxonomic relation holds between types and tokens, such as 'animal' and 'dog.'

topicalization: A construction where part of the sentence is placed in a special position for emphasis, as in *Jill, I like her*.

References

Aarts, Bas 2007. *Syntactic gradience. The nature of grammatical indeterminacy*. Oxford University Press.

Aikhenvald, Alexandra Y. 2000. *Classifiers. A typology of noun categorization devices*. Oxford University Press.

2007. Typological distinctions in word formation. In Shopen (ed.), volume III, 1–63.

Ambridge, Ben and Lieven, Elena V. M. 2011. *Child language acquisition. Contrasting theoretical approaches*. Cambridge University Press.

Andersen, Elaine 1978. Lexical universals of body-part terminology. In Greenberg *et al.* (eds.), volume III, 335–368.

Archibald, John 1998. *Second language phonology*. Amsterdam/Philadelphia: Benjamins.

Aronoff, Mark, Meir, Irit, and Sandler, Wendy 2005. The paradox of sign language morphology. *Language* 81/2: 301–344.

Ashby, Michael and Maidment, John 2005. *Introducing phonetic science*. Cambridge University Press.

Baerman, Matthew, Brown, Dunstan, and Corbett, Greville G. 2005. *The syntax-morphology interface. A study of syncretism*. Cambridge University Press.

Baker, Mark C. 1996. *The polysynthesis parameter*. Oxford University Press.

Bakker, Dik 2011. Language sampling. In Song (ed.) 100–127.

Barlow, Michael and Kemmer, Suzanne (eds.) 2000. *Usage-based models of language*. Stanford, CA: Center for the Study of Language and Information.

Bates, Elizabeth, Devescovi, Antonella, and Wulfeck, Beverly 2001. Psycholinguistics: a cross-linguistic perspective. *Annual Review of Psychology* 52: 369–396.

Behaghel, Otto 1932. *Deutsche Syntax. Eine geschichtliche Darstellung*, volume IV. Heidelberg: Carl Winter.

Bell, Alan 1978. Syllabic consonants. In Greenberg *et al.* (eds.), volume II, 153–201.

Berlin, Brent and Kay, Paul 1969, 1991. *Basic color terms. Their universality and evolution*. The University of California Press.

Bhat, D. N. S. 2004. *Pronouns*. Oxford University Press.

Bickel, Balthasar 2011. Grammatical relations typology. In Song (ed.) 399–445.

Bickel, Balthasar and Nichols, Johanna 2005. Fusion of selected inflectional formatives. In Haspelmath *et al.* (eds.) 86–89.

2007. Inflectional morphology. In Shopen (ed.), volume III: 169–240.

Bisang, Walter 2011. Word classes. In Song (ed.) 280–302.

Blevins, Juliette 1995. The syllable in phonological theory. In Goldsmith (ed.) 206–244.

2004. *Evolutionary phonology. The emergence of sound patterns*. Cambridge University Press.

Booij, Geert, Lehmann, Christian, Mugdan, Joachim, and Skopetea, Stavros (eds.) 2000. *Morphology. An international handbook on inflection and word formation*, volume II. Berlin, New York: Walter de Gruyter.

Boroditsky, Lera 2009. How does our language shape the way we think? In Brockman, Max (ed.) *What's next? Dispatches on the future of science*. Vintage Press.

Bowerman, Melissa 1996. The origins of children's spatial semantic categories: cognitive versus linguistic determinants. In Gumperz, John J. and Levinson, Stephen C. (eds.) *Rethinking linguistic relativity*, 145–176. Cambridge University Press.

Bowerman, Melissa and Choi, Soonja 2001. Shaping meanings for language: Universal and language-specific in the acquisition of semantic categories. In Bowerman, Melissa, and Levinson, Stephen C. (eds.), *Language acquisition and conceptual development*, 475–511. Cambridge University Press.

Breen, Gavan and Pensalfini, Bob 1999. Arrente: a language with no syllable onsets. *Linguistic Inquiry* 30/1: 1–25.

Brentari, Diane 1995. Sign language phonology: ASL. In Goldsmith (ed.) 615–639.

Brown, Cecil H. 1976. General principles of human anatomical partonomy and speculations on the growth of partonomic nomenclature. *American Ethnologist* 3/3: 400–424.

2005a. Hand and arm. In Haspelmath *et al.* (eds.) 522–525.

2005b. Finger and hand. In Haspelmath *et al.* (eds.) 526–529.

Brown, Cecil H. and Witkowski, Stanley R. 1981. Figurative language in a universalist perspective. *American Ethnologist* 8/3: 596–610.

Brown, Dunstan. 2011. Morphological typology. In Song (ed.) 487–503.

Brown, Roger and Gilman, Albert 1960. The pronouns of power and solidarity. In Sebeok, Thomas A. (ed.) *Style in language*, 253–276. Cambridge, MA: The MIT Press.

Burenhult, Niclas 2006. Body part terms in Jahai. *Language Sciences* 28/203: 162–189.

Butskhrikidze, Marika 2010. The nature of consonant sequences in Georgian. In Wohlgemuth *et al.* (eds.), 2010a, 23–46.

Butterworth, Brian, Comrie, Bernard and Dahl, Östen (eds.) 1984. *Explanations for language universals*. New York: Mouton.

Bybee, Joan 1985. *Morphology. A study of the relation between meaning and form*. Amsterdam/Philadelphia: Benjamins.

1988. The diachronic dimension in explanation. In Hawkins (ed.) 350–379.

2010. *Language, usage, and cognition*. Cambridge University Press.

Bynon, Theodora 1977. *Historical linguistics*. Cambridge University Press.

Cairns, Charles E. and Raimy, Eric 2011. *Handbook of the syllable*. Leiden: Brill.

Chadwick, John 1970. *The decipherment of Linear B*. Cambridge University Press.

Chapin, Paul G. 1978. Easter Island: a characteristic VSO language. In Lehmann, Winfred P. (ed.) *Syntactic typology. Studies in the phenomenology of language*. 139–168. The University of Texas Press.

Chappell, Hilary and McGregor, William (eds.) 1996. *The grammar of inalienability. A typological perspective on body part terms and the part-whole relation*. Berlin: Mouton de Gruyter.

Chomsky, Noam 2002. *On nature and language*. Cambridge University Press.

2007. Approaching UG from below. In Sauerland, Uli and Gärtner, Hans-Martin (eds.) *Interfaces + Recursion = Language*, 1–19. Berlin: Mouton de Gruyter.

Cinque, Guglielmo and Kayne, Richard S. 2005. *The Oxford handbook of comparative syntax*. Oxford University Press.

Clark, Eve V. 1971. On the acquisition of the meaning of *before* and *after*. *Journal of Verbal Learning and Verbal Behavior* 10/3: 266–275.

2003. *First language acquisition*. Cambridge University Press.

Claudi, Ulrike 1994. Word order change as category change. In Pagliuca (ed.) 193–231.

Comrie, Bernard 1980. The order of case and possessive suffixes in Uralic languages: an approach to the comparative-historical problem. *Lingua Posnaniensis* 23: 81–86.

1986. Markedness, grammar, people, and the world. In Eckman, Fred R., Moravcsik, Edith A., and Wirth, Jessica R. (eds.) *Markedness*, 85–106. New York: Plenum.

1989. *Language universals and linguistic typology*. Second edition. University of Chicago Press.

(ed.) 1990. *The major languages of the world*. Oxford University Press.

2005a. Alignment of case markers. In Haspelmath *et al.* (eds.) 398–405.

2005b. Writing systems. In Haspelmath *et al.* (eds.) 568–571.

Comrie, Bernard and Kuteva, Tania 2005. Relativization strategies. In Haspelmath *et al.* (ed.) 494–501.

Comrie, Bernard, Matthews, Stephen, and Polinsky, Maria (eds.) 2003. *The atlas of languages. The origin and development of languages throughout the world*. Second edition. New York: Facts on File, Inc.

Cooke, Joseph R. 1968. *Pronominal reference in Thai, Burmese, and Vietnamese*. University of California Press.

Corbett, Greville G. 2000. *Number*. Cambridge University Press.

2006. *Agreement*. Cambridge University Press.

2011. Implicational hierarchies. In Song (ed.), 190–205.

Craig, Colette G. 1986. Jacaltec noun classifiers: a study in language and culture. In Craig (ed.) 363–393.

(ed.) 1986. *Noun classes and categorization.* Amsterdam/Philadelphia: Benjamins.

Croft, William 2000. *Explaining language change. An evolutionary approach.* Harlow: Longman.

2001. *Radical construction grammar. Syntactic theory in typological perspective.* Oxford University Press.

2002. On being a student of Joe Greenberg. *Linguistic Typology* 6/1: 3–8.

2003. *Typology and universals.* Cambridge University Press.

Cysouw, Michael 2003. *The paradigmatic structure of person marking.* Oxford University Press.

Dalmi, Grete 2010. *Copular sentences, predication, and cyclic agree: a comparative approach.* Saarbrücken.

Daniel, Michael 2005. Plurality in independent personal pronouns. In Haspelmath *et al.* (eds.) 146–149.

Daniels, Peter T. and Bright, William (eds.) 1996. *The world's writing systems.* Oxford University Press.

Davis, Garry W. and Iverson, Gregory K. (eds.) 1992. *Explanation in historical linguistics.* Amsterdam/Philadelphia: Benjamins.

Dell, François and Elmedlaoui, Mohamed. 2002. *Syllables in Tashlhiyt Berber and in Moroccan Arabic.* Dordrecht: Kluwer.

Deutscher, Guy 2005. *The unfolding of language. An evolutionary tour of mankind's greatest invention.* New York: Henry Holt and Co.

2010. *Through the language glass. Why the world looks different in other languages.* New York: Henry Holt and Co.

Diessel, Holger 1999. *Demonstratives. Form, function, and grammaticalization.* Amsterdam/Philadelphia: Benjamins.

2012. Diachronic change and language acquisition. In Bergs, Alexander and Brinton, Laurel (eds.) *Historical linguistics of English: an international handbook,* volume II. Berlin: Mouton de Gruyter.

Di Sciullo, Anna-Maria and Williams, Edwin 1987. *On the definition of word.* The MIT Press.

Dixon, R. M. W. 1972. *The Dyirbal language of North Queensland.* Cambridge University Press.

1988. *A grammar of Boumaa Fijian.* The University of Chicago Press.

1997. *The rise and fall of languages.* Cambridge University Press.

2010. *Basic linguistic theory.* Volume I: *Methodology,* volume II: *Grammatical topics.* Oxford University Press.

Dixon, R. M. W. and Aikhenvald, Alexandra Y. (eds.) 2002. *Word. A cross-linguistic typology.* Cambridge University Press.

Donaldson, Margaret and Wales, Roger 1970. On the acquisition of some relational terms. In Hayes, John R. (ed.) *Cognition and the development of language,* 235–268. New York: John Wiley.

Downing, Pamela 1996. *Numeral classifier systems. The case of Japanese.* Amsterdam/Philadelphia: Benjamins.

Dressler, Wolfgang U. 1995. Interactions between iconicity and other semiotic parameters in language. In Simone (ed.) 21–37.

2003. Naturalness and morphological change. In Joseph and Janda (eds.) 461–471.

Dryer, Matthew S. 1989. Large linguistic areas and language sampling. *Studies in Language* 13/2: 257–292.

1992. The Greenbergian word order correlations. *Language* 68/1: 81–138.

2005a. Order of subject, object, and verb. In Haspelmath *et al.* (eds.) 330–333.

2005b. Order of adposition and noun phrase. In Haspelmath *et al.* (eds.) 346–349.

2005c. Order of genitive and noun. In Haspelmath *et al.* (eds.) 350–353.

2005d. Relationship between the order of object and verb and the order of adposition and noun phrase. In Haspelmath *et al.* (eds.) 386–389.

2005e. Relationship between the order of object and verb and the order of relative clause and noun. In Haspelmath *et al.* (eds.) 390–393.

2005f. Position of case affixes. In Haspelmath *et al.* (eds.) 210–213.

2005g. Definite articles. In Haspelmath *et al.* (eds.) 154–157.

2005h. Indefinite articles. In Haspelmath *et al.* (eds.) 158–161.

2005i. Prefixing versus suffixing in inflectional morphology. In Haspelmath *et al.* (eds.) 110–113.

2007. Word order. In Shopen (ed.), volume I, 61–131.

Du Bois, John W. 1985. Competing motivations. In Haiman (ed.) 343–365.

Eagleman, David 2011. *Incognito. The secret lives of the brain.* New York: Pantheon Books.

Eckman, Fred 1977. Markedness and the Contrastive Analysis Hypothesis. *Language Learning* 27: 315–330.

1991. The Structural Conformity Hypothesis and the acquisition of consonant clusters in the interlanguage of ESL learners. *Studies in Second Language Acquisition* 13/1: 23–41.

2011. Linguistic typology and second language acquisition. In Song (ed.) 618–633.

Eckman, Fred, Moravcsik, Edith, and Wirth, Jessica R. 1989. Implicational universals and interrogative structures in the interlanguage of ESL learners. *Language Learning* 39: 173–205.

Emmorey, Karen 2002. *Language, cognition, and the brain. Insights from sign language research.* Mahwah, NJ: Erlbaum.

Enfield, N. J. (ed.) 2002. *Ethnosyntax. Explorations in grammar and culture.* Oxford University Press.

Epstein, Richard 1994. The development of the definite article in French. In Pagliuca (ed.) 63–78.

Evans, Nicholas 1998. Aborigines speak a primitive language. In Bauer, Laurie and Trudgill, Peter (eds.) *Language myths*, 159–168. London: Penguin Books.

2000. Word classes in the world's languages. In Booij *et al.* (eds.) 708–731.

2010. *Dying words. Endangered languages and what they have to tell us.* Chichester, West Sussex: Wiley-Blackwell.

2011. Semantic typology. In Song (ed.) 505–533.

Evans, Nicholas and Levinson, Stephen C. 2009. The myth of language universals: language diversity and its importance for cognitive science. *Behavioral and Brain Sciences* 32: 429–492.

Evans, Nicholas and Osada, Toshiki 2005. Mundari: the myth of a language without word classes. *Linguistic Typology* 9/3: 351–390.

Everett, Daniel 2008. *Don't sleep, there are snakes. Life and language in the Amazonian jungle.* New York: Random House.

2012. *Language: the cultural tool.* New York: Pantheon Books.

Ferguson, Charles A. 1975. Universal tendencies and 'normal' nasality. In Ferguson *et al.* (ed.) 175–196.

Ferguson, Charles A., Hyman, Larry M., and Ohala, John J. (eds.) 1975. *Nasálfest.* Stanford University.

Filipović, Luna 2007. *Talking about motion. A crosslinguistic investigation of lexicalization patterns.* Amsterdam/Philadelphia: Benjamins.

Fox, Barbara A. and Robert Jasperson 1995. A syntactic exploration of repair in English conversation. In Davis, P. W. (ed.) *Alternative linguistics. Descriptive and theoretical modes*, 77–134. Amsterdam/Philadelphia: Benjamins.

Fox, Barbara A., Hayashi, Makoto, and Jasperson, Robert 1996. Resources and repair: a crosslinguistic study of syntax and repair. In Ochs, Elinor, Schegloff, Emanuel A., and Thompson, Sandra A. (eds.) *Interaction and grammar*, 285–237. Cambridge University Press.

Fox, Barbara A., Maschler, Yael, and Uhmann, Susanne 2009. Morpho-syntactic resources for the organization of same-turn self-repair: cross-linguistic variation in English, German, and Hebrew. *Gesprächsforschung. Online Zeitschrift zur verbalen Interaktion* 10: 245–291. www.gespraechsforschung-ozs.de/heft2009/ga-fox.pdf

Fox, Barbara A. *et al.* 2012. A crosslinguistic investigation of the site of initiation in same-turn self-repair. In Sidnell, Jack (ed.) *Conversation analysis: comparative perspectives.* Cambridge University Press.

Frauenfelder, Ulli, Segui, Juan, and Mehler, Jacques 1980. Monitoring around the relative clause. *Journal of Verbal Learning and Verbal Behavior* 19/3: 328–337.

Gelderen, Elly van 2011. *The linguistic cycle. Language change and the language faculty.* Oxford University Press.

Gell-Mann, Murray and Ruhlen, Merritt 2011. The origin and evolution of word order. *Proceedings of the National Academy of Sciences* 108/42: 17290–17295.

Gentner, Dedre and Goldin-Meadow, Susan (eds.) 2003. *Language in mind.* The MIT Press.

Giacalone Ramat, Anna (ed.) 2003. *Typology and second language acquisition.* Berlin: Mouton de Gruyter.

Gil, David 2005. Numeral classifiers. In Haspelmath *et al.* (eds.) 226–229.

Givón, Talmy 1981. The development of the numeral 'one' as an indefinite marker. *Folia Linguistica Historica* 2: 35–53.

2002. *Bio-linguistics. The Santa Barbara lectures.* Amsterdam/Philadelphia: Benjamins.

2009. *The genesis of syntactic complexity.* Amsterdam/Philadelphia: Benjamins.

Gleason, H. A. 1955. *An introduction to descriptive linguistics.* New York: Holt, Rinehart and Winston.

Gnanadesikan, Amalia E. 2009. *The writing revolution. Cuneiform to the Internet.* Chichester: Wiley-Blackwell.

Goddard, Cliff and Wierzbicka, Anna (eds.) 1994. Introducing lexical primitives. In Goddard, Cliff and Wiezbicka, Anna (eds.) *Semantic and lexical universals. Theory and empirical findings*, 31–54. Amsterdam/Philadelphia: Benjamins.
    (eds.) 2002. *Meaning and universal grammar. Theory and empirical findings.* Volumes I–II. Amsterdam/Philadelphia: Benjamins.

Goedemans, Rob and van der Hulst, Harry 2005. Rhythm types. In Haspelmath *et al.* (ed.) 74–77.

Goldsmith, John A. (ed.) 1995. *The handbook of phonological theory.* Oxford: Blackwell.

Gould, Stephen Jay 2011. *The hedgehog, the fox, and the magister's pox.* Cambridge, MA: Belknap Press.

Greenberg, Joseph H. 1966a. Some universals of grammar with particular reference to the order of meaningful elements. In Greenberg (ed.) 1966b, 73–113.
    (ed.) 1966b. *Universals of language.* Second edition. The MIT Press.
    1966c [2005, new edition]. *Language universals.* Berlin: Mouton de Gruyter.
    1977. Numeral classifiers and substantival number: problems in the genesis of a linguistic type. In Makkai, Adam, Becker Makkai, Valerie, and Hellmann, Luigi (eds.) *Linguistics at the crossroads.* 276–300. Lake Bluff, IL: Jupiter Press.
    1978a. Generalizations about numeral systems. In Greenberg *et al.* (eds.), volume III, 249–295.
    1978b. Some generalizations concerning initial and final consonant clusters. In Greenberg *et al.* (eds.), volume II, 243–279.
    1978c. How does a language acquire gender markers? In Greenberg *et al.* (eds.), volume III, 47–82.
    1980. Universals of kinship terminology: their nature and the problem of their explanation. In Jacques Maquet (ed.) *On linguistic anthropology: essays in honor of Harry Hoijer*, 9–32. Malibu: Udena.

Greenberg, Joseph H., Ferguson, Charles A. and Moravcsik, Edith A. (eds.) 1978. *Universals of human language.* Volumes I–IV. Stanford University Press.

Gregory, Bruce 1988. *Inventing reality. Physics as language.* New York: John Wiley.

Gussenhoven, Carlos and Jacobs, Haike 1998. *Understanding phonology.* Second edition. London: Hodder Arnold.

Haddon, Mark 2001. *The curious incident of the dog at night-time.* New York: Vintage Books.

Haiman, John 1994. Ritualization and the development of language. In Pagliuca (ed.) 3–28.
    (ed.) 1985. *Iconicity in syntax.* Amsterdam/Philadelphia: Benjamins.
    2003. Explaining infixation. In Moore and Polinsky (eds.) 105–120.

Hall, Christopher J. 1988. Integrating diachronic and processing principles in explaining the suffixing preference. In Hawkins (ed.) 321–349.

Hall, Rich and friends 1984. *Sniglets (snig'let): any word that does not appear in the dictionary but it should.* New York: Collier Books.

Halle, Morris and Clements, G. N. 1983. *Problem book in phonology. A workbook in introductory courses in linguistics and in modern phonology.* The MIT Press.

Hammarström, Harald 2010. Rarities in numeral systems. In Wohlgemuth and Cysouw (eds.) 2010b, 11–59.

Hanke, Thomas 2010. Additional rarities in the typology of numerals. In Wohlgemuth and Cysouw (eds.) 2010b, 61–89.

Hardin, C. L. and Maffi, Luisa (eds.) 1997. *Color categories in thought and language.* Cambridge University Press. (Review in *Linguistic Typology*, 1999, 3/2: 259–269.)

Harris, Alice C. 2010. Explaining typologically unusual structures: the role of probability. In Wohlgemuth and Cysouw (eds.) 2010b, 91–103.

Harris, Alice C. and Campbell, Lyle 1995. *Historical syntax in crosslinguistic perspective.* Cambridge University Press.

Haspelmath, Martin 2006. Against markedness (and what to replace it with). *Journal of Linguistics* 42/1: 25–70.
    2010. Comparative concepts and descriptive categories in cross-linguistic studies. *Language* 86/3: 663–688.

Haspelmath, Martin, Dryer, Matthew S., Gil, David, and Comrie, Bernard (eds.) 2005. *The world atlas of language structures.* Oxford University Press.

Haspelmath, Martin, König, Ekkehard, Oesterreicher, Wulf, and Raible, Wolfgang (eds.) 2001. *Language typology and language universals. An international handbook.* Volumes I–II. Berlin: de Gruyter.

Haspelmath, Martin and Sims, Andrea D. 2010. *Understanding morphology*. London: Hodder Education.

Hauser, Marc D., Chomsky, Noam, and Fitch, W. Tecumseh 2002. The faculty of language: what is it, who has it, and how did it evolve? *Science* 298/5598: 1569–1579.

Haviland, John B. 1979. How to talk to your brother-in-law in Guugu Yimidhirr. In Shopen (ed.) 1979a, 161–239.

Hawkins, John A. 1983. *Word order universals*. New York: Academic Press.
    1988. Explaining language universals. In Hawkins (ed.) 3–28.
    (ed.) 1988. *Explaining language universals*. Oxford: Blackwell.
    1999. Processing complexity and filler-gap dependencies across grammars. *Language* 75/2: 244–285.
    2004. *Efficiency and complexity in grammars*. Oxford University Press.

Hawkins, John A. and Gilligan, Gary 1988. Prefixing and suffixing universals in relation to basic word order. *Lingua* 74: 219–259.

Heine, Bernd and Kuteva, Tania 2002. *World lexicon of grammaticalization*. Cambridge University Press.
    2006. *The changing languages of Europe*. Oxford University Press.

Hengeveld, Kees 1992. *Non-verbal predication. Theory, typology, diachrony*. Berlin: Mouton de Gruyter.

Holmes, Virginia M. and O'Regan, J. K. 1981. Eye fixation patterns during the reading of relative clause sentences. *Journal of Verbal Learning and Verbal Behavior* 20/4: 417–430.

Hopper, Paul J. and Traugott, Elizabeth Closs 2003. *Grammaticalization*. Second edition. Cambridge University Press.

Hulst, Harry van der and Weijer, Jeroen van de. 1995. Vowel harmony. In Goldsmith (ed.) 495–534.

Hulst, Harry van der and Ritter, Nancy A. (eds.) 1999. *The syllable: views and facts*. Berlin: Walter de Gruyter.

Hurford, James R. 1975. *The linguistic theory of numerals*. Cambridge University Press.
    1987. *Language and number. The emergence of a cognitive system*. Oxford: Blackwell.

Hurford, James R., Studdert-Kennedy, Michael, and Knight, Chris (eds.) 1998. *Approaches to the evolution of language*. Cambridge University Press.

Hyltenstam, Kenneth 1984. The use of typological markedness conditions as predictors in second language acquisition: the case of pronominal copies in relative clauses. In Anderson, Roger (ed.) *Second languages. A crosslinguistic perspective*, 39–57. Rowley, MA: Newbury.

Inoue, Kyoko 1979. Japanese: a story of language and people. In Shopen (ed.) 1979a, 241–300.

Iturrioz Leza, José Luis 2001. Inkorporation. In Haspelmath *et al.* (eds.), volume I, 714–725.

Jackendoff, Ray. 2012. *A user's guide to thought and meaning*. Oxford University Press.

Jonsson, Niklas 2001. Kin terms in grammar. In Haspelmath *et al.* (eds.), volume II, 1203–1214.

Joseph, Brian 2002. 'Word' in Modern Greek. In Dixon and Aikhenvald (eds.) 243–265.

Joseph, Brian D. and Janda, Richard D. (eds.) 2003. *The handbook of historical linguistics*. Oxford: Blackwell.

Kaku, Michio. 2008. *Physics of the impossible. A scientific exploration into the world of phasers, force fields, teleportation, and time travel*. New York: Anchor Books.

Kay, Paul, Berlin, Brent, Maffi, Luisa, Merrifield, William R., and Cook, Richard 2009. *World color survey*. Stanford: Center for the Study of Language and Information.

Keenan, Edward and Comrie, Bernard 1977. Noun phrase accessibility and universal grammar. *Linguistic Inquiry* 8/1: 63–99.

Keenan, Edward L. and Hawkins, Sarah 1987. The psychological validity of the Accessibility Hierarchy. In Keenan, Edward L., *Universal grammar. 15 essays*, 60–85. London: Croom Helm.

Keller, Rudi 1994. *On language change. The invisible hand in language*. Translated by Brigitte Nerlich. London: Routledge.

Kertész, András and Rákosi, Csilla 2012. *Data and evidence in linguistics. A plausible argumentation model*. Cambridge University Press.

Kimenyi, Alexandre 1980. *A relational grammar of Kinyarwanda*. University of California Press.

Kinsella, Anna R. 2009. *Language evolution and syntactic theory*. Cambridge University Press.

Kirby, Simon 1999. *Function, selection, and innateness. The emergence of language universals*. Oxford University Press.

Klatzky, Roberta L., Clark, Eve V., and Macken, Marlys 1973. Asymmetries in the acquisition of polar adjectives: linguistic or conceptual? *Journal of Experimental Child Psychology* 16/1: 32–46.

Klima, Edward S. and Bellugi, Ursula 1979. *The signs of language*. Harvard University Press.

Koptjevskaja-Tamm, Maria (2008). Approaching lexical typology. In Vanhove, Martine (ed.) *From polysemy to semantic change: towards a typology of semantic associations*, 3–52. Amsterdam/Philadelphia: Benjamins.

Krámský, Jiři 1972. *The article and the concept of definiteness in language*. The Hague: Mouton.

Ladefoged, Peter and Maddieson, Ian 1996. *The sounds of the world's languages*. Oxford: Blackwell.

Lado, Robert 1957. *Linguistics across cultures: applied linguistics for language teachers*. University of Michigan Press.

Lahiri, Aditi 2001. Metrical patterns. In Haspelmath *et al.* (eds.), volume II, 1347–1367.

Lakoff, George 1986. Classifiers as a reflection of mind. In Craig (ed.) 13–51.

Langacker, Ronald W. 1972. *Fundamentals of linguistic analysis*. New York: Harcourt Brace Jovanovich, Inc.
    2008. *Cognitive grammar. A basic introduction*. Oxford University Press.

Lashley, K. S. 1951. The problem of serial order in behavior. In Jeffress, Lloyd A. (ed.) *Cerebral mechanisms in behavior*, 112–136. New York: John Wiley and Sons.

Leeding, Velma J. 1996. Body parts and possession in Anindilyakwa. In Chappell and McGregor (eds.) 193–250.

Lehmann, Christian 1982. Universal and typological aspects of agreement. In Seiler, Hansjakob and Stachowiak, Franz Josef (eds.) *Apprehension. Das sprachliche Erfassen von Gegenständen. Teil II. Die Techniken und ihr Zusamenhang in Einzelsprachen*, 201–267. Tübingen: Gunter Narr.
    1995. *Thoughts on grammaticalization*. Munich – Newcastle: Lincom Europa.

Lehrer, Adrienne 1974. *Semantic fields and lexical structure*. Amsterdam: American Elsevier.

Levelt, Clara C. 2011. Consonant harmony in child language. In van Oestendorp, Marc, Ewen, Colin J., Hume, Elizabeth, and Rice, Keren (ed.) *The Blackwell companion to phonology*. Blackwell.

Lewis, Geoffrey L. 1967. *Turkish grammar*. Oxford: The Clarendon Press.

Li, Charles N. and Thompson, Sandra A. 1974. An explanation of word order change SVO → SOV. *Foundations of Language* 12/2: 201–14.
    1975. Historical change in word order: a case study in Chinese and its implications. In Anderson, John M. and Jones, C. (eds.) *Historical linguistics. Proceedings of the first international conference on historical linguistics, volume I: Syntax, morphology, internal and comparative reconstruction*, 199–217. Amsterdam: North Holland.
    1981. *Mandarin Chinese. A functional reference grammar*. The University of California Press.

Lindblom, Björn, MacNeilage, Michael, and Studdert-Kennedy, Michael 1984. Self-organizing processes and the explanation of phonological universals. In Butterworth *et al.* (eds.) 181–203.

Lucy, John A. 1997. The linguistics of "color." In Hardin and Maffi (eds.) 320–345.

Luraghi, Silvia, Thornton, Anna and Voghera, Miriam 2003. *Esercizi di linguistica*. Rome: Carocci.

MacLaury, Robert 2001. Color terms. In Haspelmath *et al.* (eds.), volume II, 1227–1251.

MacWhinney, Brian 1999. The emergence of language from embodiment. In MacWhinney, Brian (ed.) *The emergence of language*, 213–256. Mahwah, NJ: Erlbaum.

MacWhinney, Brian and Bates, Elizabeth 1989. *The crosslinguistic study of sentence processing*. Cambridge University Press.

MacWhinney, Brian, Malchukov, Andrej, and Moravcsik, Edith (eds.). To appear. *Competing motivations in grammar, acquisition, and usage*. Oxford University Press.

Maddieson, Ian 2005a. Consonant inventories. In Haspelmath *et al.* (eds.) 10–13.
    2005b. Consonant-vowel ratio. In Haspelmath *et al.* (eds.) 18–21.
    2005c. Voicing in plosives and fricatives. In Haspelmath *et al.* (eds.) 22–25.
    2005d. Front rounded vowels. In Haspelmath *et al.* (eds.) 50–53.
    2005e. Syllable structure. In Haspelmath *et al.* (eds.) 54–57.
    2005f. Tone. In Haspelmath *et al.* (eds.) 58–61.
    2005g. Presence of uncommon consonants. In Haspelmath *el al.* (ed.) 82–85.

2011. Typology of phonological systems. In Song (ed.) 534–548.

Major, Roy Coleman. 2001. *Foreign accent. The ontology and phylogeny of second language acquisition*. Mahwah, NJ: Erlbaum.

Malchukov, Andrej and Spencer, Andrew (eds.) 2009. *The Oxford handbook of case*. Oxford University Press.

Malchukov, Andrej 2011. Interaction of verbal categories: resolution of infelicitous grammeme combinations. *Linguistics* 49/1: 229–282.

Mattes, Veronika 2006. One form – opposite meanings? Diminutive and augmentative interpretation of full reduplication in Bikol. http://reduplication.uni-graz.at

Matthews, S. and Yip, V. 2003. Relative clauses in early bilingual development: transfer and universals. In Giacalone Ramat (ed.), 39–81.

Merrifield, Willam R. *et al.* 1987. *Laboratory manual for morphology and syntax*. Revised edition. Dallas, TX: Summer Institute of Linguistics.

Mithun, Marianne 1984. The evolution of noun incorporation. *Language* 60: 847–894.
1999. *The languages of Native North America*. Cambridge University Press.

Moore, John and Polinsky, Maria 2003. Explanations in linguistics. In Moore and Polinsky (eds.) 1–30.
(eds.) 2003. *The nature of explanation in linguistic theory*. Stanford, CA: The Center for the Study of Language and Information.

Moravcsik, Edith 1978. Reduplicative constructions. In Greenberg *et al.* (eds.), volume III, 297–334.
2006a. *An introduction to syntax*. London: Continuum.
2006b. *An introduction to syntactic theory*. London: Continuum.
2007. What is universal about typology? *Linguistic Typology* 11/1, 27–41.
2009. Partonomic structures in syntax. In Evans, Vyvyan and Pourcel, Stéphanie (eds.) *New directions in cognitive linguistics*, 269–285. Amsterdam/Philadelphia: Benjamins.
2010. Explaining language universals. In Song (ed.) 69–89.

Nathan, Geoffrey S. 2008. *Phonology. A cognitive grammar introduction*. Amsterdam/Philadelphia: Benjamins.

Nedjalkov, Vladimir K. (ed.) *Reciprocal constructions*. Volume III. Amsterdam/Philadelphia: Benjamins.

Nettle, Daniel. 1998. Functionalism and its difficulties in biology and linguistics. In Darnell, Michael *et al.* (eds.) *Functionalism and formalism in linguistics*, volume I, 445–467. Amsterdam/Philadelphia: Benjamins.

Nevins, Andrew 2010. *Locality in vowel harmony*. The MIT Press.

Newman, John (ed.) 1998. *The linguistics of giving*. Amsterdam/Philadelphia: Benjamins.
(ed.) 2002. *The linguistics of sitting, standing, and lying*. Amsterdam/Philadelphia: Benjamins.
(ed.) 2009. *The linguistics of eating and drinking*. Amsterdam/Philadelphia: Benjamins.

Newman, Paul 2000. *The Hausa language. An encyclopedic reference grammar*. Yale University Press.

Newmeyer, Frederick J. 1998. *Language form and language function*. The MIT Press.
2003. Theoretical implications of grammatical category – grammatical relations mismatched. In Francis, Elaine J. and Michaelis, Laura A. (eds.) *Mismatch: form-function incongruity and the architecture of grammar*, 149–178. Stanford, CA: Center for the Study of Language and Information.
2005. *Probable and possible languages. A generative perspective on linguistic typology*. Oxford University Press. (Review in *Linguistic Typology*, 2006, 10/2, 277–286.)
2010. On comparative concepts and descriptive categories. *Language* 86:3, 688–695.

Nichols, Johanna. 1992. *Linguistic diversity in space and time*. The University of Chicago Press.

Nida, Eugene (ed.) 1972. *The book of a thousand tongues*. Revised edition. United Bible Societies.

Niemeier, Susanne and René Dirven (eds.) (2000). *Evidence for linguistic relativity*. Amsterdam/Philadelphia: Benjamins.

Odden, David 2005. *Introducing phonology*. Cambridge University Press.

Ogloblin, Alexandr K. and Nedjalkov, Vladimir P. 2007. Reciprocal constructions in Indonesian. In Nedjalkov (ed.) 1437–1476.

Ohala, John 1975. Phonetic explanations for nasal sound patterns. In Ferguson *et al.* (eds.) 289–316.

Ohala, Manjari 1975. Nasals and nasalization in Hindi. In Ferguson *et al.* (eds.) 317–332.

Pagliuca, William (ed.) 1994. *Perspectives on grammaticalization*. Amsterdam/Philadelphia: Benjamins.

Pérez-Leroux, Ana Teresa 1995. Resumptives in the acquisition of relative clauses. *Language Acquisition* 4: 105–138.

Peters, Ann M. 1983. *The units of language acquisition*. Cambridge University Press.

Pfeiffer, Martin C. To appear. Formal and functional motivations for the structure of self-repair in German. In MacWhinney *et al.* (eds).

Pereltsvaig, Asya 2012. *Languages of the world. An introduction*. Cambridge University Press.

Pinker, Steven and Jackendoff, Ray 2009. The reality of the universal language faculty. *Behavior and Brain Sciences* 32: 465–466.

Plank, Frans 1984. 24 grundsätzliche Bemerkungen zur Wortarten-Frage. *Leuvense Bijdragen* 73: 489–520.

  1999. Split morphology: how agglutination and flexion mix. *Linguistic Typology* 3/3: 279–340.

Plank, Frans and Schellinger, Wolfgang 1997. The uneven distribution of genders over numbers. Greenberg Nos. 37 and 45. *Linguistic Typology* 1/1: 53–101.

Ramat, Paolo 1987. *Linguistic typology*. Berlin: Mouton de Gruyter.

Randall, Lisa 2011. How science can lead the way. *TIME Magazine*, October 3, 2011, 20.

Rijkhoff, Jan 2002. *The noun phrase*. Oxford University Press.

Roca, Iggy and Johnson, Wyn 1999. *A workbook in phonology*. Oxford: Blackwell.

Rogers, Henry 2005. Writing *systems. A linguistic approach*. Oxford: Blackwell.

Rubba, Johanna 2001. Introflection. In Haspelmath *et al.* (eds.) 678–694.

Sanders, Gerald A. 1977. Functional constraints on grammar. In Juilland, Alphonse (ed.) *Linguistic studies offered to Joseph Greenberg on the occasion of his sixtieth birthday*, 161–178. Saratoga: ANMA LIBRI.

Sandler, Wendy 1996. Representing handshapes. *International Review of Sign Linguistics* 1: 115–158.

Sandler, Wendy and Lillo-Martin, Diane. 2006. *Sign language and linguistic universals*. Cambridge University Press.

Saxe, Geoffrey B. 1981. Body parts as numerals. A developmental analysis of numeration among the Oksapmin in Papua New Guinea. *Child Development*, 52/1: 206–316.

Schachter, Paul 1976. The subject in Philippine languages: topic, actor, actor-topic, or none of the above? In Li, Charles N. (ed.) *Subject and topic*, 491–518. New York: Academic Press.

Schachter, Paul and Otanes, Fe T. 1972. *Tagalog reference grammar*. University of California Press.

Seiler, Hansjakob 2000. *Language universals research; a synthesis*. Tübingen: Gunter Narr Verlag.

Shibatani, Masayoshi and Bynon, Theodora (eds.) 1995. *Approaches to language typology*. Oxford: Clarendon Press.

Schieffelin, Bambi B. 1985. The acquisition of Kaluli. In Slobin (ed.), volume I, 525–594.

Shkarban, Lina I. and Rachkov, Gennadij E. 2007. Reciprocal, sociative, and comitative constructions in Tagalog. In Nedjalkov (ed.) 887–931.

Shopen, Timothy (ed.) 1979a. *Languages and their speakers*. Cambridge, MA: Winthrop.

  (ed.) 1979b. *Languages and their status*. Cambridge, MA: Winthrop.

  (ed.) 2007. *Language typology and syntactic fieldwork*, volumes I–III. Second edition. Cambridge University Press.

Siewierska, Anna 2004. *Person*. Cambridge University Press.

  2005a. Gender distinctions in independent personal pronouns. In Haspelmath *et al.* (eds.) 182–185.

  2005b. Alignment in verbal person marking. In Haspelmath *et al.* (eds.) 406–409.

Siewierska, Anna and Bakker, Dik 1996. The distribution of subject and object agreement and word order type. *Studies in Language* 20/1: 115–161.

Simon, Herbert 1962. The architecture of complexity. *Proceedings of the American Philosophical Society* 106/6: 467–482.

Simone, Raffaele (ed.) 1995. *Iconicity in language*. Amsterdam/Philadelphia: Benjamins.

Slobin, Dan Isaac (ed.) 1985. *The crosslinguistic study of language acquisition*. Volumes I–V. Hillsdale: Erlbaum.

  1985a. Crosslinguistic evidence for the language-making capacity. In Slobin (ed.), volume II, 1157–1256.

1985b. The universal, the typological, and the particular in acquisition. In Slobin (ed.), volume V, 1–39.

2003. Language and thought online: cognitive consequences of linguistic relativity. In Gentner and Goldin-Meadow (eds.) 157–191.

Song, Jae Jung 2001. *Linguistic typology: morphology and syntax*. Harlow: Pearson.

(ed.) 2011. *The Oxford handbook of linguistic typology*. Oxford University Press.

2012. *Word order*. Cambridge University Press.

Spencer, Andrew and Zwicky, Arnold M. (ed.) 1998. *The handbook of morphology*. Oxford: Blackwell.

Stassen, Leon 2009. *Predicative possession*. Oxford University Press.

Sun, Chaofen. 1996. *Word-order change and grammaticalization in the history of Chinese*. Stanford University Press.

Supalla, Ted. 1986. The classifier system in American Sign Language. In Craig (ed.) 181–214.

Talmy, Leonard 2007. Lexical typologies. In Shopen (ed.), volume III, 66–168.

Tarallo, Fernando and Myhill, John. 1983. Interference and natural language processing in second language acquisition. *Language Learning* 33/1: 55–76.

Taylor, John R. 2003. *Linguistic categorization*. Third edition. Oxford University Press.

Terrill, Angela. 2006. Body part terms in Lavukaleve, a Papuan language of the Solomon Island. *Language Sciences* 28/2–3: 304–322.

Thomason, Sarah G. 2001. *Language contact. An introduction*. Georgetown University Press.

Tomasello, Michael 2003. *Constructing a language. A usage-based theory of language acquisition*. Harvard University Press.

Traugott, Elizabeth Closs 1972. *The history of English syntax*. New York: Holt, Rinehart and Winston, Inc.

Underhill, Robert 1976. *Turkish grammar*. The MIT Press.

Vennemann, Theo 1973. Explanation in syntax. In Kimball, John (ed.) *Syntax and semantics*, volume II, 1–50. New York: Academic Press.

Vogel, Petra M. and Comrie, Bernard (eds.) 2000. *Approaches to the typology of word classes*. Berlin: Mouton de Gruyter.

Völkel, Svenja. 2010. *Social structure, space and possession in Tongan culture. An ethnolinguistic study*. Amsterdam/Philadelphia: Benjamins.

Wanner, Eric and Maratsos, Michael. 1978. An ATN approach to comprehension. In Halle, Morris, Bresnan, Joan, and Miller, George A. (eds.) *Linguistic theory and psychological reality*, 119–161. The MIT Press.

Weber, David John 1989. *A grammar of Huallaga (Huánuco) Quechua*. University of California Press.

Whaley, Lindsay J. 1997. *Introduction to typology. The unity and diversity of language*. Thousand Oaks: Sage.

Whitelock, Doris 1982. *White Hmong language lessons*. University of Minnesota.

Wierzbicka, Anna 1997. *Understanding cultures through their key words. English, Russian, Polish, German, and Japanese*. Oxford University Press.

2008. Why there are no 'colour universals' in language and thought. *Journal of the Royal Anthropological Institute* 14/2: 407–425.

Wiese, Heike 2003. *Numbers, language, and the human mind*. Cambridge University Press.

Winawer, Jonathan, Witthof, Nathan, Frank, Michael C., Wu, Lisa, Wade, Alex R., and Boroditsky, Lera 2007. Russian blues reveal effects of language on color discrimination. *Proceedings of the National Academy of Sciences of the United States of America* 104/19: 7780–7785.

Wirth, Jessica R. 1983. Toward universal principles of word formation: a look at antonyms. In Shiroó Hattori and Kazuko Inoue (eds.) *Proceedings of the XIIIth international congress of linguists, August 29– September 4 1982, Tokyo*. Tokyo.

Witkowski, Stanley and Brown, Cecil H. 1982. Whorf and universals of color nomenclature. *Journal of Anthropological Research* 38/4: 411–420.

Wohlgemuth, Jan and Cysouw, Michael (eds.) 2010a. *Rara and rarissima. Documenting the fringes of linguistic diversity*. Berlin: De Gruyter Mouton.

(eds.) 2010b. *Rethinking universals. How rarities affect linguistic theory*. Berlin: De Gruyter Mouton.

Zeshan, Ulrike 2004a. Hand, head, and face: negative constructions in sign language. *Linguistic Typology* 8/1: 1–58.

2004b. Interrogative constructions in signed languages: crosslinguistic perspectives. *Language* 80/1: 7–39.

2005a. Sign languages. In Haspelmath *et al.* (eds.) 558–559.

2005b. Irregular negatives in sign languages. In Haspelmath *et al.* (eds.) 560–563.

2005c. Question particles in sign languages. In Haspelmath *et al.* (eds.) 564–567.

Subject index

Language index

Author index

This index includes only the authors' names mentioned in the running text. For additional author references, please see the sections titled **Further reading** *following each chapter.*